Hyde & Closer

HYDE & CLOSER
Volume 1
Shonen Sunday Edition

Story and Art by
HARO ASO

© 2008 Haro ASO/Shogakukan
All rights reserved.
Original Japanese edition "JUHOU KAIKIN!! HYDE AND CLOSER"
published by SHOGAKUKAN Inc.

English Adaptation/AJ Glasser, Honyaku Center Inc.

Translation/Labaaman, Honyaku Center Inc.
Touch-up & Lettering Chapter 1/Susan Daigle-Leach
Touch-up & Lettering Chapter 2–8/Annaliese Christman
Design/Hidemi Sahara
Editor/Jann Jones

VP, Production/Alvin Lu
VP, Sales & Product Marketing/Gonzalo Ferreyra
VP, Creative/Linda Espinosa
Publisher/Hyoe Narita

Printed in Canada

Published by VIZ Media, LLC
P.O. Box 77010
San Francisco, CA 94107

10 9 8 7 6 5 4 3 2 1
First printing, July 2010

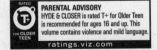

www.viz.com

WWW.SHONENSUNDAY.COM

Hyde & Closer

1

Story & Art by
Haro Aso

Hyde & Closer

1

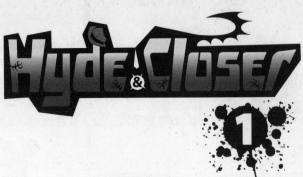

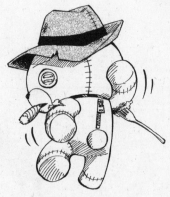

Table of Contents

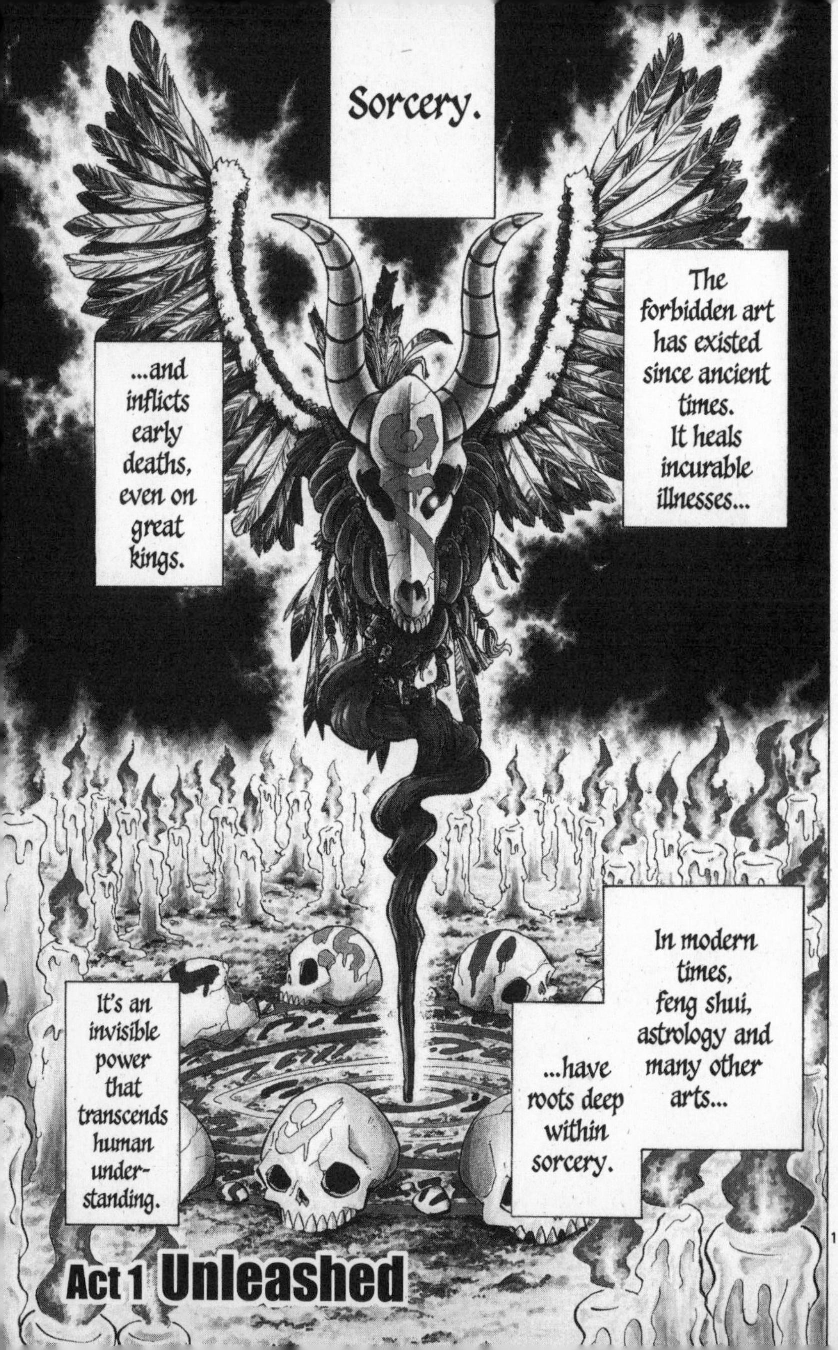
Sorcery.
The forbidden art has existed since ancient times. It heals incurable illnesses...
...and inflicts early deaths, even on great kings.
In modern times, feng shui, astrology and many other arts...
...have roots deep within sorcery.
It's an invisible power that transcends human under-standing.
Act 1 Unleashed

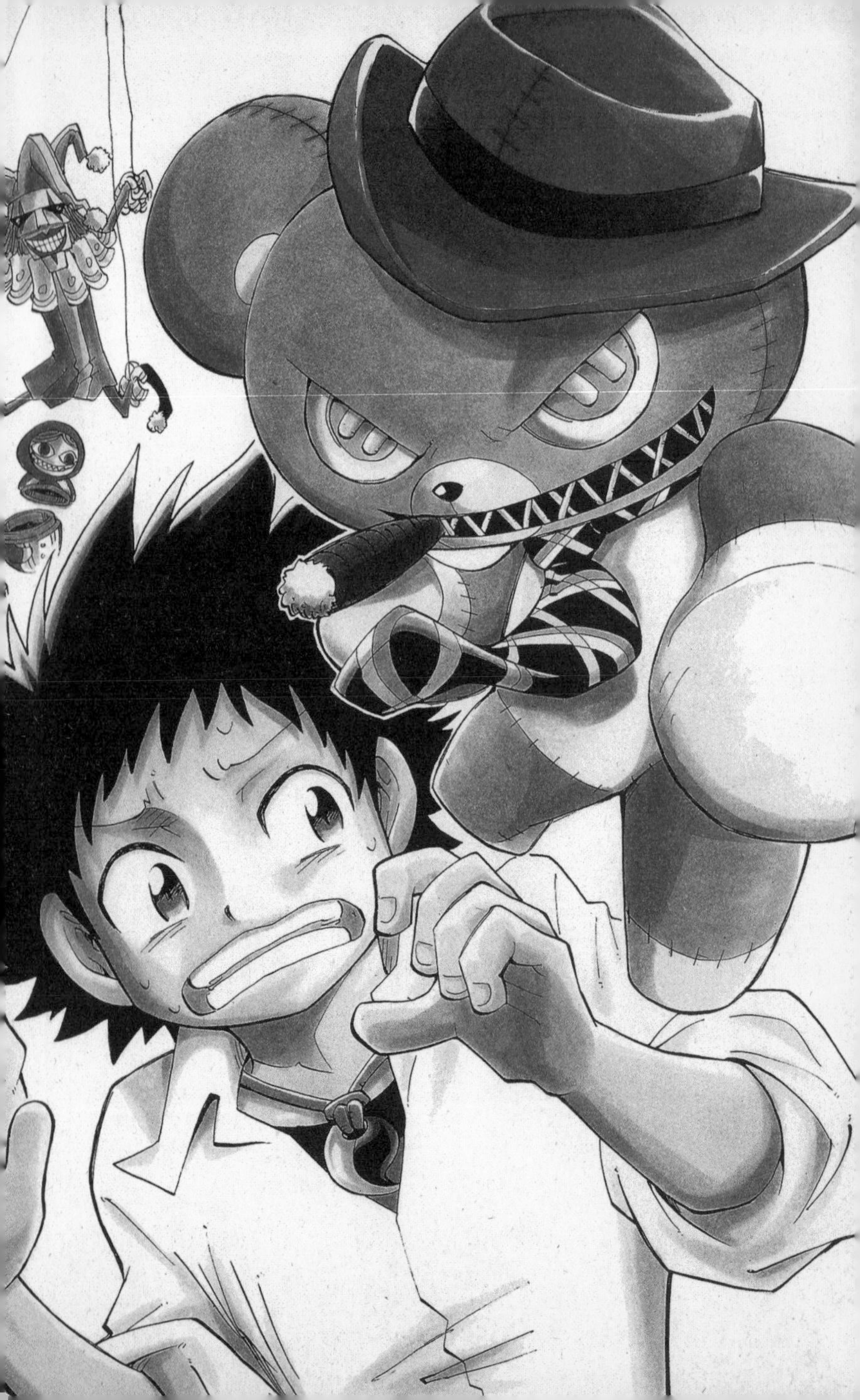

Act 1
Unleashed

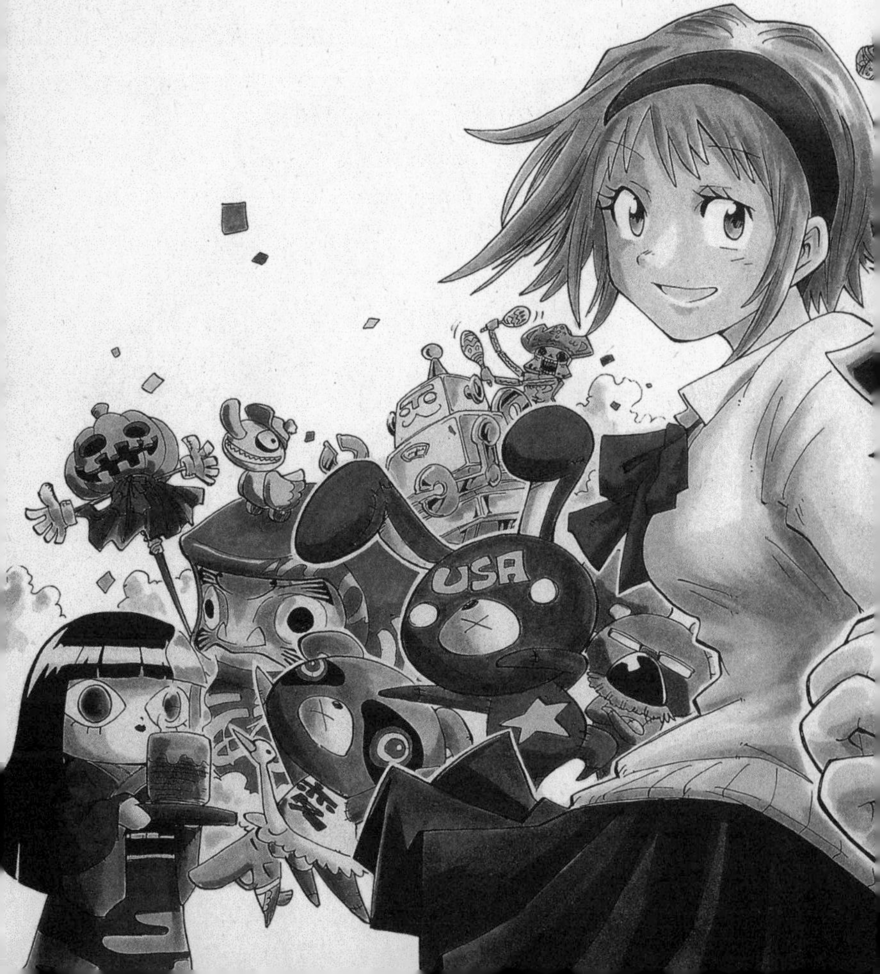
USA

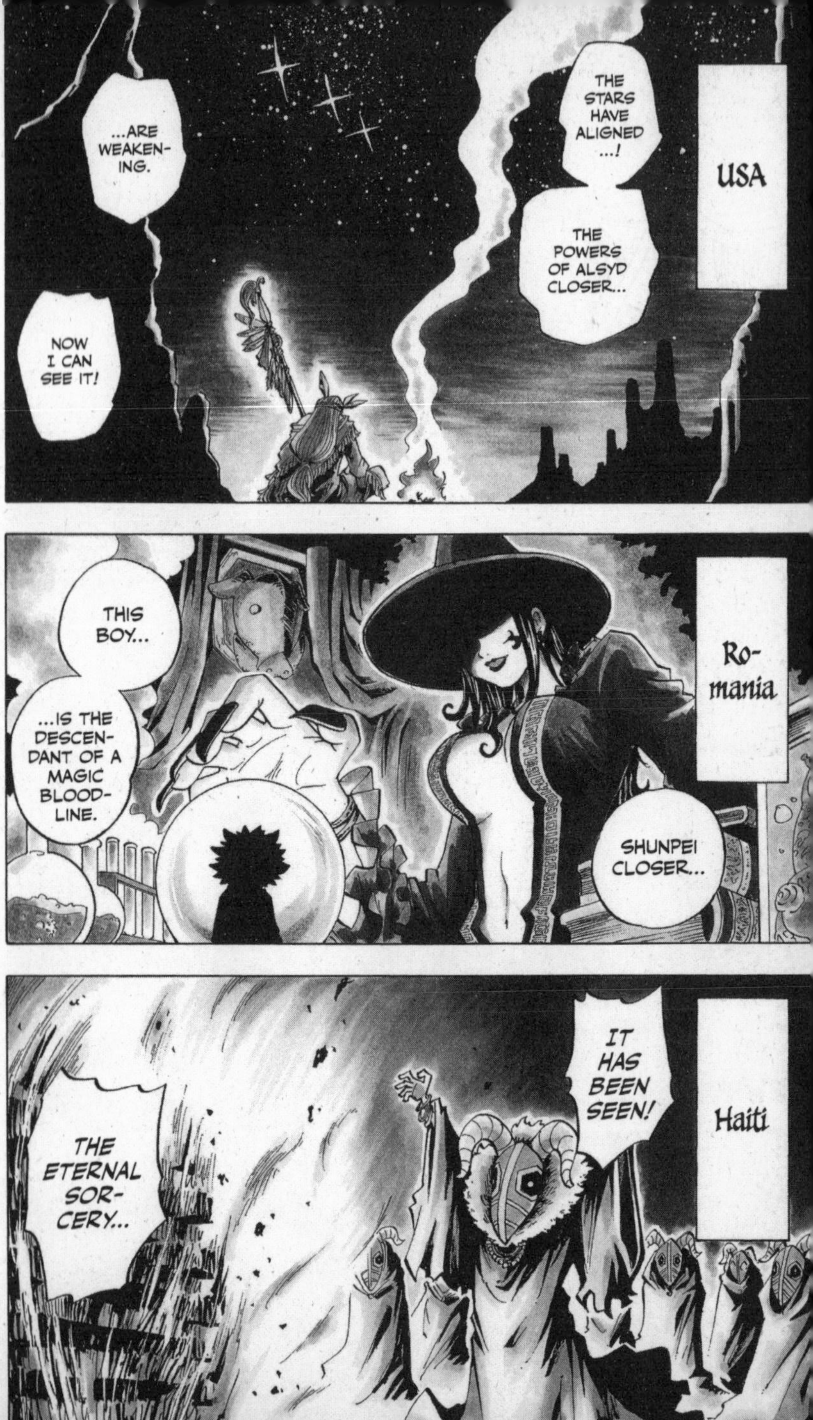
USA
THE STARS HAVE ALIGNED ...!
THE POWERS OF ALSYD CLOSER...
...ARE WEAKEN-ING.
NOW I CAN SEE IT!
Ro-mania
THIS BOY...
...IS THE DESCEN-DANT OF A MAGIC BLOOD-LINE.
SHUNPEI CLOSER...
Haiti
IT HAS BEEN SEEN!
THE ETERNAL SOR-CERY...

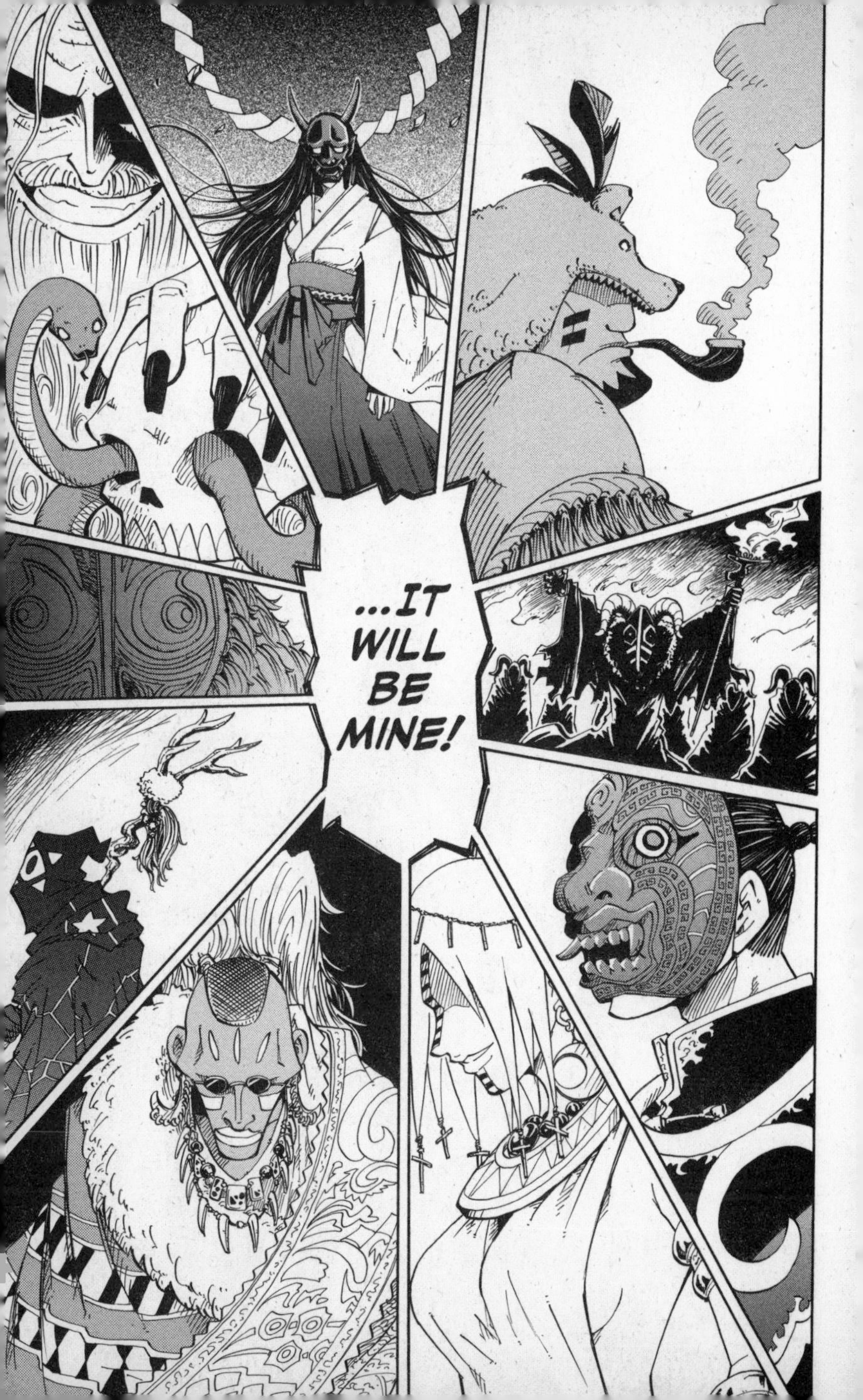
...IT WILL BE MINE!

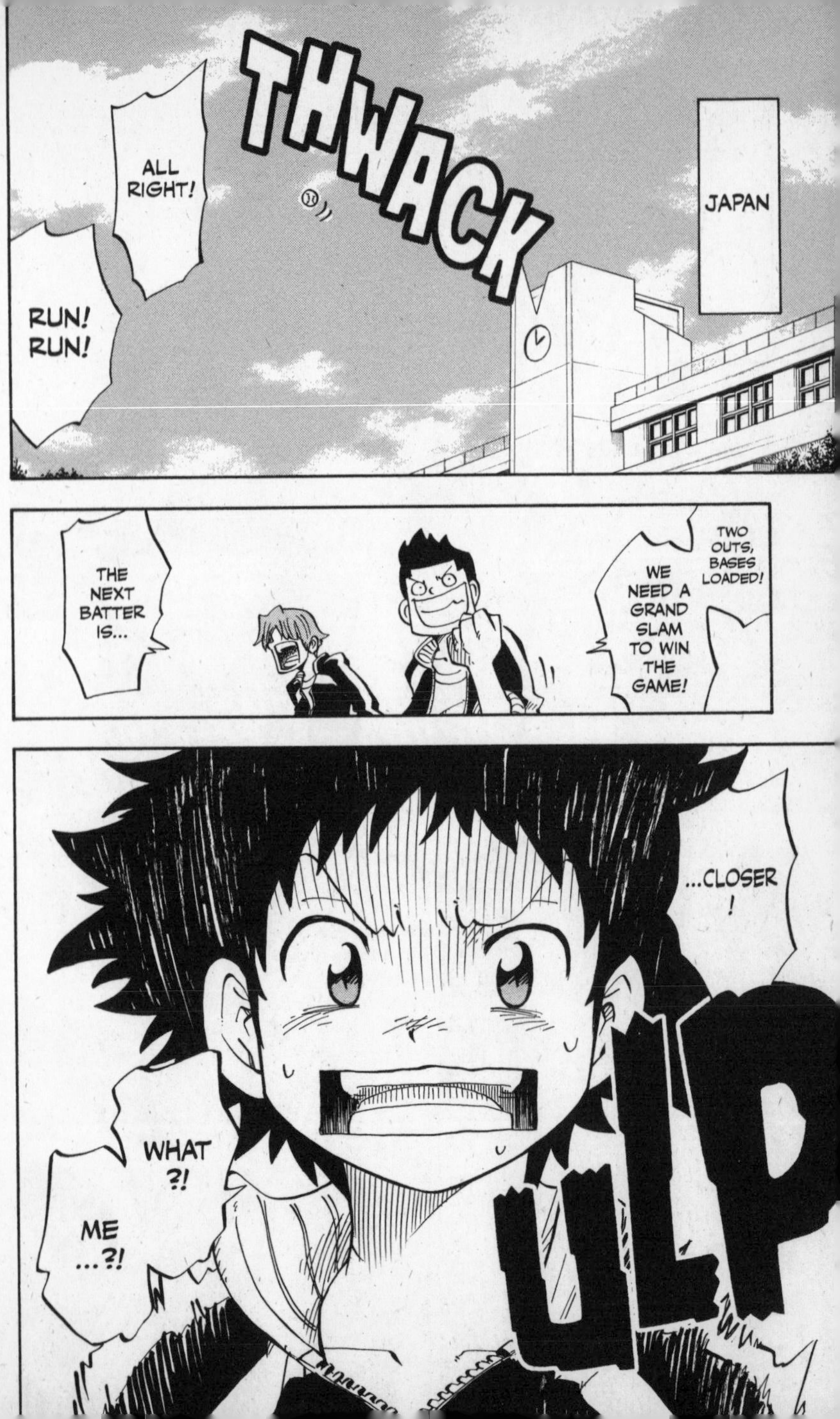
JAPAN
THWACK
ALL RIGHT!
RUN! RUN!
TWO OUTS, BASES LOADED!
WE NEED A GRAND SLAM TO WIN THE GAME!
THE NEXT BATTER IS...
...CLOSER!
GULP
WHAT?!
ME...?!

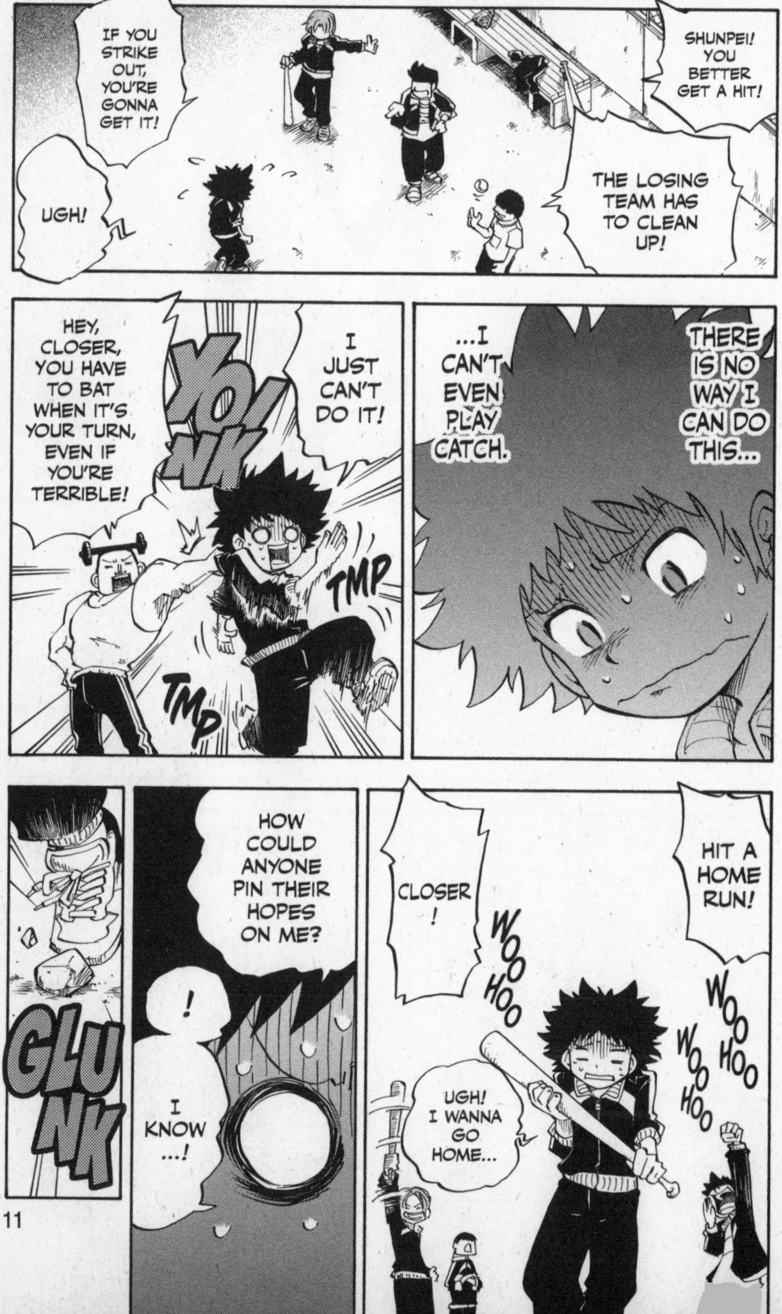
SHUNPEI! YOU BETTER GET A HIT!
THE LOSING TEAM HAS TO CLEAN UP!
IF YOU STRIKE OUT, YOU'RE GONNA GET IT!
UGH!
THERE IS NO WAY I CAN DO THIS...
...I CAN'T EVEN PLAY CATCH.
I JUST CAN'T DO IT!
YOINK
HEY, CLOSER, YOU HAVE TO BAT WHEN IT'S YOUR TURN, EVEN IF YOU'RE TERRIBLE!
TMP
TMP
HIT A HOME RUN!
WOO HOO
WOO HOO
CLOSER!
WOO HOO
UGH! I WANNA GO HOME...
HOW COULD ANYONE PIN THEIR HOPES ON ME?
!
I KNOW ...!
GLUNK

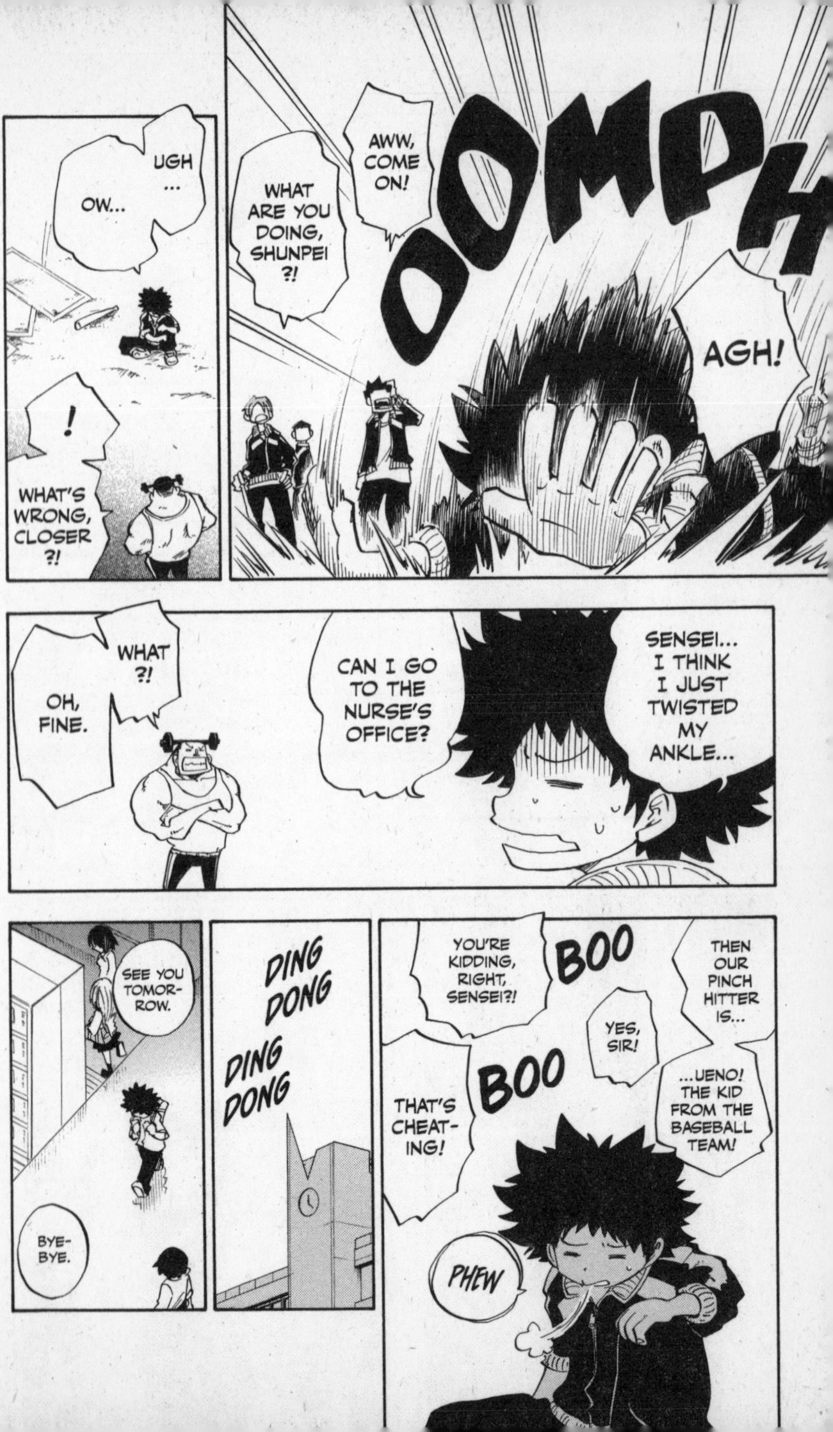
OOMPH
AGH!
AWW, COME ON!
WHAT ARE YOU DOING, SHUNPEI?!
UGH...
OW...
!
WHAT'S WRONG, CLOSER?!
SENSEI... I THINK I JUST TWISTED MY ANKLE...
CAN I GO TO THE NURSE'S OFFICE?
WHAT?!
OH, FINE.
THEN OUR PINCH HITTER IS...
...UENO! THE KID FROM THE BASEBALL TEAM!
YES, SIR!
BOO
YOU'RE KIDDING, RIGHT, SENSEI?!
BOO
THAT'S CHEAT-ING!
PHEW
DING DONG
DING DONG
SEE YOU TOMOR-ROW.
BYE-BYE.

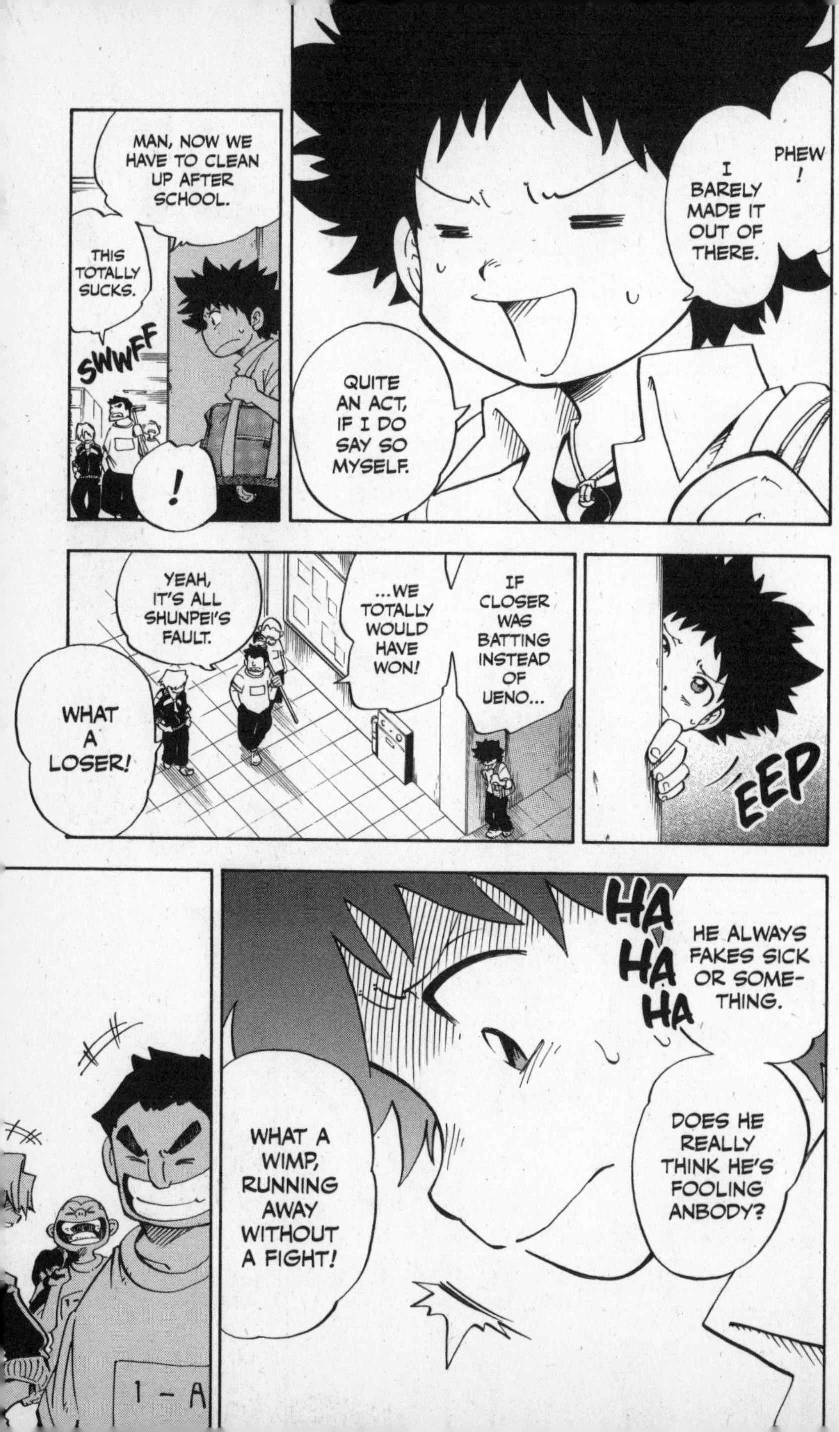
PHEW!
I BARELY MADE IT OUT OF THERE.
QUITE AN ACT, IF I DO SAY SO MYSELF.
MAN, NOW WE HAVE TO CLEAN UP AFTER SCHOOL.
THIS TOTALLY SUCKS.
SWWFF
!
EEP
IF CLOSER WAS BATTING INSTEAD OF UENO...
...WE TOTALLY WOULD HAVE WON!
YEAH, IT'S ALL SHUNPEI'S FAULT.
WHAT A LOSER!
HA HA HA
HE ALWAYS FAKES SICK OR SOME-THING.
DOES HE REALLY THINK HE'S FOOLING ANBODY?
WHAT A WIMP, RUNNING AWAY WITHOUT A FIGHT!
1-A

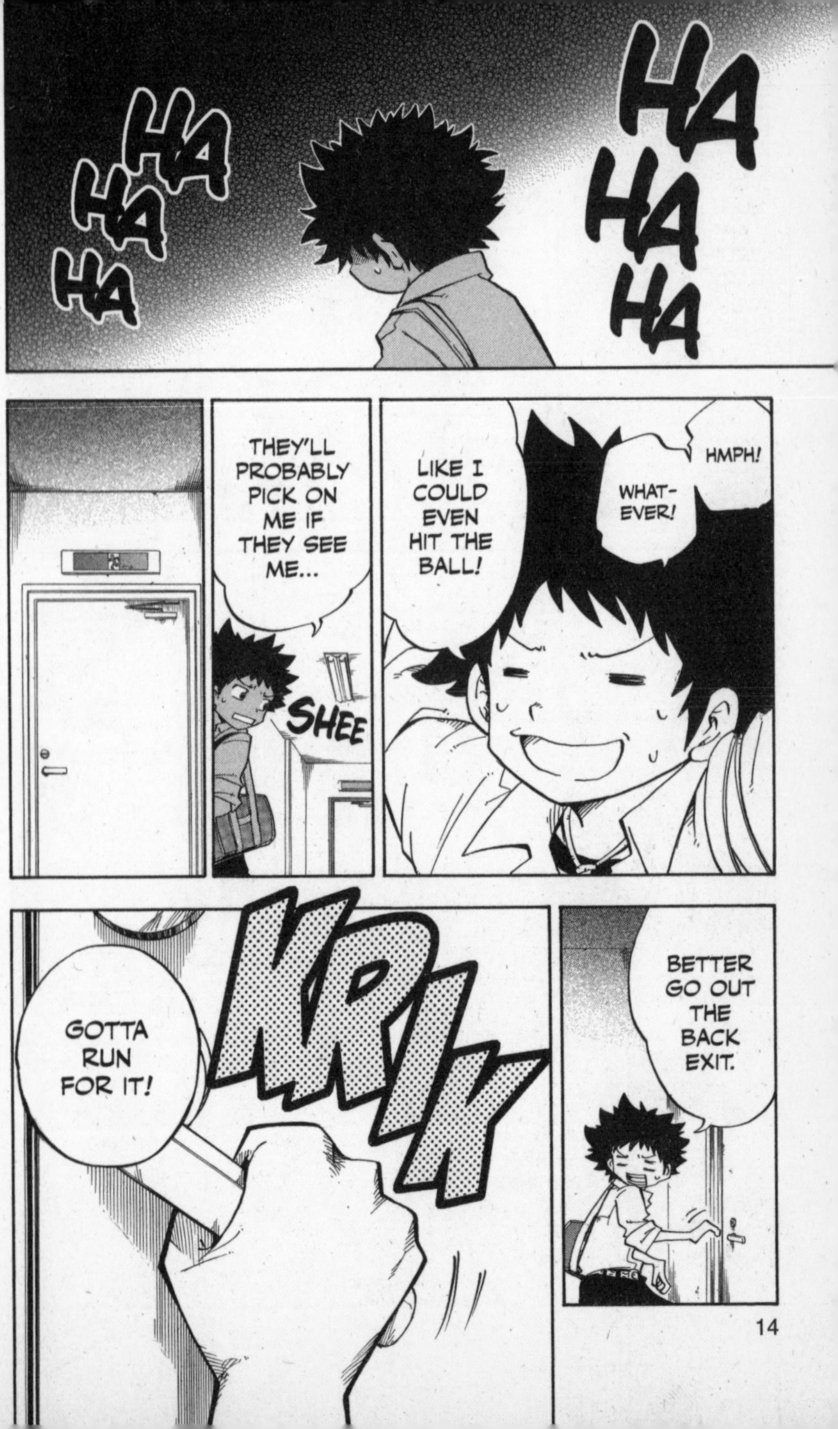
HA HA HA
HA HA HA
HMPH!
WHAT-EVER!
LIKE I COULD EVEN HIT THE BALL!
THEY'LL PROBABLY PICK ON ME IF THEY SEE ME...
SHEE
BETTER GO OUT THE BACK EXIT.
KRIK
GOTTA RUN FOR IT!

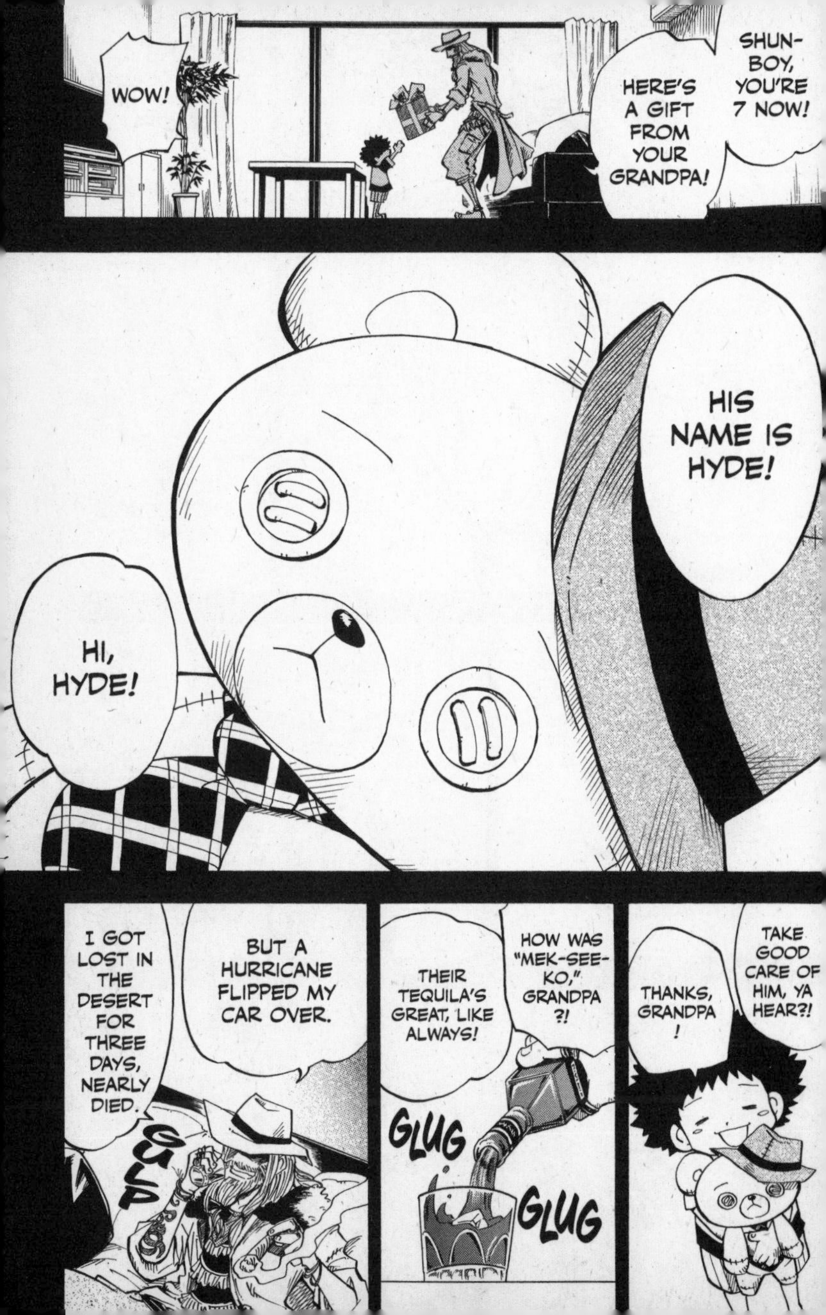
SHUN-BOY, YOU'RE 7 NOW!
HERE'S A GIFT FROM YOUR GRANDPA!
WOW!
HIS NAME IS HYDE!
HI, HYDE!
TAKE GOOD CARE OF HIM, YA HEAR?!
THANKS, GRANDPA!
HOW WAS "MEK-SEE-KO," GRANDPA?!
THEIR TEQUILA'S GREAT, LIKE ALWAYS!
GLUG
GLUG
BUT A HURRICANE FLIPPED MY CAR OVER.
I GOT LOST IN THE DESERT FOR THREE DAYS, NEARLY DIED.
GULP

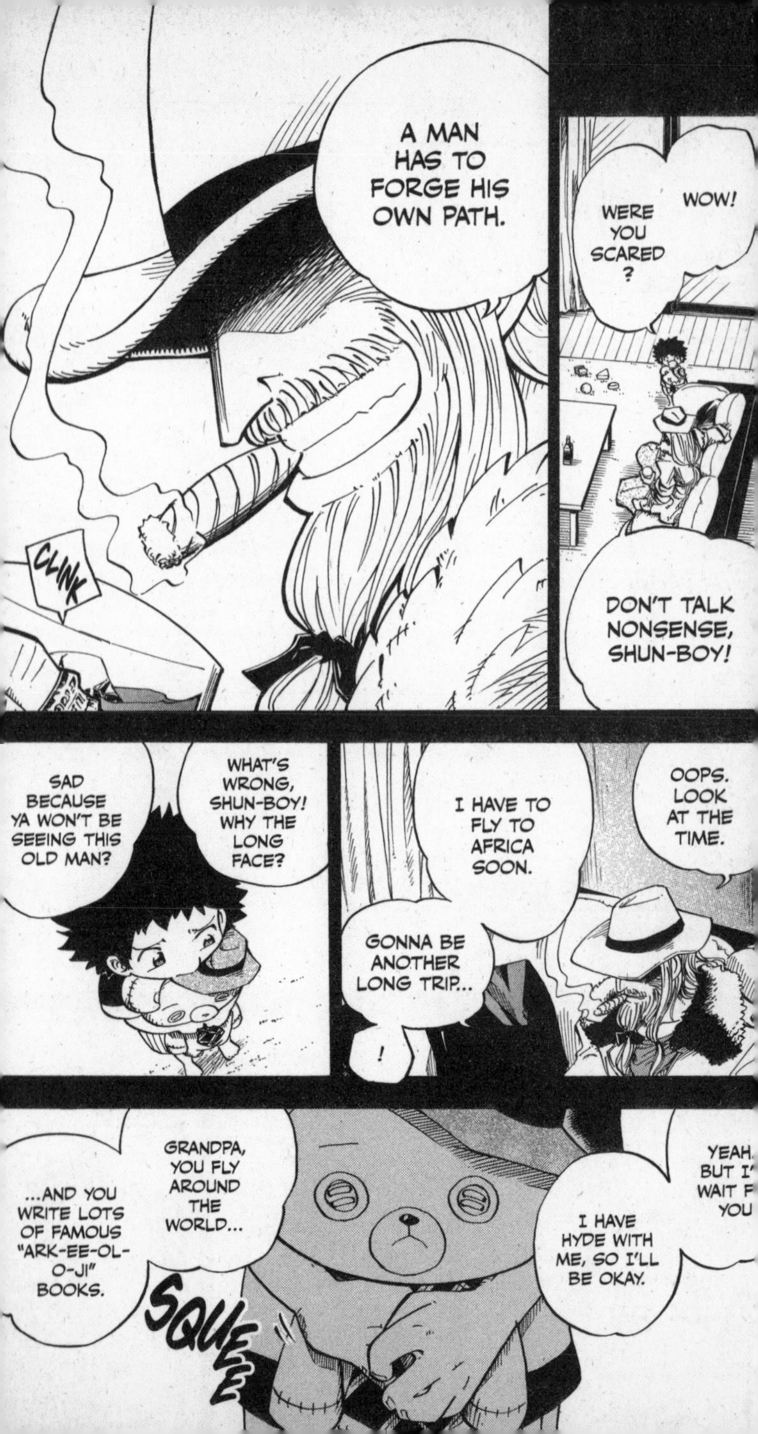
WOW!
WERE YOU SCARED?
DON'T TALK NONSENSE, SHUN-BOY!
A MAN HAS TO FORGE HIS OWN PATH.
CLINK
OOPS. LOOK AT THE TIME.
I HAVE TO FLY TO AFRICA SOON.
GONNA BE ANOTHER LONG TRIP...
!
WHAT'S WRONG, SHUN-BOY! WHY THE LONG FACE?
SAD BECAUSE YA WON'T BE SEEING THIS OLD MAN?
YEAH. BUT I' WAIT F YOU
I HAVE HYDE WITH ME, SO I'LL BE OKAY.
GRANDPA, YOU FLY AROUND THE WORLD...
...AND YOU WRITE LOTS OF FAMOUS "ARK-EE-OL-O-JI" BOOKS.
SQUEE

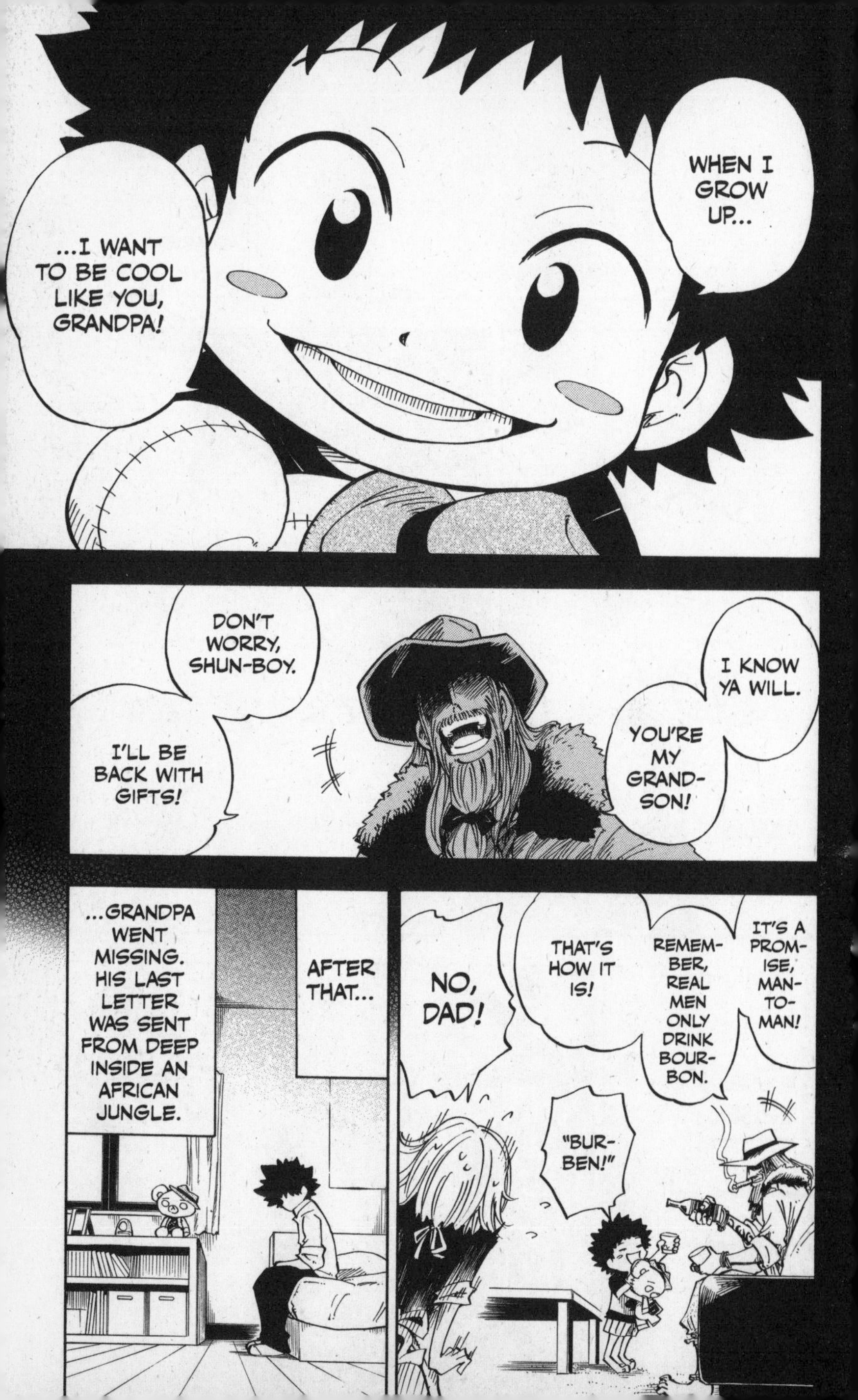
WHEN I GROW UP...
...I WANT TO BE COOL LIKE YOU, GRANDPA!
I KNOW YA WILL.
YOU'RE MY GRAND-SON!
DON'T WORRY, SHUN-BOY.
I'LL BE BACK WITH GIFTS!
IT'S A PROM-ISE, MAN-TO-MAN!
REMEM-BER, REAL MEN ONLY DRINK BOUR-BON.
THAT'S HOW IT IS!
NO, DAD!
"BUR-BEN!"
AFTER THAT...
...GRANDPA WENT MISSING. HIS LAST LETTER WAS SENT FROM DEEP INSIDE AN AFRICAN JUNGLE.

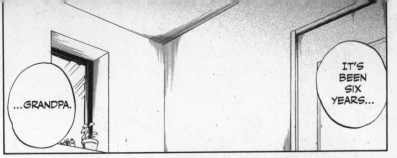

...GRANDPA.

IT'S BEEN SIX YEARS...

BUT...

...I REALLY...

I GUESS I WON'T EVER BE COOL...

...LIKE YOU, GRANDPA.

CLOSER

VROOM

KRUNCH

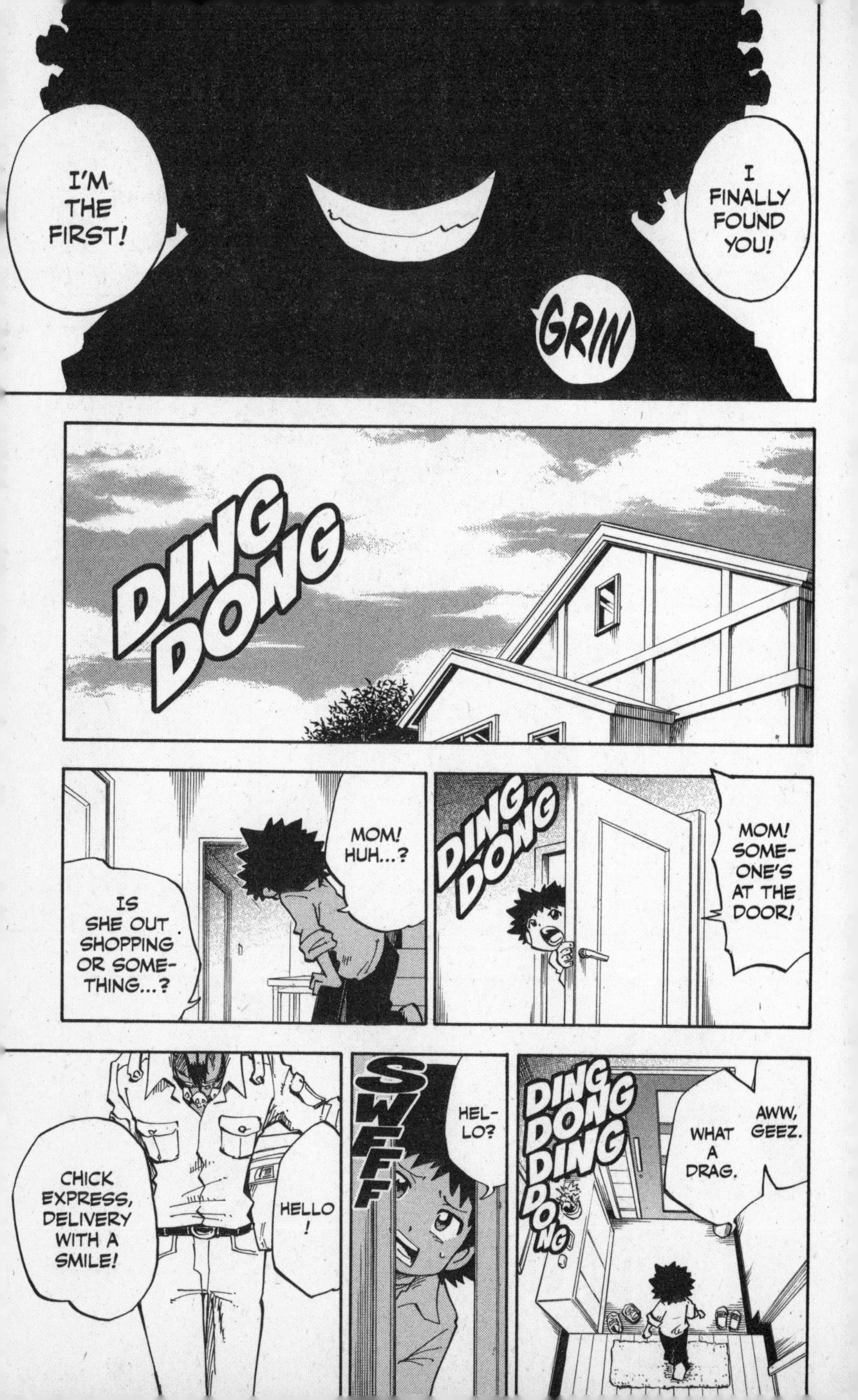
I FINALLY FOUND YOU!
I'M THE FIRST!
GRIN
DING DONG
MOM! SOMEONE'S AT THE DOOR!
DING DONG
MOM! HUH...?
IS SHE OUT SHOPPING OR SOMETHING...?
AWW, GEEZ.
WHAT A DRAG.
DING DONG DING DONG
HEL-LO?
SWFFF
HELLO!
CHICK EXPRESS, DELIVERY WITH A SMILE!

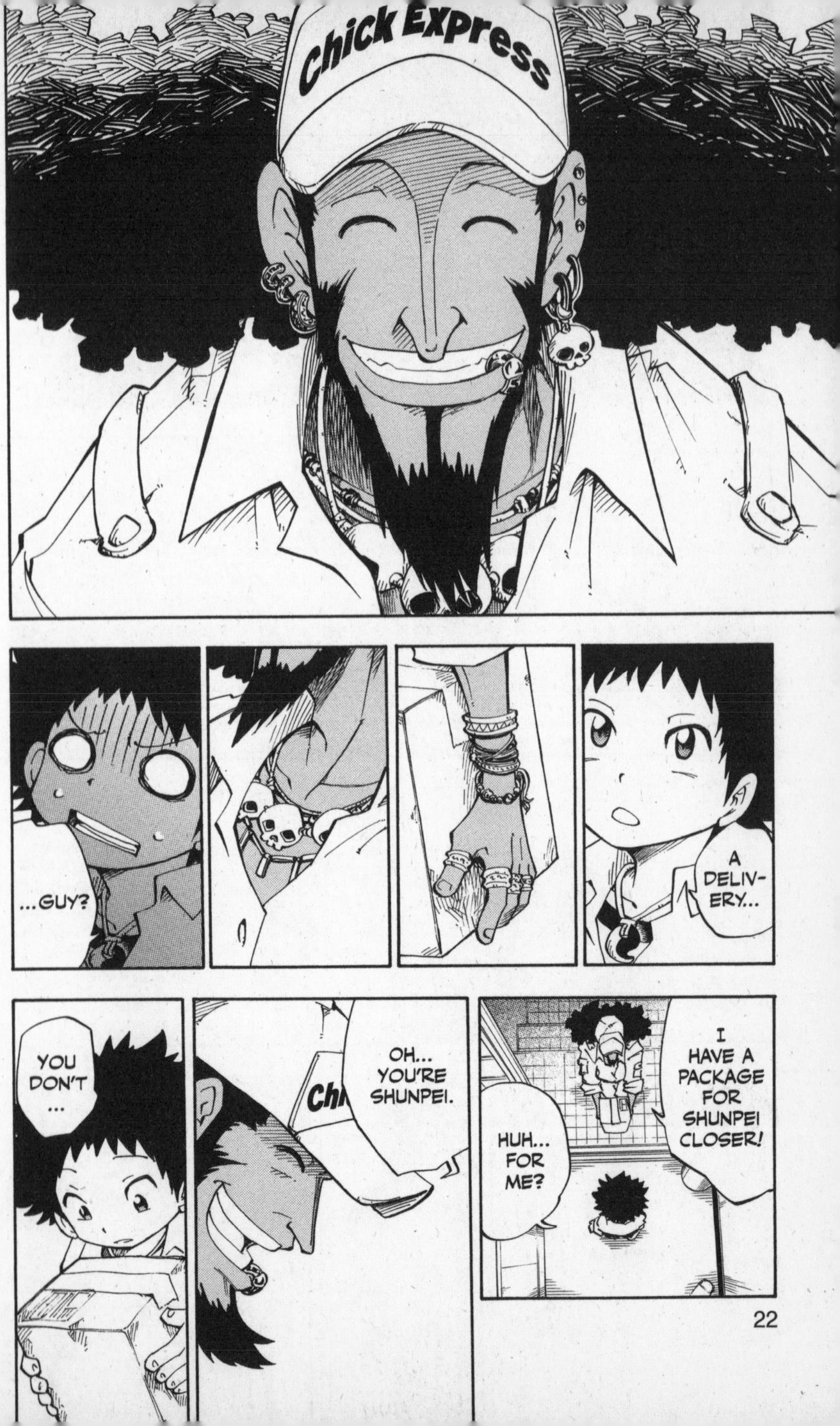
Chick Express
A DELIVERY...
...GUY?
I HAVE A PACKAGE FOR SHUNPEI CLOSER!
HUH... FOR ME?
OH... YOU'RE SHUNPEI.
YOU DON'T ...

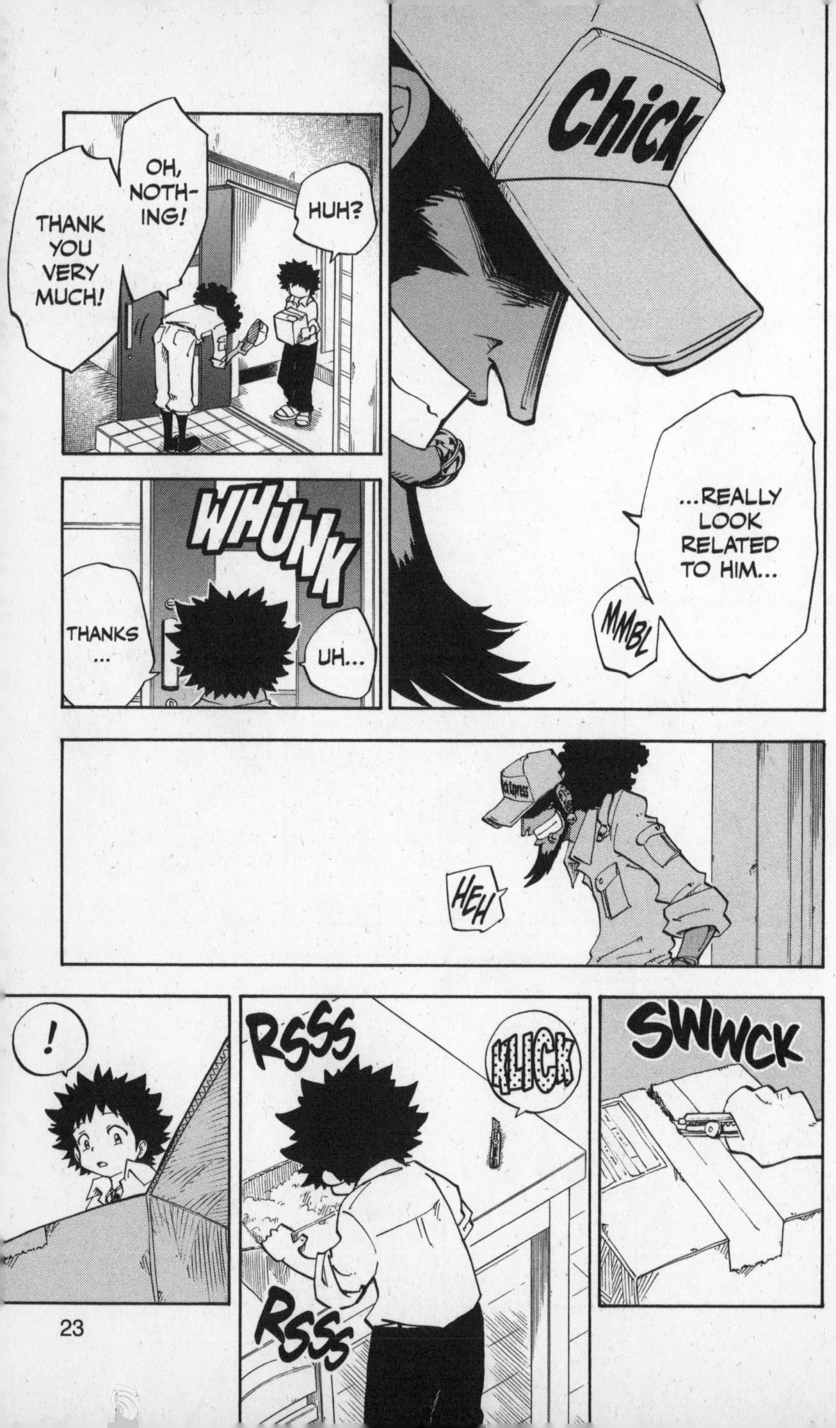
Chick
...REALLY LOOK RELATED TO HIM...
MMBL
HUH?
OH, NOTHING!
THANK YOU VERY MUCH!
WHUNK
UH...
THANKS ...
HEH
SWWCK
KLICK
RSSS
RSSS
!

A STUFFED...

...MONKEY...

OW!

WHO'S IT FROM?

THERE'S NO RETURN ADDRESS.

?

WHAT IS THIS...?

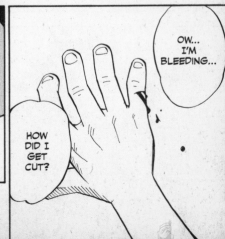

OW... I'M BLEEDING...

HOW DID I GET CUT?

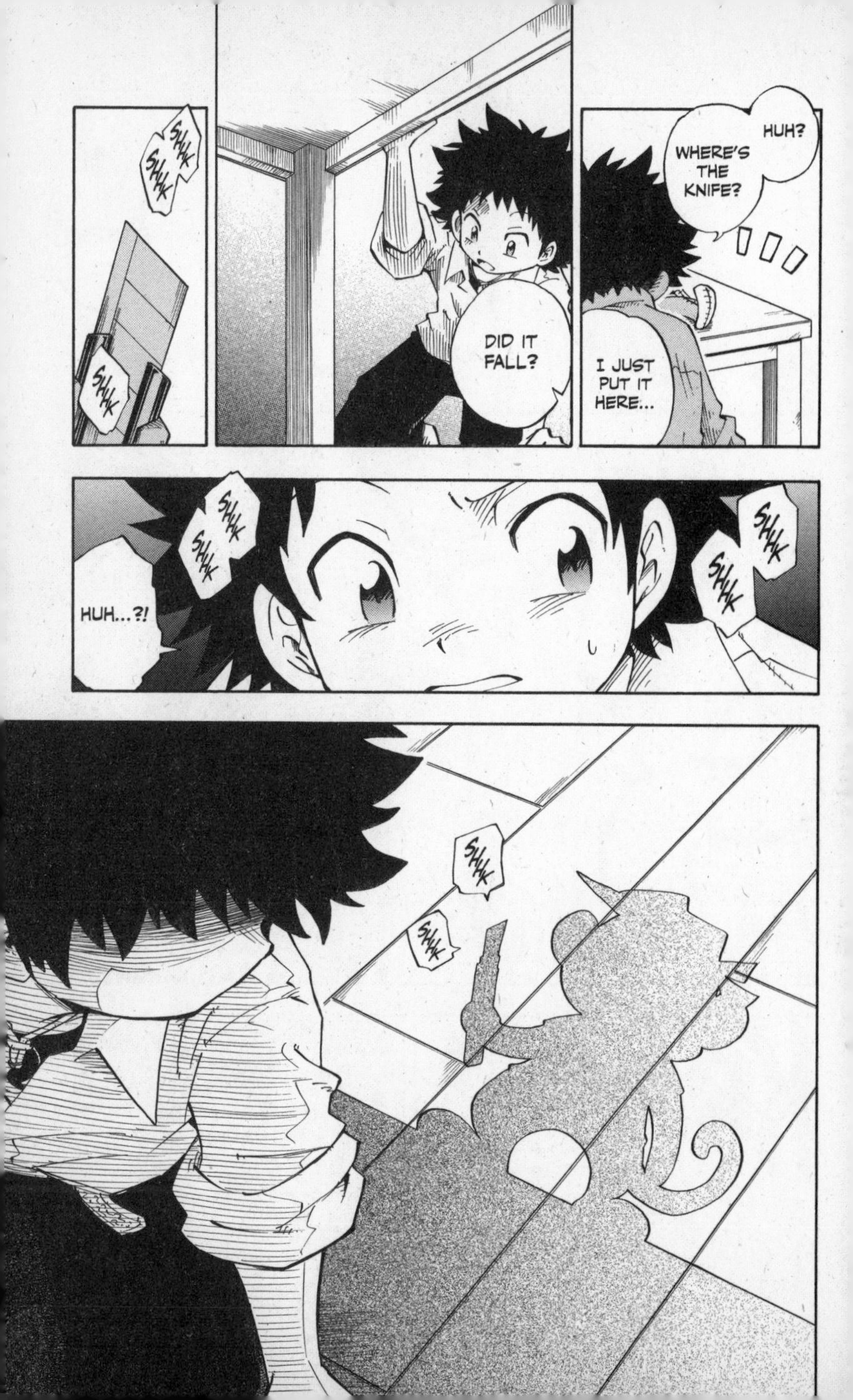
HUH?
WHERE'S THE KNIFE?
I JUST PUT IT HERE...
DID IT FALL?
SHUK SHUK
SHUK
SHUK SHUK
SHUK SHUK
HUH...?!
SHUK
SHUK

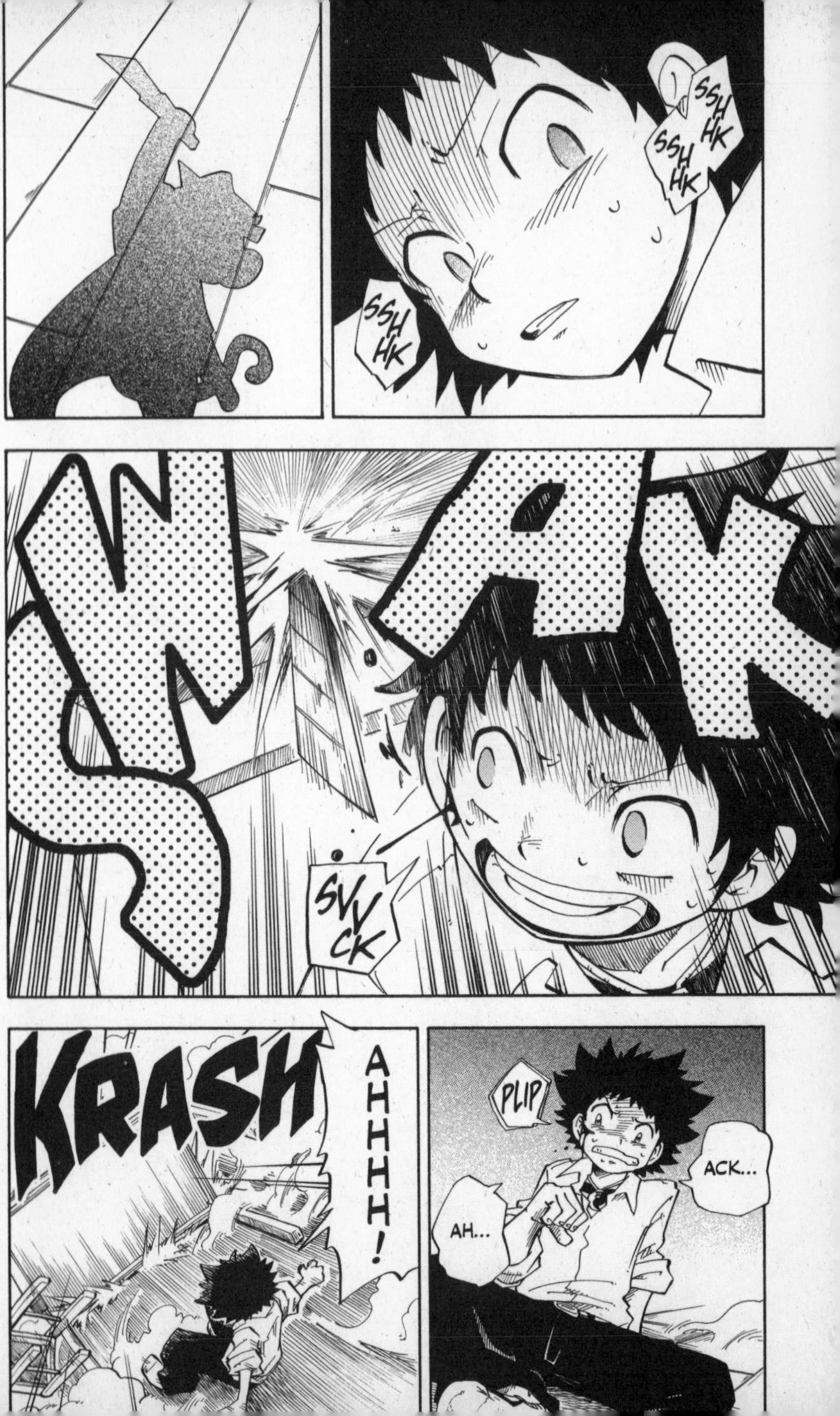
SSHHK
SSHHK
SSHHK
SVVCK
PLIP
ACK...
AH...
KRASH
AHHHHH!

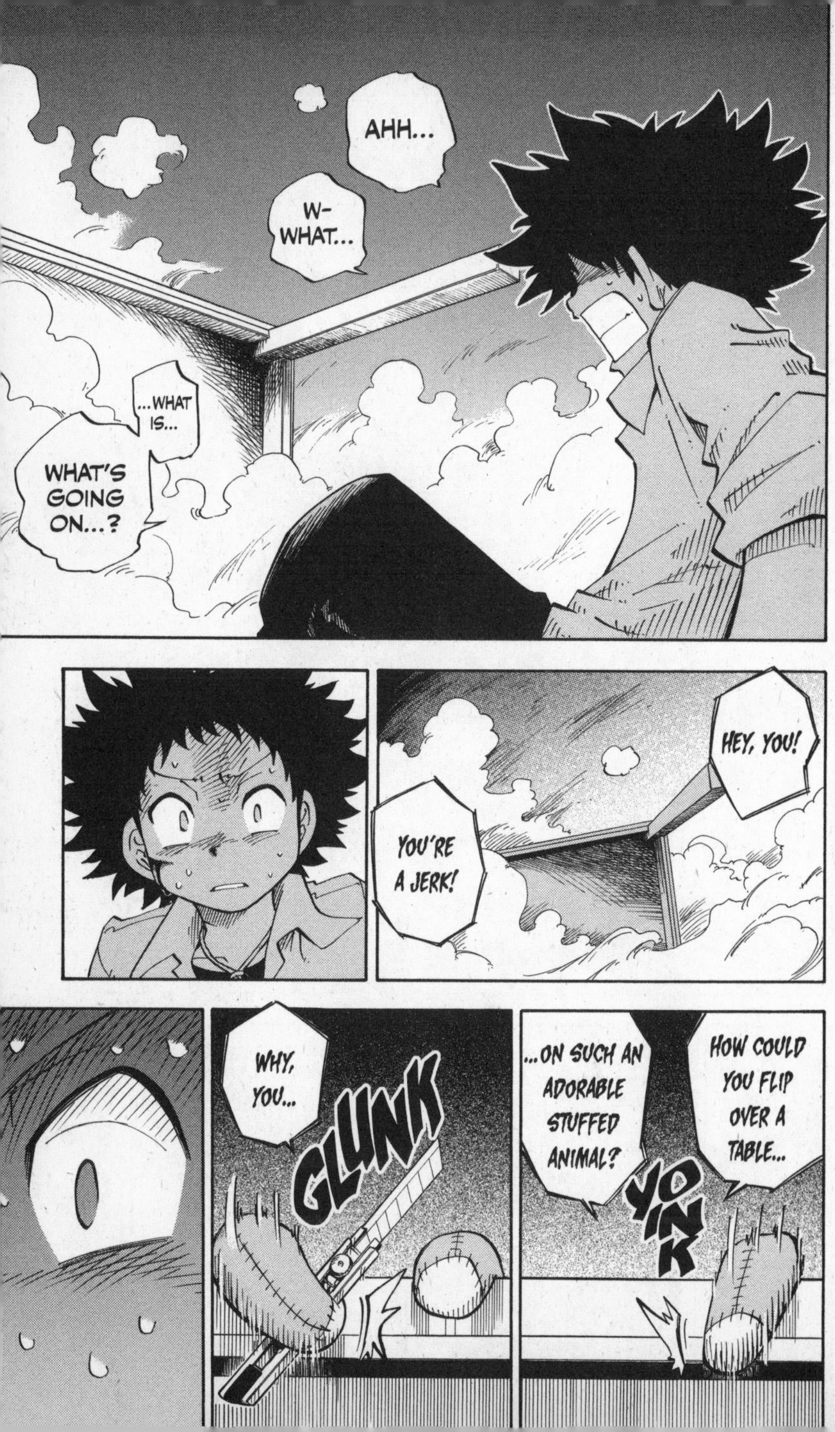
AHH...
W- WHAT...
...WHAT IS...
WHAT'S GOING ON...?
HEY, YOU!
YOU'RE A JERK!
HOW COULD YOU FLIP OVER A TABLE...
...ON SUCH AN ADORABLE STUFFED ANIMAL?
YOINK
WHY, YOU...
GLUNK

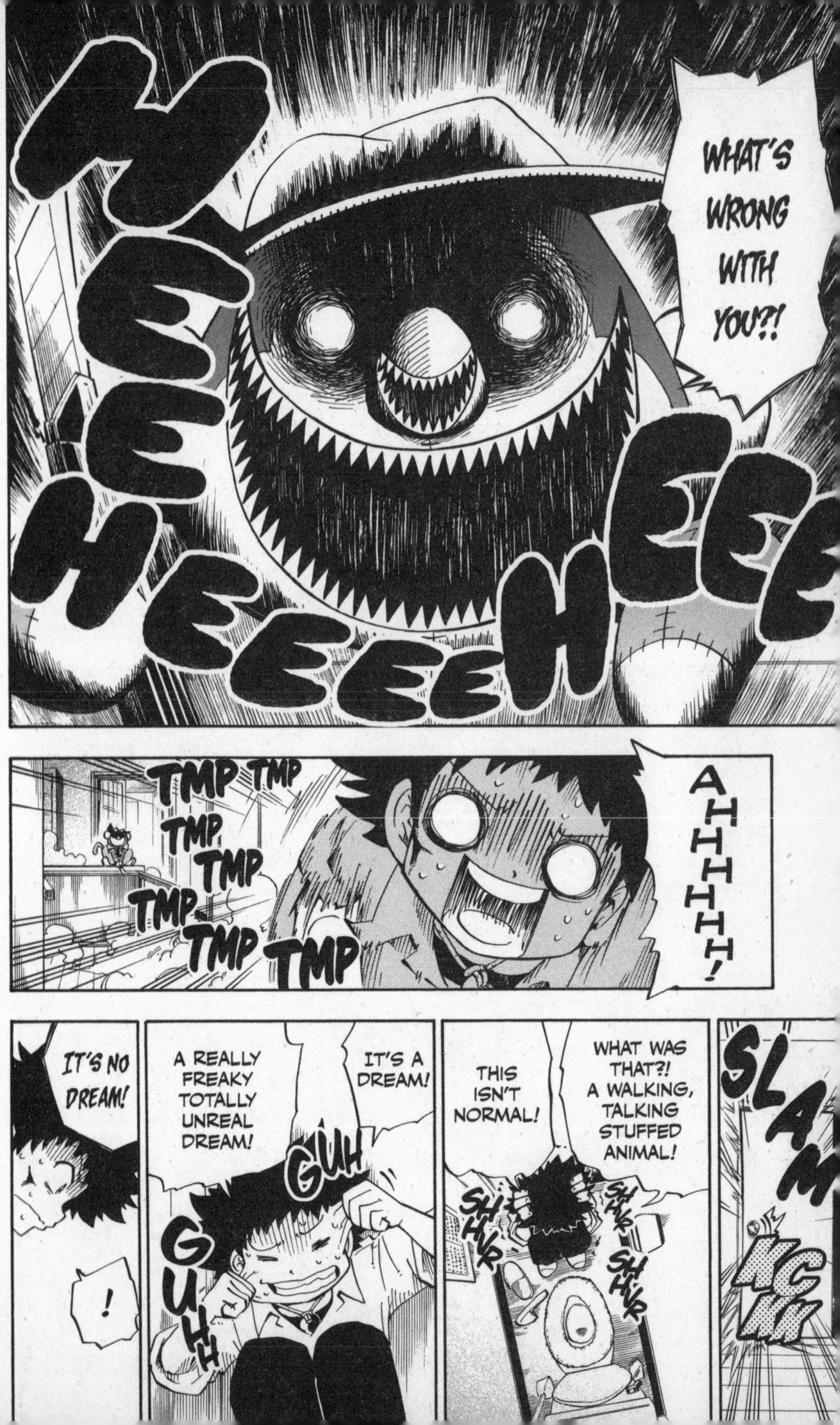
WHAT'S WRONG WITH YOU?!
HEEHEEEEHEEE
AHHHHHH!
TMP TMP TMP TMP TMP TMP TMP
SLAM
KCHK
WHAT WAS THAT?! A WALKING, TALKING STUFFED ANIMAL!
THIS ISN'T NORMAL!
SHHVR SHHVR SHHVR
IT'S A DREAM!
A REALLY FREAKY TOTALLY UNREAL DREAM!
GUH GUHH
IT'S NO DREAM!
!

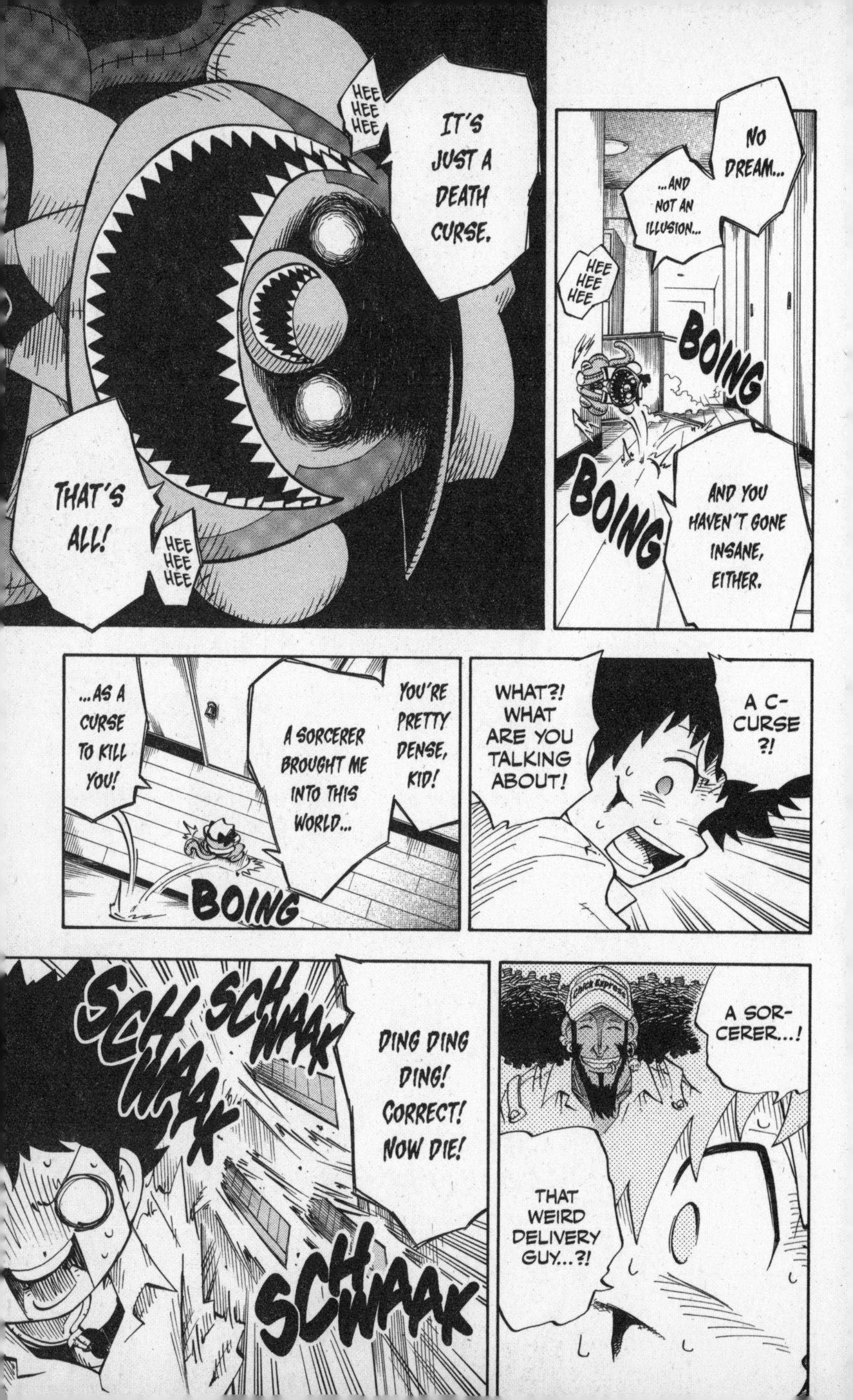
NO DREAM...
...AND NOT AN ILLUSION...
HEE HEE HEE
BOING
BOING
AND YOU HAVEN'T GONE INSANE, EITHER.
HEE HEE HEE
IT'S JUST A DEATH CURSE.
THAT'S ALL!
HEE HEE HEE
A C-CURSE?!
WHAT?! WHAT ARE YOU TALKING ABOUT!
YOU'RE PRETTY DENSE, KID!
A SORCERER BROUGHT ME INTO THIS WORLD...
...AS A CURSE TO KILL YOU!
BOING
A SOR-CERER...!
THAT WEIRD DELIVERY GUY...?!
DING DING DING! CORRECT! NOW DIE!
SCHWAAK
SCHWAAK
SCHWAAK
SCHWAAK

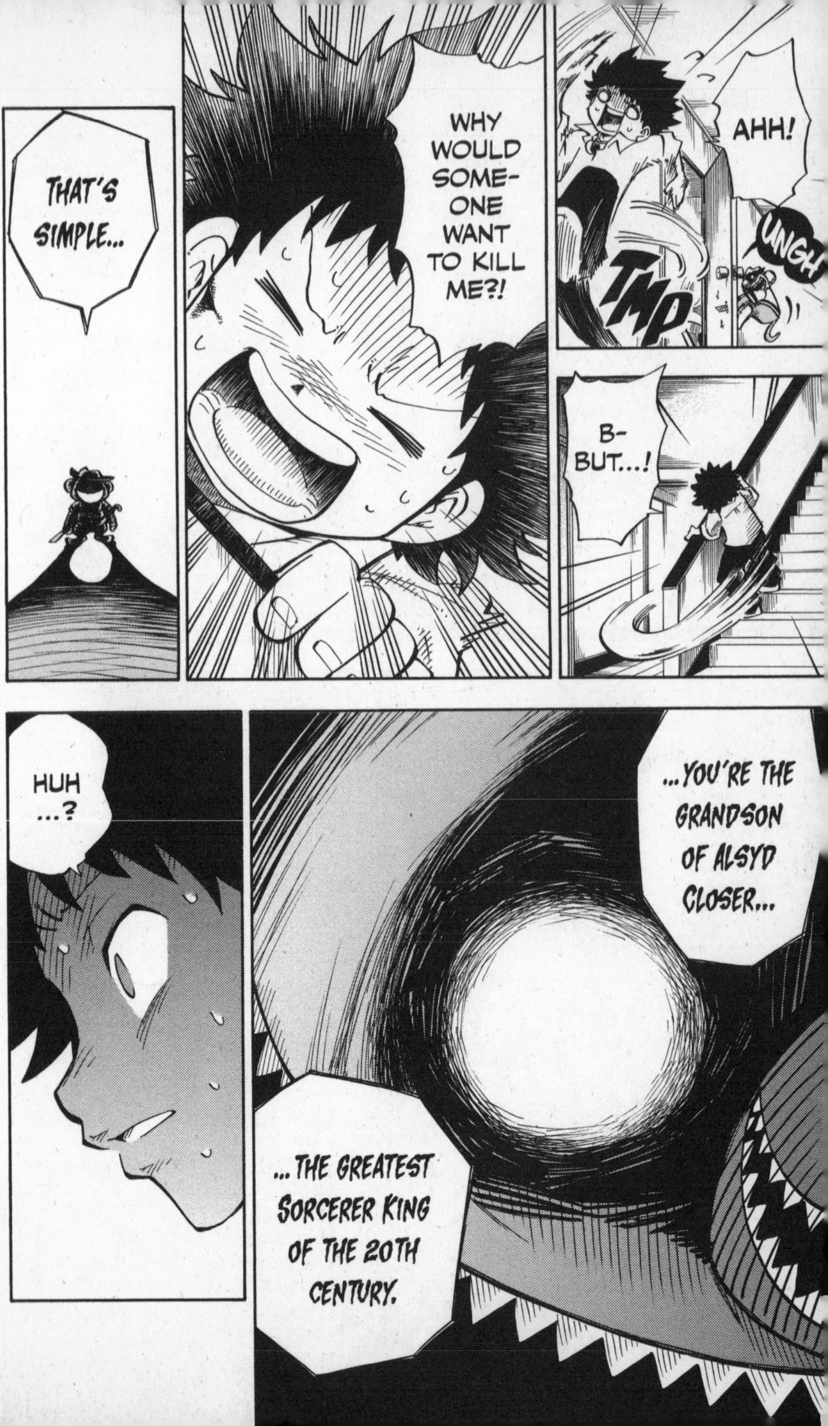
AHH!
UNGH
TMP
B-BUT...!
WHY WOULD SOME-ONE WANT TO KILL ME?!
THAT'S SIMPLE...
...YOU'RE THE GRANDSON OF ALSYD CLOSER...
...THE GREATEST SORCERER KING OF THE 20TH CENTURY.
HUH ...?

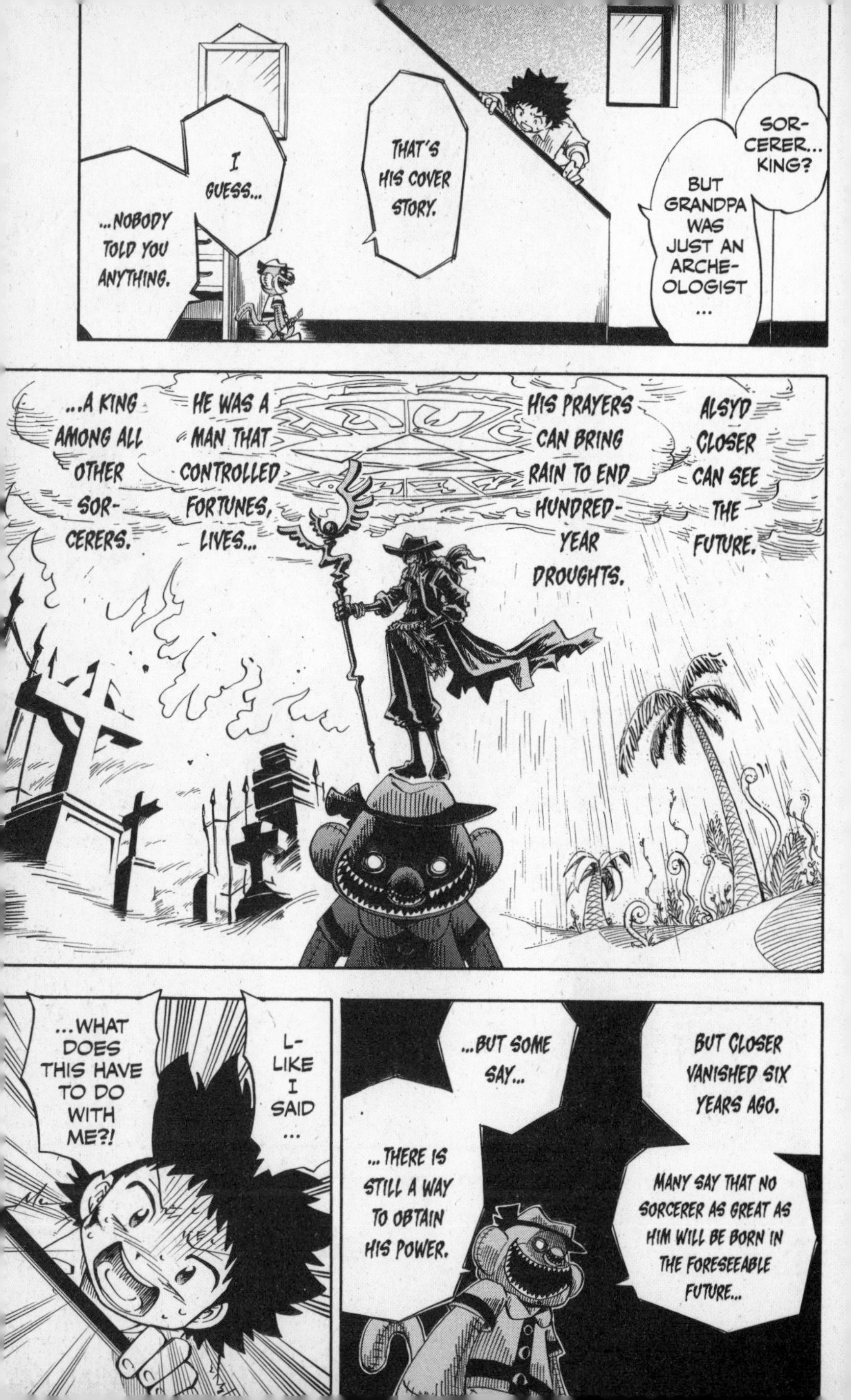
SORCERER... KING?
BUT GRANDPA WAS JUST AN ARCHEOLOGIST...
THAT'S HIS COVER STORY.
I GUESS...
...NOBODY TOLD YOU ANYTHING.
ALSYD CLOSER CAN SEE THE FUTURE.
HIS PRAYERS CAN BRING RAIN TO END HUNDRED-YEAR DROUGHTS.
HE WAS A MAN THAT CONTROLLED FORTUNES, LIVES...
...A KING AMONG ALL OTHER SORCERERS.
BUT CLOSER VANISHED SIX YEARS AGO.
MANY SAY THAT NO SORCERER AS GREAT AS HIM WILL BE BORN IN THE FORESEEABLE FUTURE...
...BUT SOME SAY...
...THERE IS STILL A WAY TO OBTAIN HIS POWER.
L-LIKE I SAID...
...WHAT DOES THIS HAVE TO DO WITH ME?!

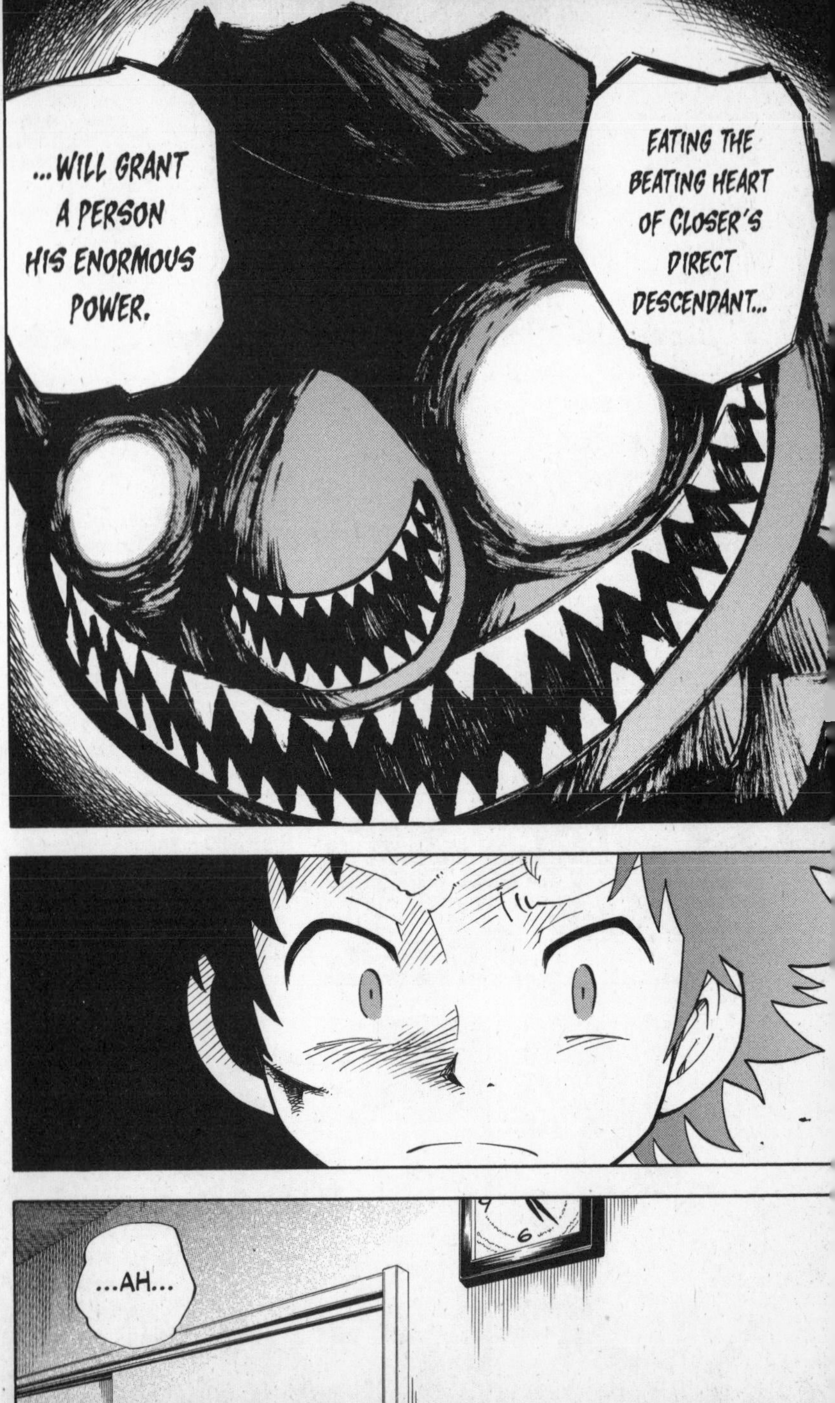
EATING THE BEATING HEART OF CLOSER'S DIRECT DESCENDANT...
...WILL GRANT A PERSON HIS ENORMOUS POWER.
...AH...

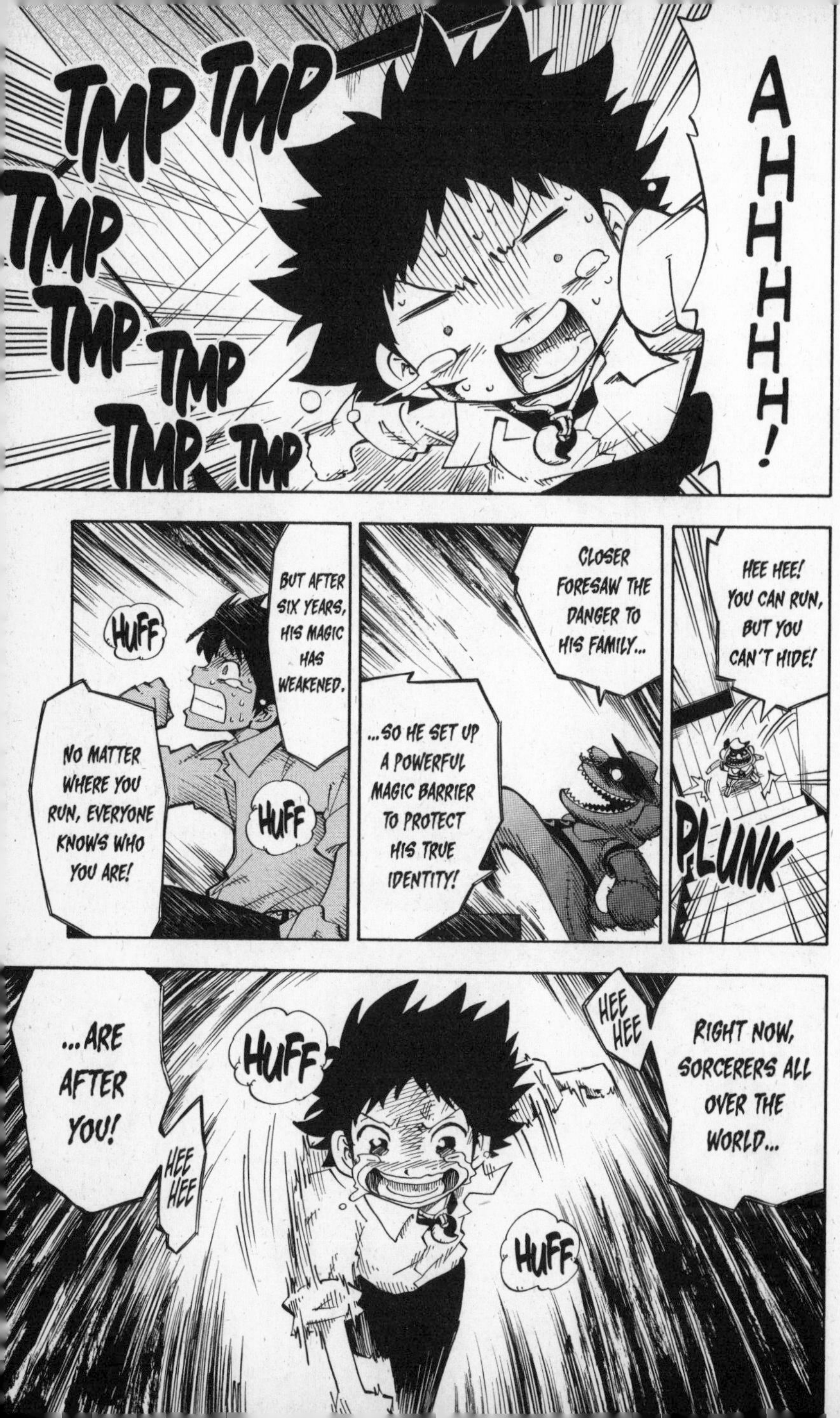
AHHHHH!
TMP TMP
TMP
TMP
TMP
TMP TMP
HEE HEE! YOU CAN RUN, BUT YOU CAN'T HIDE!
PLUNK
CLOSER FORESAW THE DANGER TO HIS FAMILY...
...SO HE SET UP A POWERFUL MAGIC BARRIER TO PROTECT HIS TRUE IDENTITY!
BUT AFTER SIX YEARS, HIS MAGIC HAS WEAKENED.
HUFF
HUFF
NO MATTER WHERE YOU RUN, EVERYONE KNOWS WHO YOU ARE!
RIGHT NOW, SORCERERS ALL OVER THE WORLD...
HEE HEE
HUFF
HUFF
...ARE AFTER YOU!
HEE HEE

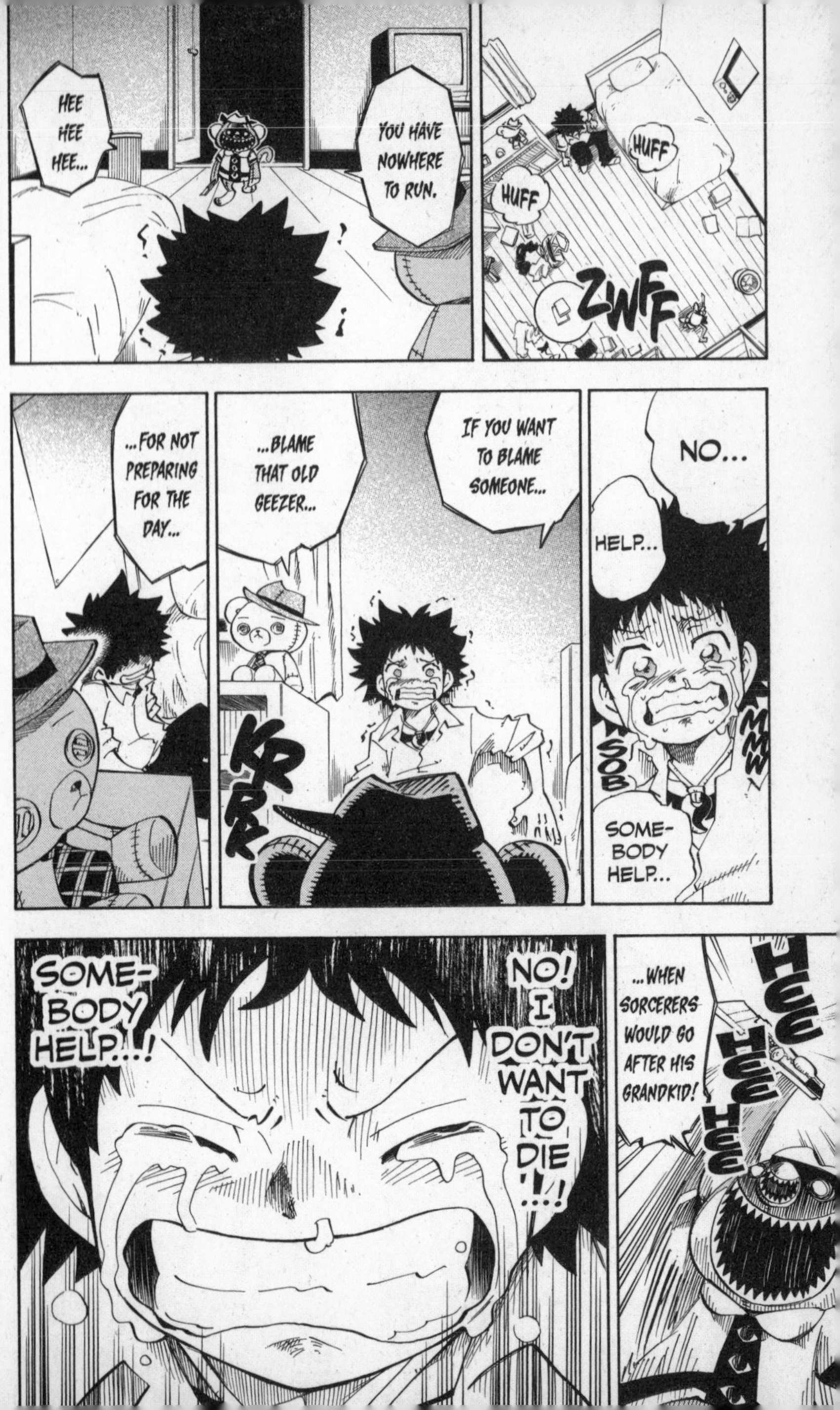
HUFF
HUFF
ZWFF
YOU HAVE NOWHERE TO RUN.
HEE HEE HEE...
NO...
HELP...
MMW
SOB
SOME-BODY HELP...
IF YOU WANT TO BLAME SOMEONE...
...BLAME THAT OLD GEEZER...
KRKK
...FOR NOT PREPARING FOR THE DAY...
HEE HEE HEE HEE
...WHEN SORCERERS WOULD GO AFTER HIS GRANDKID!
NO! I DON'T WANT TO DIE!!!
SOME-BODY HELP...!

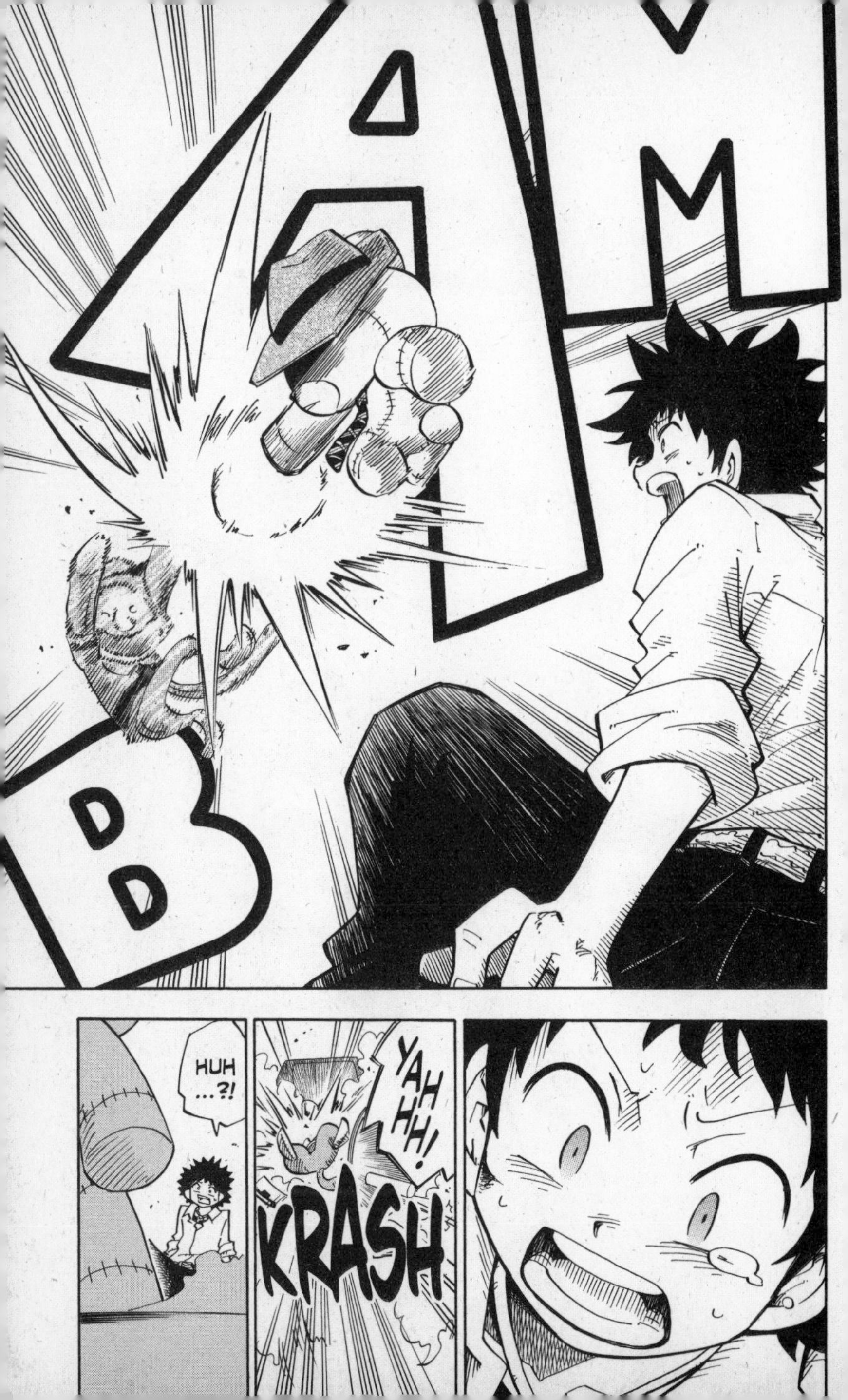
YAHHH!
KRASH
HUH ...?!

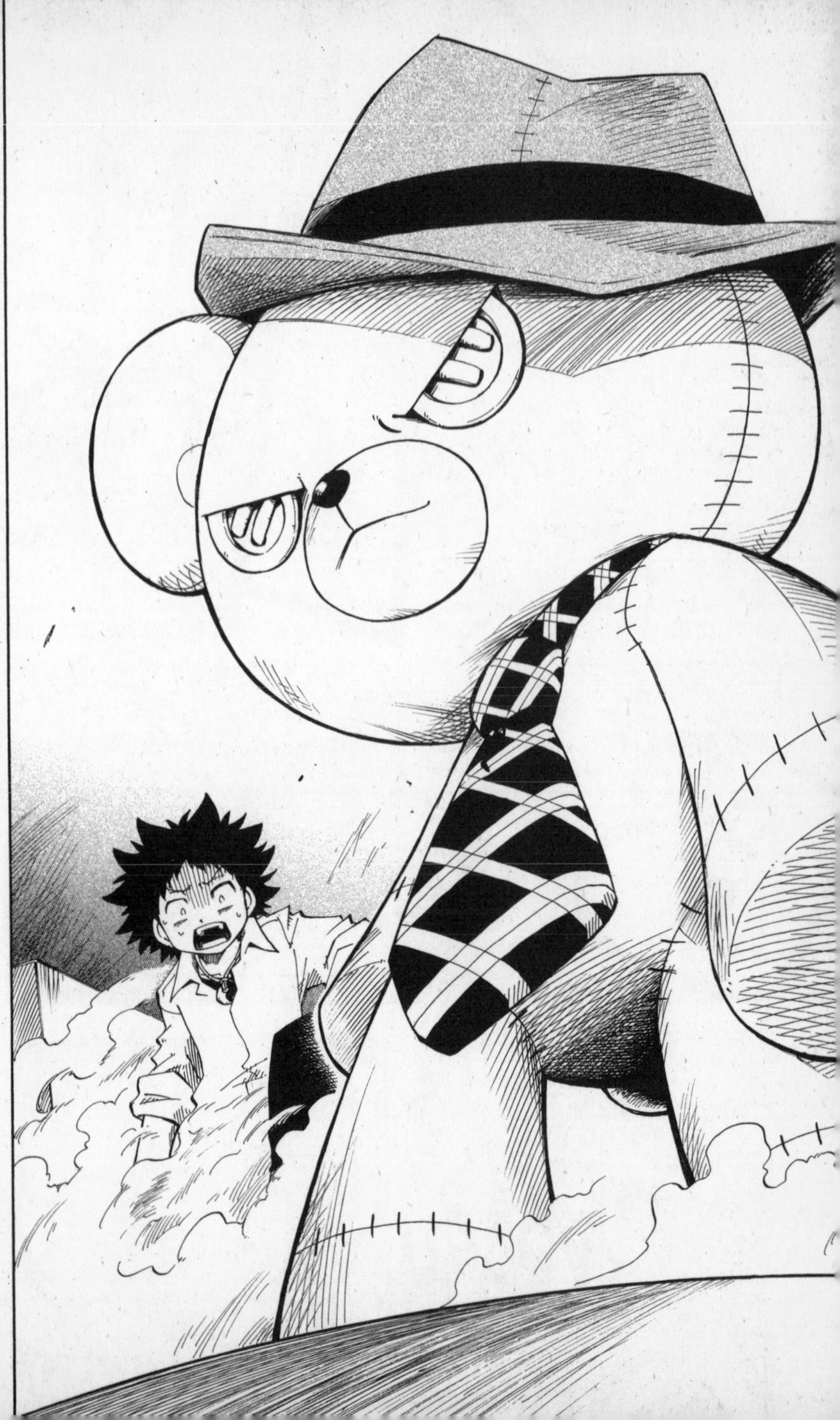

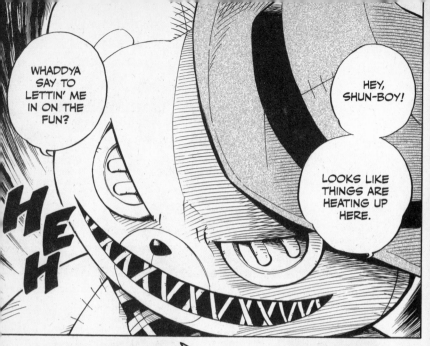

HEY, SHUN-BOY!
LOOKS LIKE THINGS ARE HEATING UP HERE.
WHADDYA SAY TO LETTIN' ME IN ON THE FUN?
HEH
HYDE ...?!
H-H-H...
...HYDE CAN TALK NOW!
AHHH
HEY HEY. WHERE YA GOING, SHUN-BOY?
HMPH ...
WHATTA WIMP HE TURNED OUT TO BE.
PTMP
PTMP

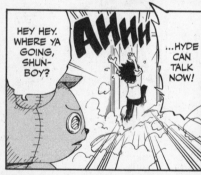

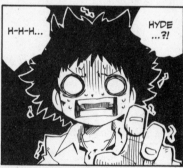

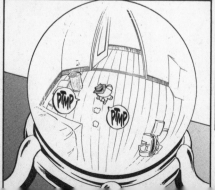

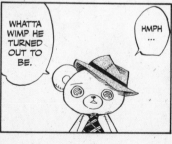

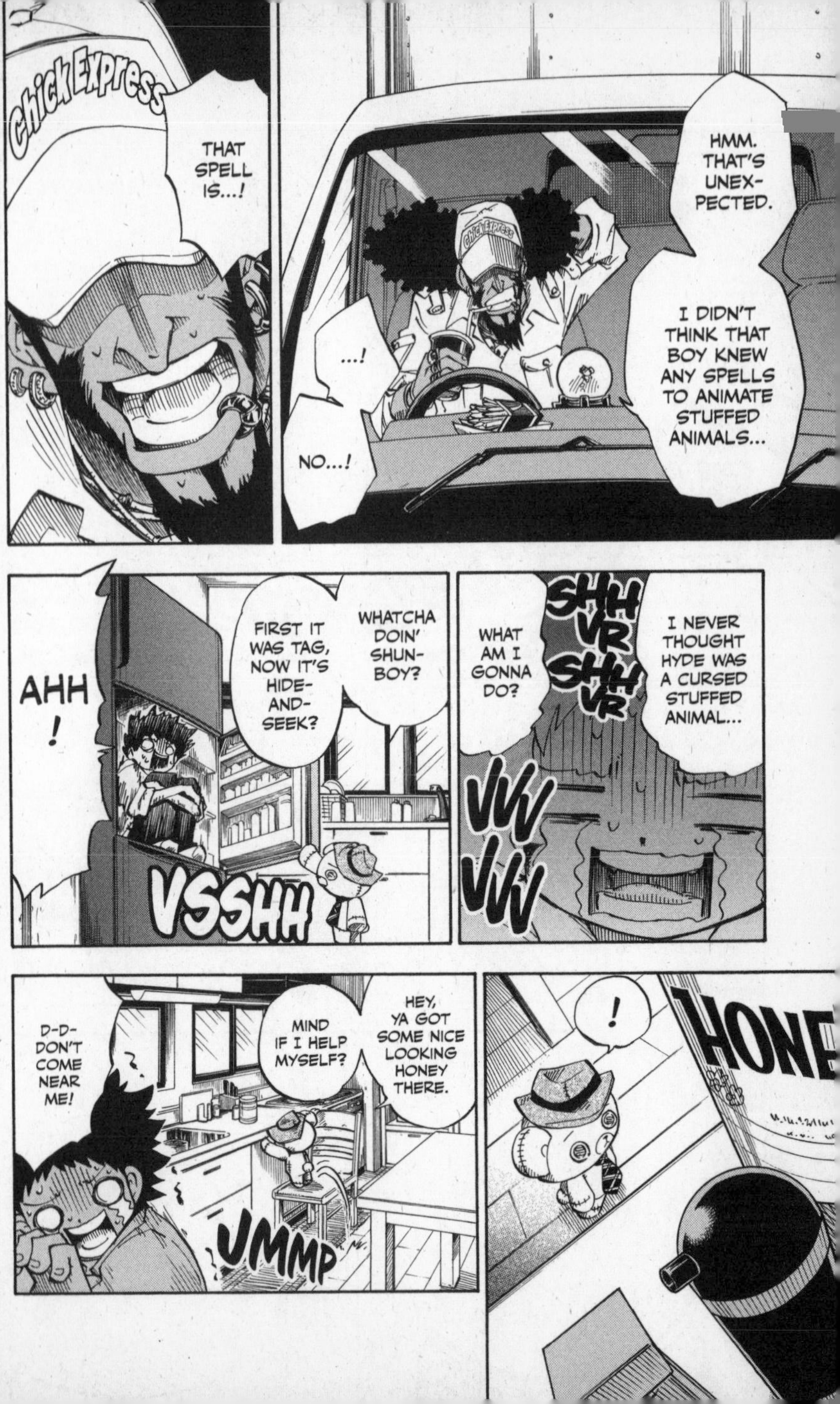
HMM. THAT'S UNEXPECTED.
I DIDN'T THINK THAT BOY KNEW ANY SPELLS TO ANIMATE STUFFED ANIMALS...
...!
NO...!
Chick Express
THAT SPELL IS...!
I NEVER THOUGHT HYDE WAS A CURSED STUFFED ANIMAL...
SHH VR SHH VR
WHAT AM I GONNA DO?
VVV VVV
WHATCHA DOIN' SHUN-BOY?
FIRST IT WAS TAG, NOW IT'S HIDE-AND-SEEK?
AHH!
VSSHH
!
HONE
HEY, YA GOT SOME NICE LOOKING HONEY THERE.
MIND IF I HELP MYSELF?
D-D-DON'T COME NEAR ME!
UMMP

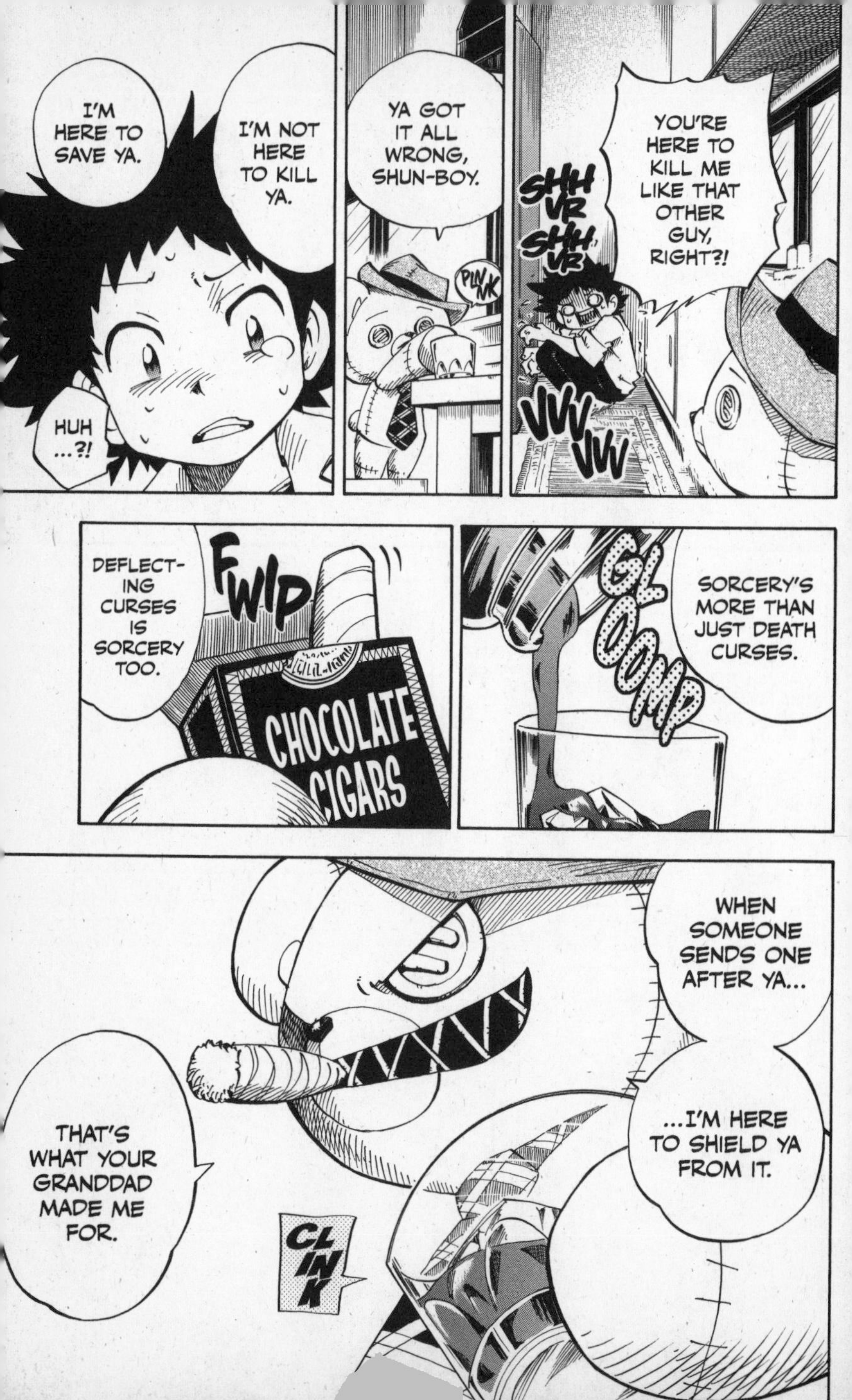
YOU'RE HERE TO KILL ME LIKE THAT OTHER GUY, RIGHT?!
SHHVR SHHVR
VVV VVV
YA GOT IT ALL WRONG, SHUN-BOY.
PLINK
I'M NOT HERE TO KILL YA.
I'M HERE TO SAVE YA.
HUH ...?!
SORCERY'S MORE THAN JUST DEATH CURSES.
GLOOMP
FWIP
DEFLECT-ING CURSES IS SORCERY TOO.
CHOCOLATE CIGARS
WHEN SOMEONE SENDS ONE AFTER YA...
...I'M HERE TO SHIELD YA FROM IT.
CLINK
THAT'S WHAT YOUR GRANDDAD MADE ME FOR.

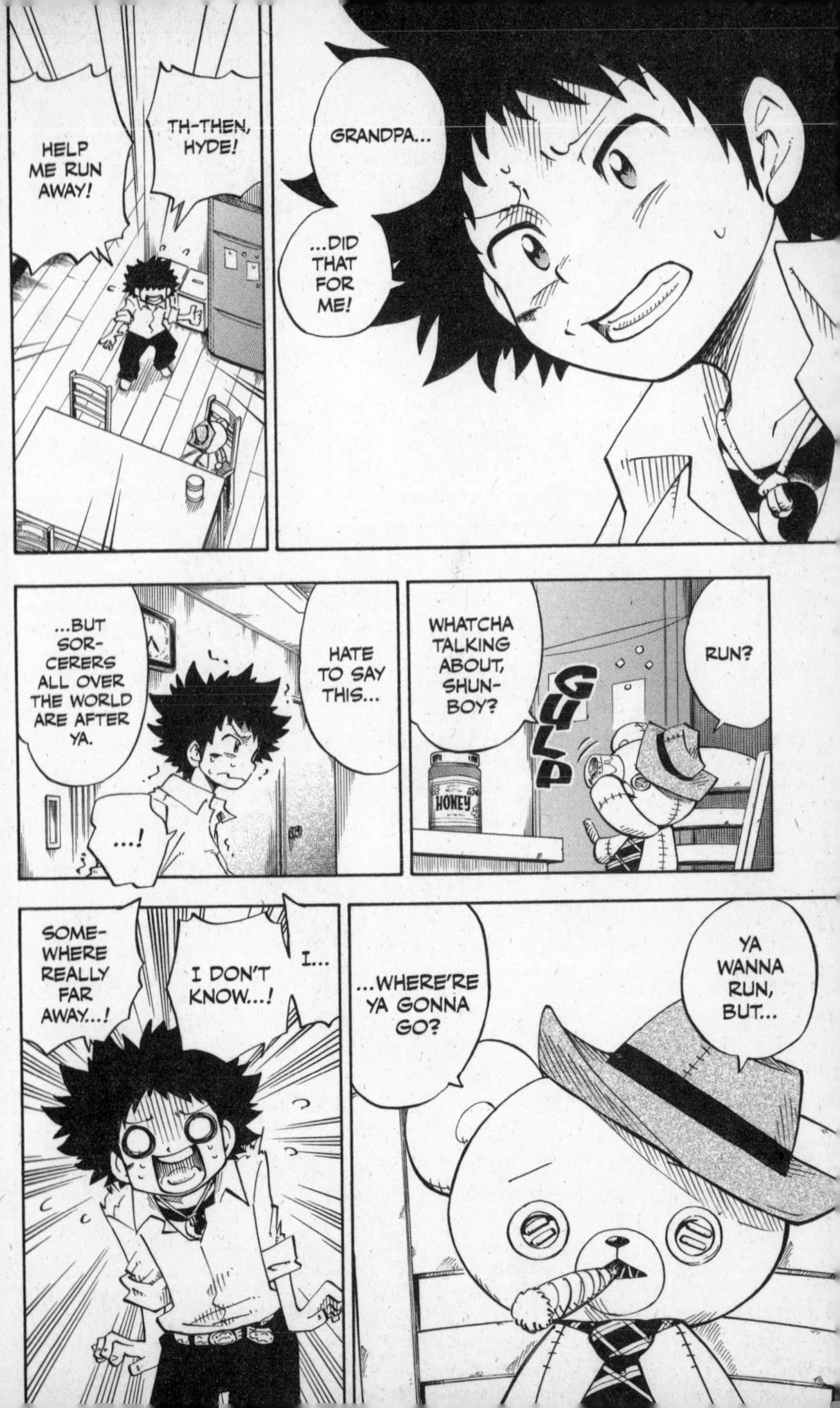
GRANDPA...
...DID THAT FOR ME!
TH-THEN, HYDE!
HELP ME RUN AWAY!
RUN?
GULP
WHATCHA TALKING ABOUT, SHUN-BOY?
HONEY
HATE TO SAY THIS...
...BUT SORCERERS ALL OVER THE WORLD ARE AFTER YA.
...!
YA WANNA RUN, BUT...
...WHERE'RE YA GONNA GO?
I...
I DON'T KNOW...!
SOMEWHERE REALLY FAR AWAY...!

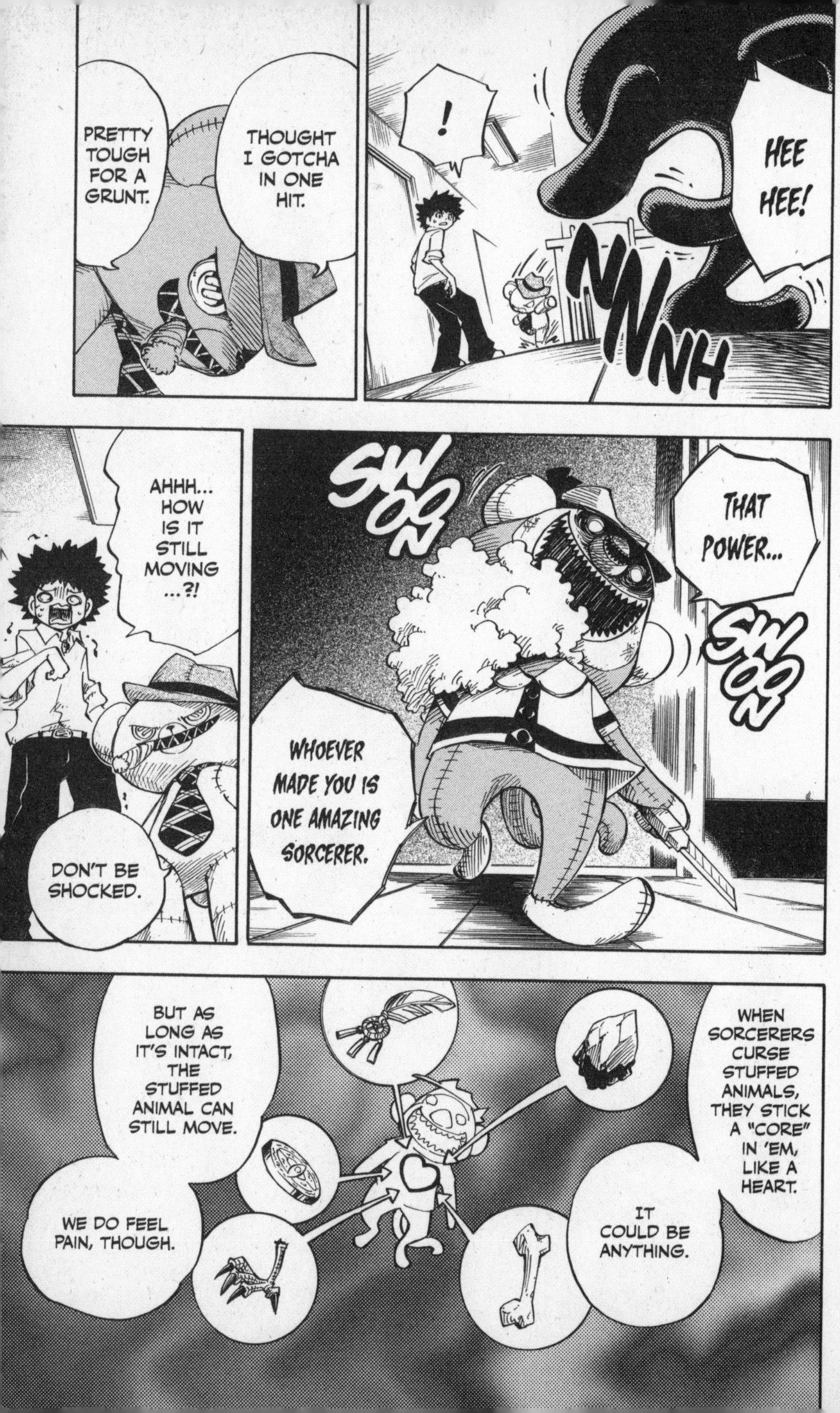
!
HEE HEE!
NNNNH
THOUGHT I GOTCHA IN ONE HIT.
PRETTY TOUGH FOR A GRUNT.
SWOON
THAT POWER...
SWOON
WHOEVER MADE YOU IS ONE AMAZING SORCERER.
AHHH... HOW IS IT STILL MOVING ...?!
DON'T BE SHOCKED.
WHEN SORCERERS CURSE STUFFED ANIMALS, THEY STICK A "CORE" IN 'EM, LIKE A HEART.
IT COULD BE ANYTHING.
BUT AS LONG AS IT'S INTACT, THE STUFFED ANIMAL CAN STILL MOVE.
WE DO FEEL PAIN, THOUGH.

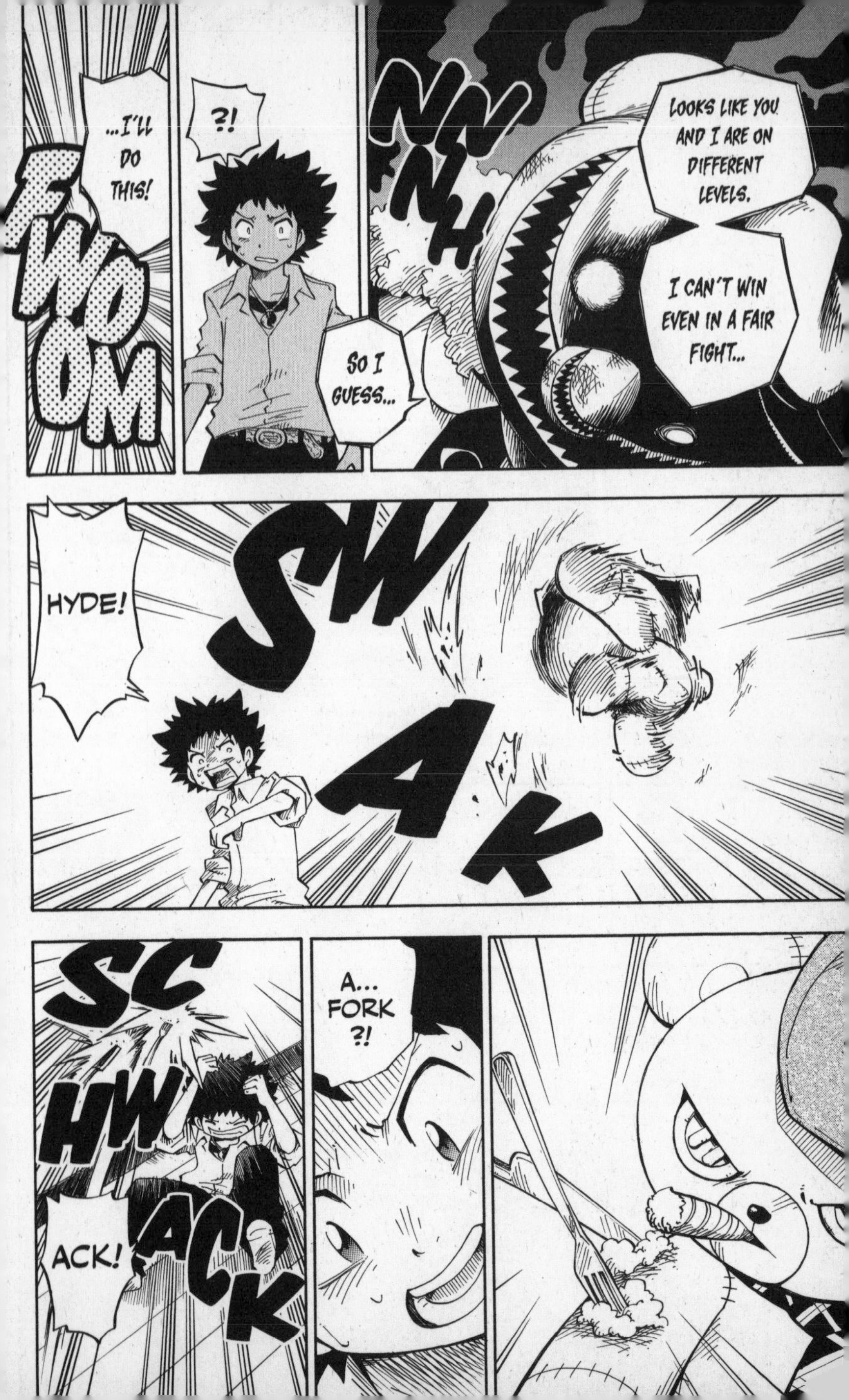
LOOKS LIKE YOU AND I ARE ON DIFFERENT LEVELS.
I CAN'T WIN EVEN IN A FAIR FIGHT...
NNNNH
SO I GUESS...
?!
...I'LL DO THIS!
FWOOM
SWAK
HYDE!
A... FORK ?!
SCHWACK
ACK!

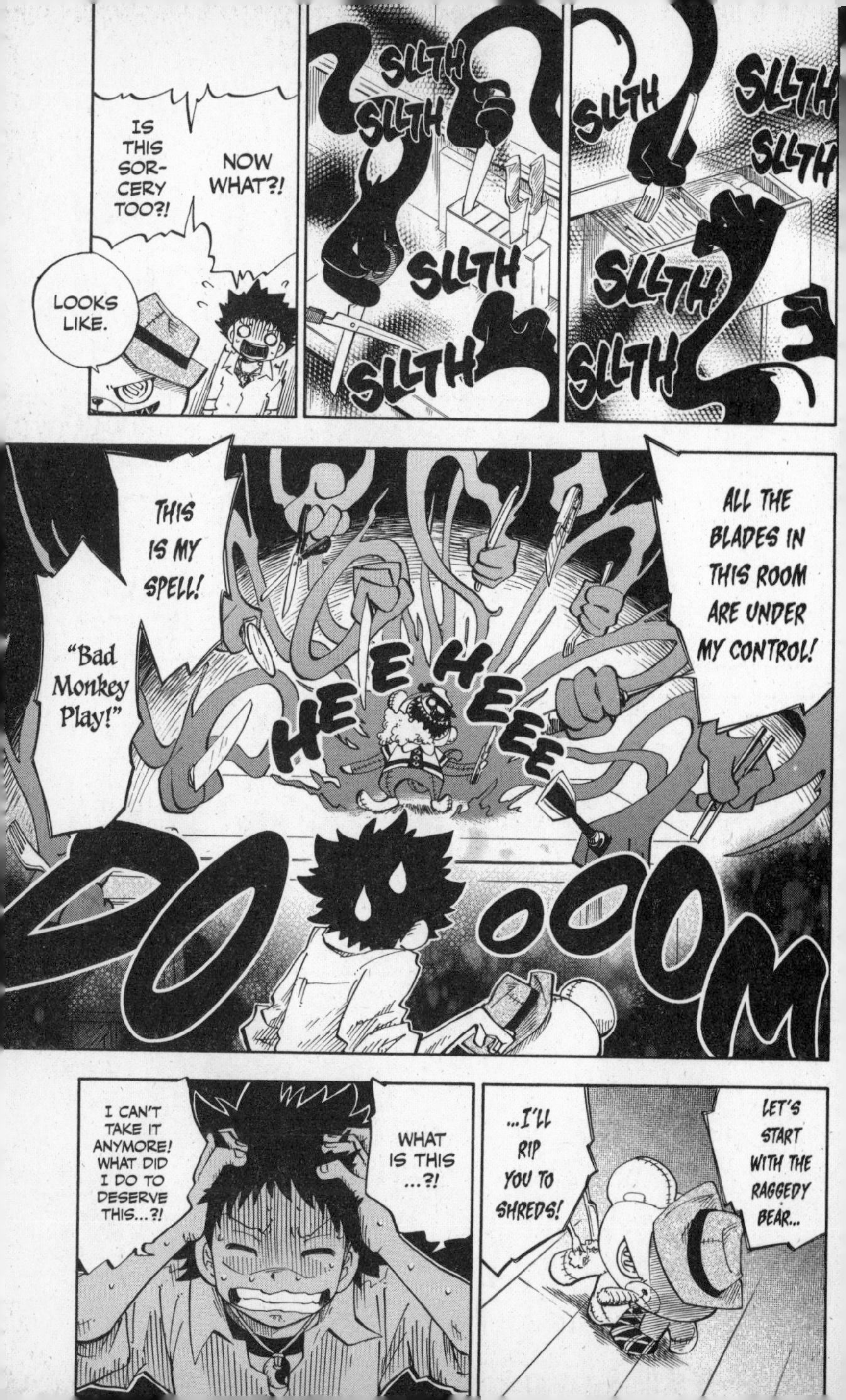

SLLTH
SLLTH
SLLTH
SLLTH
SLLTH
SLLTH
SLLTH
SLLTH
SLLTH
NOW WHAT?!
IS THIS SORCERY TOO?!
LOOKS LIKE.
ALL THE BLADES IN THIS ROOM ARE UNDER MY CONTROL!
HEE HEEE
THIS IS MY SPELL!
"Bad Monkey Play!"
DOOOOM
LET'S START WITH THE RAGGEDY BEAR...
...I'LL RIP YOU TO SHREDS!
WHAT IS THIS ...?!
I CAN'T TAKE IT ANYMORE! WHAT DID I DO TO DESERVE THIS...?!

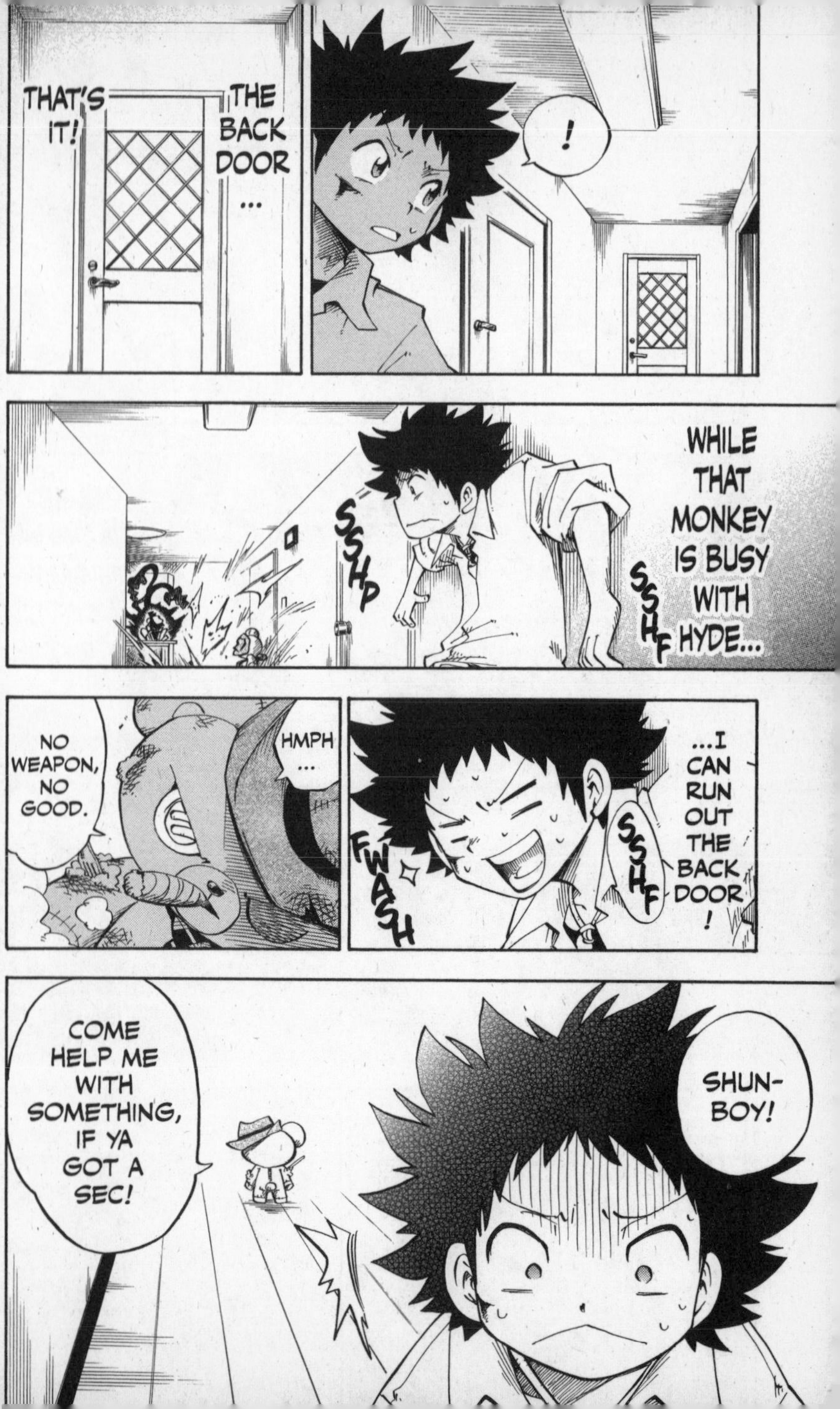
!
THE BACK DOOR...
THAT'S IT!
WHILE THAT MONKEY IS BUSY WITH HYDE...
SSHF
SSHP
...I CAN RUN OUT THE BACK DOOR!
SSHF
FWASH
HMPH...
NO WEAPON, NO GOOD.
SHUN-BOY!
COME HELP ME WITH SOMETHING, IF YA GOT A SEC!

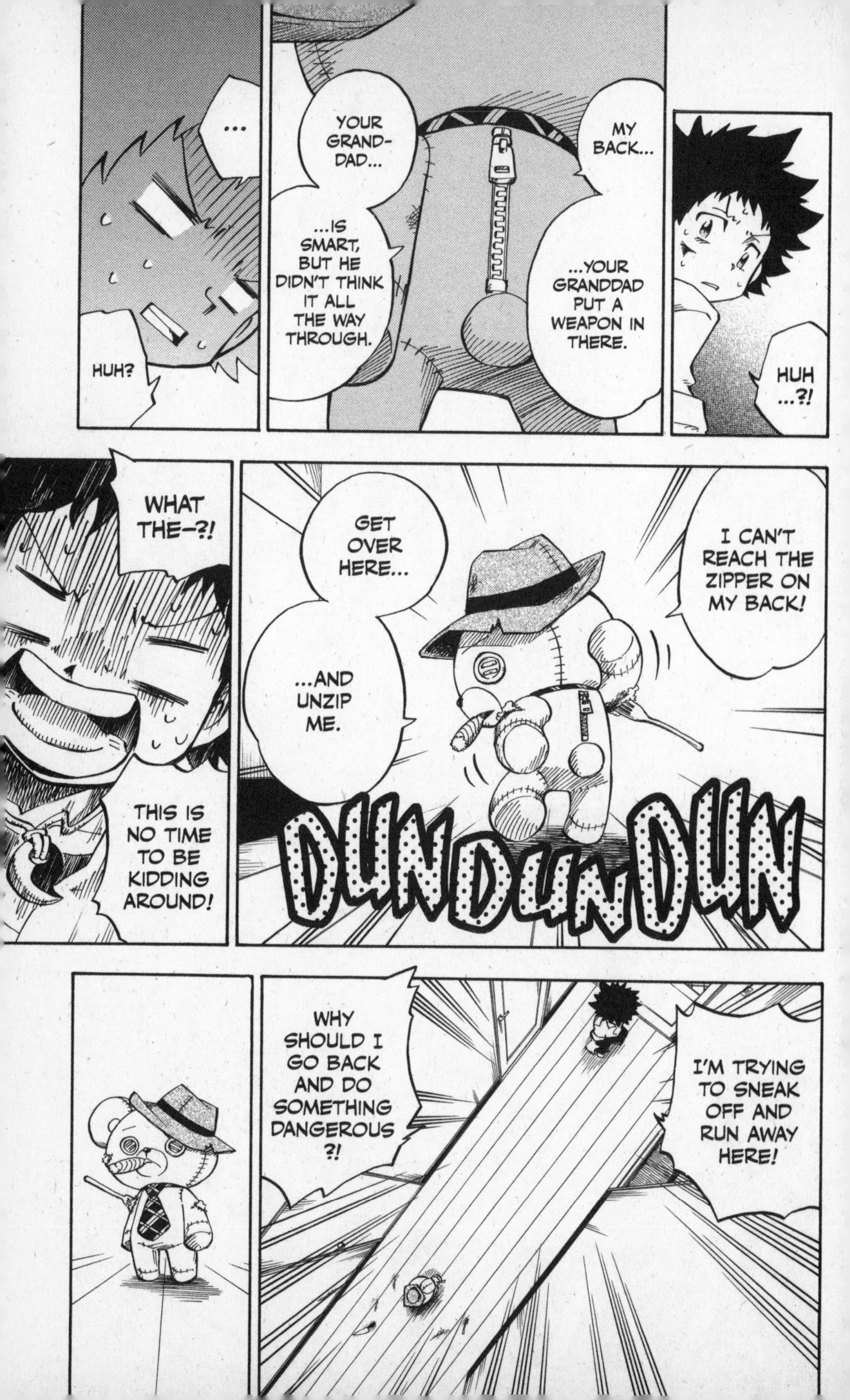
HUH ...?!
MY BACK...
...YOUR GRANDDAD PUT A WEAPON IN THERE.
YOUR GRAND-DAD...
...IS SMART, BUT HE DIDN'T THINK IT ALL THE WAY THROUGH.
...
HUH?
I CAN'T REACH THE ZIPPER ON MY BACK!
GET OVER HERE...
...AND UNZIP ME.
DUN DUN DUN
WHAT THE–?!
THIS IS NO TIME TO BE KIDDING AROUND!
I'M TRYING TO SNEAK OFF AND RUN AWAY HERE!
WHY SHOULD I GO BACK AND DO SOMETHING DANGEROUS ?!

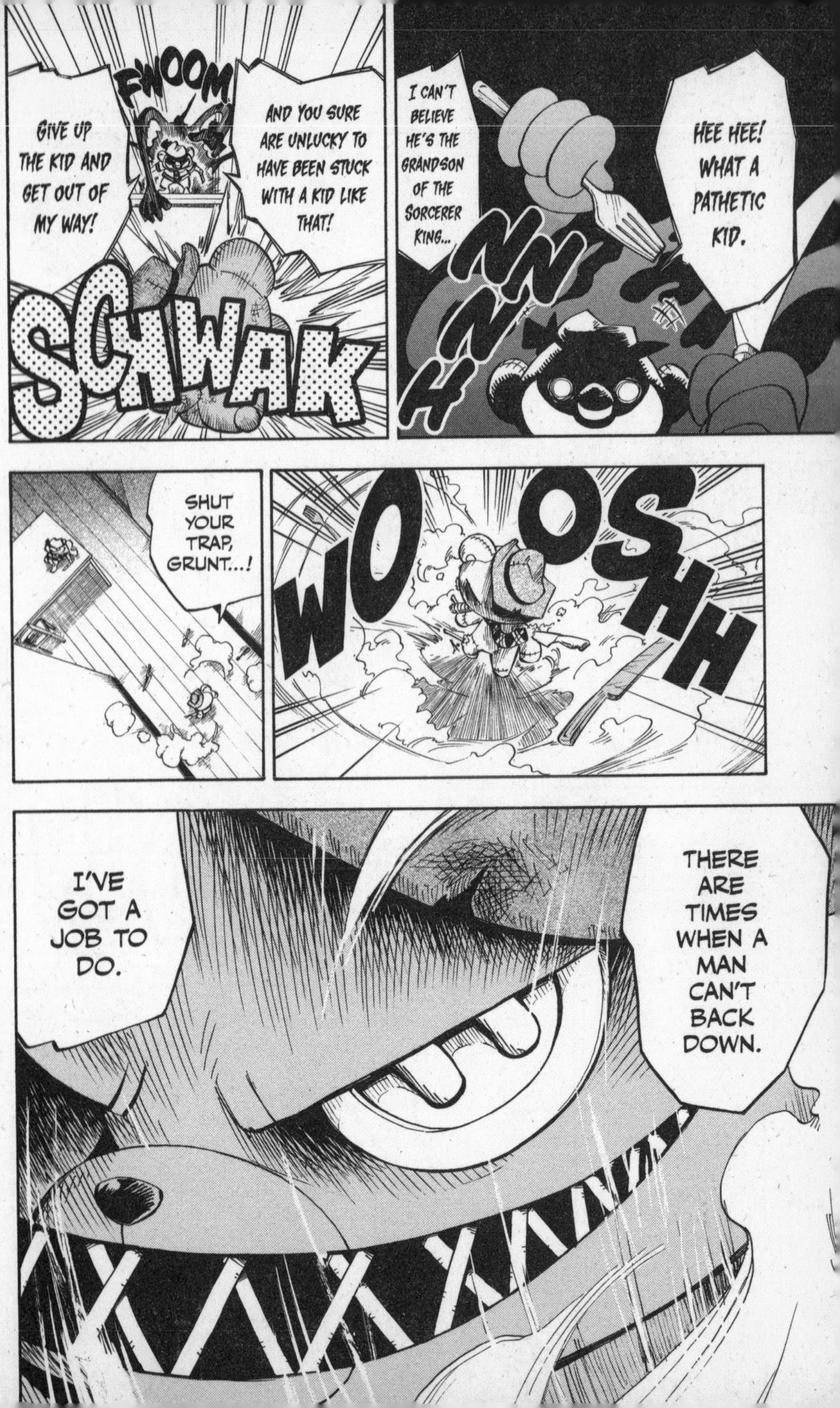
HEE HEE! WHAT A PATHETIC KID.
I CAN'T BELIEVE HE'S THE GRANDSON OF THE SORCERER KING...
NNNH
FWOOM
AND YOU SURE ARE UNLUCKY TO HAVE BEEN STUCK WITH A KID LIKE THAT!
GIVE UP THE KID AND GET OUT OF MY WAY!
SCHWAK
WOOSHH
SHUT YOUR TRAP, GRUNT...!
THERE ARE TIMES WHEN A MAN CAN'T BACK DOWN.
I'VE GOT A JOB TO DO.

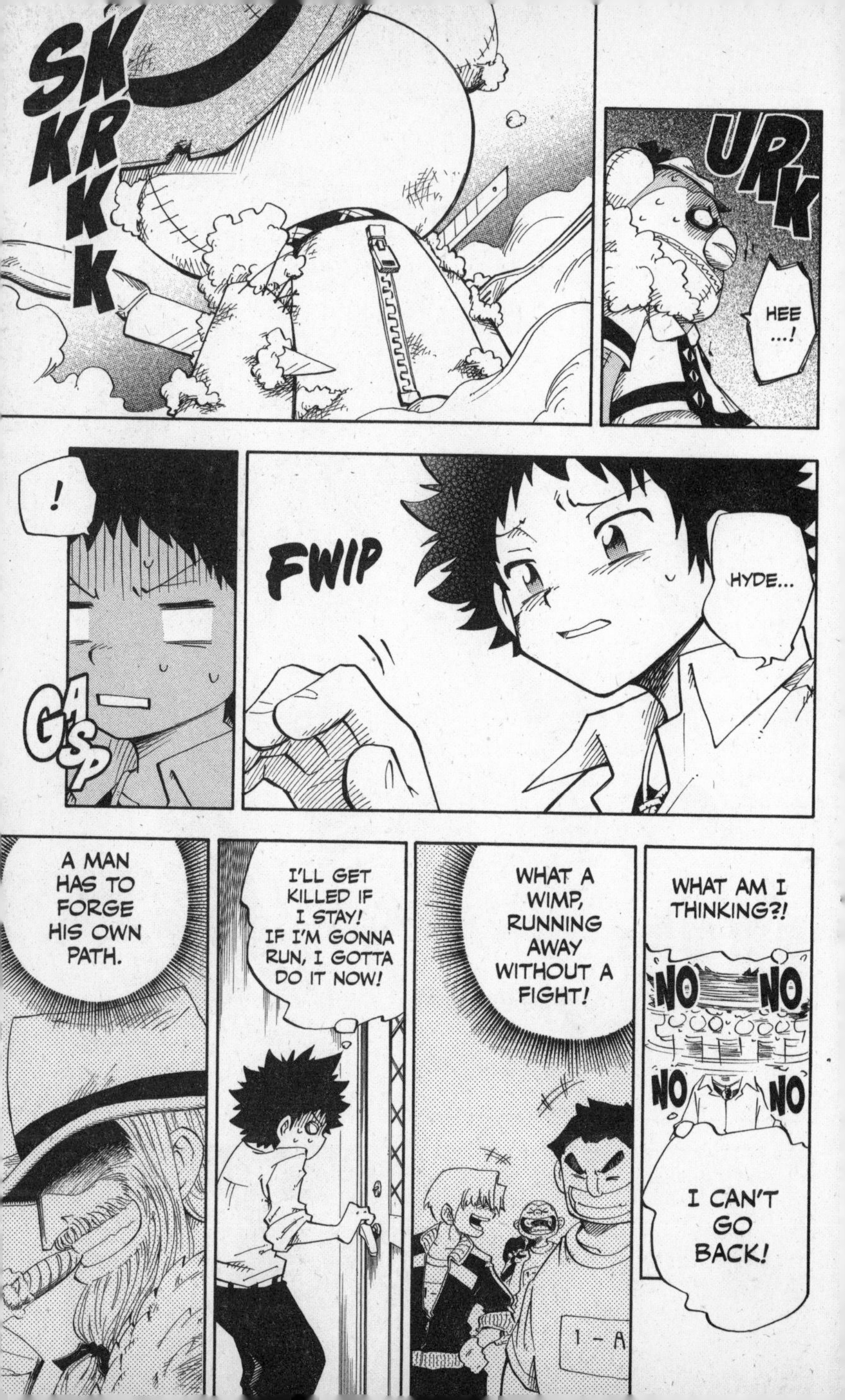
URK
HEE ...!
SKKRKKK
HYDE...
FWIP
!
GASP
WHAT AM I THINKING?!
NO NO NO NO
I CAN'T GO BACK!
WHAT A WIMP, RUNNING AWAY WITHOUT A FIGHT!
1-A
I'LL GET KILLED IF I STAY! IF I'M GONNA RUN, I GOTTA DO IT NOW!
A MAN HAS TO FORGE HIS OWN PATH.

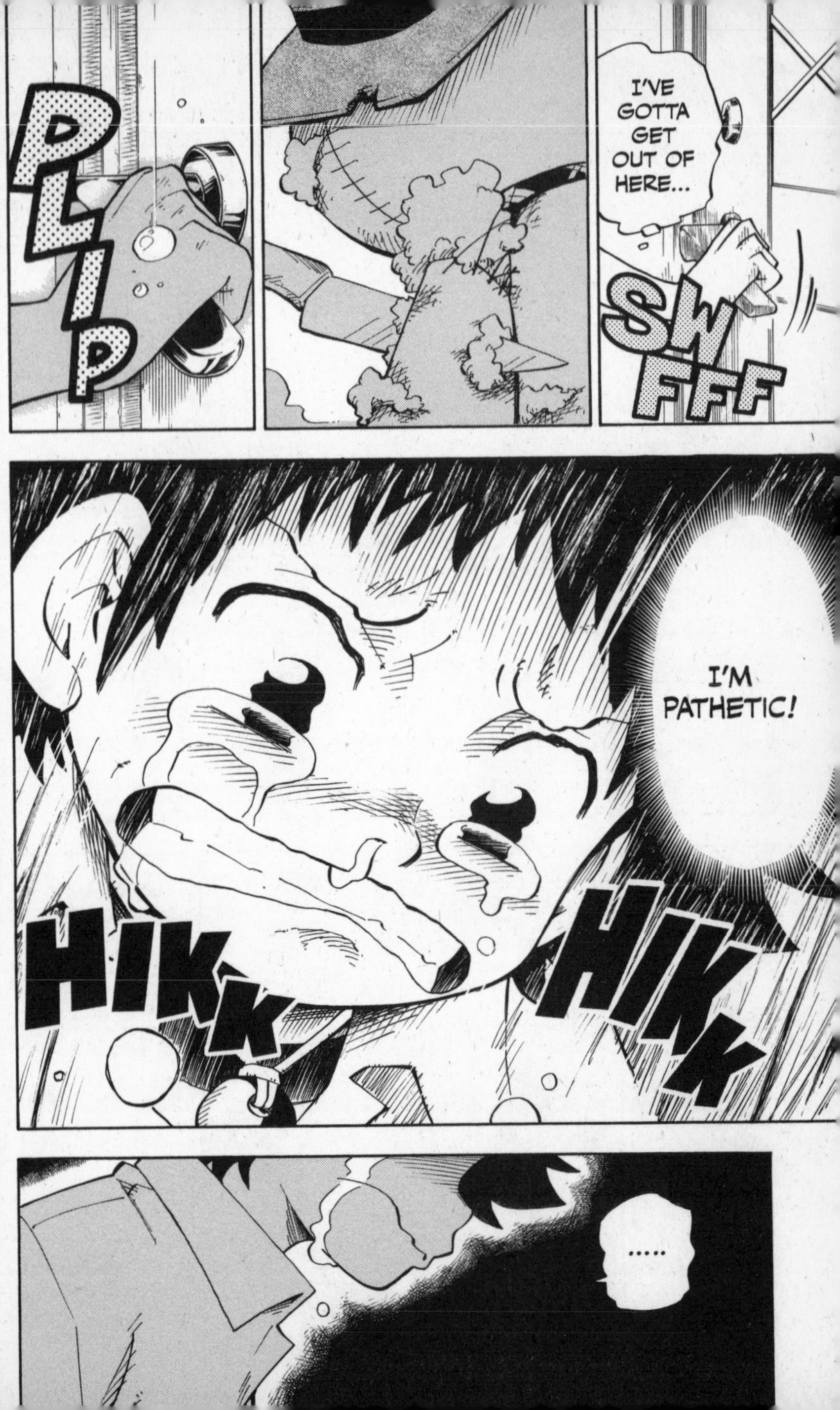
I'VE GOTTA GET OUT OF HERE...
SWFFF
PLIP
I'M PATHETIC!
HIKK
HIKK
......

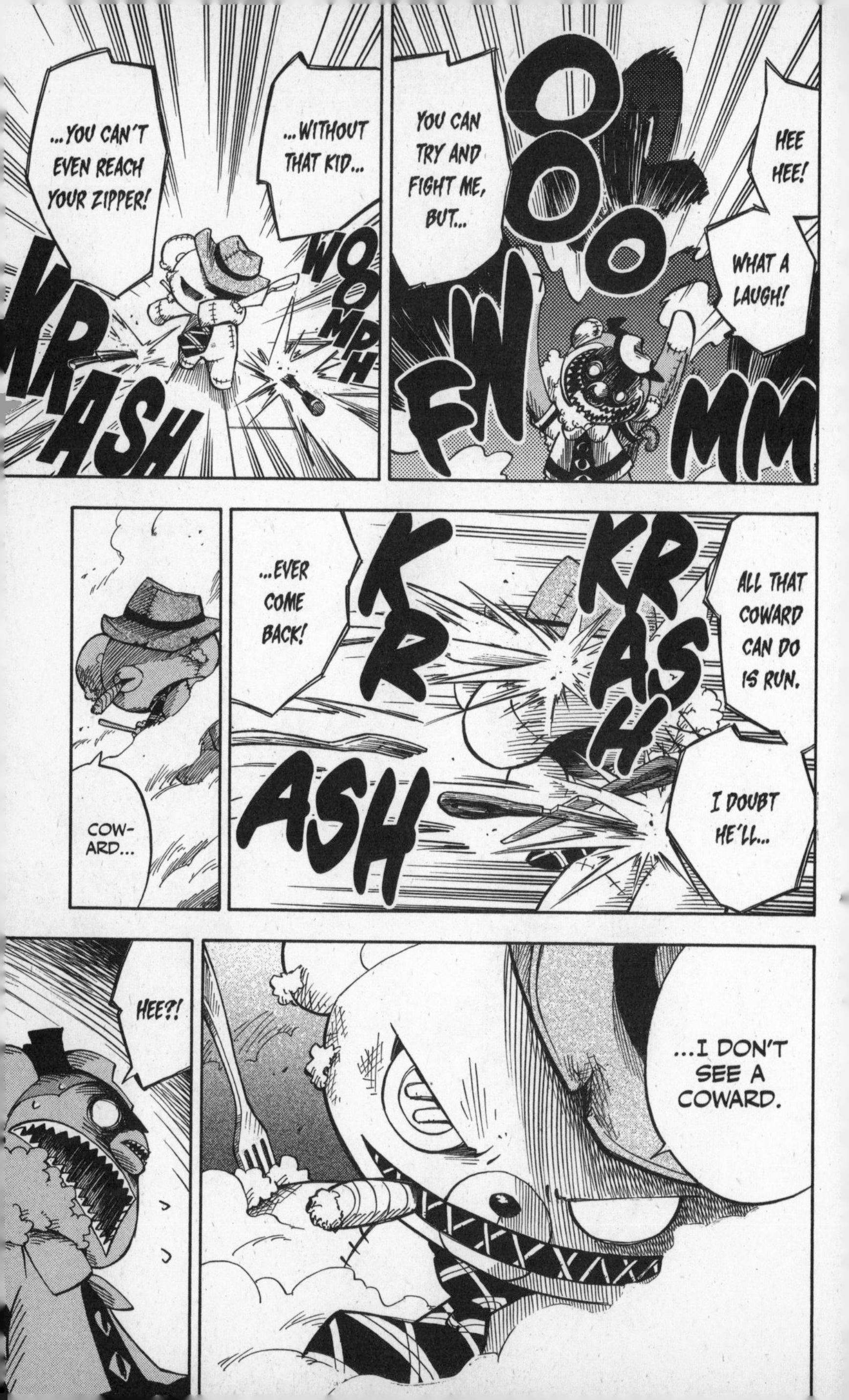
HEE HEE!
WHAT A LAUGH!
FWOOOMM
YOU CAN TRY AND FIGHT ME, BUT...
...WITHOUT THAT KID...
...YOU CAN'T EVEN REACH YOUR ZIPPER!
WOOMPH
KRASH
ALL THAT COWARD CAN DO IS RUN.
I DOUBT HE'LL...
KRASH
...EVER COME BACK!
KRASH
COW-ARD...
...I DON'T SEE A COWARD.
HEE?!

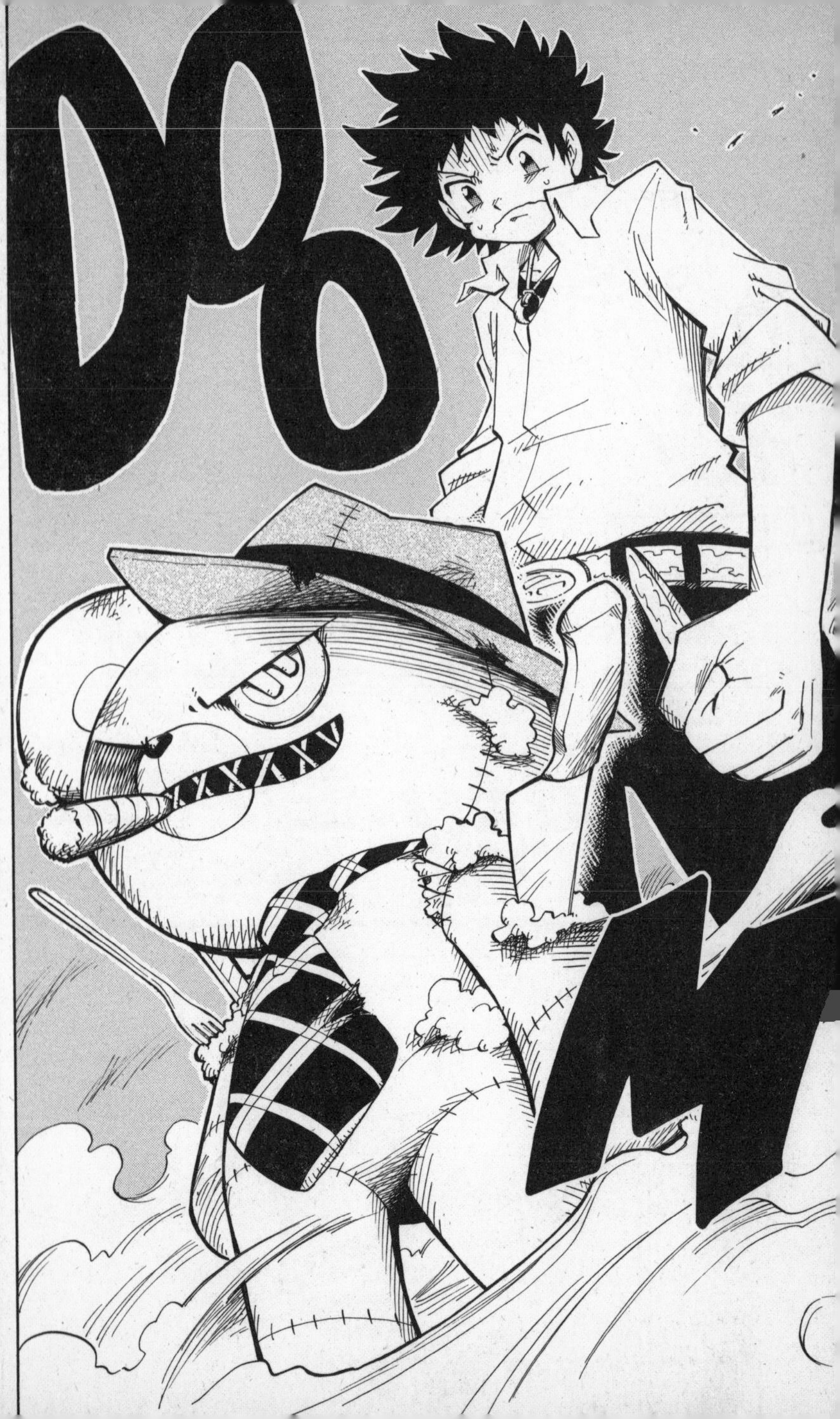
DO
M

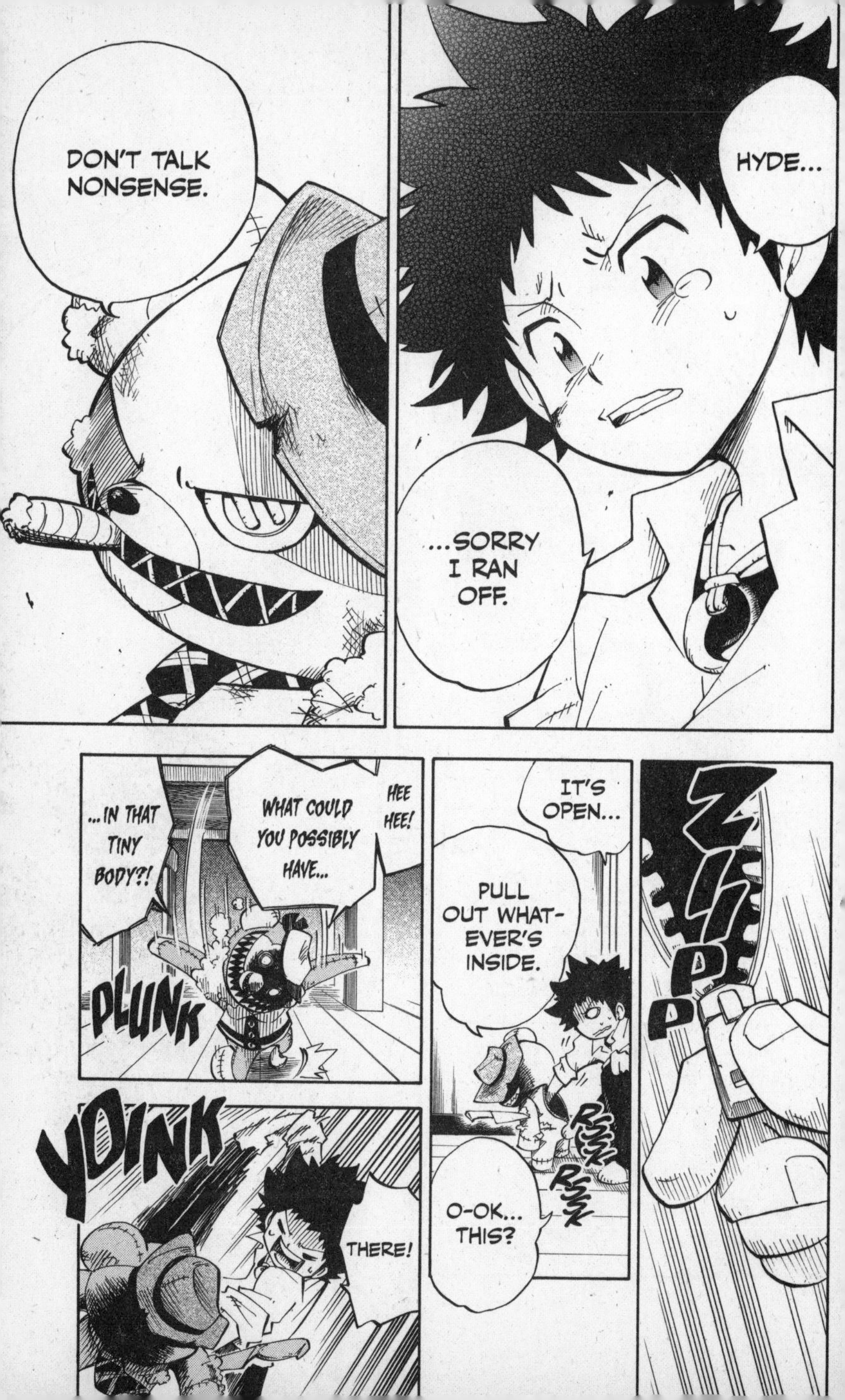
HYDE...
...SORRY I RAN OFF.
DON'T TALK NONSENSE.
ZIPPP
IT'S OPEN...
PULL OUT WHAT-EVER'S INSIDE.
RSSK RSSK
O-OK... THIS?
HEE HEE!
WHAT COULD YOU POSSIBLY HAVE...
...IN THAT TINY BODY?!
PLUNK
YOINK
THERE!

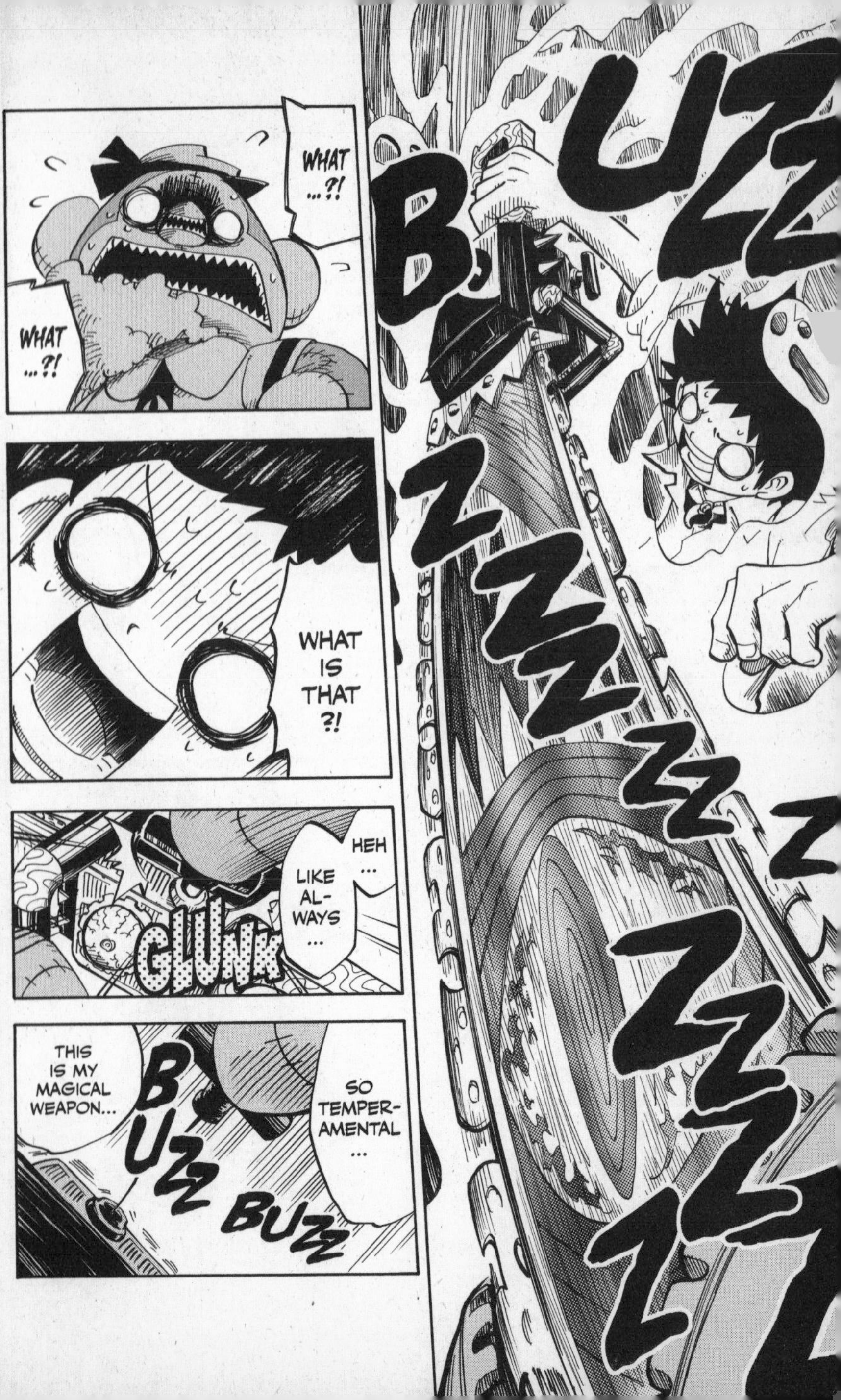
BUZZZZZZZZZZZZZ
WHAT ...?!
WHAT ...?!
WHAT IS THAT ?!
HEH ...
LIKE AL- WAYS ...
GLUNK
SO TEMPER- AMENTAL ...
THIS IS MY MAGICAL WEAPON...
BUZZ BUZZ

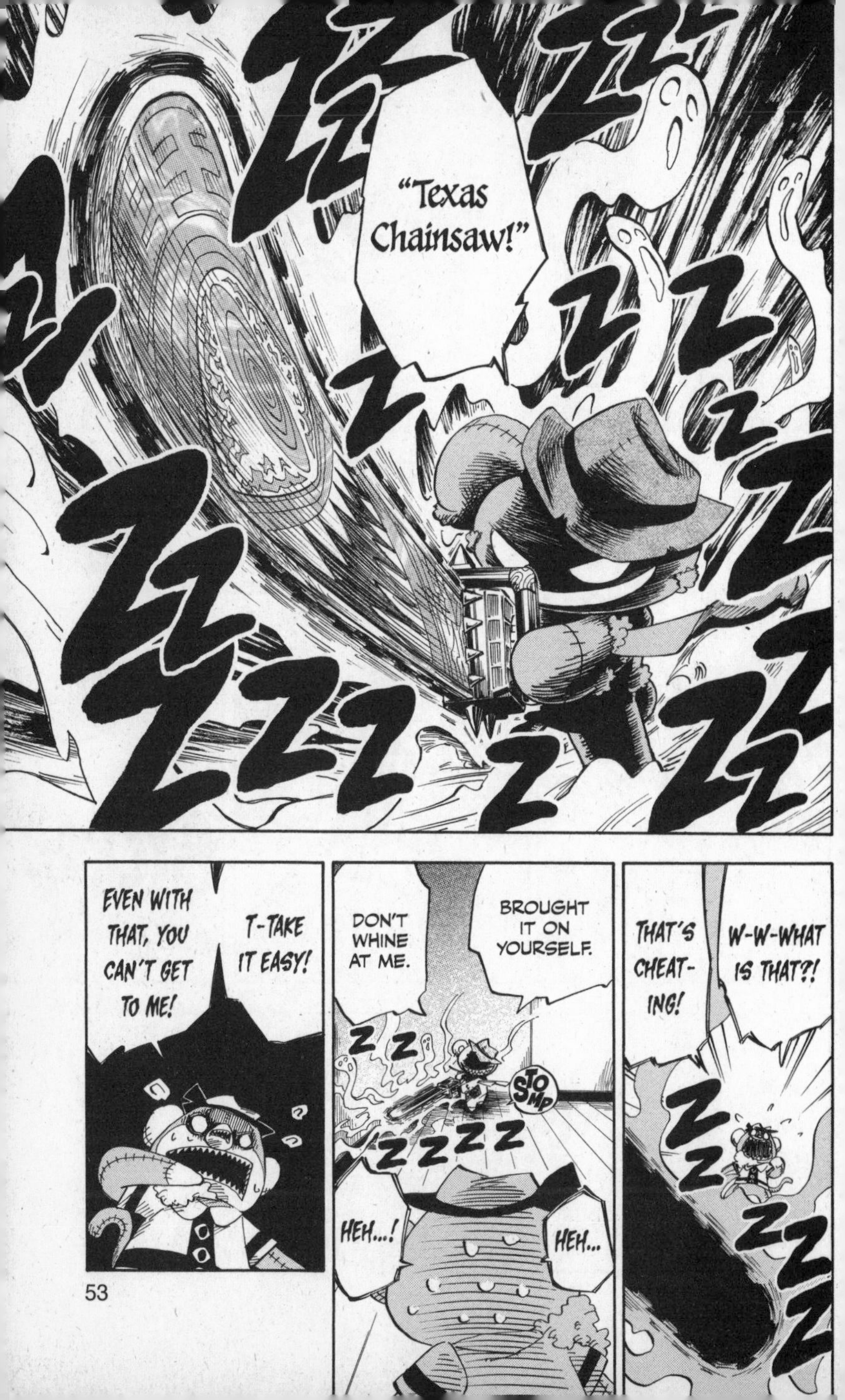
"Texas Chainsaw!"
W-W-WHAT IS THAT?!
THAT'S CHEATING!
BROUGHT IT ON YOURSELF.
DON'T WHINE AT ME.
STOMP
HEH...
HEH...!
T-TAKE IT EASY!
EVEN WITH THAT, YOU CAN'T GET TO ME!

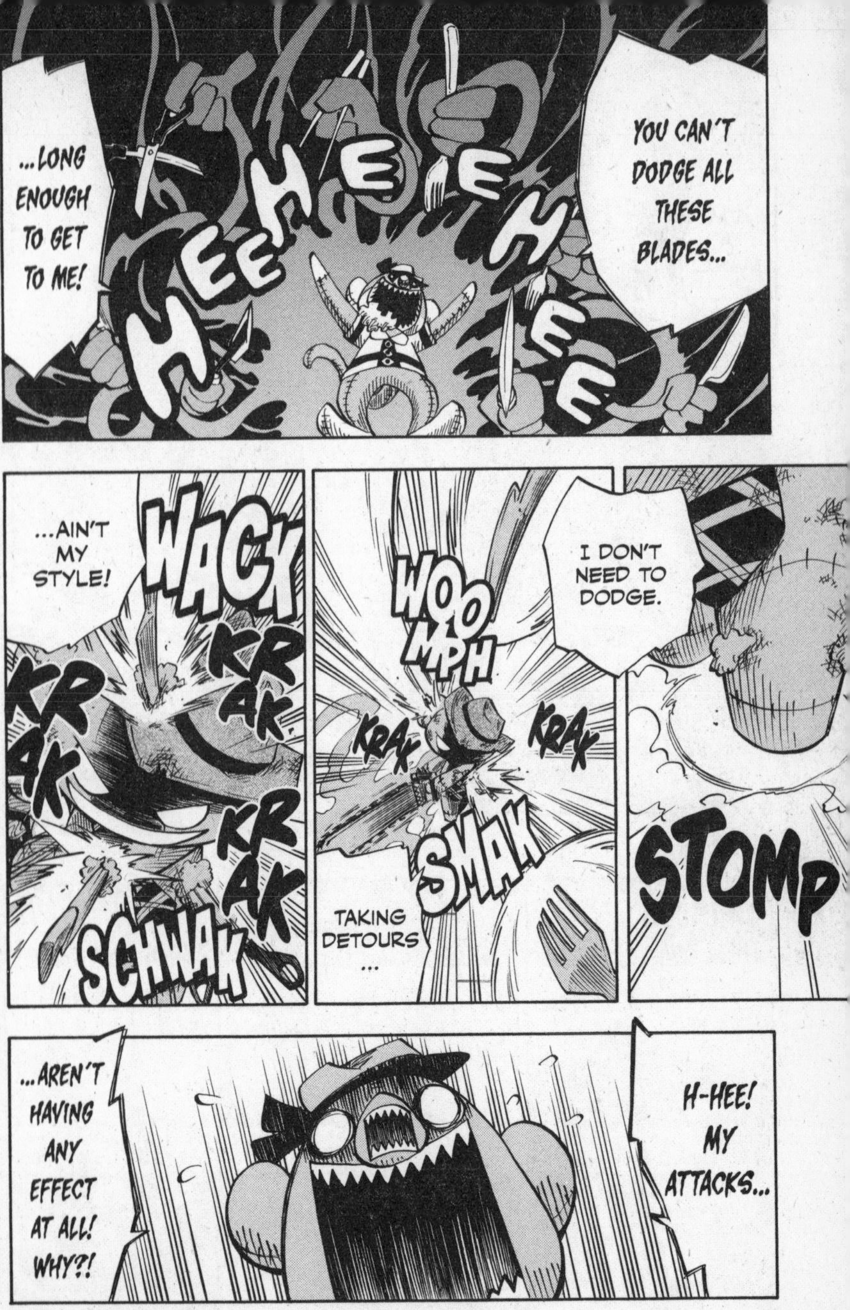
YOU CAN'T DODGE ALL THESE BLADES...
HEEHEEHEEHEE
...LONG ENOUGH TO GET TO ME!
STOMP
I DON'T NEED TO DODGE.
WOOMPH
KRAK
KRAK
SMAK
TAKING DETOURS ...
...AIN'T MY STYLE!
WACK
KRAK
KRAK
KRAK
SCHWAK
H-HEE! MY ATTACKS...
...AREN'T HAVING ANY EFFECT AT ALL! WHY?!

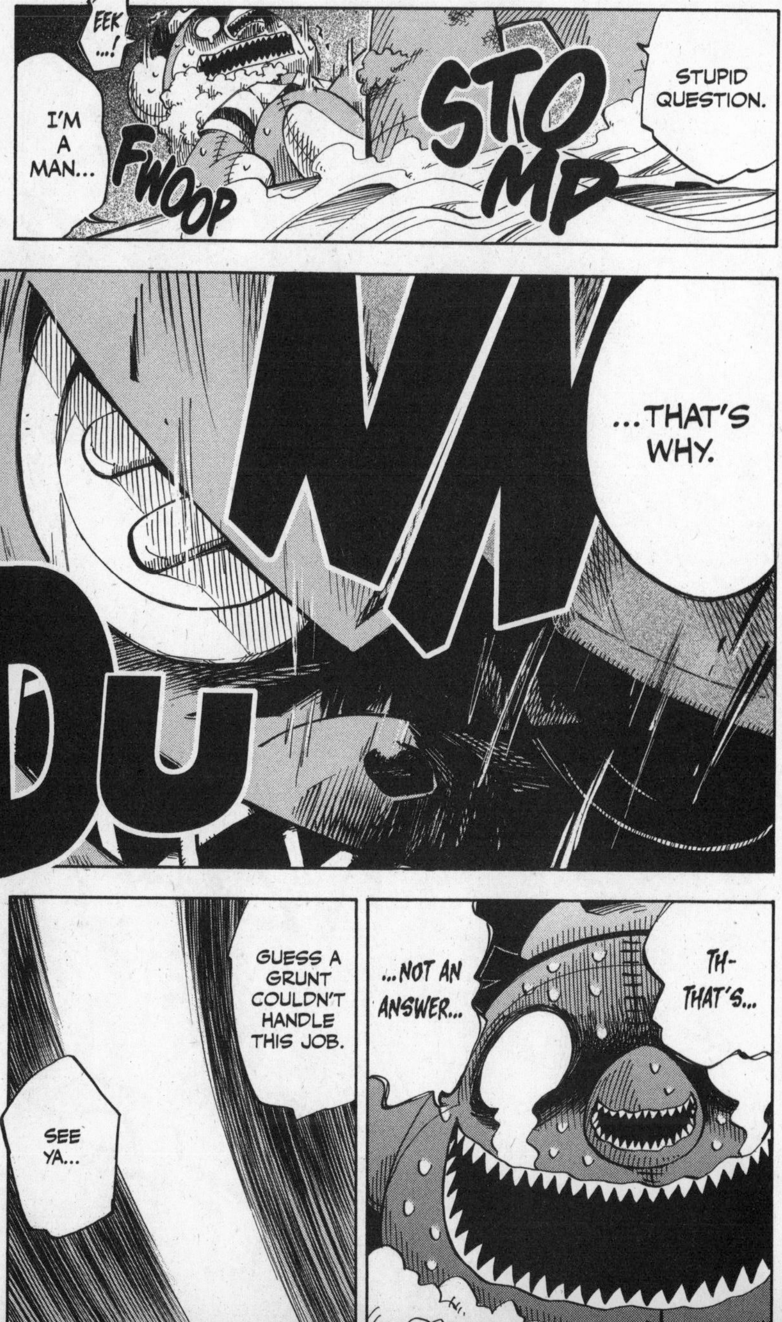
STUPID QUESTION.
STO MP
EEK ...!
I'M A MAN...
FWOOP
...THAT'S WHY.
DU
TH- THAT'S...
...NOT AN ANSWER...
GUESS A GRUNT COULDN'T HANDLE THIS JOB.
SEE YA...

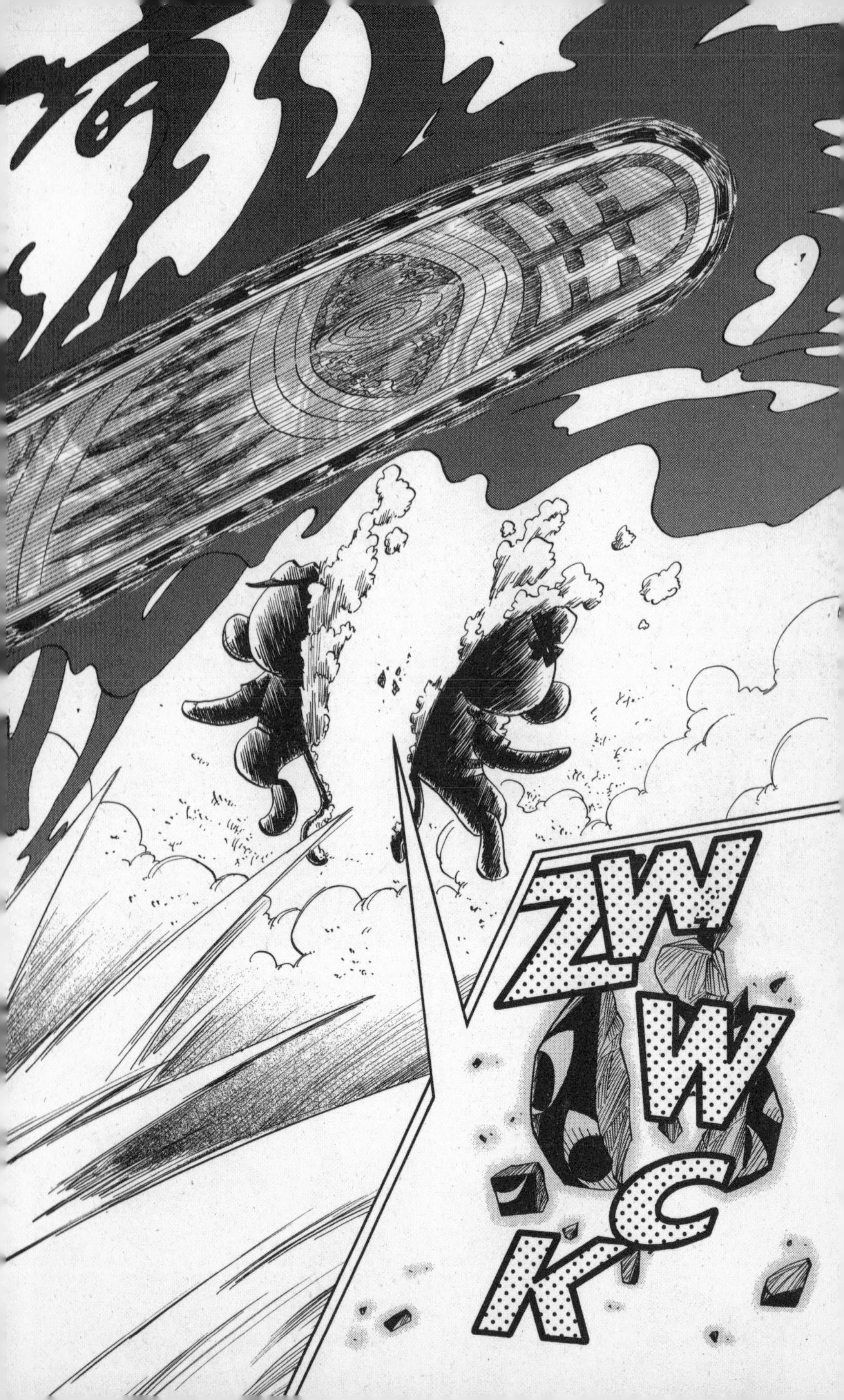
ZWWCK

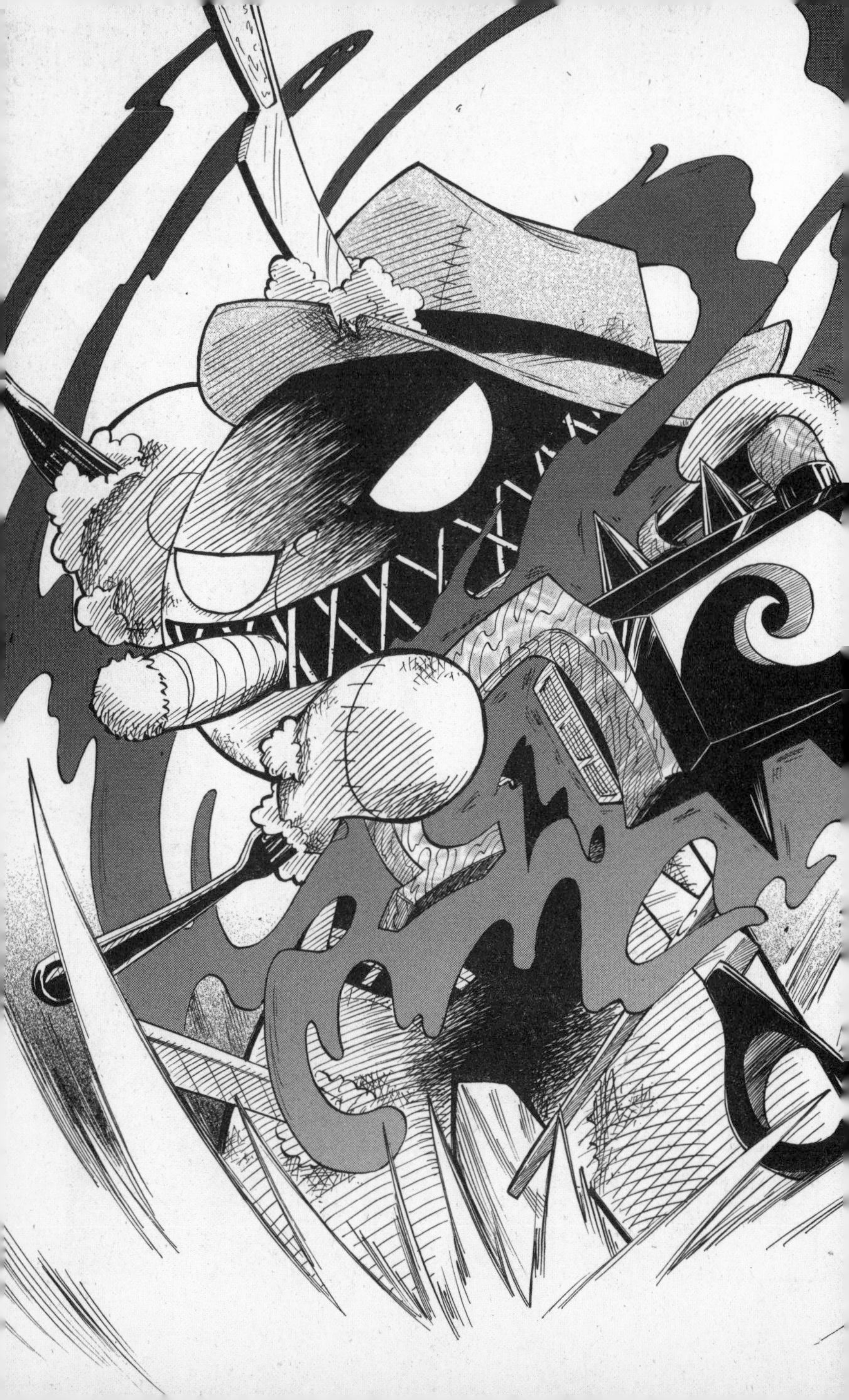

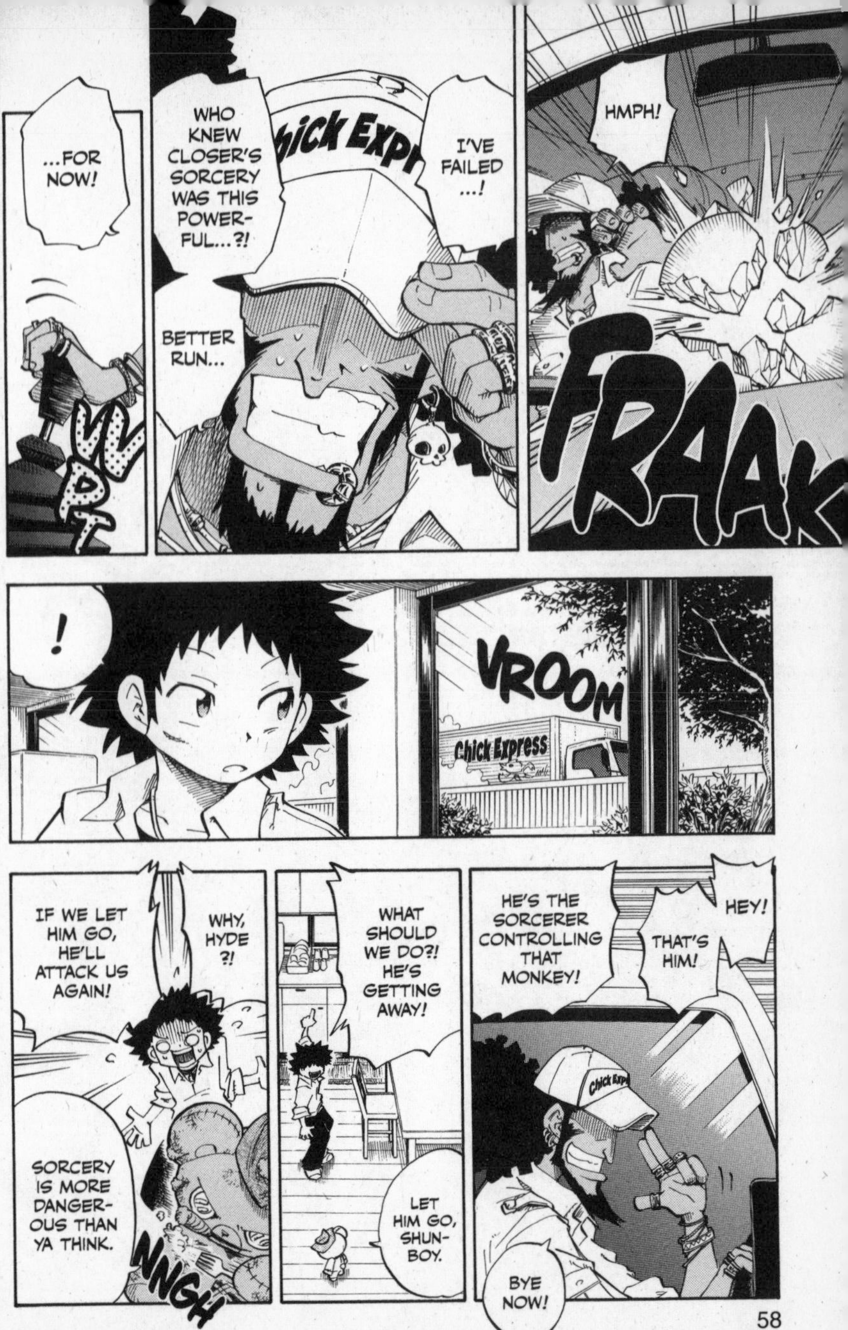
HMPH!
FRAAK
I'VE FAILED ...!
WHO KNEW CLOSER'S SORCERY WAS THIS POWER-FUL...?!
Chick Expr
BETTER RUN...
...FOR NOW!
VROOM
Chick Express
!
HEY!
THAT'S HIM!
HE'S THE SORCERER CONTROLLING THAT MONKEY!
Chick Expr
BYE NOW!
WHAT SHOULD WE DO?! HE'S GETTING AWAY!
LET HIM GO, SHUN-BOY.
WHY, HYDE ?!
IF WE LET HIM GO, HE'LL ATTACK US AGAIN!
SORCERY IS MORE DANGER-OUS THAN YA THINK.
NNGH

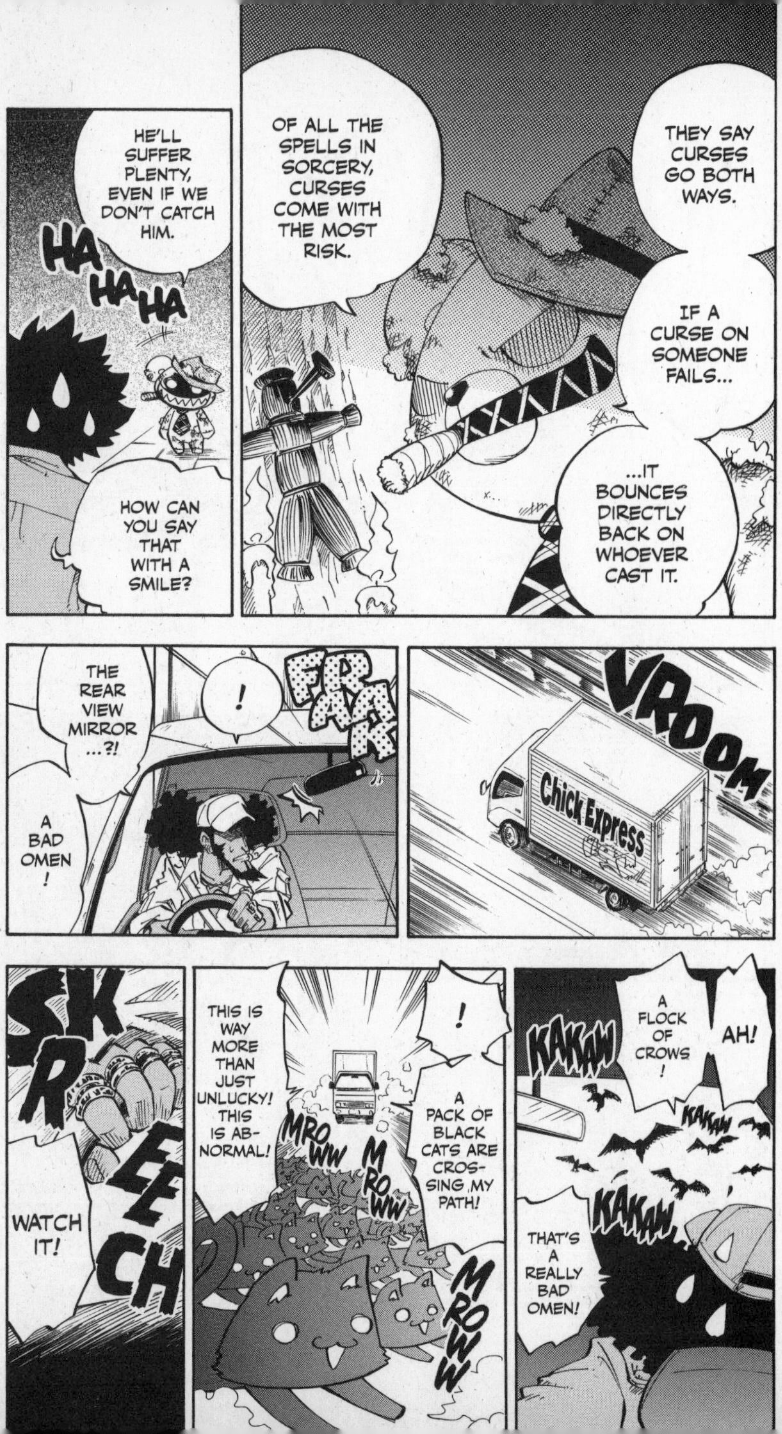
OF ALL THE SPELLS IN SORCERY, CURSES COME WITH THE MOST RISK.
THEY SAY CURSES GO BOTH WAYS.
IF A CURSE ON SOMEONE FAILS...
...IT BOUNCES DIRECTLY BACK ON WHOEVER CAST IT.
HE'LL SUFFER PLENTY, EVEN IF WE DON'T CATCH HIM.
HA HA HA
HOW CAN YOU SAY THAT WITH A SMILE?
VROOM
Chick Express
FRAAK
!
THE REAR VIEW MIRROR...?!
A BAD OMEN!
A FLOCK OF CROWS!
AH!
KAKAW
KAKAW
KAKAW
THAT'S A REALLY BAD OMEN!
!
A PACK OF BLACK CATS ARE CROSSING MY PATH!
THIS IS WAY MORE THAN JUST UNLUCKY! THIS IS ABNORMAL!
MROWW
MROWW
MROWW
SKREEECH
WATCH IT!

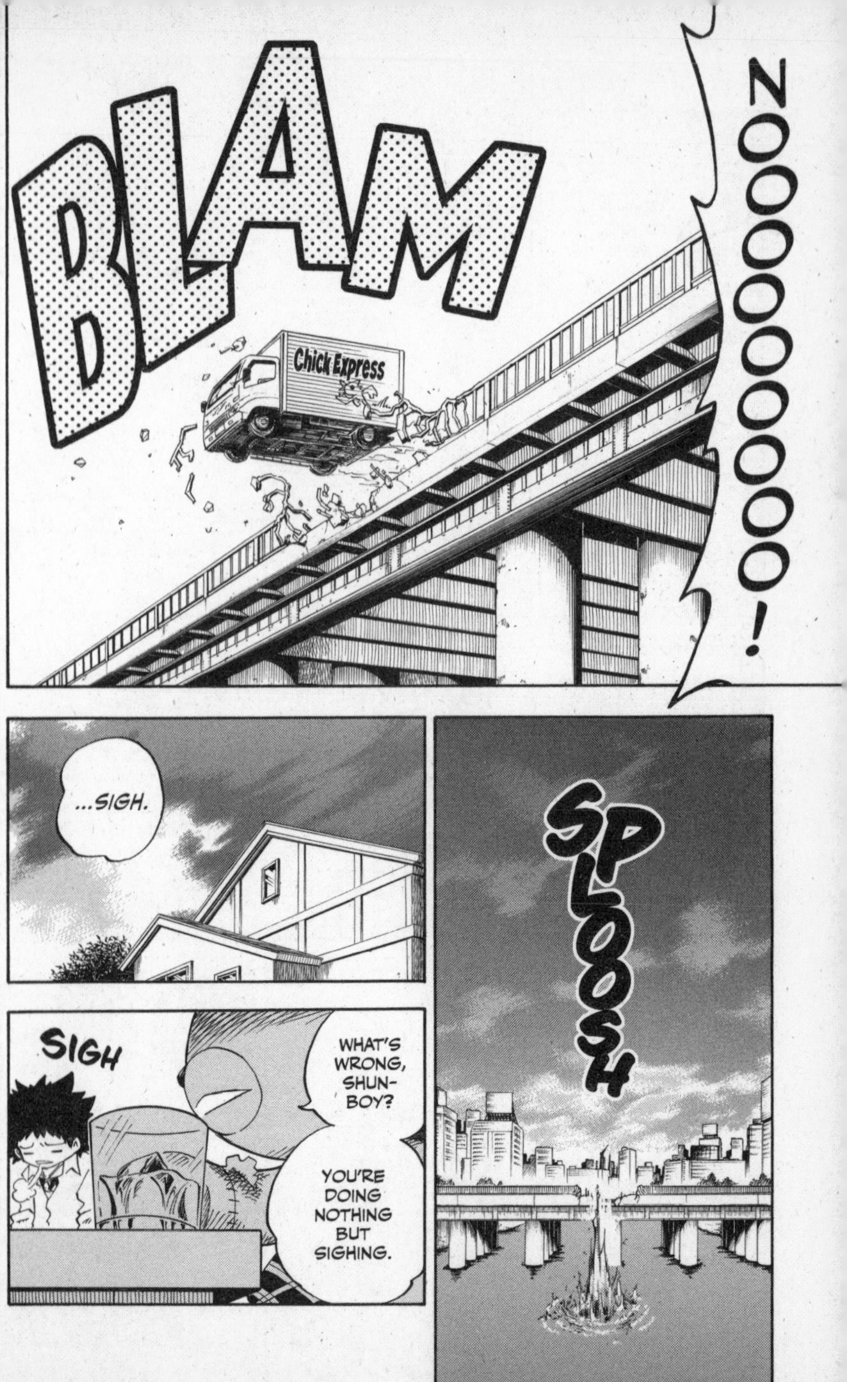

NOOOOOOOOO!
BLAM
Chick Express
SPLOOSH
...SIGH.
WHAT'S WRONG, SHUN-BOY?
YOU'RE DOING NOTHING BUT SIGHING.
SIGH

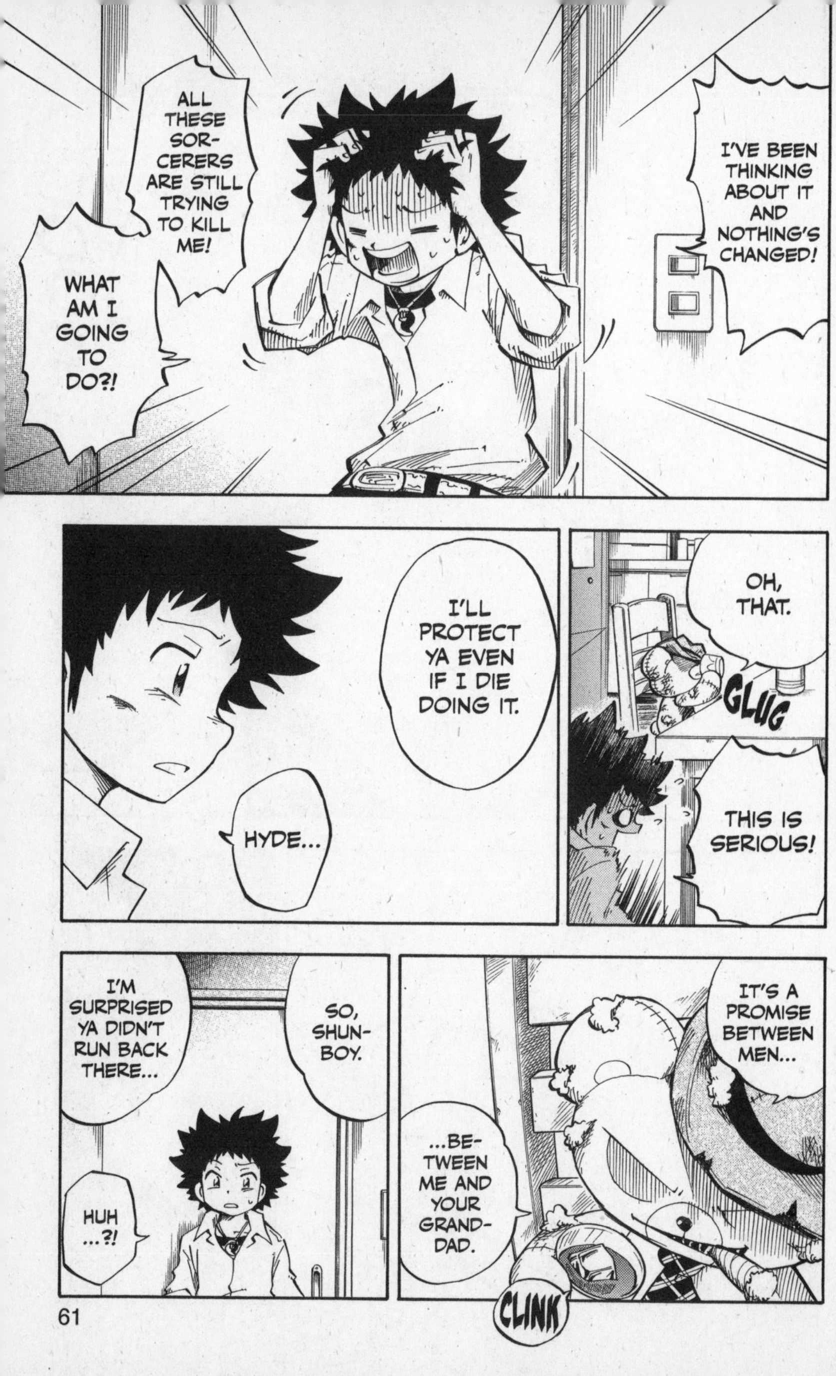
I'VE BEEN THINKING ABOUT IT AND NOTHING'S CHANGED!
ALL THESE SOR-CERERS ARE STILL TRYING TO KILL ME!
WHAT AM I GOING TO DO?!
OH, THAT.
GLUG
THIS IS SERIOUS!
I'LL PROTECT YA EVEN IF I DIE DOING IT.
HYDE...
IT'S A PROMISE BETWEEN MEN...
...BE-TWEEN ME AND YOUR GRAND-DAD.
CLINK
SO, SHUN-BOY.
I'M SURPRISED YA DIDN'T RUN BACK THERE...
HUH ...?!

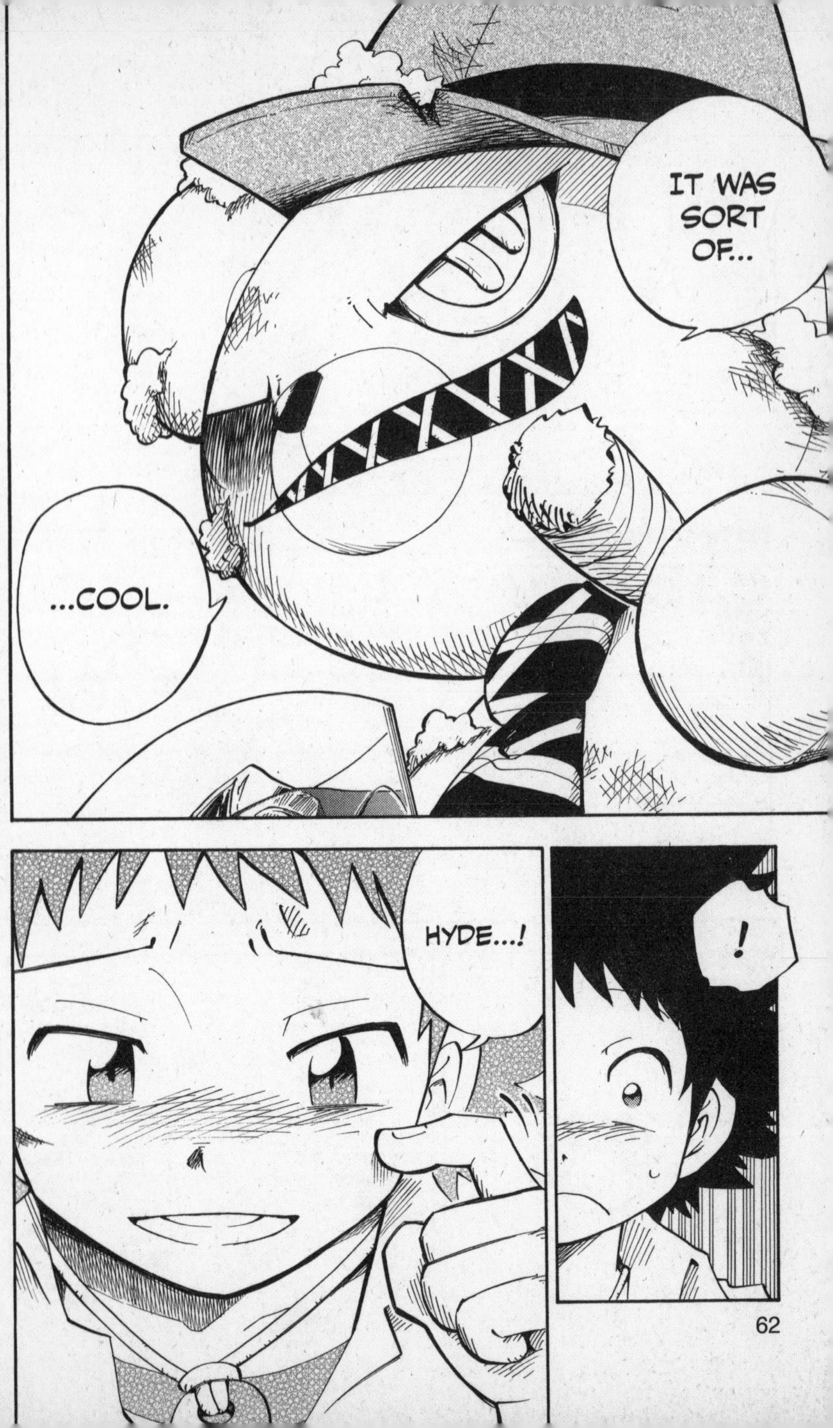
IT WAS SORT OF...
...COOL.
!
HYDE...!

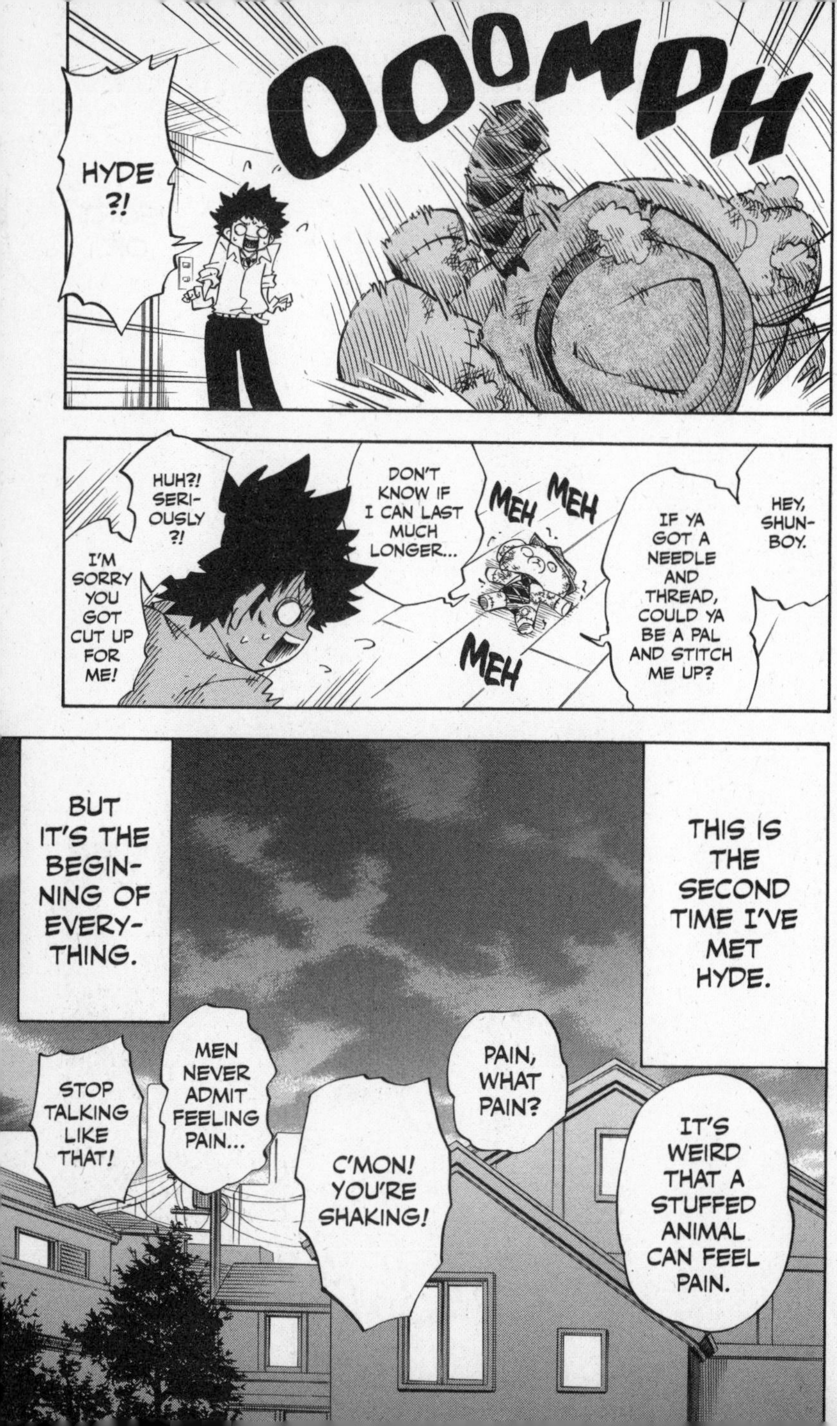
OOOMPH
HYDE ?!
HEY, SHUN-BOY.
IF YA GOT A NEEDLE AND THREAD, COULD YA BE A PAL AND STITCH ME UP?
MEH MEH
MEH
DON'T KNOW IF I CAN LAST MUCH LONGER...
HUH?! SERIOUSLY ?!
I'M SORRY YOU GOT CUT UP FOR ME!
THIS IS THE SECOND TIME I'VE MET HYDE.
BUT IT'S THE BEGINNING OF EVERYTHING.
IT'S WEIRD THAT A STUFFED ANIMAL CAN FEEL PAIN.
PAIN, WHAT PAIN?
C'MON! YOU'RE SHAKING!
MEN NEVER ADMIT FEELING PAIN...
STOP TALKING LIKE THAT!

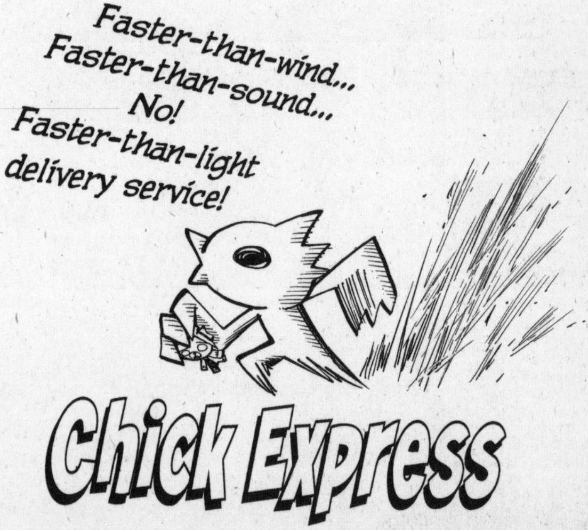
Faster-than-wind...
Faster-than-sound...
No!
Faster-than-light delivery service!
Chick Express

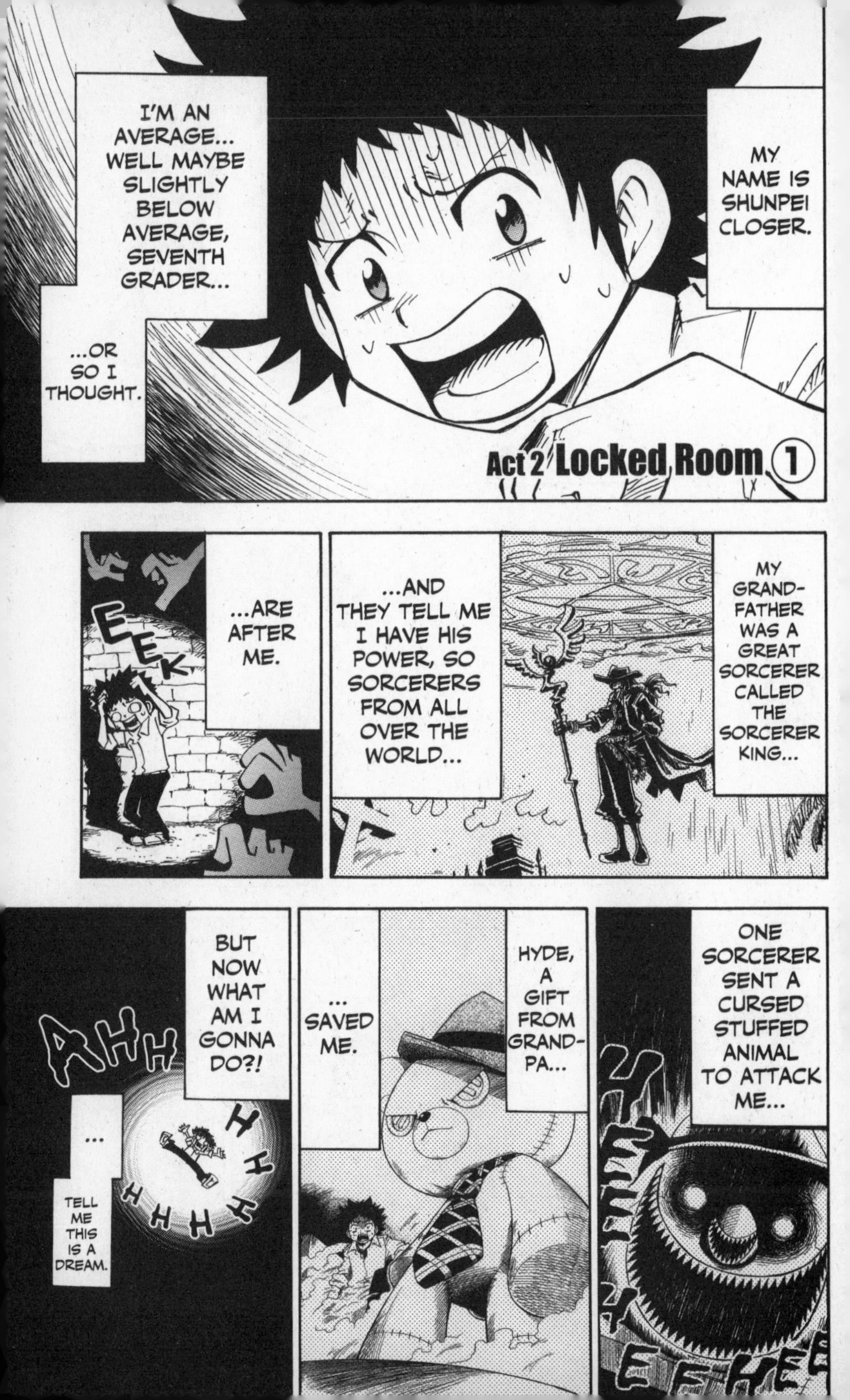
MY NAME IS SHUNPEI CLOSER.
I'M AN AVERAGE... WELL MAYBE SLIGHTLY BELOW AVERAGE, SEVENTH GRADER...
...OR SO I THOUGHT.
Act 2 Locked Room 1
MY GRAND-FATHER WAS A GREAT SORCERER CALLED THE SORCERER KING...
...AND THEY TELL ME I HAVE HIS POWER, SO SORCERERS FROM ALL OVER THE WORLD...
EEEK
...ARE AFTER ME.
ONE SORCERER SENT A CURSED STUFFED ANIMAL TO ATTACK ME...
HYDE, A GIFT FROM GRAND-PA...
... SAVED ME.
BUT NOW WHAT AM I GONNA DO?!
AHHHHHHHHHH
...
TELL ME THIS IS A DREAM.

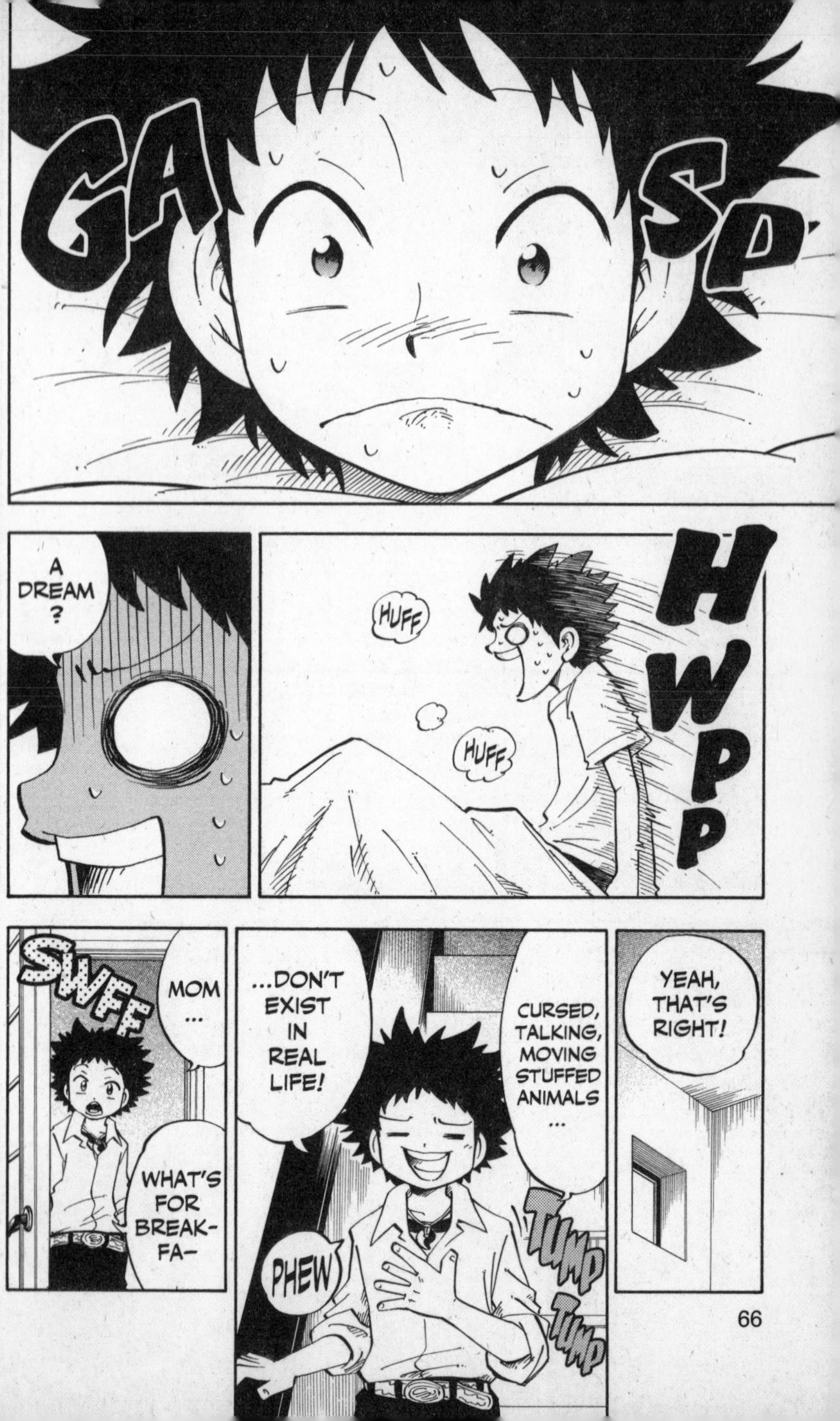
GASP
HWPP
HUFF
HUFF
A DREAM?
YEAH, THAT'S RIGHT!
CURSED, TALKING, MOVING STUFFED ANIMALS...
...DON'T EXIST IN REAL LIFE!
PHEW
TUMP
TUMP
SWFF
MOM...
WHAT'S FOR BREAK-FA-

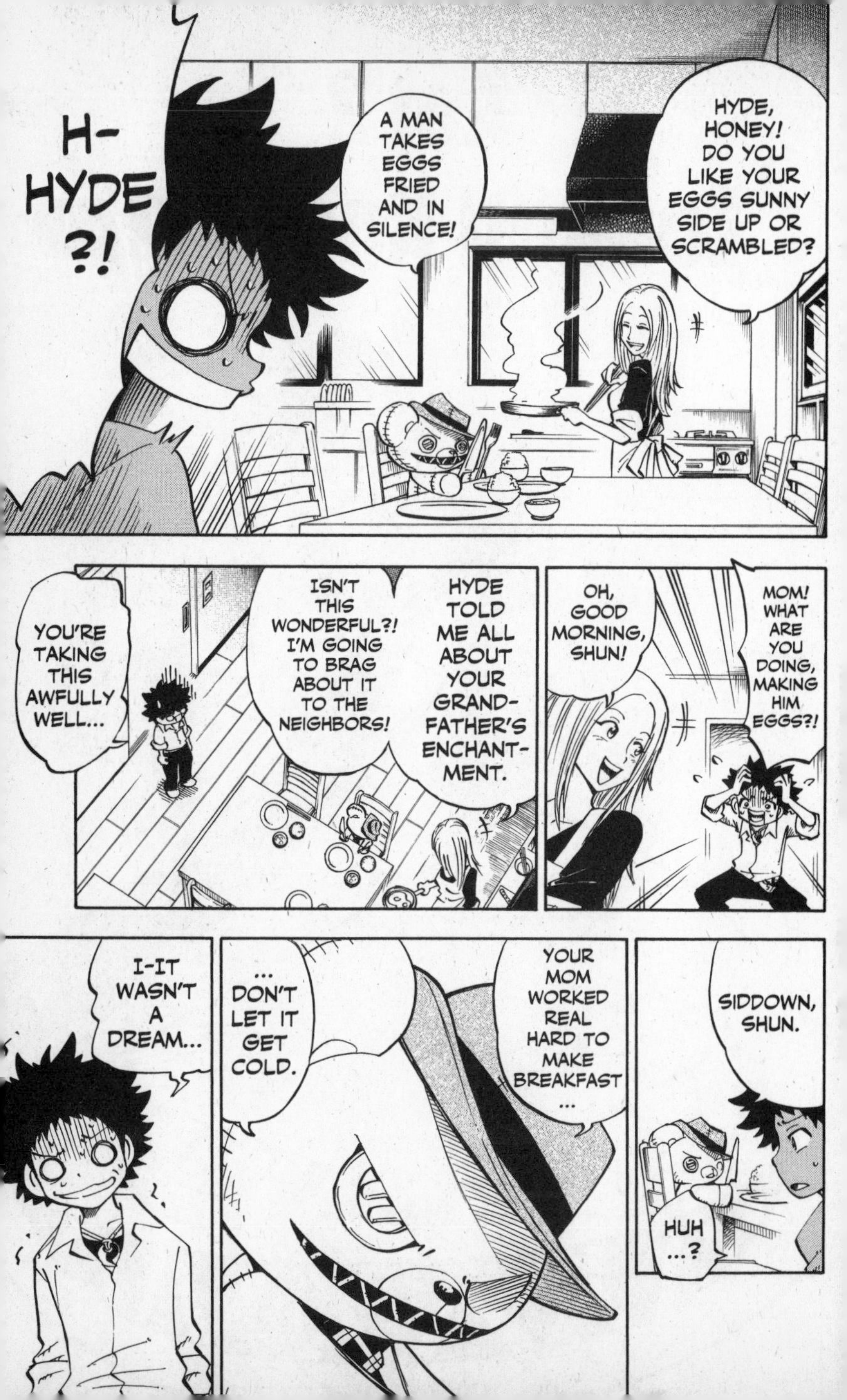
HYDE, HONEY! DO YOU LIKE YOUR EGGS SUNNY SIDE UP OR SCRAMBLED?
A MAN TAKES EGGS FRIED AND IN SILENCE!
H-HYDE?!
MOM! WHAT ARE YOU DOING, MAKING HIM EGGS?!
OH, GOOD MORNING, SHUN!
HYDE TOLD ME ALL ABOUT YOUR GRANDFATHER'S ENCHANTMENT.
ISN'T THIS WONDERFUL?! I'M GOING TO BRAG ABOUT IT TO THE NEIGHBORS!
YOU'RE TAKING THIS AWFULLY WELL...
SIDDOWN, SHUN.
HUH ...?
YOUR MOM WORKED REAL HARD TO MAKE BREAKFAST ...
... DON'T LET IT GET COLD.
I-IT WASN'T A DREAM...

Act 2
Locked Room (1)

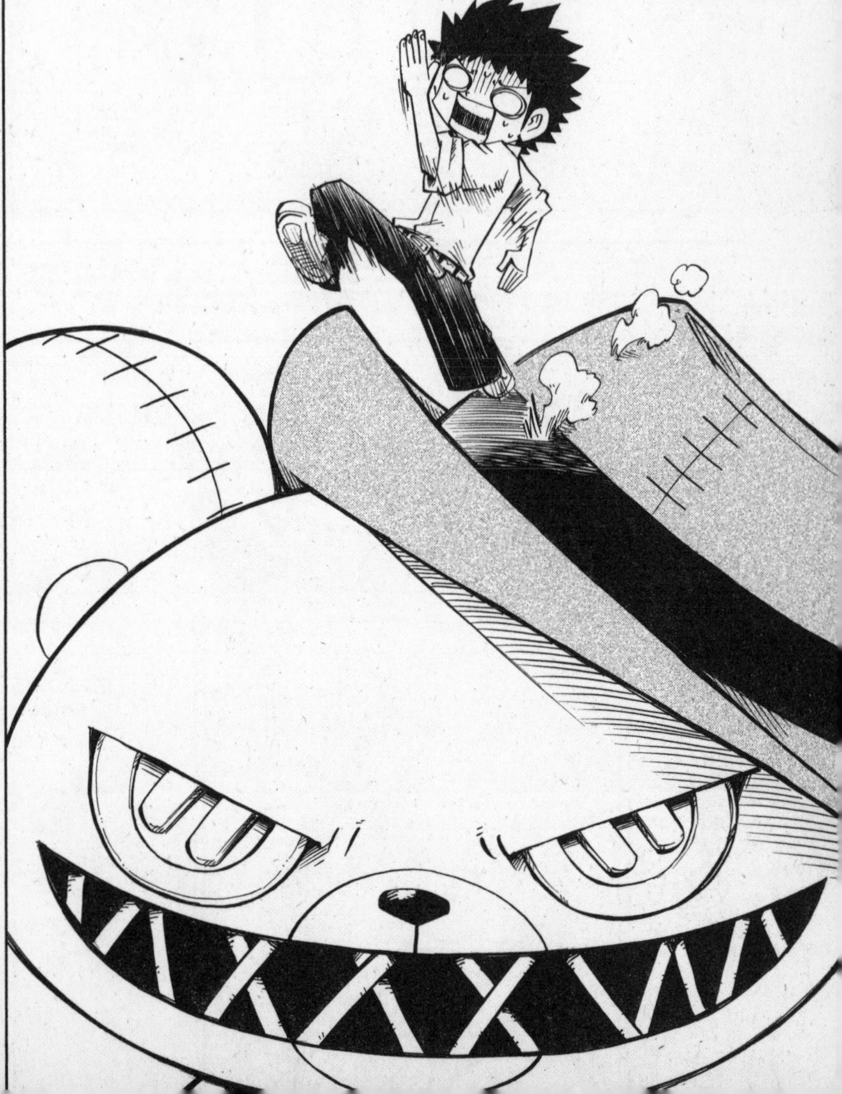

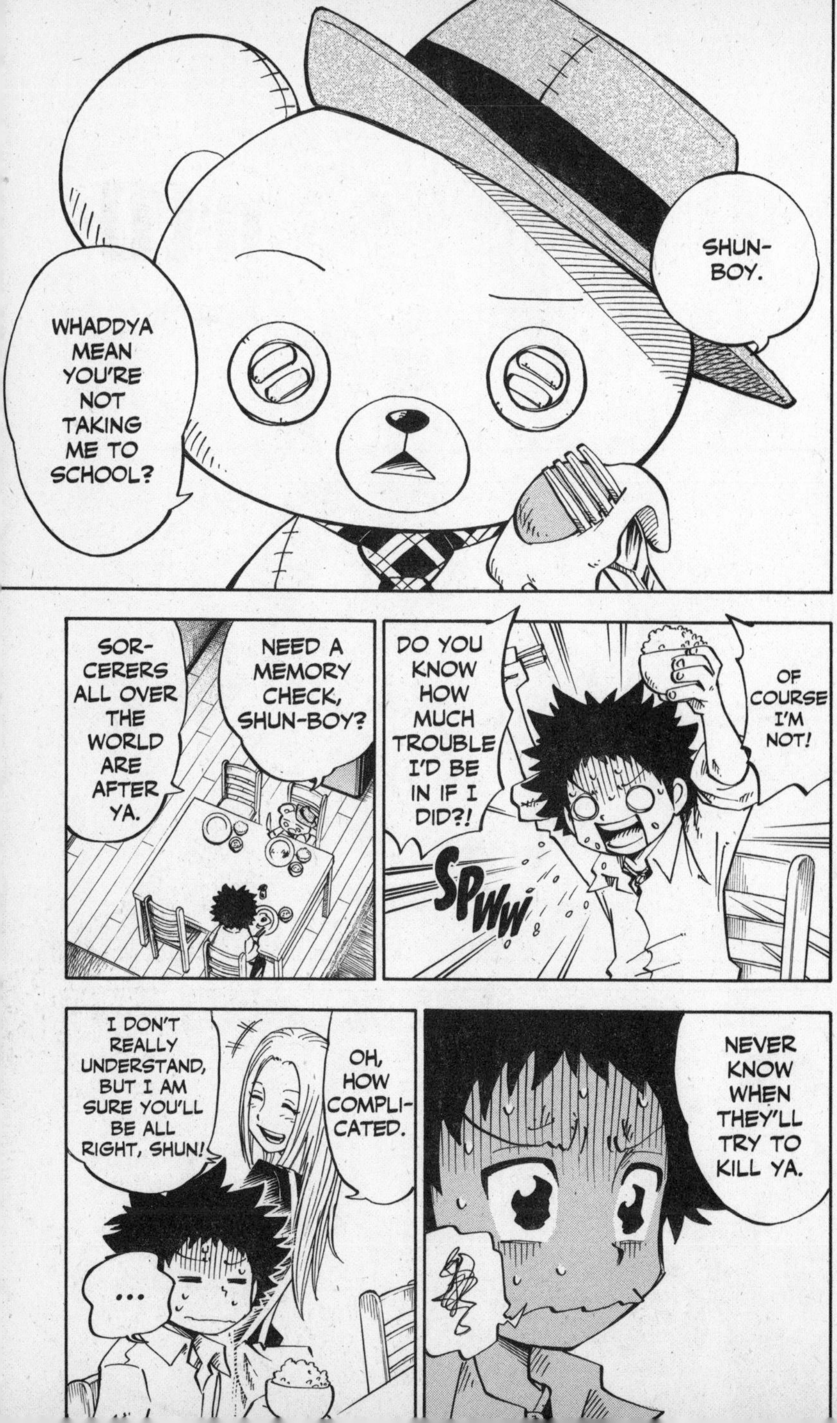
SHUN-BOY.
WHADDYA MEAN YOU'RE NOT TAKING ME TO SCHOOL?
OF COURSE I'M NOT!
DO YOU KNOW HOW MUCH TROUBLE I'D BE IN IF I DID?!
SPWW
NEED A MEMORY CHECK, SHUN-BOY?
SORCERERS ALL OVER THE WORLD ARE AFTER YA.
NEVER KNOW WHEN THEY'LL TRY TO KILL YA.
OH, HOW COMPLICATED.
I DON'T REALLY UNDERSTAND, BUT I AM SURE YOU'LL BE ALL RIGHT, SHUN!
...

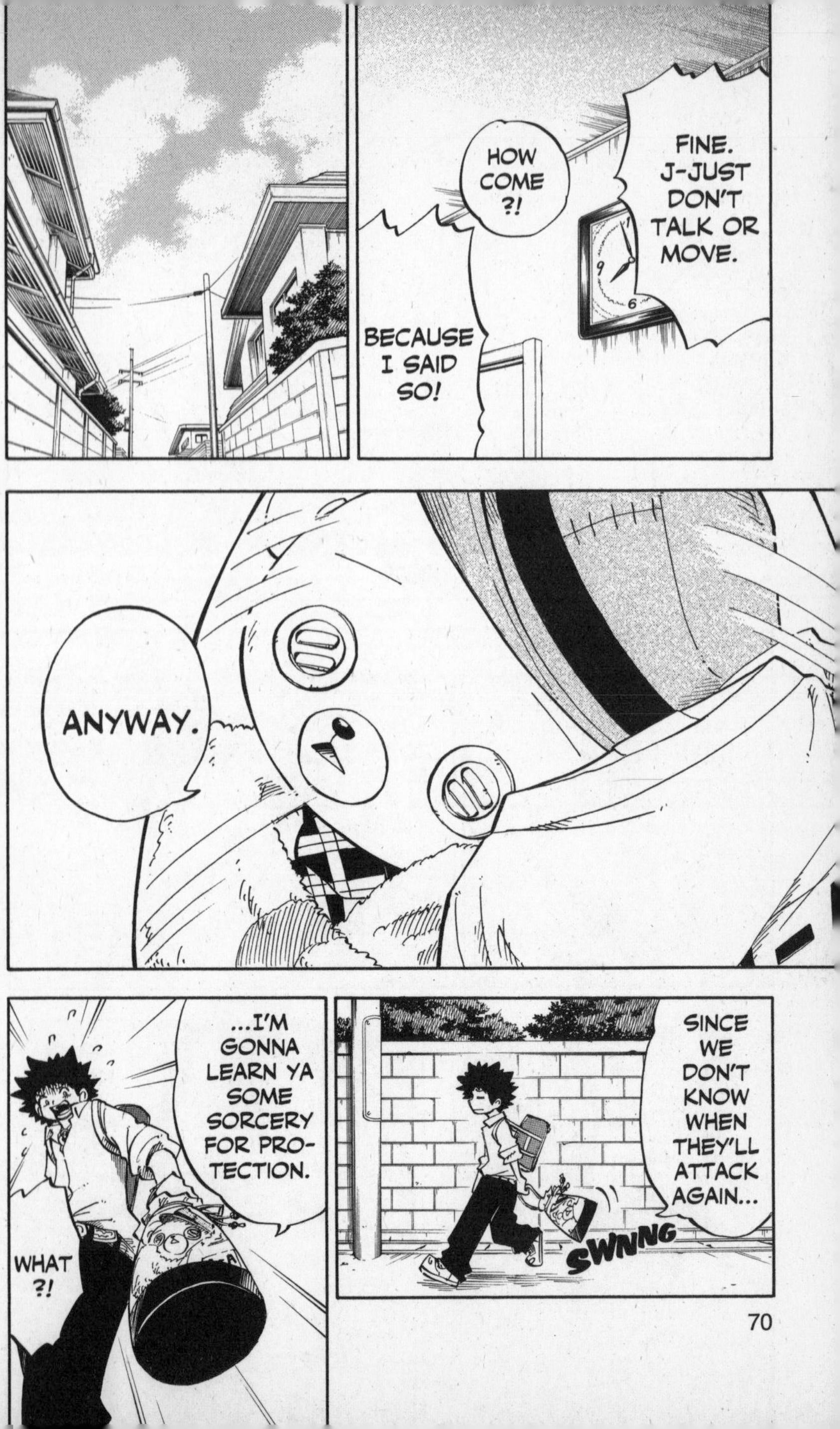
FINE. J-JUST DON'T TALK OR MOVE.
HOW COME?!
BECAUSE I SAID SO!
ANYWAY.
SINCE WE DON'T KNOW WHEN THEY'LL ATTACK AGAIN...
SWNNG
...I'M GONNA LEARN YA SOME SORCERY FOR PRO-TECTION.
WHAT?!

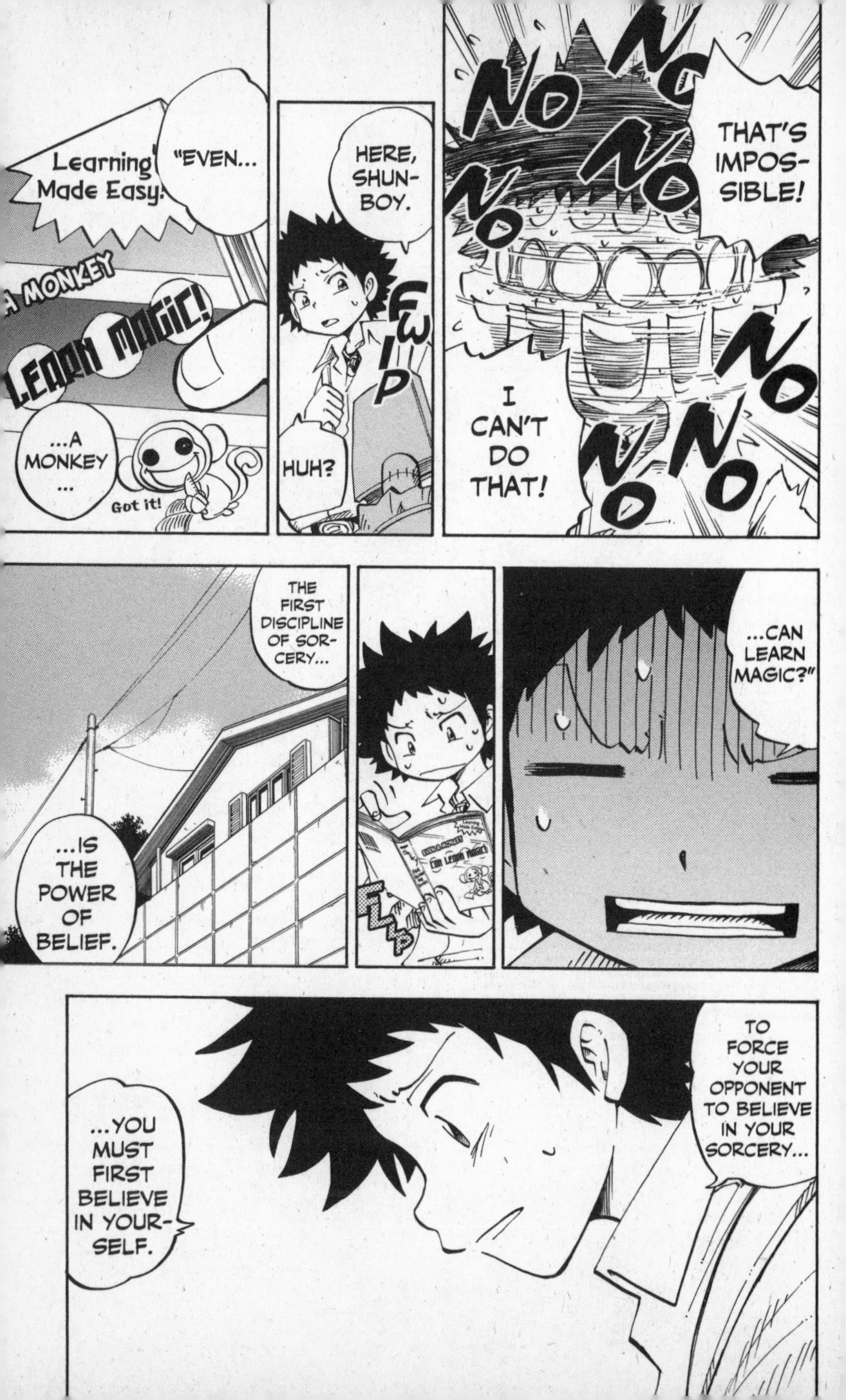
THAT'S IMPOSSIBLE!
NO NO NO NO NO
I CAN'T DO THAT!
NO NO NO NO
HERE, SHUN-BOY.
FWIP
HUH?
"EVEN...
Learning Made Easy!
A MONKEY
LEARN MAGIC!
...A MONKEY ...
Got it!
...CAN LEARN MAGIC?"
FLIP
THE FIRST DISCIPLINE OF SORCERY...
...IS THE POWER OF BELIEF.
TO FORCE YOUR OPPONENT TO BELIEVE IN YOUR SORCERY...
...YOU MUST FIRST BELIEVE IN YOURSELF.

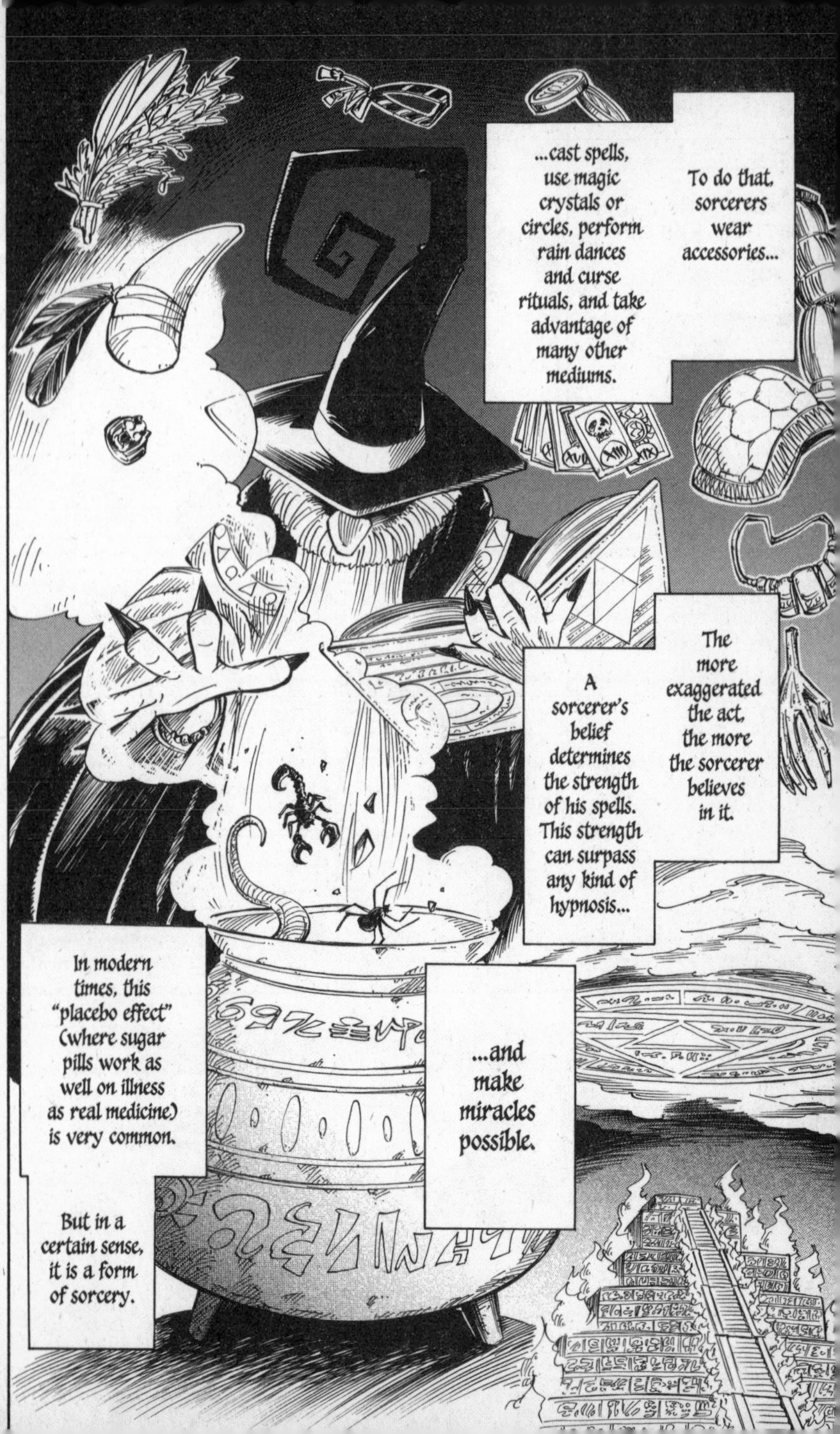
To do that, sorcerers wear accessories...
...cast spells, use magic crystals or circles, perform rain dances and curse rituals, and take advantage of many other mediums.
The more exaggerated the act, the more the sorcerer believes in it.
A sorcerer's belief determines the strength of his spells. This strength can surpass any kind of hypnosis...
...and make miracles possible.
In modern times, this "placebo effect" (where sugar pills work as well on illness as real medicine) is very common.
But in a certain sense, it is a form of sorcery.

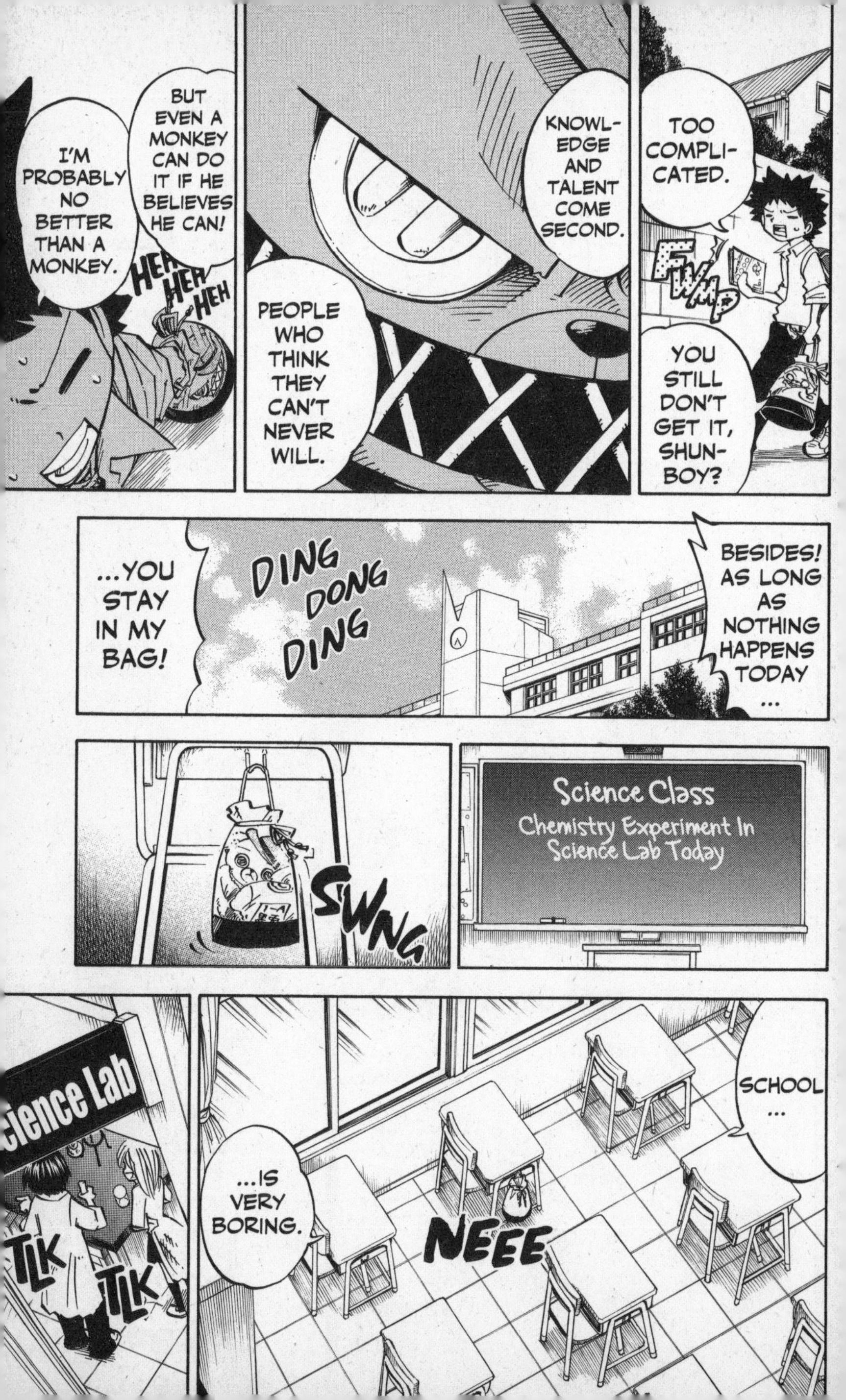

TOO COMPLICATED.
FWMP
YOU STILL DON'T GET IT, SHUN-BOY?
KNOWLEDGE AND TALENT COME SECOND.
PEOPLE WHO THINK THEY CAN'T NEVER WILL.
BUT EVEN A MONKEY CAN DO IT IF HE BELIEVES HE CAN!
I'M PROBABLY NO BETTER THAN A MONKEY.
HEH HEH HEH
BESIDES! AS LONG AS NOTHING HAPPENS TODAY ...
DING DONG DING
...YOU STAY IN MY BAG!
Science Class
Chemistry Experiment In Science Lab Today
SWNG
SCHOOL ...
...IS VERY BORING.
NEEE
Science Lab
TLK TLK

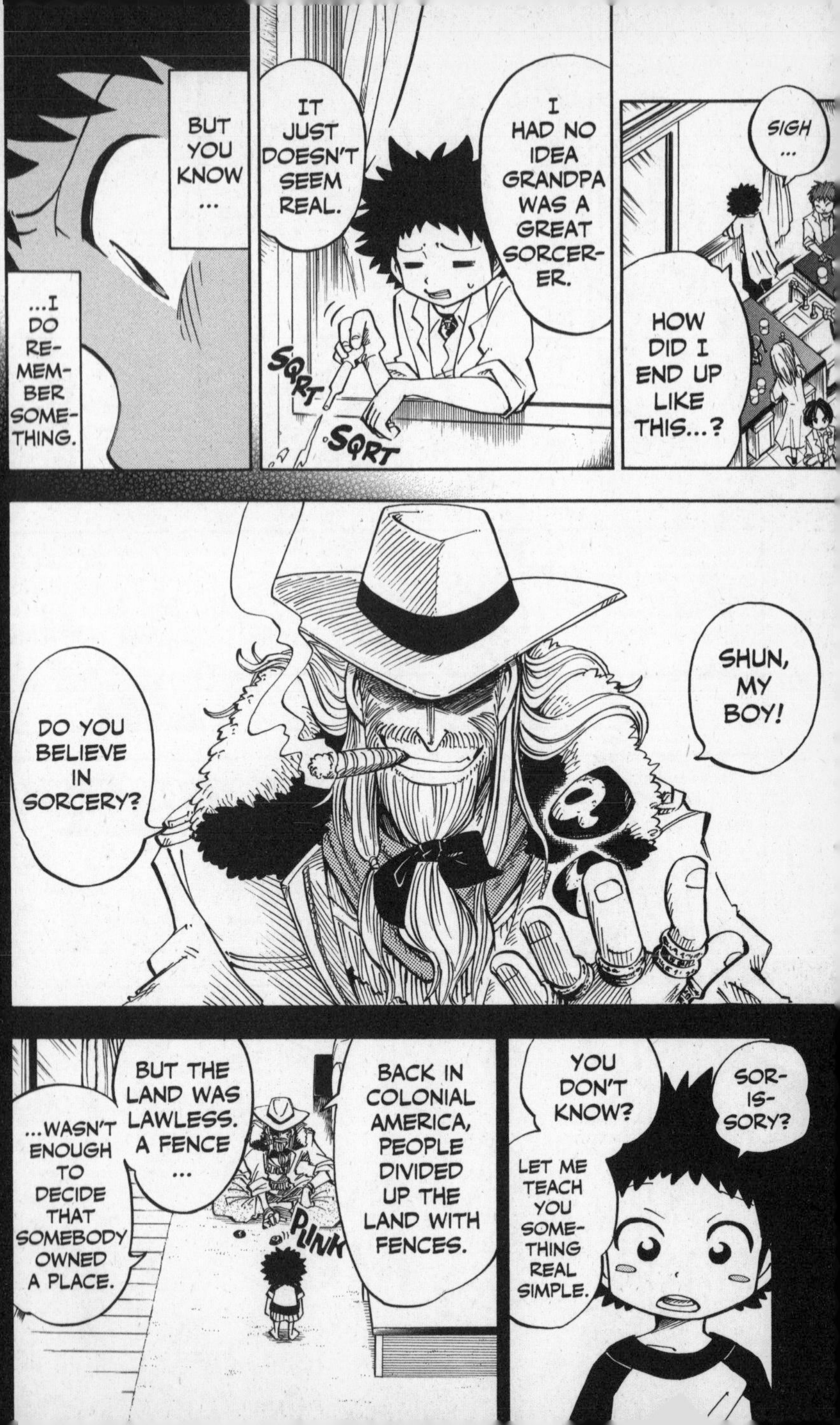
SIGH ...
HOW DID I END UP LIKE THIS...?
I HAD NO IDEA GRANDPA WAS A GREAT SORCERER.
IT JUST DOESN'T SEEM REAL.
SQRT
SQRT
BUT YOU KNOW ...
...I DO REMEMBER SOMETHING.
SHUN, MY BOY!
DO YOU BELIEVE IN SORCERY?
SOR-IS-SORY?
YOU DON'T KNOW?
LET ME TEACH YOU SOMETHING REAL SIMPLE.
BACK IN COLONIAL AMERICA, PEOPLE DIVIDED UP THE LAND WITH FENCES.
PLINK
BUT THE LAND WAS LAWLESS. A FENCE ...
...WASN'T ENOUGH TO DECIDE THAT SOMEBODY OWNED A PLACE.

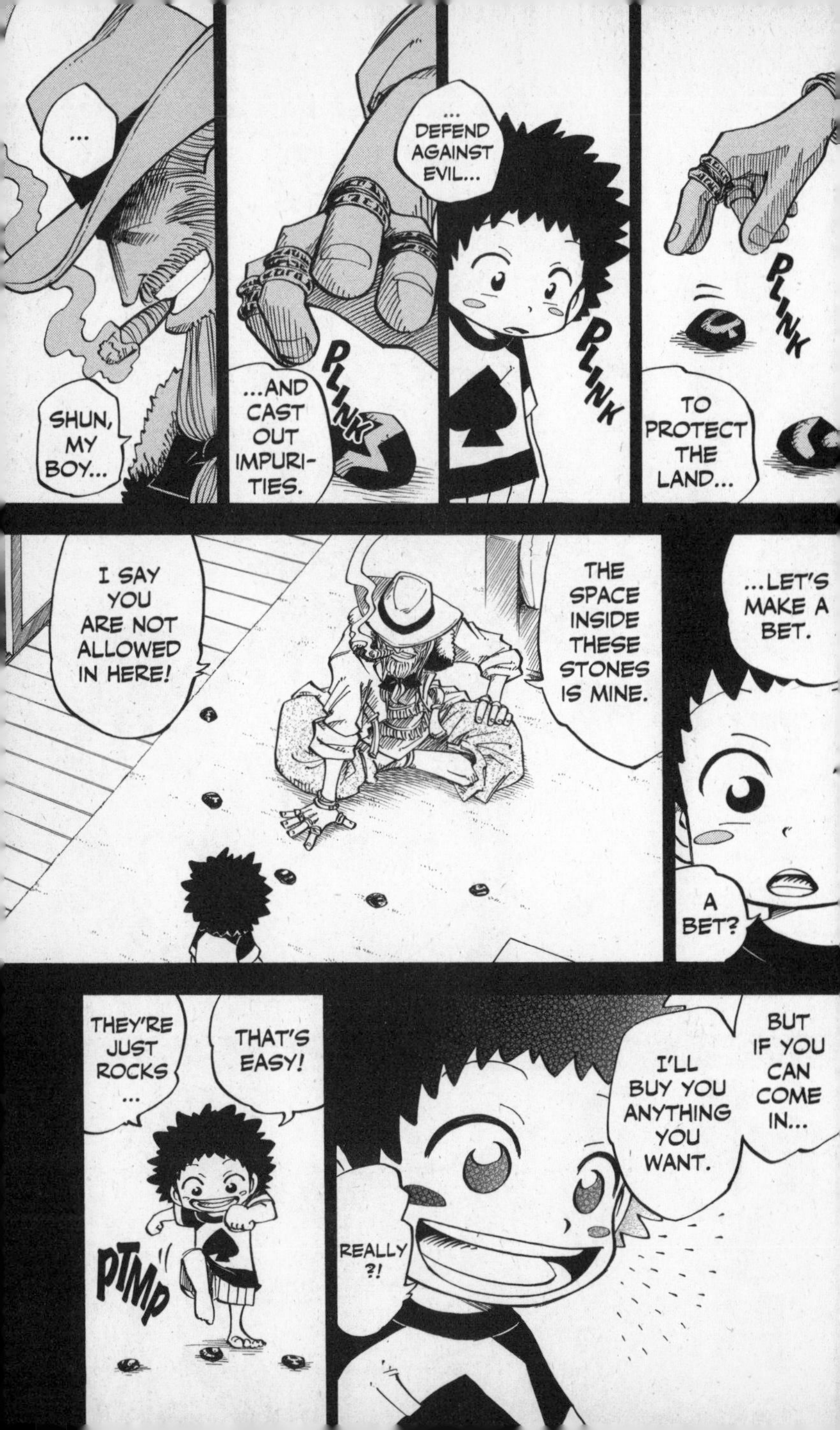
PLINK
TO PROTECT THE LAND...
...DEFEND AGAINST EVIL...
PLINK
PLINK
...AND CAST OUT IMPURI-TIES.
...
SHUN, MY BOY...
...LET'S MAKE A BET.
A BET?
THE SPACE INSIDE THESE STONES IS MINE.
I SAY YOU ARE NOT ALLOWED IN HERE!
BUT IF YOU CAN COME IN...
I'LL BUY YOU ANYTHING YOU WANT.
REALLY?!
THAT'S EASY!
THEY'RE JUST ROCKS...
PTMP

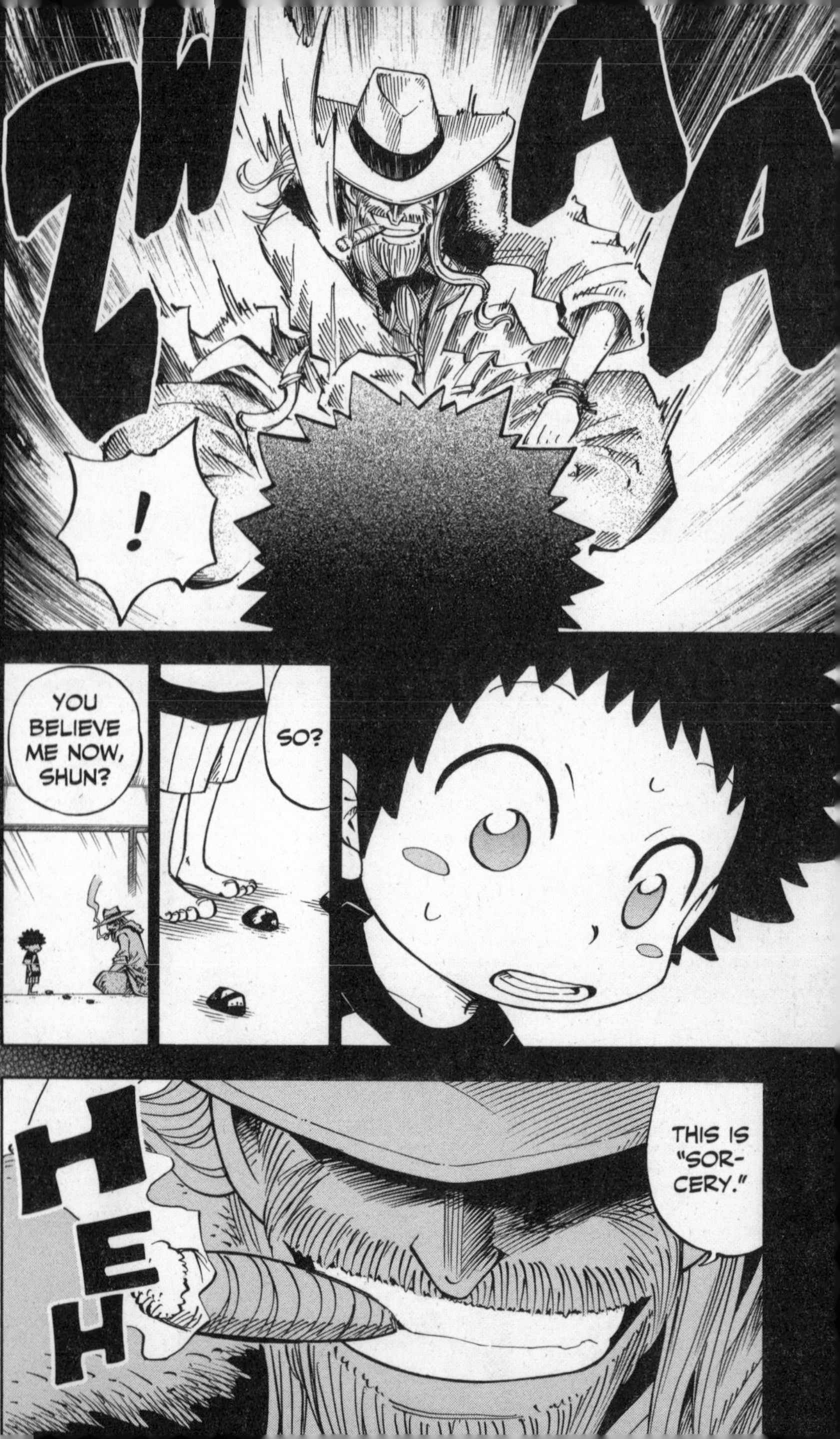
ZWAA
!
SO?
YOU BELIEVE ME NOW, SHUN?
THIS IS "SORCERY."
HEH

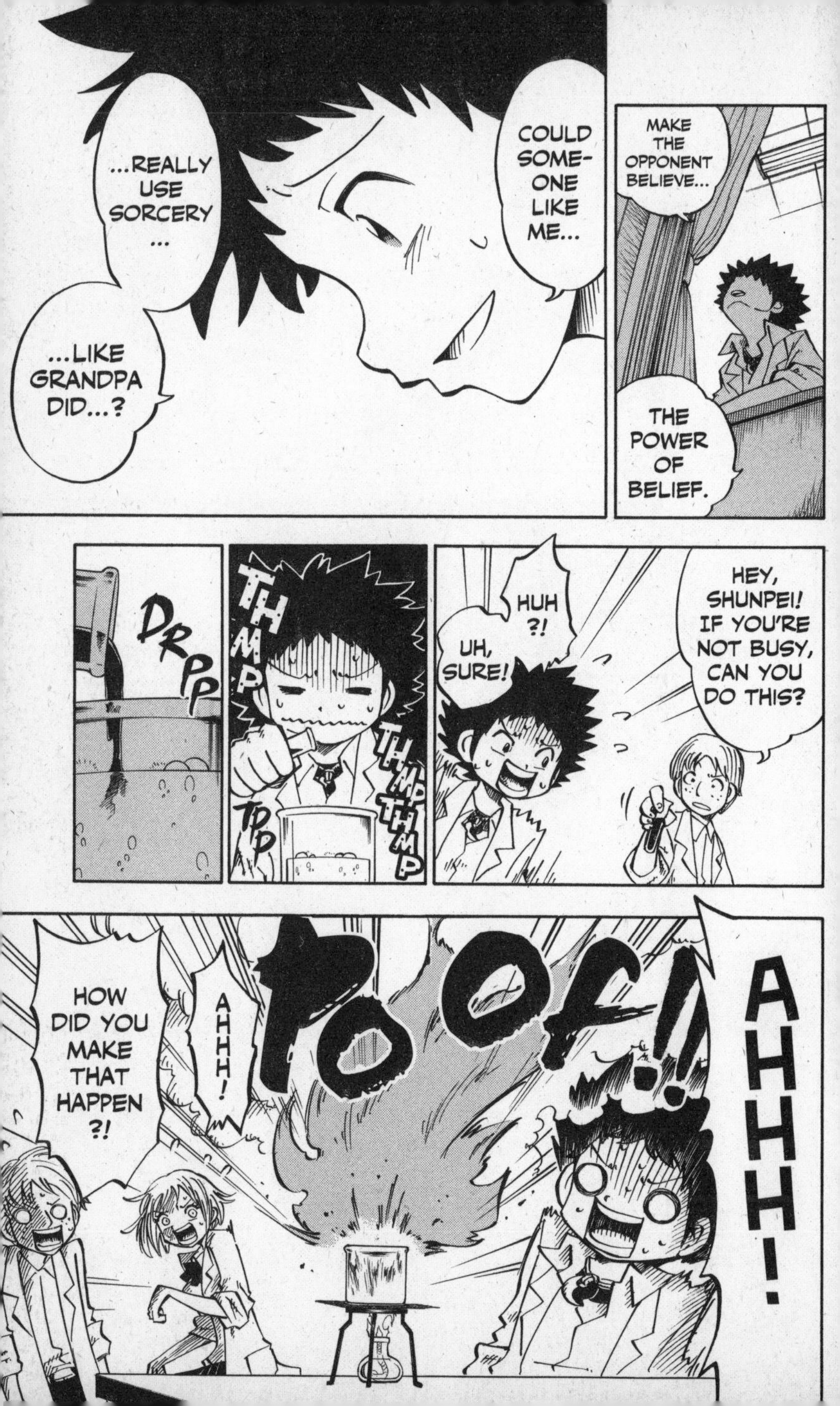

MAKE THE OPPONENT BELIEVE...
THE POWER OF BELIEF.
COULD SOME-ONE LIKE ME...
...REALLY USE SORCERY ...
...LIKE GRANDPA DID...?
HEY, SHUNPEI! IF YOU'RE NOT BUSY, CAN YOU DO THIS?
HUH ?!
UH, SURE!
THMP
THMP THMP
TPP
DRPP
AHHH!
POOF!!
AHHH!
HOW DID YOU MAKE THAT HAPPEN ?!

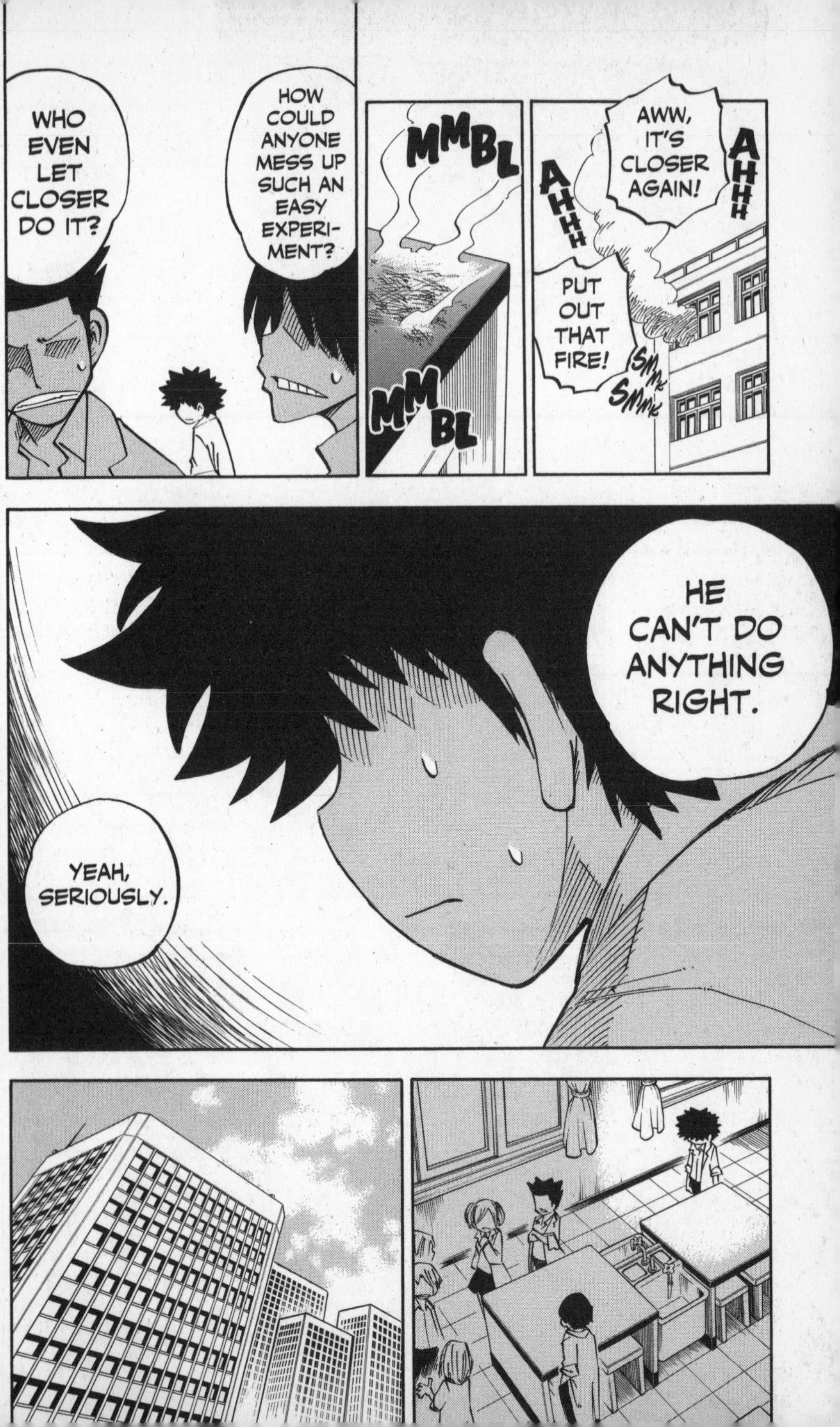
AHHHH
AWW, IT'S CLOSER AGAIN!
AHHHH
PUT OUT THAT FIRE!
SMMK
SMMK
MMBL
MMBL
HOW COULD ANYONE MESS UP SUCH AN EASY EXPERIMENT?
WHO EVEN LET CLOSER DO IT?
HE CAN'T DO ANYTHING RIGHT.
YEAH, SERIOUSLY.

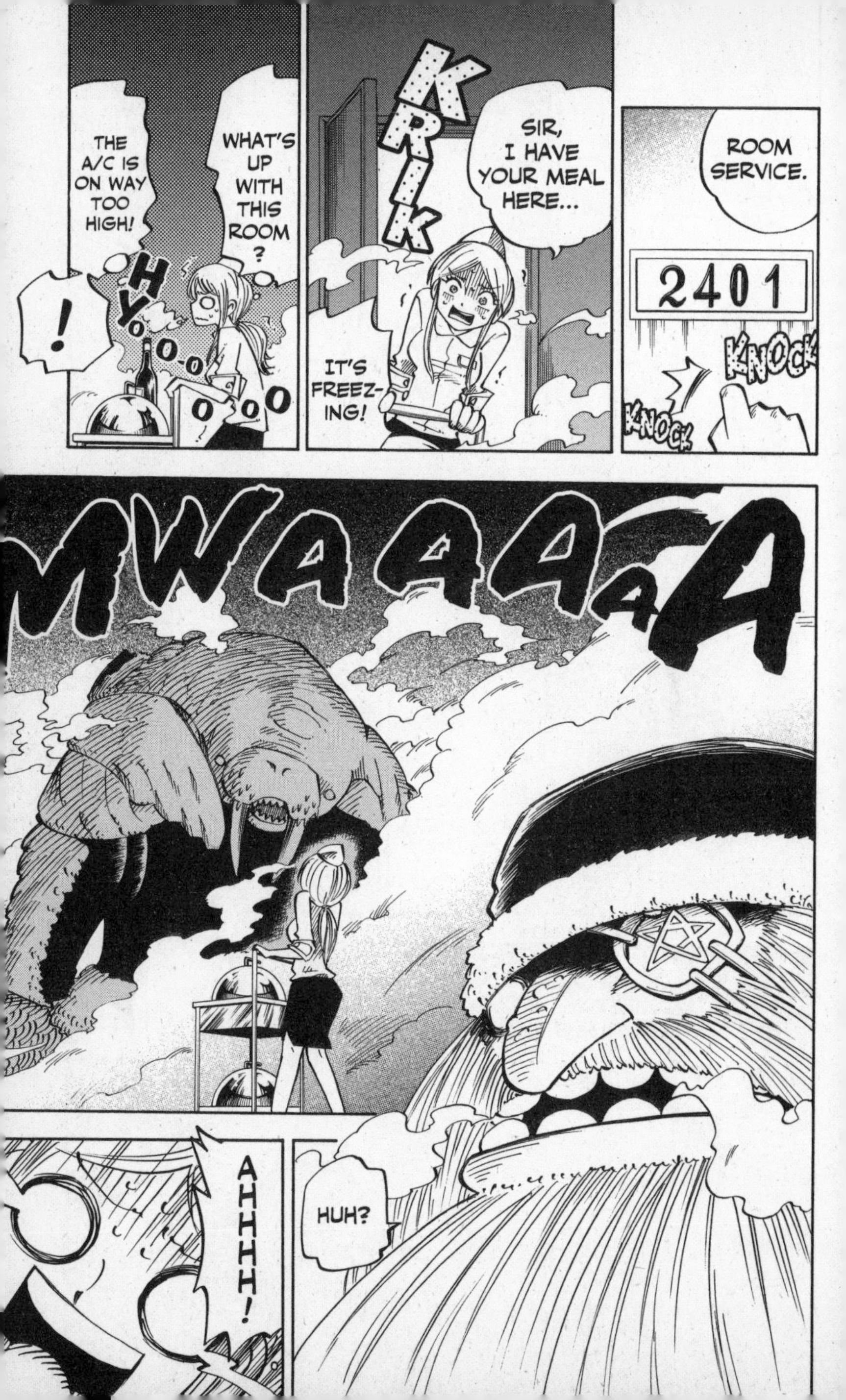
ROOM SERVICE.
2401
KNOCK
KNOCK
SIR, I HAVE YOUR MEAL HERE...
KRIK
IT'S FREEZ-ING!
WHAT'S UP WITH THIS ROOM?
THE A/C IS ON WAY TOO HIGH!
HYOOO-OOOOO
!
MWAAAAAA
HUH?
AHHHH!

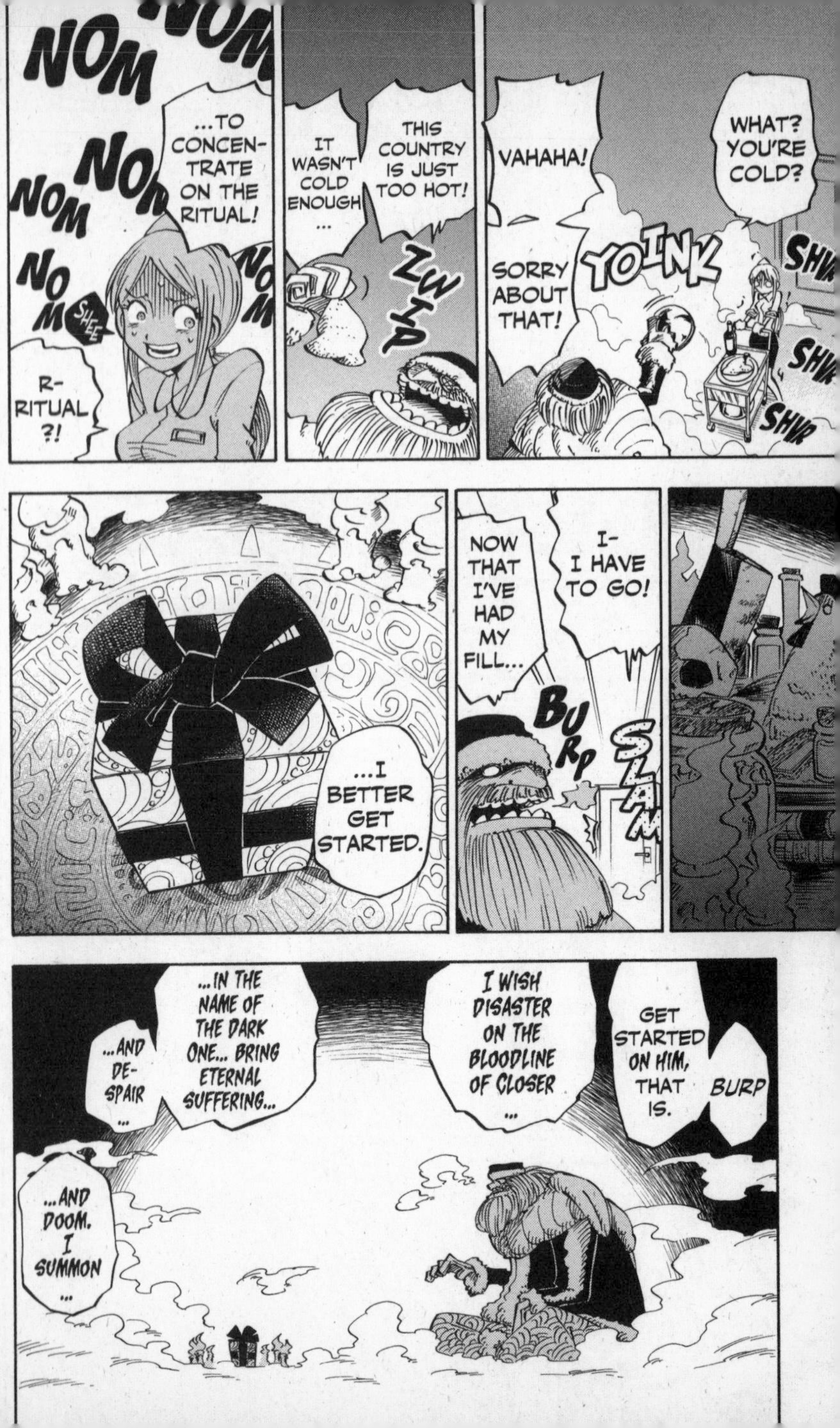
WHAT? YOU'RE COLD?
SHVR
SHVR
SHVR
VAHAHA!
YOINK
SORRY ABOUT THAT!
THIS COUNTRY IS JUST TOO HOT!
IT WASN'T COLD ENOUGH...
ZWIP
NOM NOM
...TO CONCENTRATE ON THE RITUAL!
NOM NOM NOM NOM NOM
SHEE
R-RITUAL?!
I- I HAVE TO GO!
NOW THAT I'VE HAD MY FILL...
BURP
SLAM
...I BETTER GET STARTED.
GET STARTED ON HIM, THAT IS.
BURP
I WISH DISASTER ON THE BLOODLINE OF CLOSER...
...IN THE NAME OF THE DARK ONE... BRING ETERNAL SUFFERING...
...AND DESPAIR...
...AND DOOM. I SUMMON...

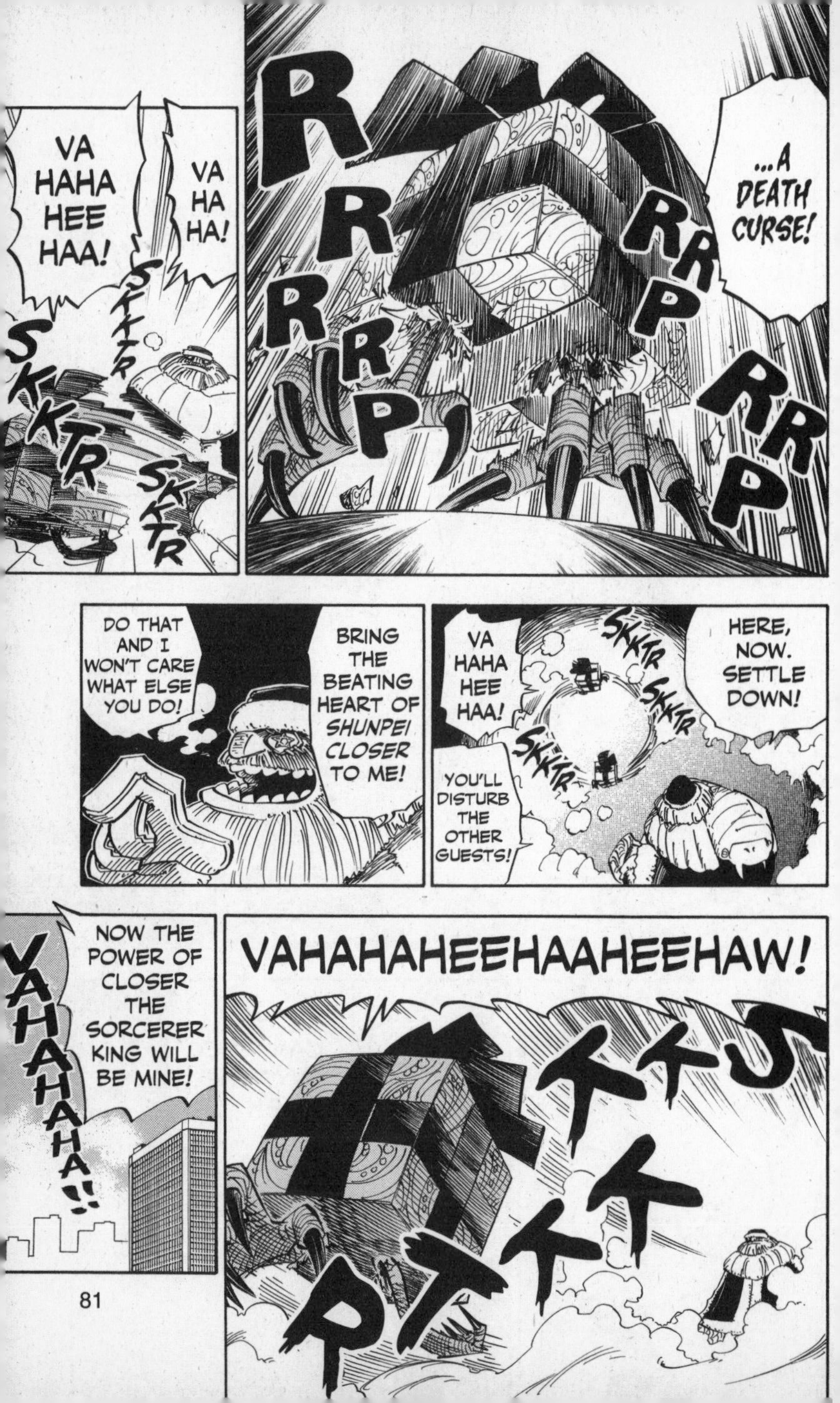

...A DEATH CURSE!
RRRRP
RRRP
RRRP
RRP
VA HA HA!
VA HAHA HEE HAA!
SKKTR
SKKTR
SKKTR
HERE, NOW. SETTLE DOWN!
VA HAHA HEE HAA!
YOU'LL DISTURB THE OTHER GUESTS!
SKKKR
SKKKR
SKKKR
BRING THE BEATING HEART OF SHUNPEI CLOSER TO ME!
DO THAT AND I WON'T CARE WHAT ELSE YOU DO!
VAHAHAHEEHAAHEEHAW!
SKKKKRT
NOW THE POWER OF CLOSER THE SORCERER KING WILL BE MINE!
VAHAHAHAHA!!

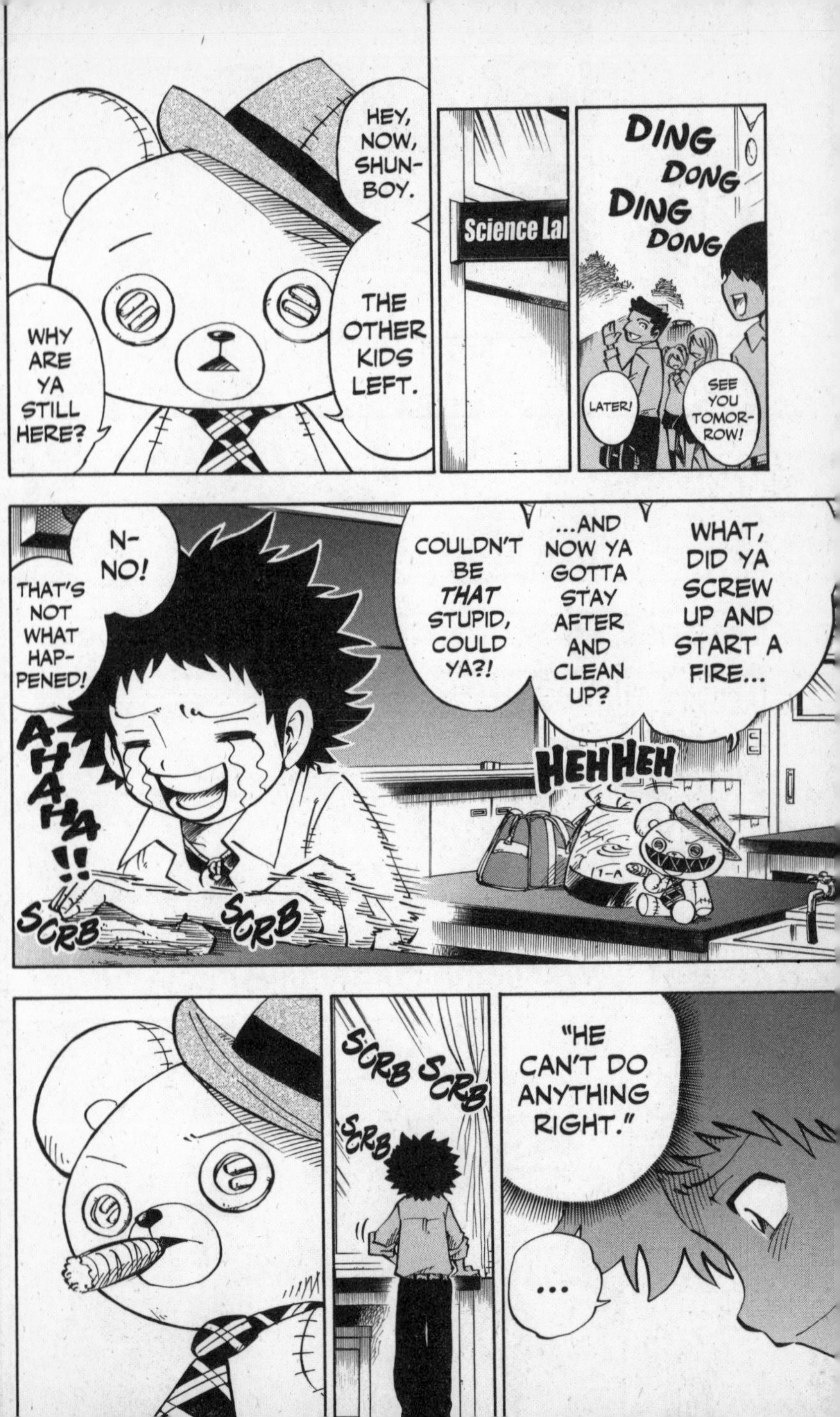
DING DONG DING DONG
SEE YOU TOMOR-ROW!
LATER!
Science La
HEY, NOW, SHUN-BOY.
THE OTHER KIDS LEFT.
WHY ARE YA STILL HERE?
WHAT, DID YA SCREW UP AND START A FIRE...
...AND NOW YA GOTTA STAY AFTER AND CLEAN UP?
COULDN'T BE *THAT* STUPID, COULD YA?!
HEHHEH
1-A
N-NO!
THAT'S NOT WHAT HAP-PENED!
AHAHAHA!!
SCRB
SCRB
"HE CAN'T DO ANYTHING RIGHT."
...
SCRB SCRB
SCRB

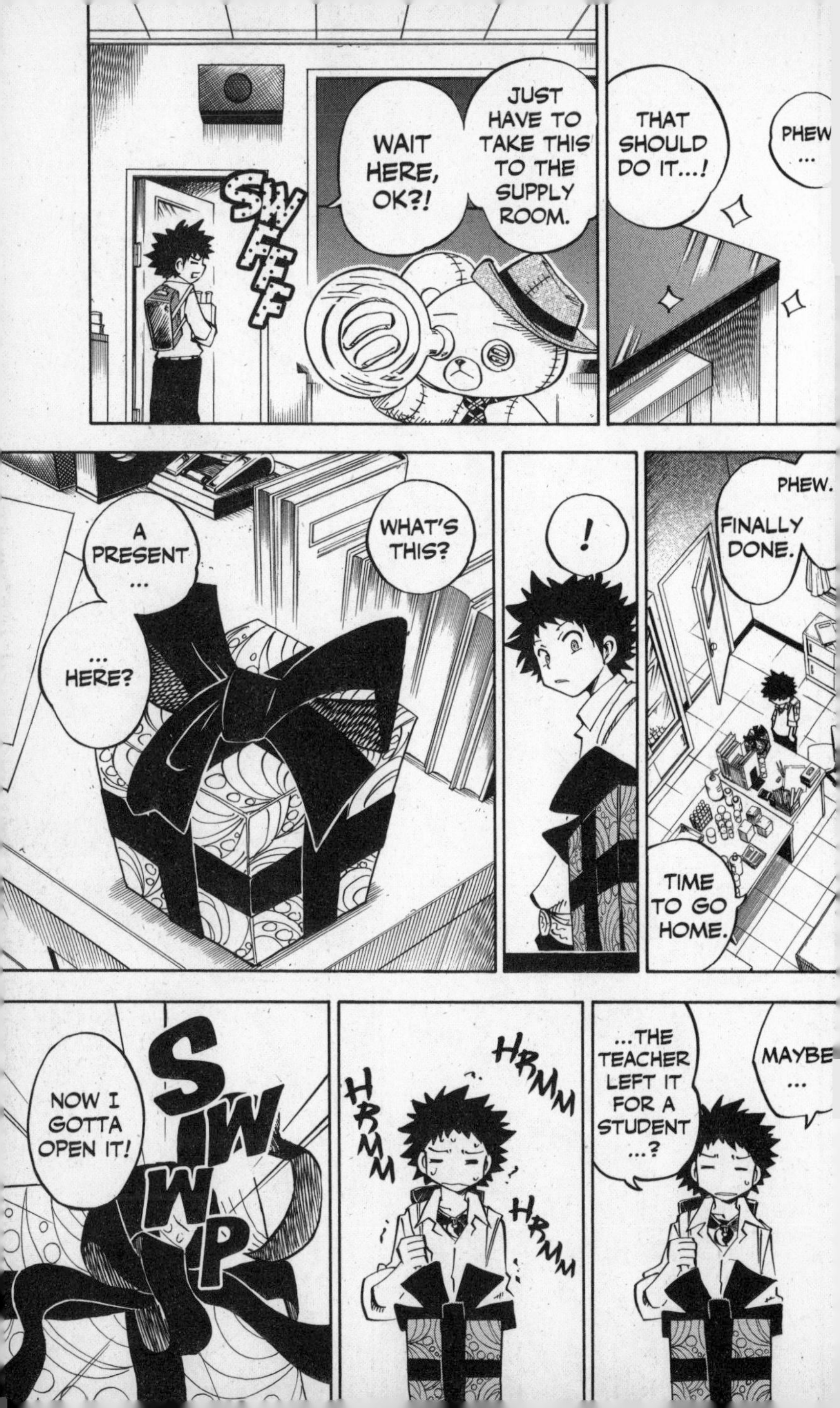
PHEW ...
THAT SHOULD DO IT...!
JUST HAVE TO TAKE THIS TO THE SUPPLY ROOM.
WAIT HERE, OK?!
SWFFF
PHEW.
FINALLY DONE.
TIME TO GO HOME.
!
WHAT'S THIS?
A PRESENT ...
... HERE?
MAYBE ...
...THE TEACHER LEFT IT FOR A STUDENT ...?
HRMM
HRMM
HRMM
SWWP
NOW I GOTTA OPEN IT!

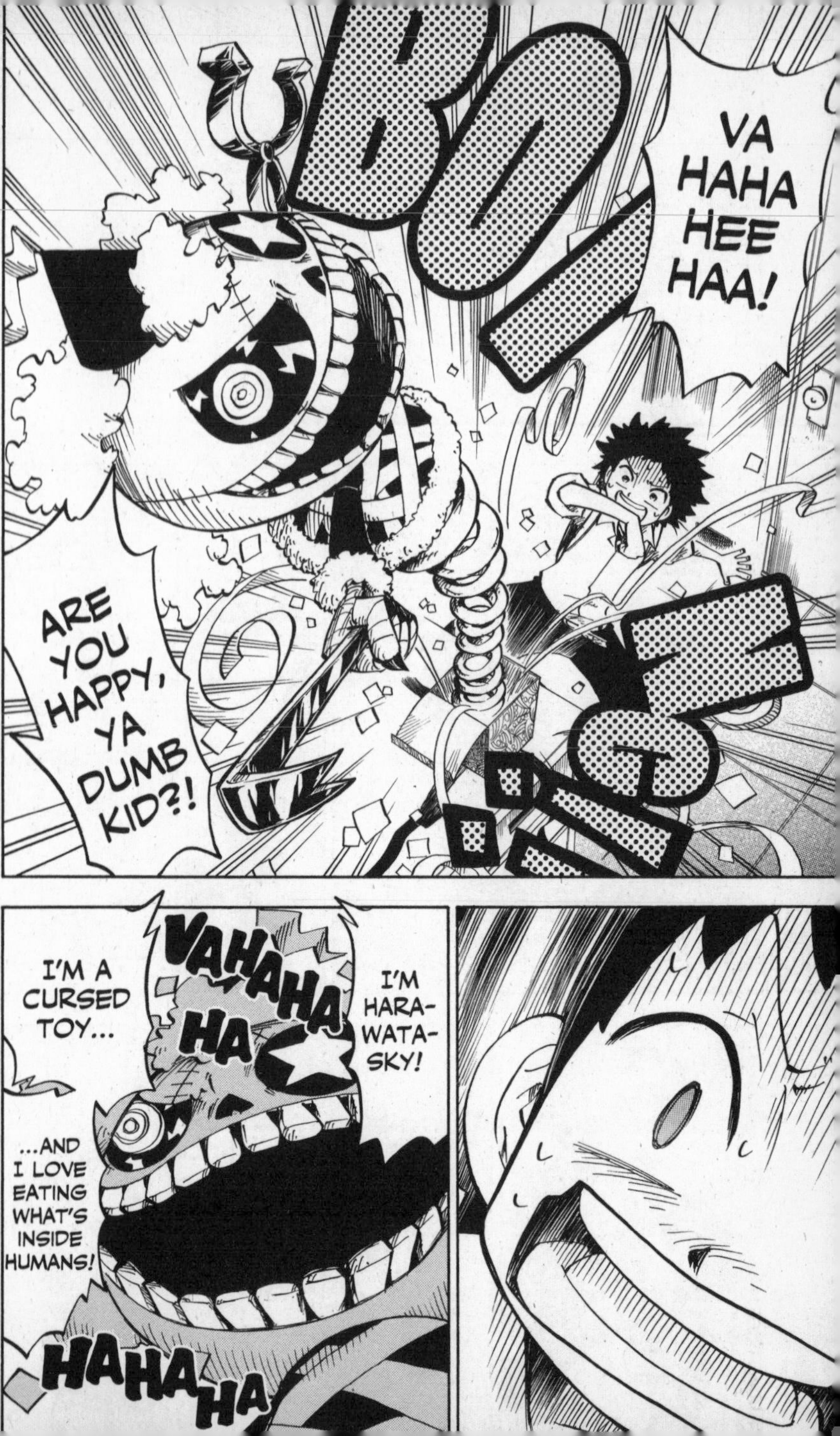
VA HAHA HEE HAA!
ARE YOU HAPPY, YA DUMB KID?!
I'M HARA-WATA-SKY!
VAHAHAHA HA
I'M A CURSED TOY...
...AND I LOVE EATING WHAT'S INSIDE HUMANS!
HAHAHA

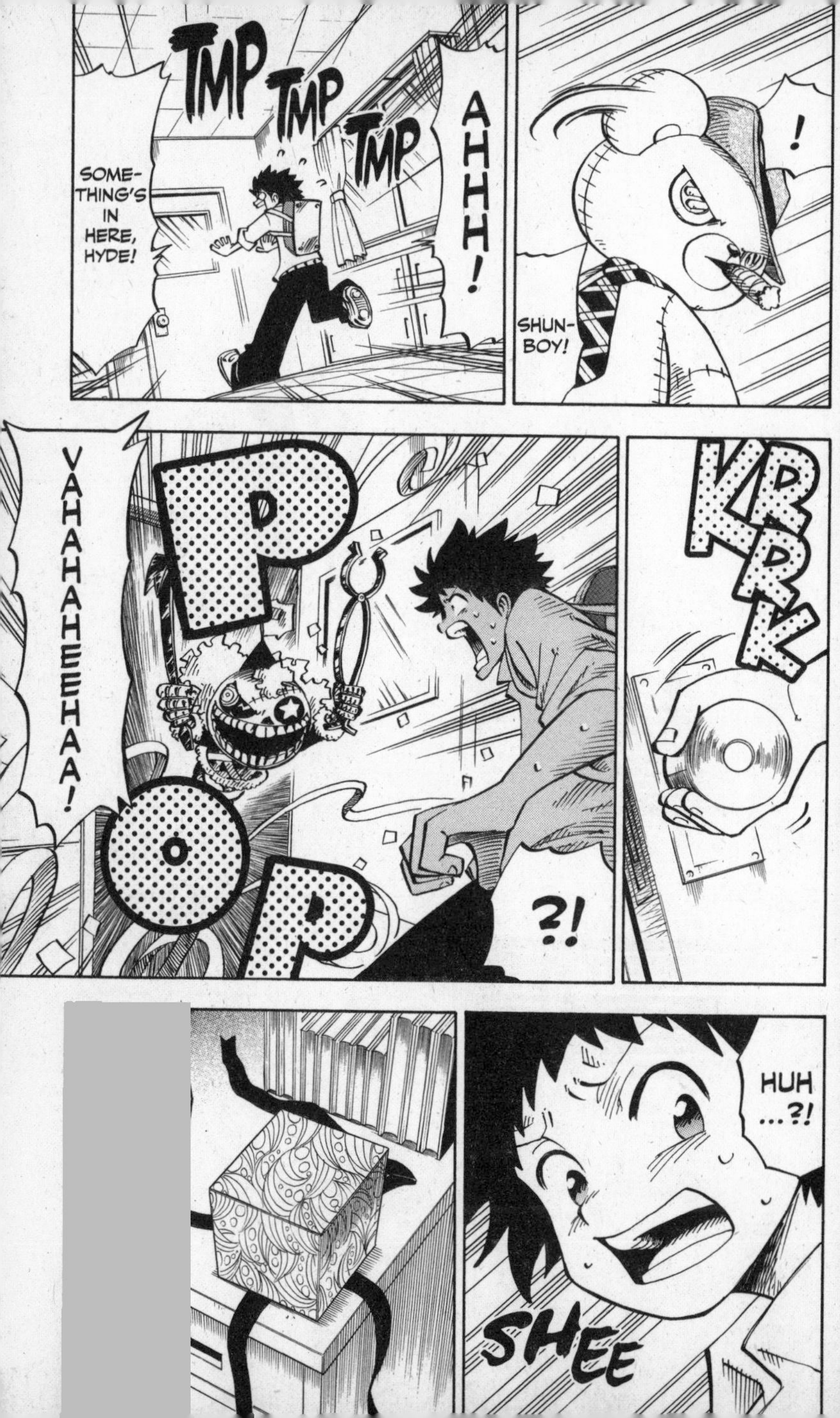
!
SHUN-BOY!
TMP TMP TMP
AHHH!
SOME-THING'S IN HERE, HYDE!
KRRK
?!
POP
VAHAHAHEEHAA!
HUH ...?!
SHEE

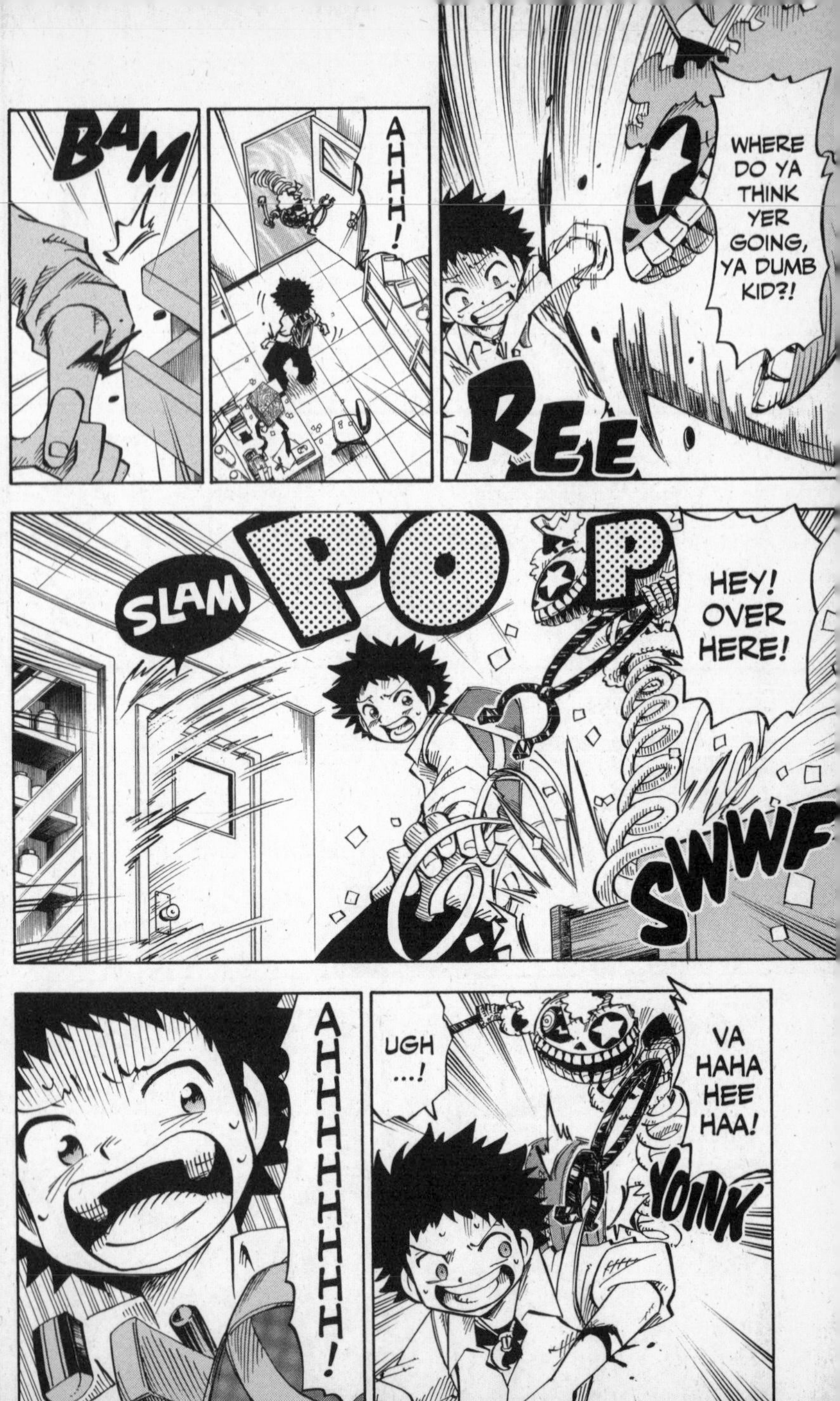
WHERE DO YA THINK YER GOING, YA DUMB KID?!
REE
AHHH!
BAM
HEY! OVER HERE!
POP
SLAM
SWWF
VA HAHA HEE HAA!
YOINK
UGH ...!
AHHHHHHHHH!

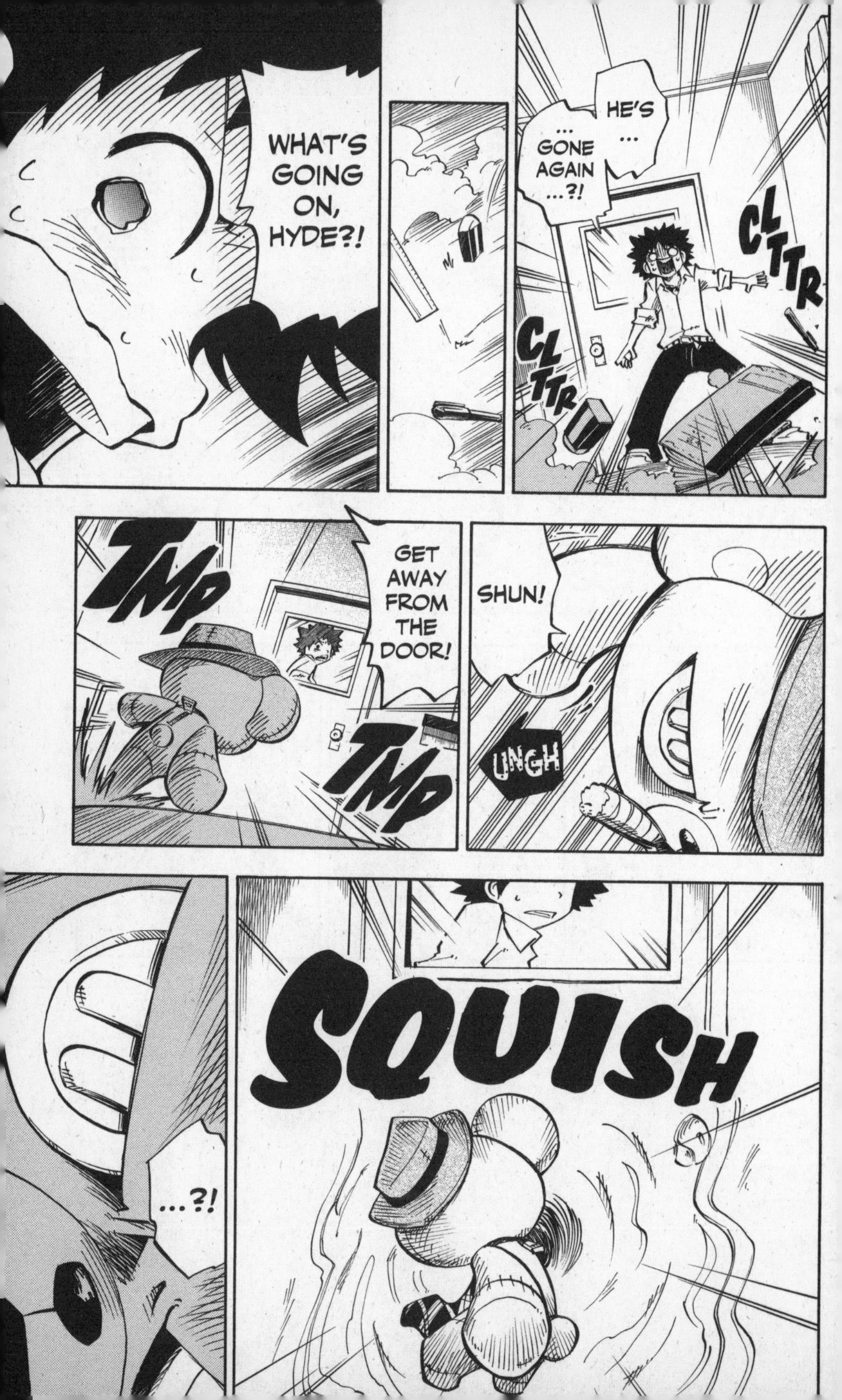
HE'S ...
... GONE AGAIN ...?!
CLTTR
CLTTR
WHAT'S GOING ON, HYDE?!
SHUN!
UNGH
TMP
GET AWAY FROM THE DOOR!
TMP
SQUISH
...?!

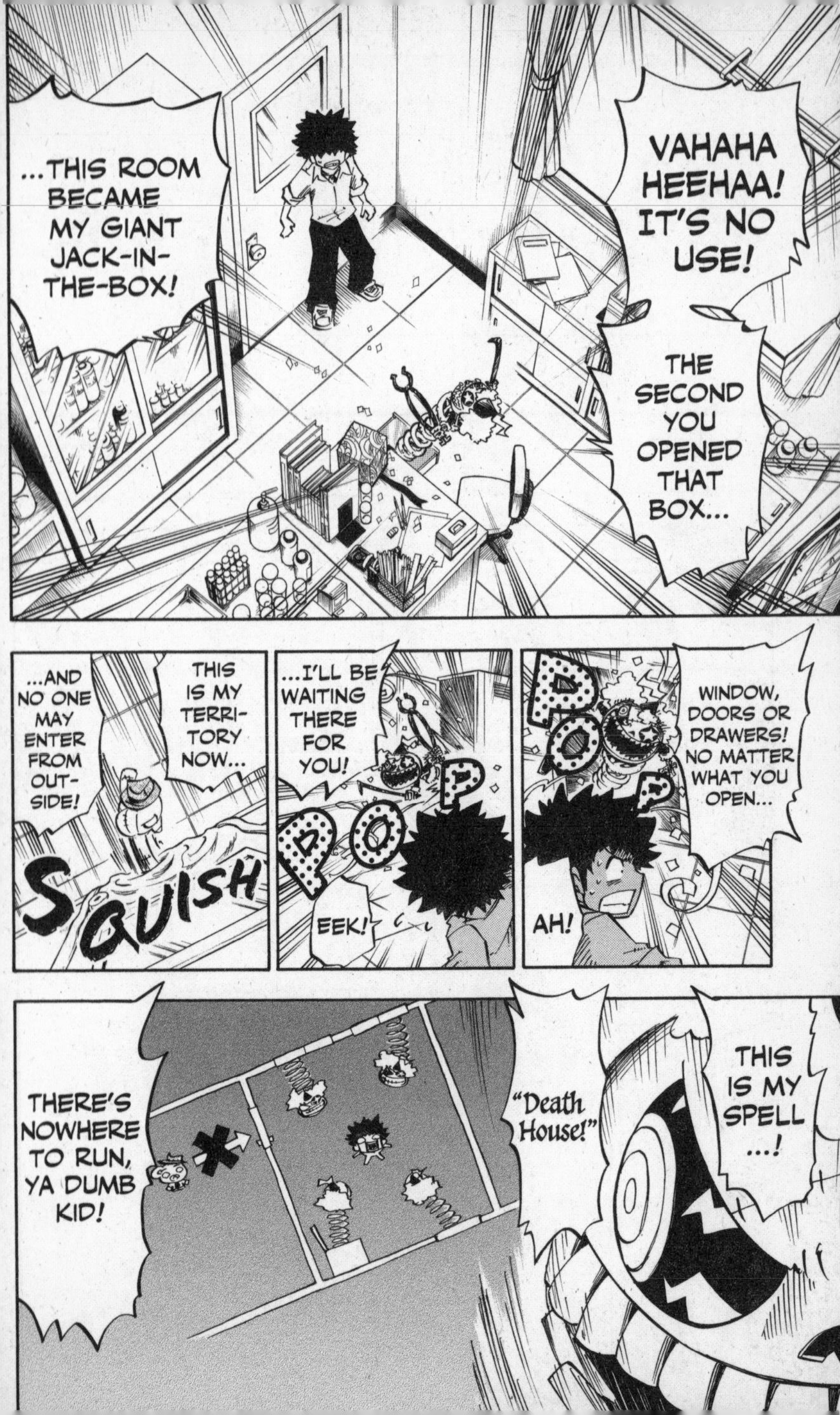
VAHAHA HEEHAA! IT'S NO USE!
THE SECOND YOU OPENED THAT BOX...
...THIS ROOM BECAME MY GIANT JACK-IN-THE-BOX!
WINDOW, DOORS OR DRAWERS! NO MATTER WHAT YOU OPEN...
POP
AH!
...I'LL BE WAITING THERE FOR YOU!
POP
EEK!
THIS IS MY TERRITORY NOW...
...AND NO ONE MAY ENTER FROM OUTSIDE!
SQUISH
THIS IS MY SPELL ...!
"Death House!"
THERE'S NOWHERE TO RUN, YA DUMB KID!

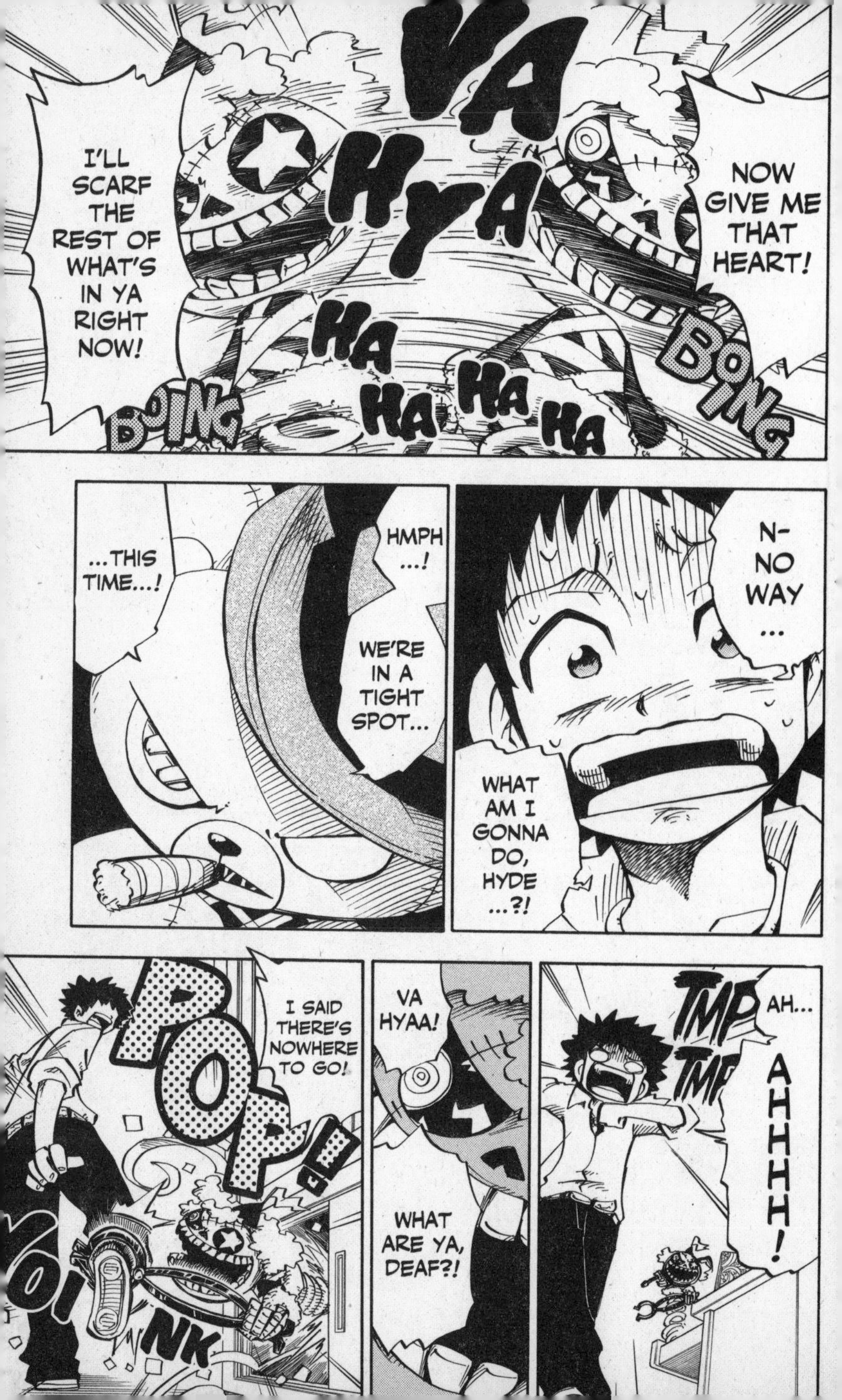
NOW GIVE ME THAT HEART!
VA HYA
I'LL SCARF THE REST OF WHAT'S IN YA RIGHT NOW!
BOING
HA HA HA HA HA
BOING
N-NO WAY...
WHAT AM I GONNA DO, HYDE...?!
HMPH...!
WE'RE IN A TIGHT SPOT...
...THIS TIME...!
TMP TMP
AH...AHHHH!
VA HYAA!
WHAT ARE YA, DEAF?!
I SAID THERE'S NOWHERE TO GO!
POP!!
BOINK

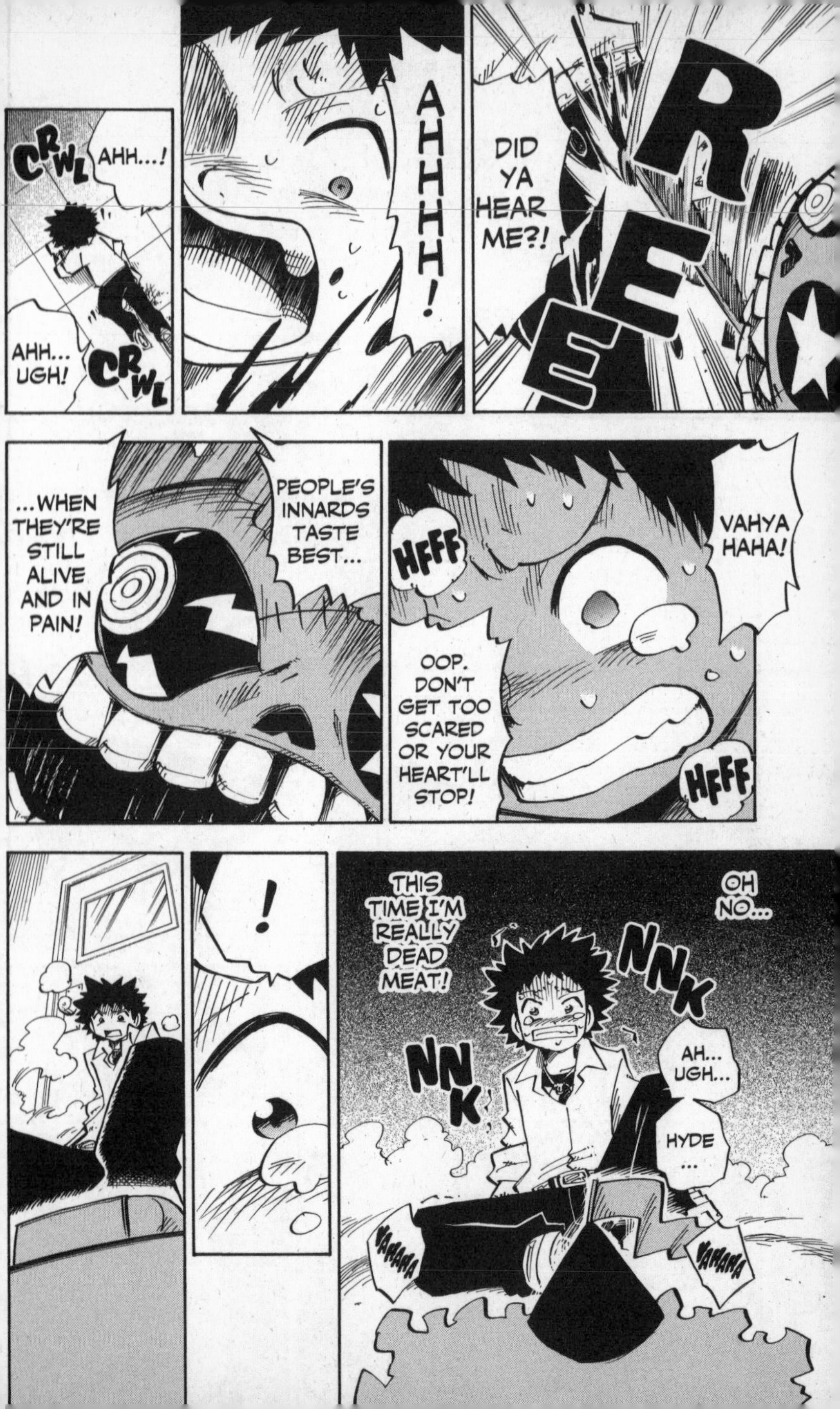
REE
DID YA HEAR ME?!
AHHHHH!
AHH...!
CRWL
AHH... UGH!
CRWL
VAHYA HAHA!
HFFF
OOP. DON'T GET TOO SCARED OR YOUR HEART'LL STOP!
HFFF
PEOPLE'S INNARDS TASTE BEST...
...WHEN THEY'RE STILL ALIVE AND IN PAIN!
OH NO...
THIS TIME I'M REALLY DEAD MEAT!
NNK
AH... UGH...
NNK
HYDE ...
VAHAHA
VAHAHA
!

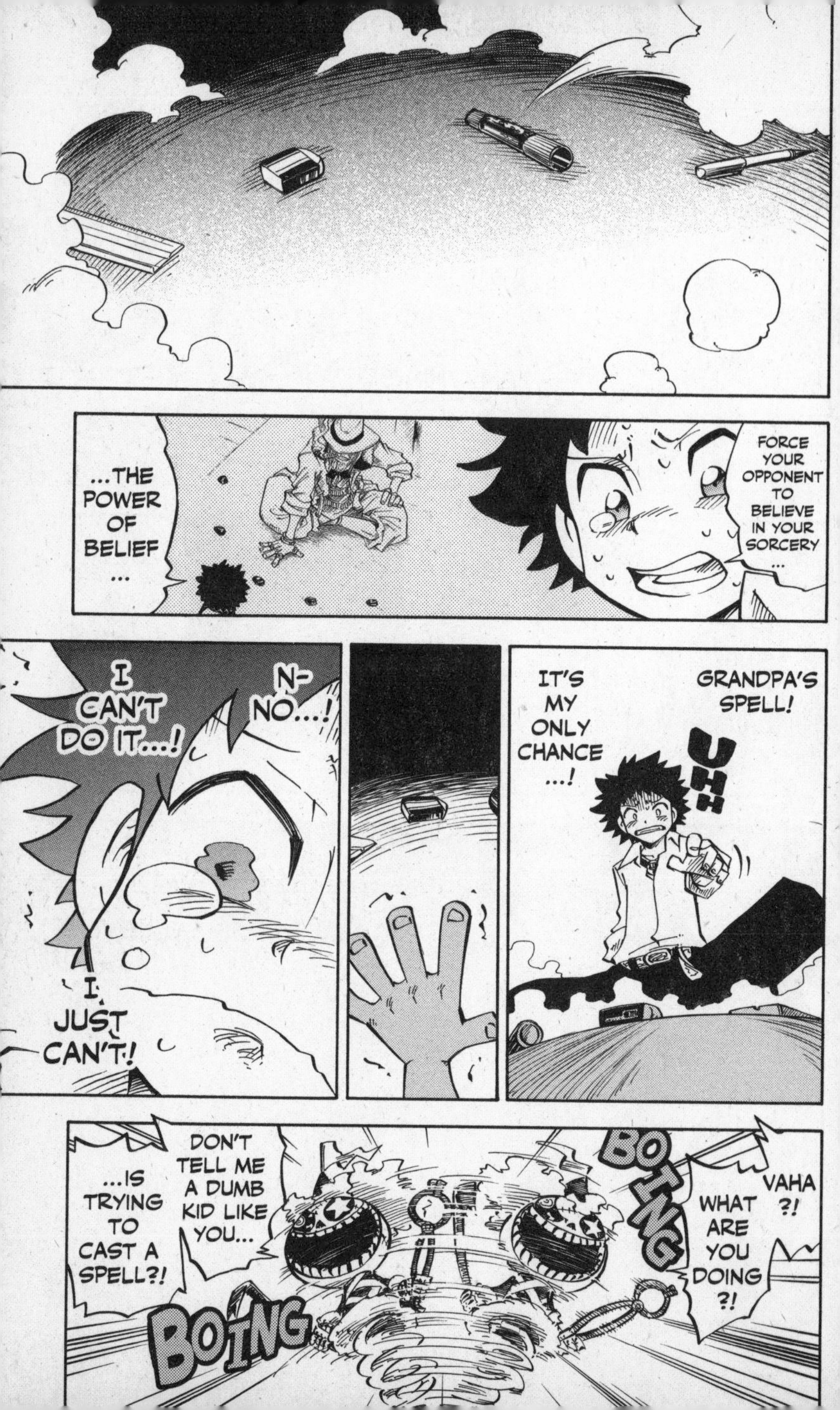
FORCE YOUR OPPONENT TO BELIEVE IN YOUR SORCERY ...
...THE POWER OF BELIEF ...
GRANDPA'S SPELL!
UHH
IT'S MY ONLY CHANCE ...!
N-NO...!
I CAN'T DO IT...!
I JUST CAN'T!
BOING
VAHA ?!
WHAT ARE YOU DOING ?!
DON'T TELL ME A DUMB KID LIKE YOU...
...IS TRYING TO CAST A SPELL?!
BOING

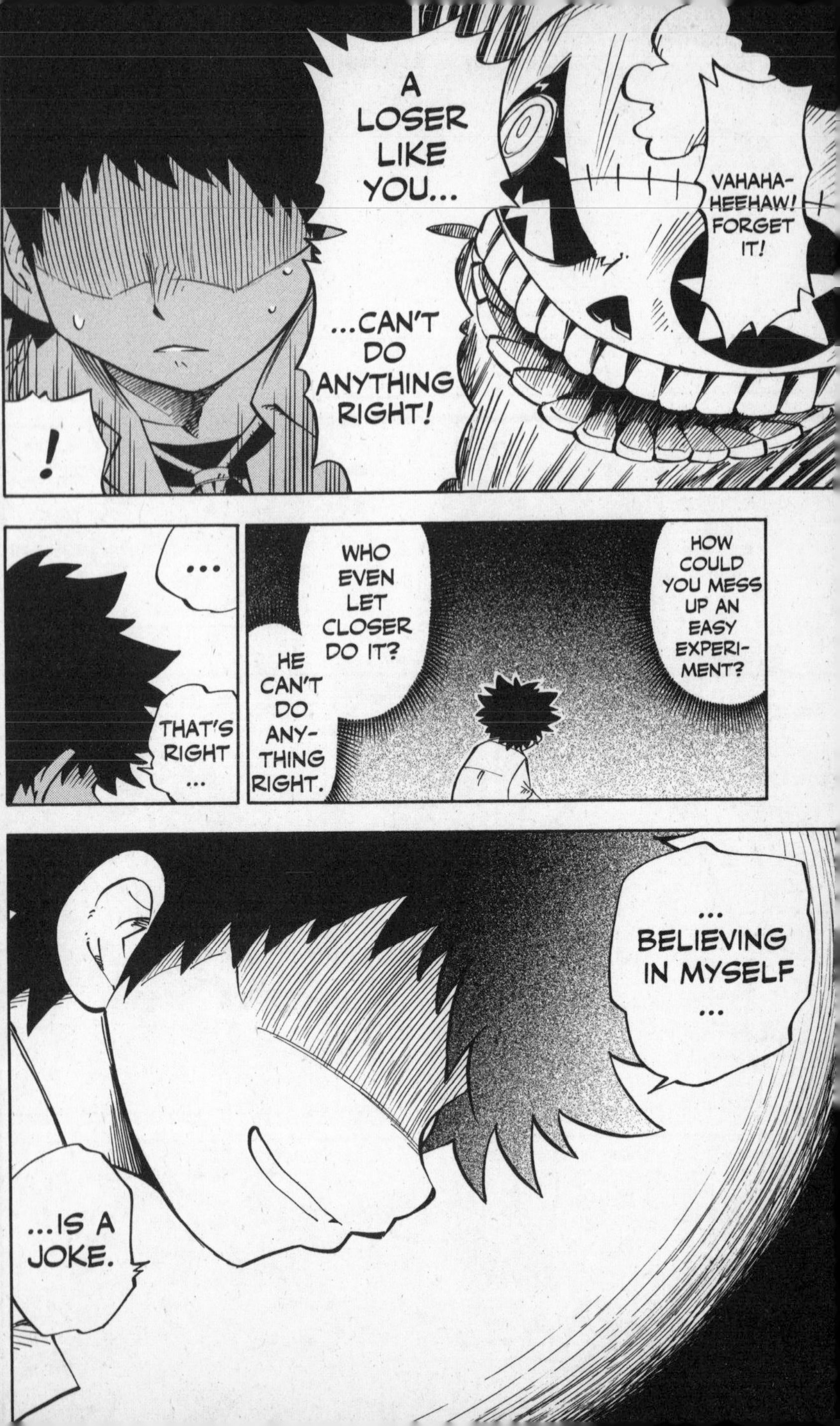
VAHAHA-HEEHAW! FORGET IT!
A LOSER LIKE YOU...
...CAN'T DO ANYTHING RIGHT!
!
HOW COULD YOU MESS UP AN EASY EXPERI-MENT?
WHO EVEN LET CLOSER DO IT?
HE CAN'T DO ANY-THING RIGHT.
...
THAT'S RIGHT ...
... BELIEVING IN MYSELF ...
...IS A JOKE.

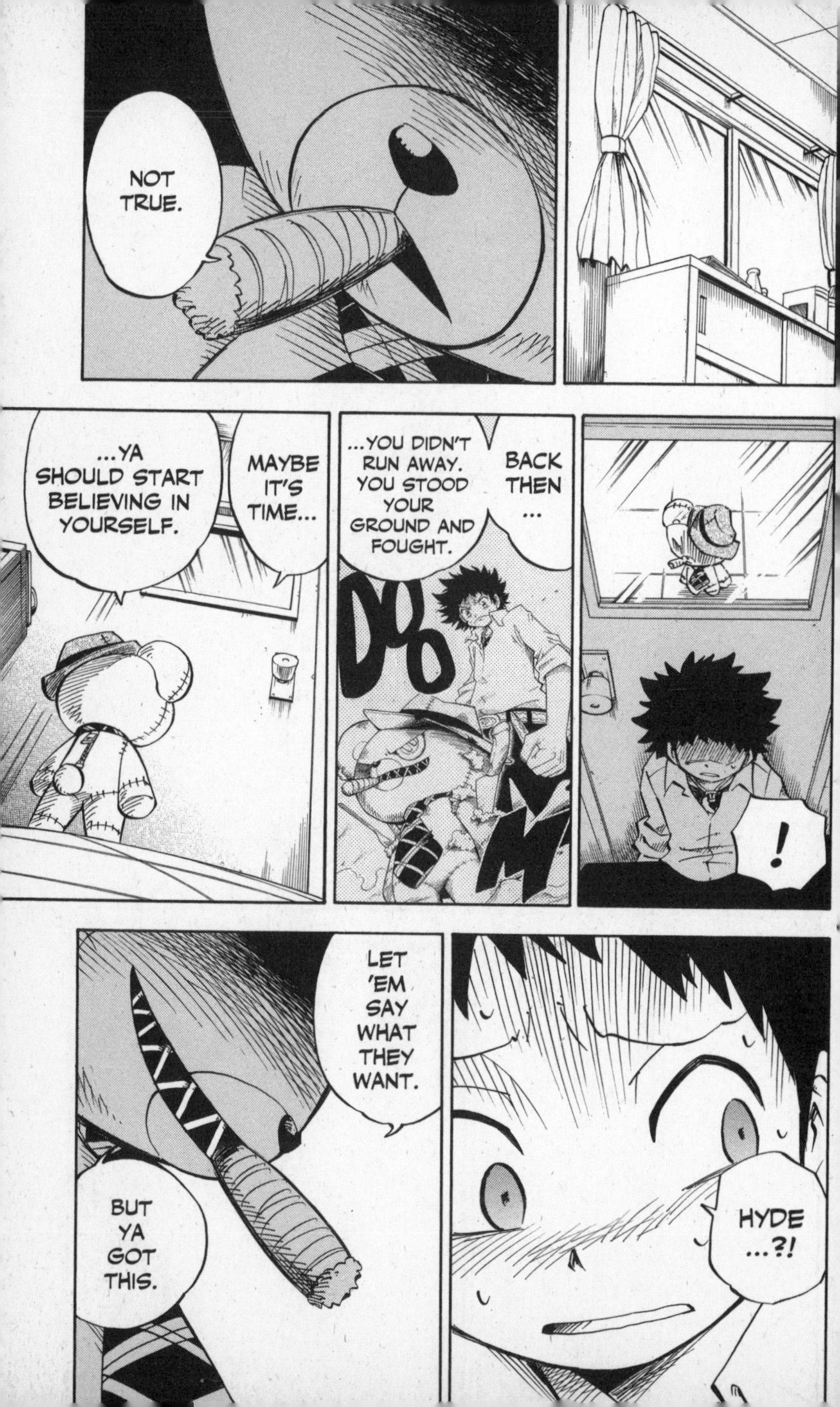
NOT TRUE.
!
BACK THEN ...
...YOU DIDN'T RUN AWAY. YOU STOOD YOUR GROUND AND FOUGHT.
MAYBE IT'S TIME...
...YA SHOULD START BELIEVING IN YOURSELF.
HYDE ...?!
LET 'EM SAY WHAT THEY WANT.
BUT YA GOT THIS.

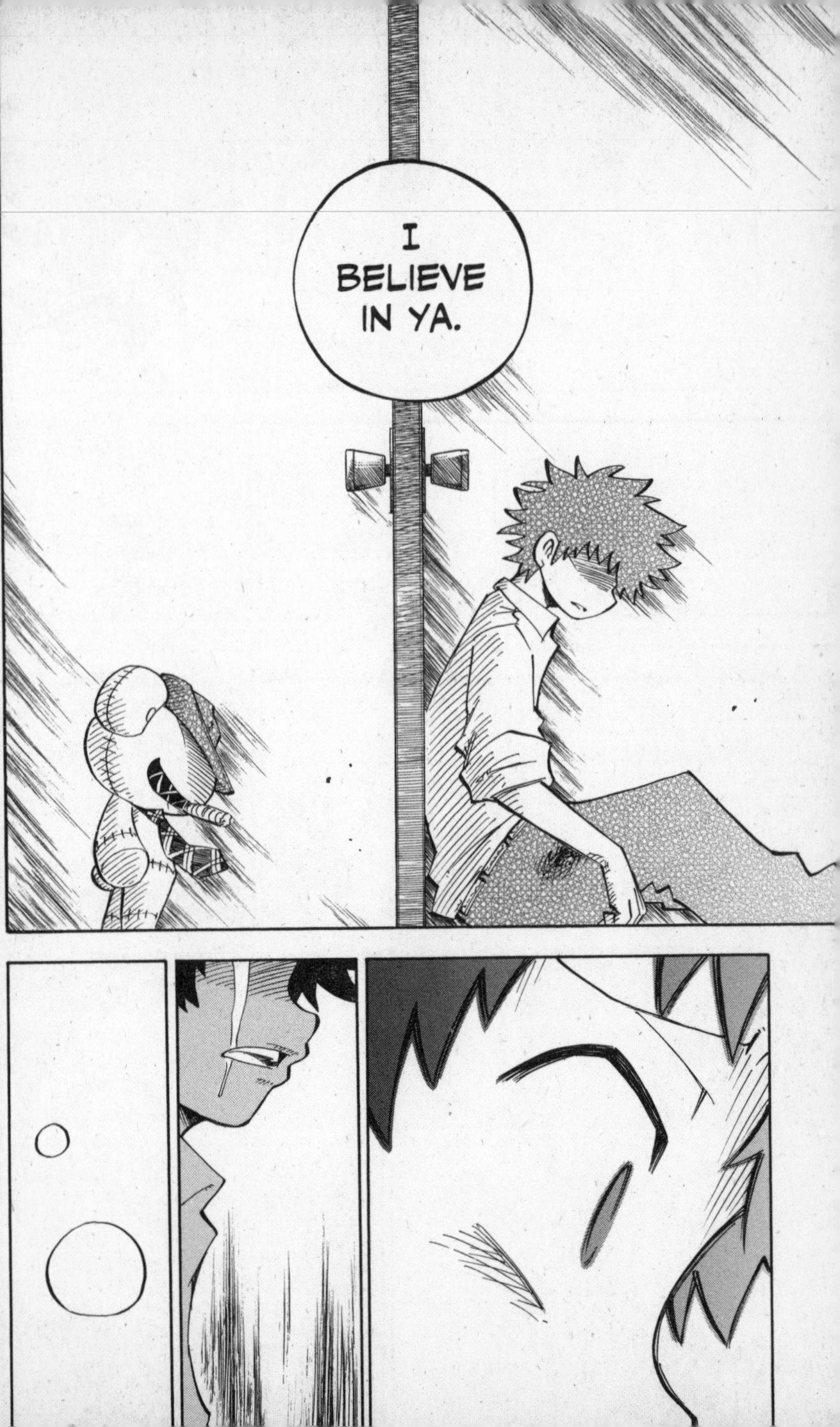
I BELIEVE IN YA.

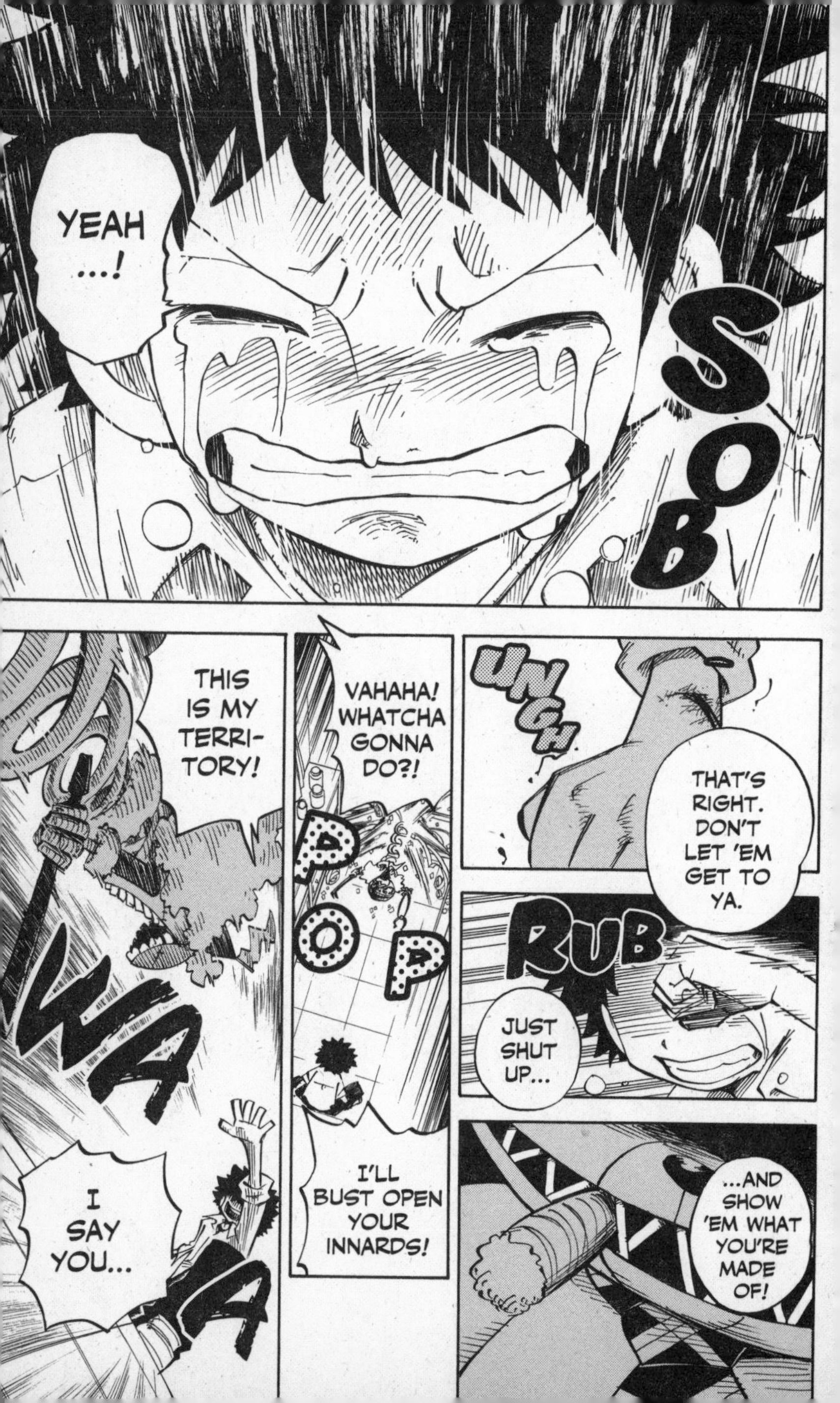
YEAH ...!
SOB
UNGH
THAT'S RIGHT. DON'T LET 'EM GET TO YA.
RUB
JUST SHUT UP...
...AND SHOW 'EM WHAT YOU'RE MADE OF!
VAHAHA! WHATCHA GONNA DO?!
POP
I'LL BUST OPEN YOUR INNARDS!
THIS IS MY TERRI-TORY!
WA
I SAY YOU...

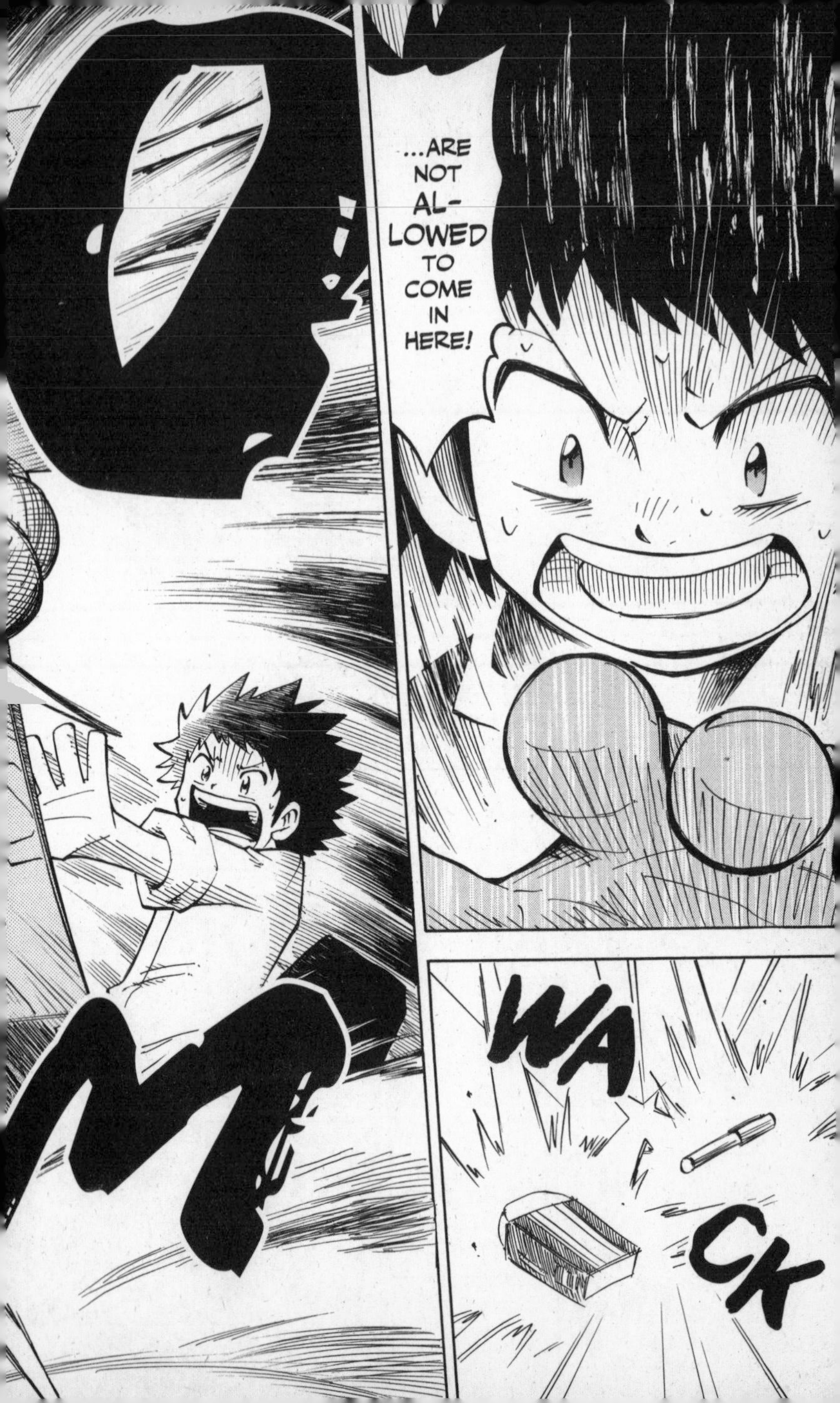
...ARE NOT AL-LOWED TO COME IN HERE!
WA
CK

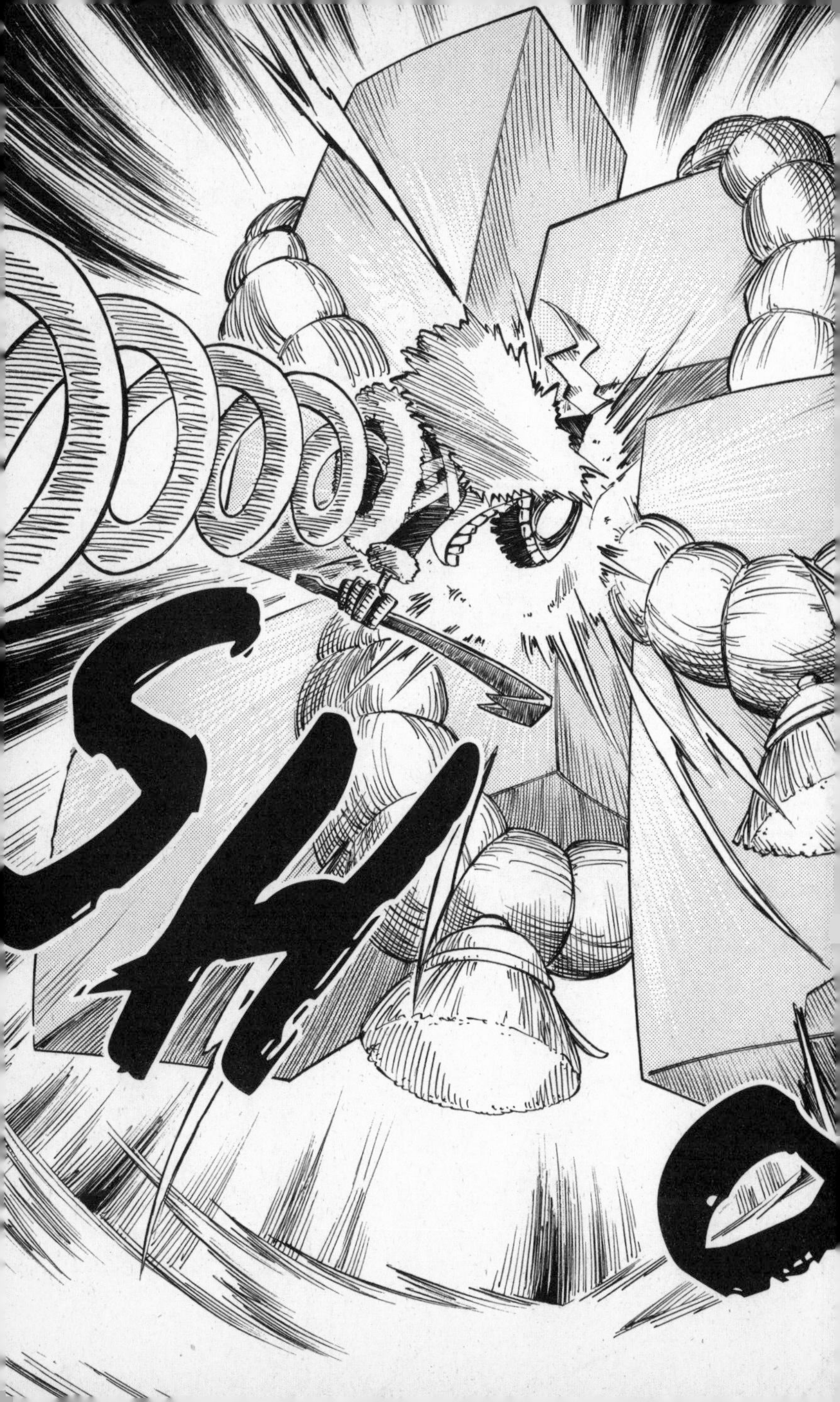
SH

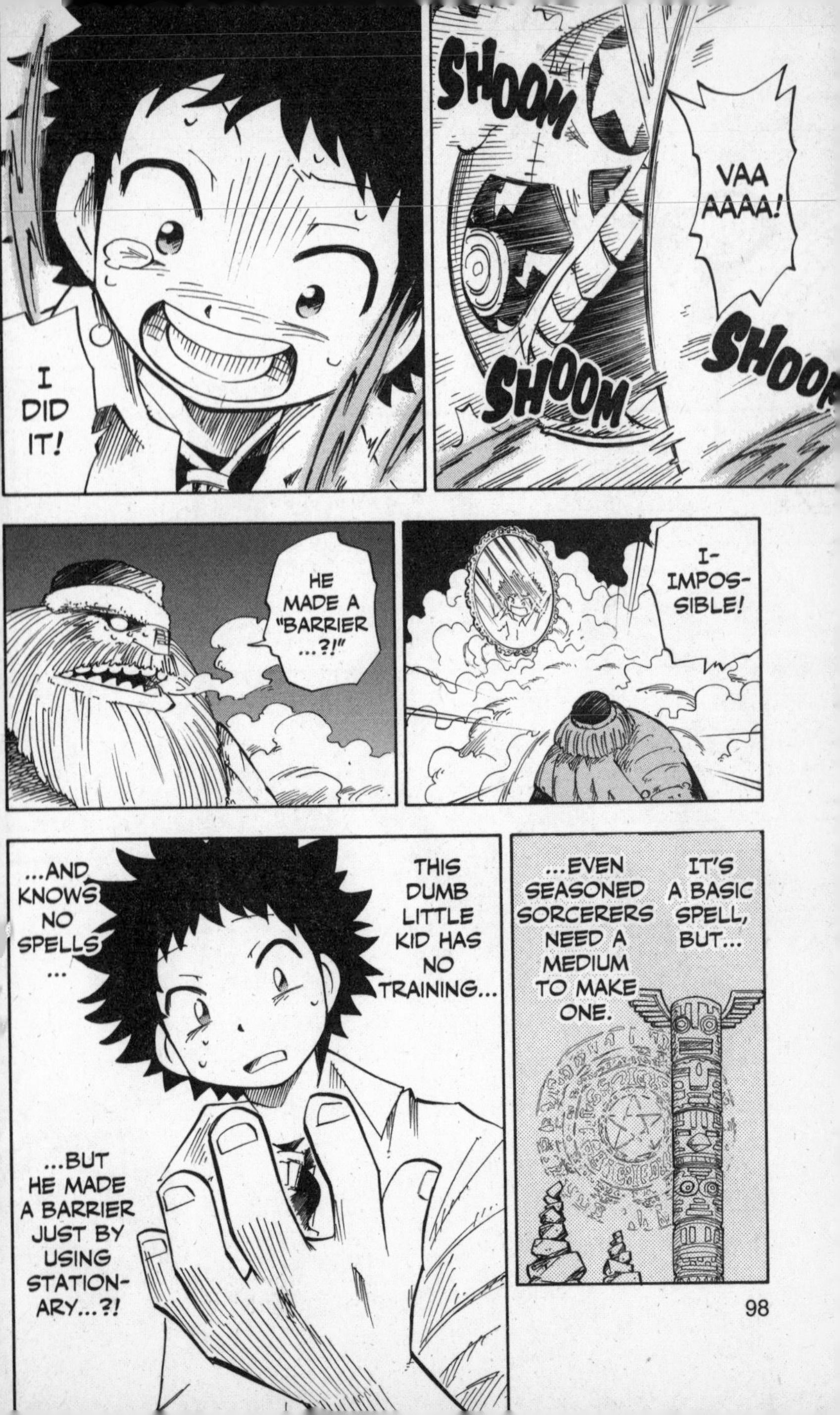
VAA AAAA!
SHOOM
SHOO
SHOOM
I DID IT!
I- IMPOSSIBLE!
HE MADE A "BARRIER ...?!"
IT'S A BASIC SPELL, BUT...
...EVEN SEASONED SORCERERS NEED A MEDIUM TO MAKE ONE.
THIS DUMB LITTLE KID HAS NO TRAINING...
...AND KNOWS NO SPELLS ...
...BUT HE MADE A BARRIER JUST BY USING STATION- ARY...?!

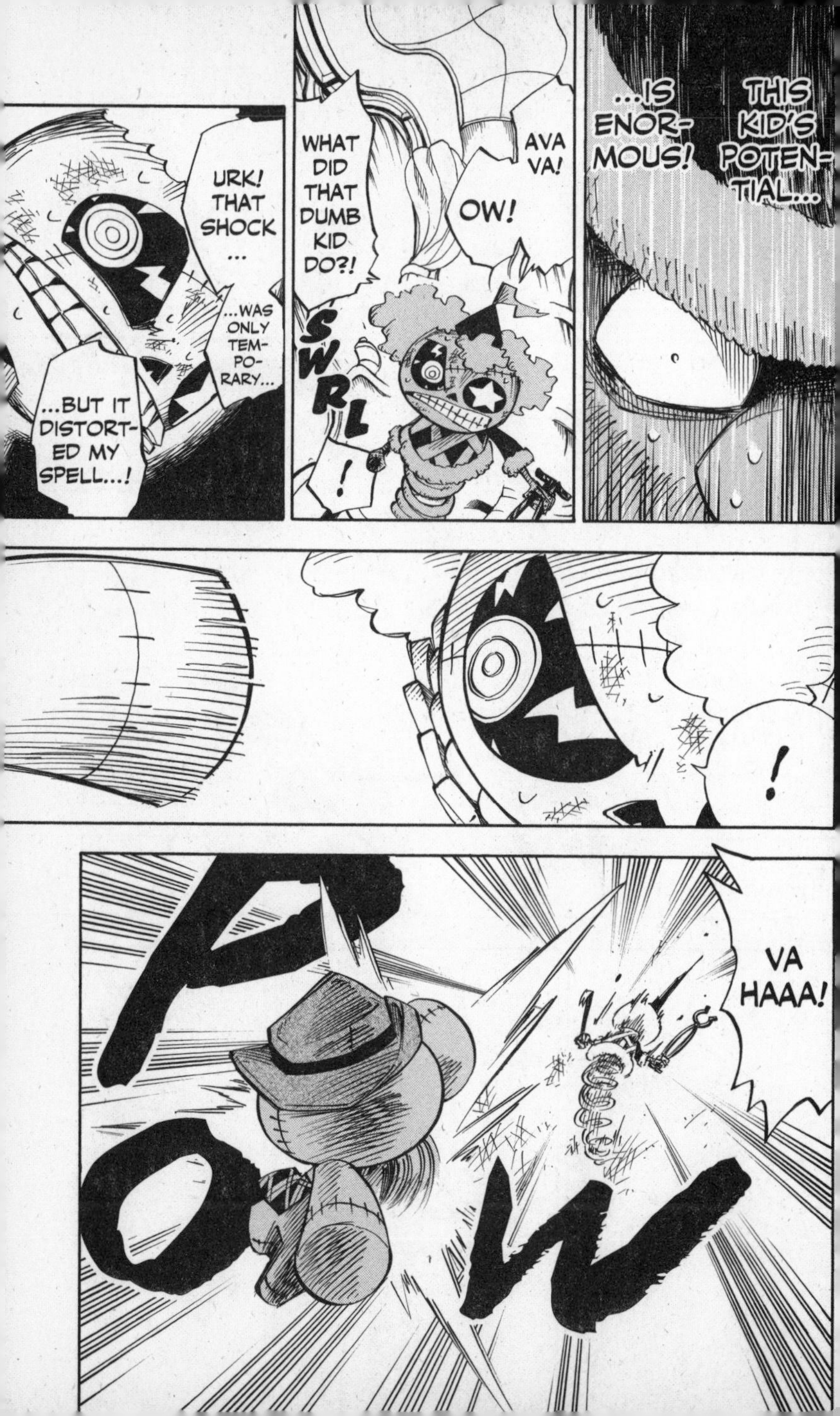
THIS KID'S POTEN-TIAL...
...IS ENOR-MOUS!
AVA VA!
OW!
WHAT DID THAT DUMB KID DO?!
SWRL
!
URK! THAT SHOCK...
...WAS ONLY TEM-PO-RARY...
...BUT IT DISTORT-ED MY SPELL...!
!
VA HAAA!

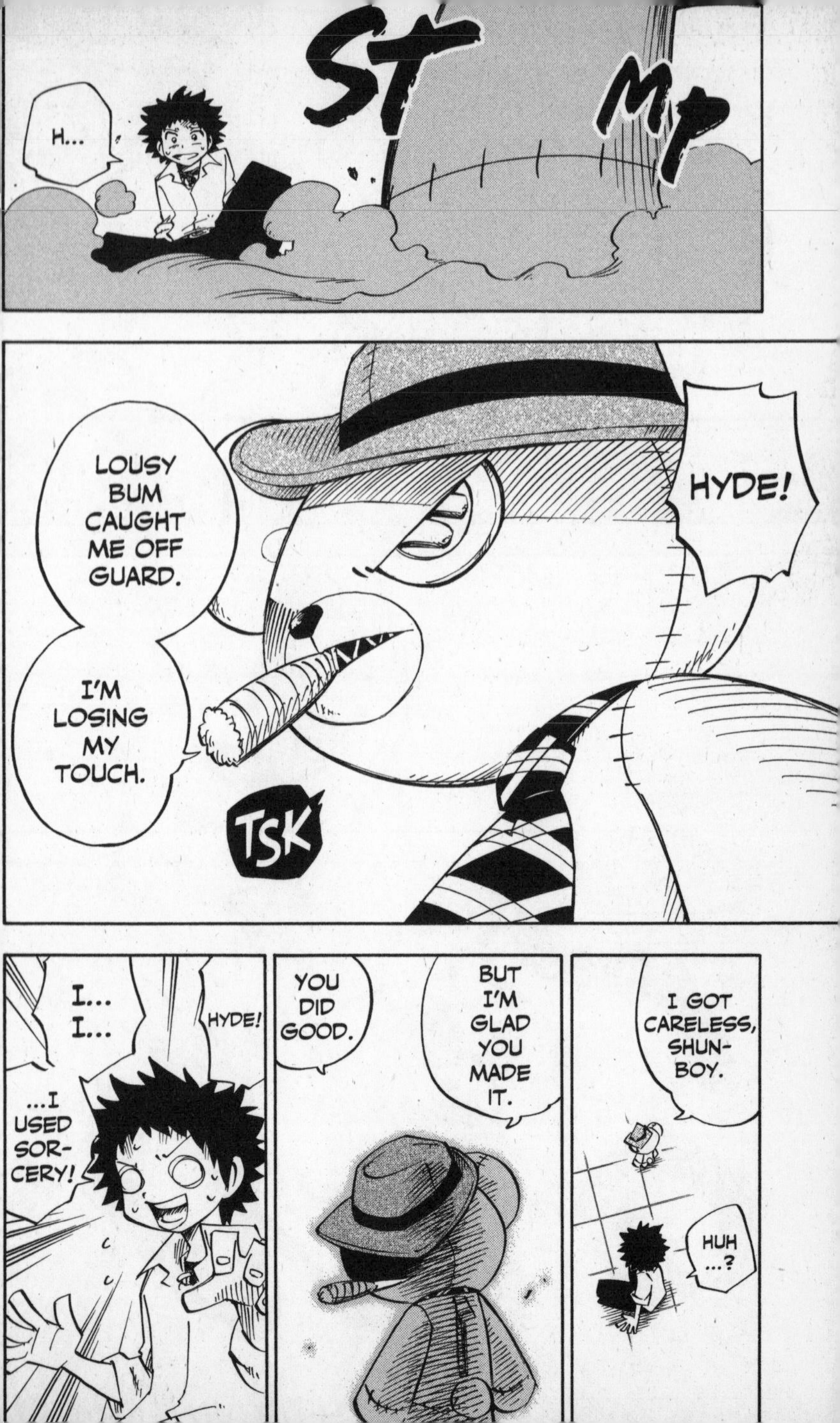
ST MP
H...
HYDE!
LOUSY BUM CAUGHT ME OFF GUARD.
I'M LOSING MY TOUCH.
TSK
I GOT CARELESS, SHUN-BOY.
HUH ...?
BUT I'M GLAD YOU MADE IT.
YOU DID GOOD.
HYDE!
I... I...
...I USED SORCERY!

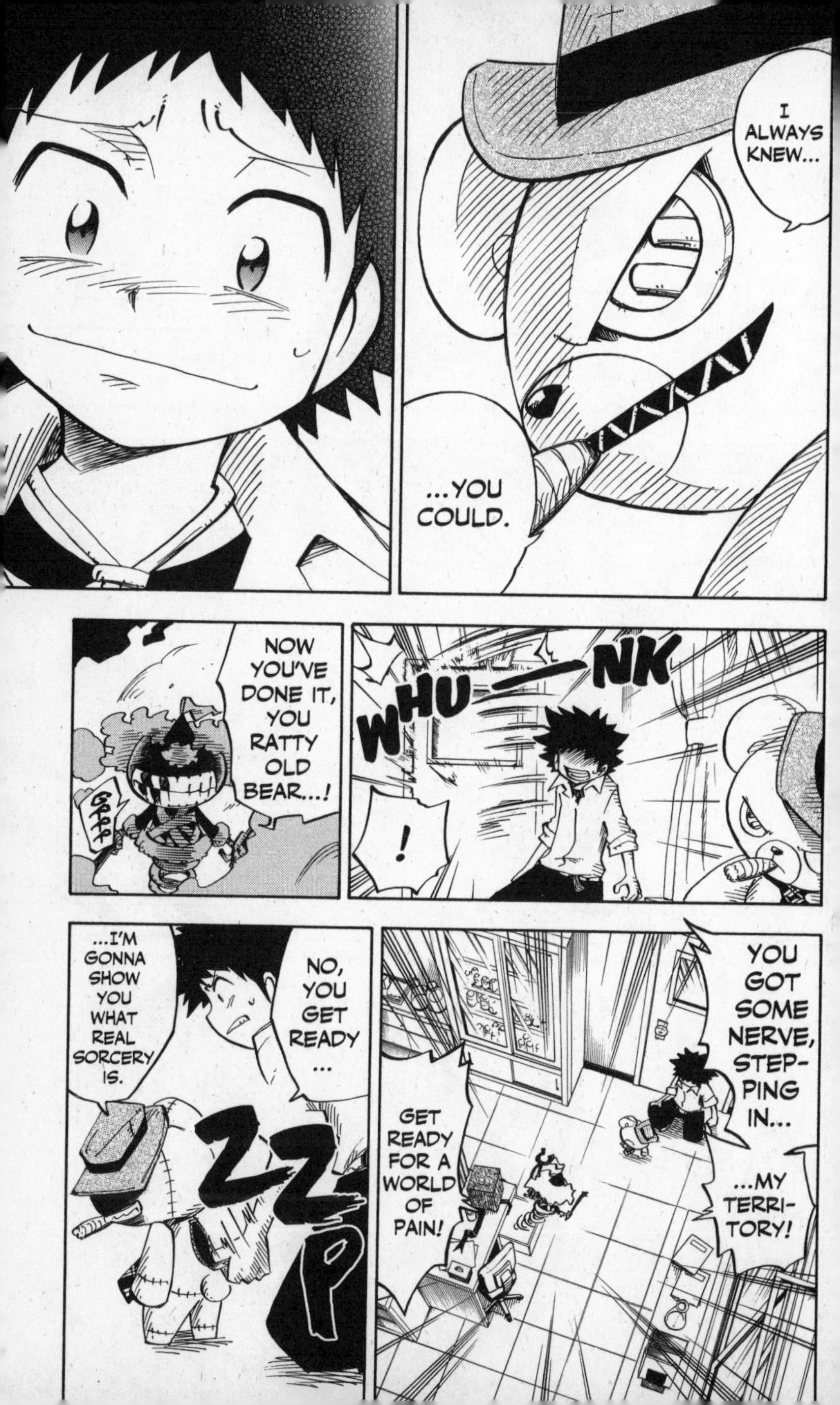
I ALWAYS KNEW...
...YOU COULD.
WHU—NK
!
NOW YOU'VE DONE IT, YOU RATTY OLD BEAR...!
YOU GOT SOME NERVE, STEP-PING IN...
...MY TERRI-TORY!
GET READY FOR A WORLD OF PAIN!
NO, YOU GET READY ...
...I'M GONNA SHOW YOU WHAT REAL SORCERY IS.
ZZP

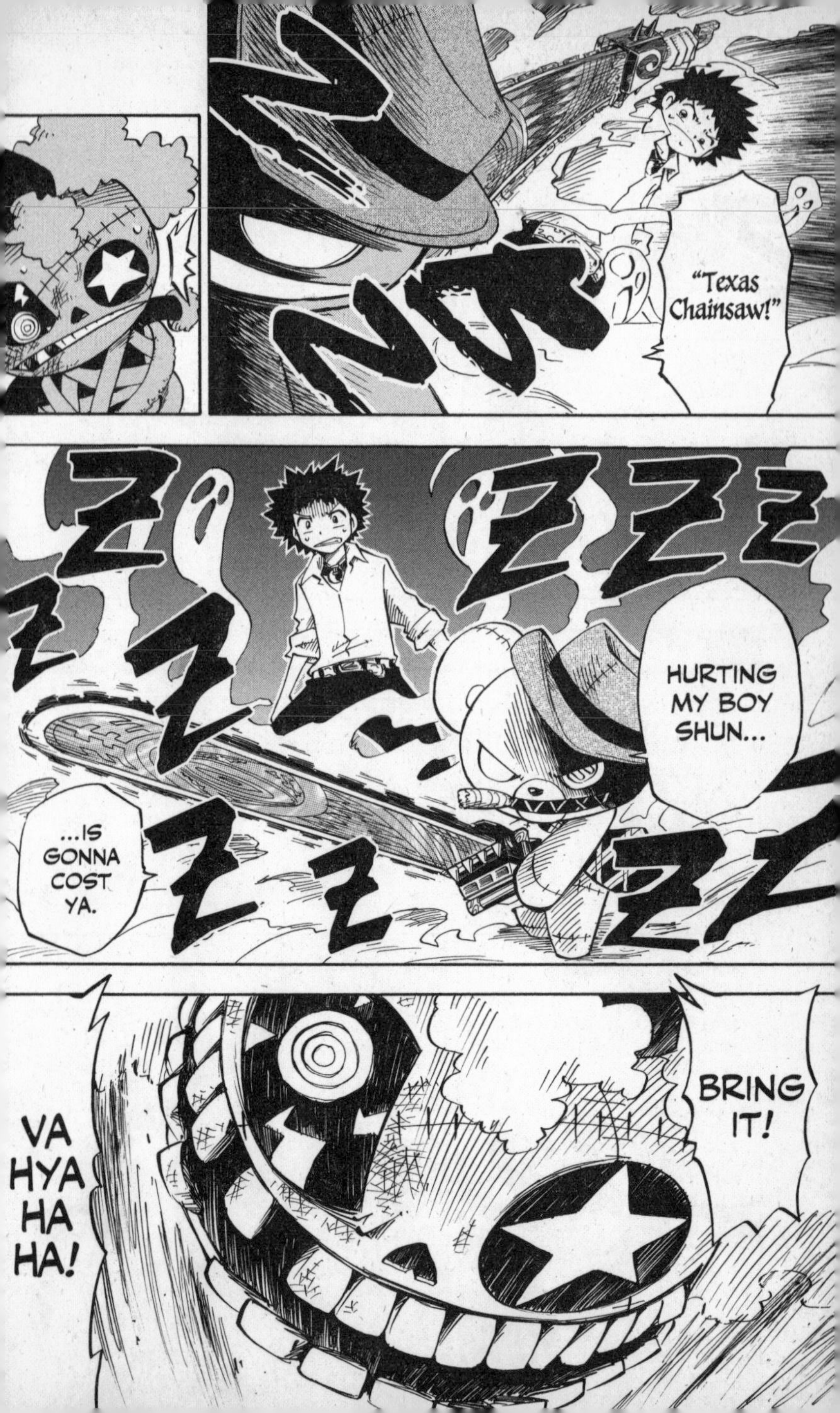

"Texas Chainsaw!"
HURTING MY BOY SHUN...
...IS GONNA COST YA.
BRING IT!
VA HYA HA HA!

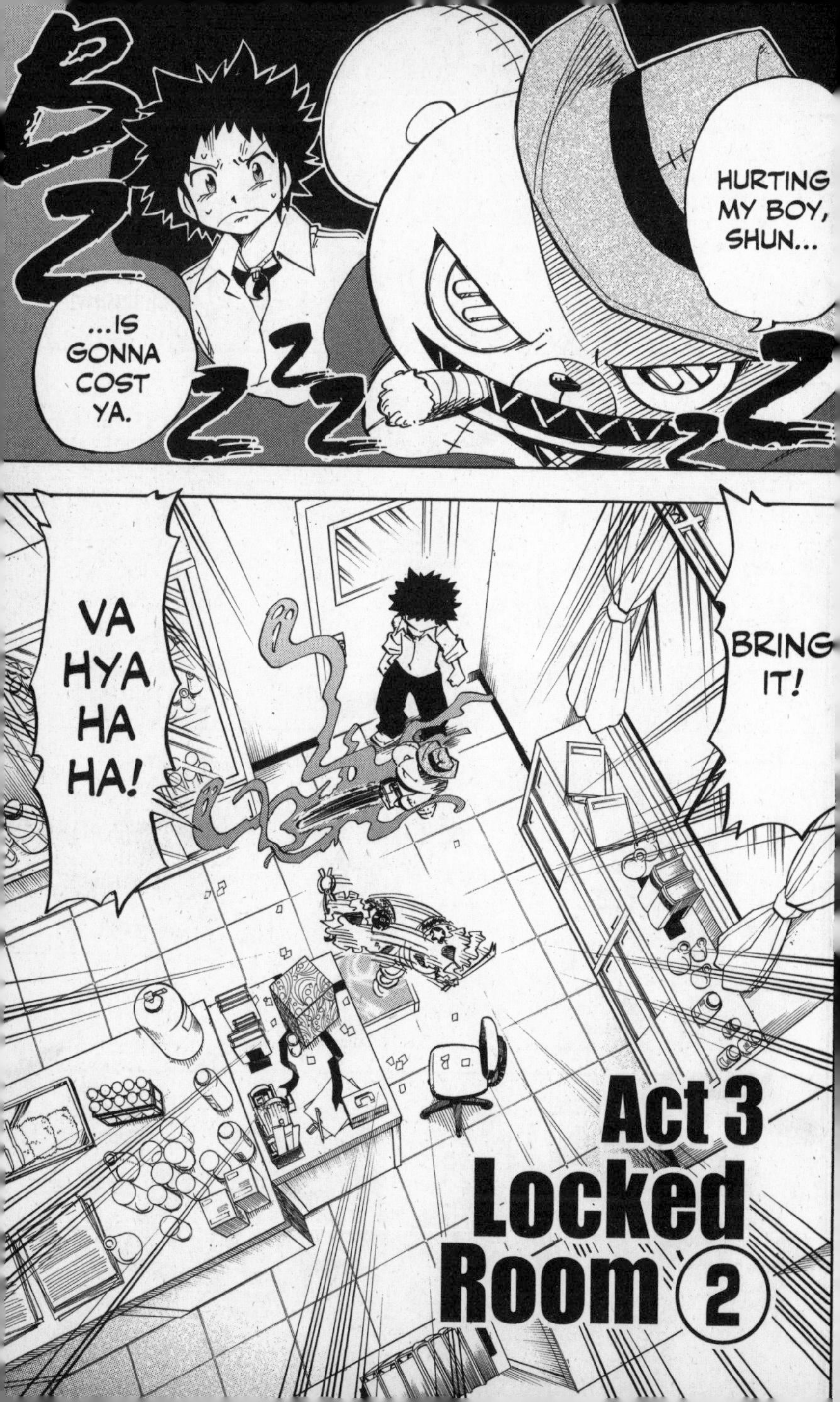
HURTING MY BOY, SHUN...
...IS GONNA COST YA.
BRING IT!
VA HYA HA HA HA!
Act 3 Locked Room ②

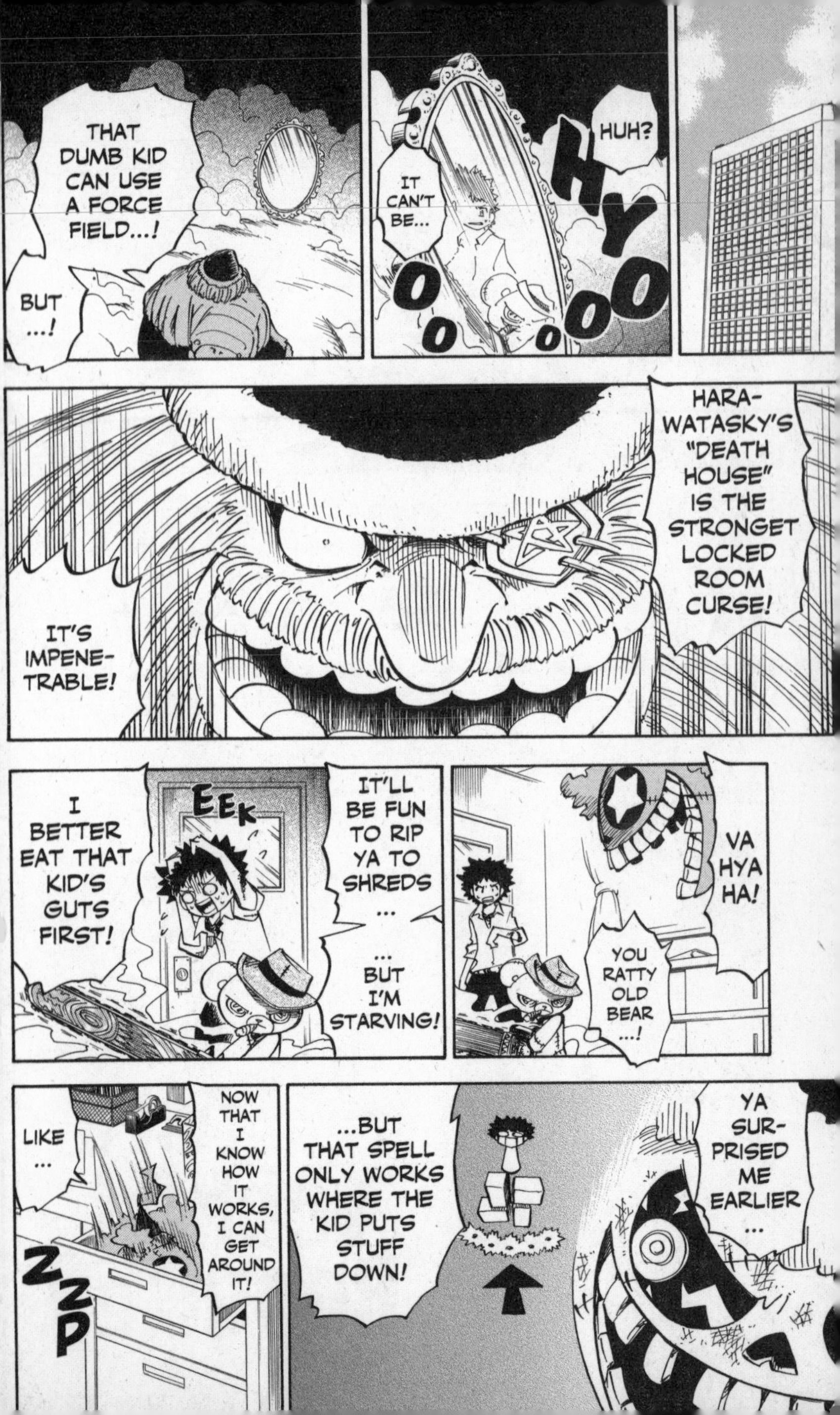
HUH?
HYOOOOO
IT CAN'T BE...
THAT DUMB KID CAN USE A FORCE FIELD...!
BUT...!
HARA-WATASKY'S "DEATH HOUSE" IS THE STRONGET LOCKED ROOM CURSE!
IT'S IMPENE-TRABLE!
VA HYA HA!
YOU RATTY OLD BEAR...!
EEK
IT'LL BE FUN TO RIP YA TO SHREDS...
...BUT I'M STARVING!
I BETTER EAT THAT KID'S GUTS FIRST!
YA SUR-PRISED ME EARLIER...
...BUT THAT SPELL ONLY WORKS WHERE THE KID PUTS STUFF DOWN!
NOW THAT I KNOW HOW IT WORKS, I CAN GET AROUND IT!
LIKE...
ZZP

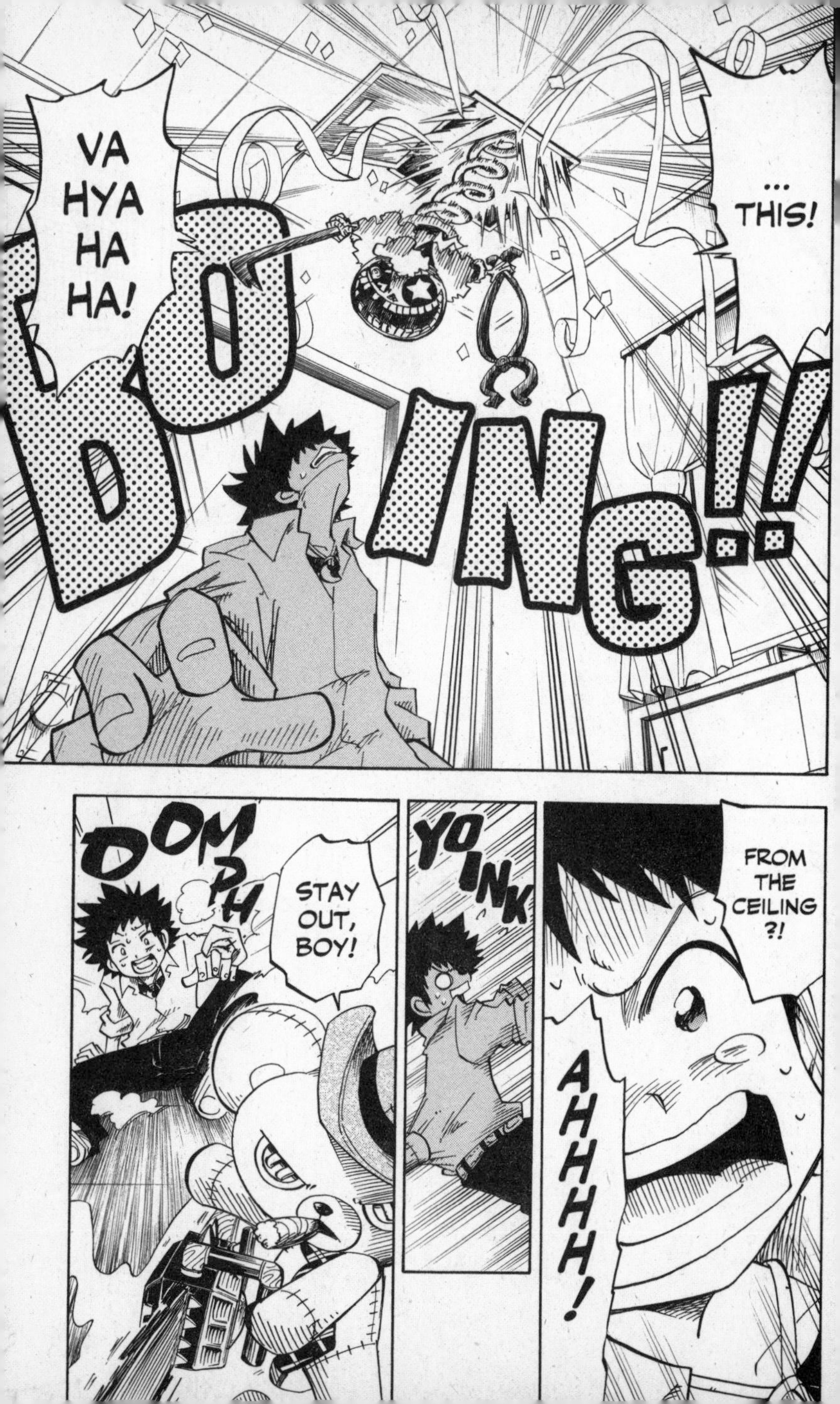
... THIS!
VA HYA HA HA!
DOING!!
FROM THE CEILING ?!
AHHHHH!
YOINK
STAY OUT, BOY!
DOOMPH

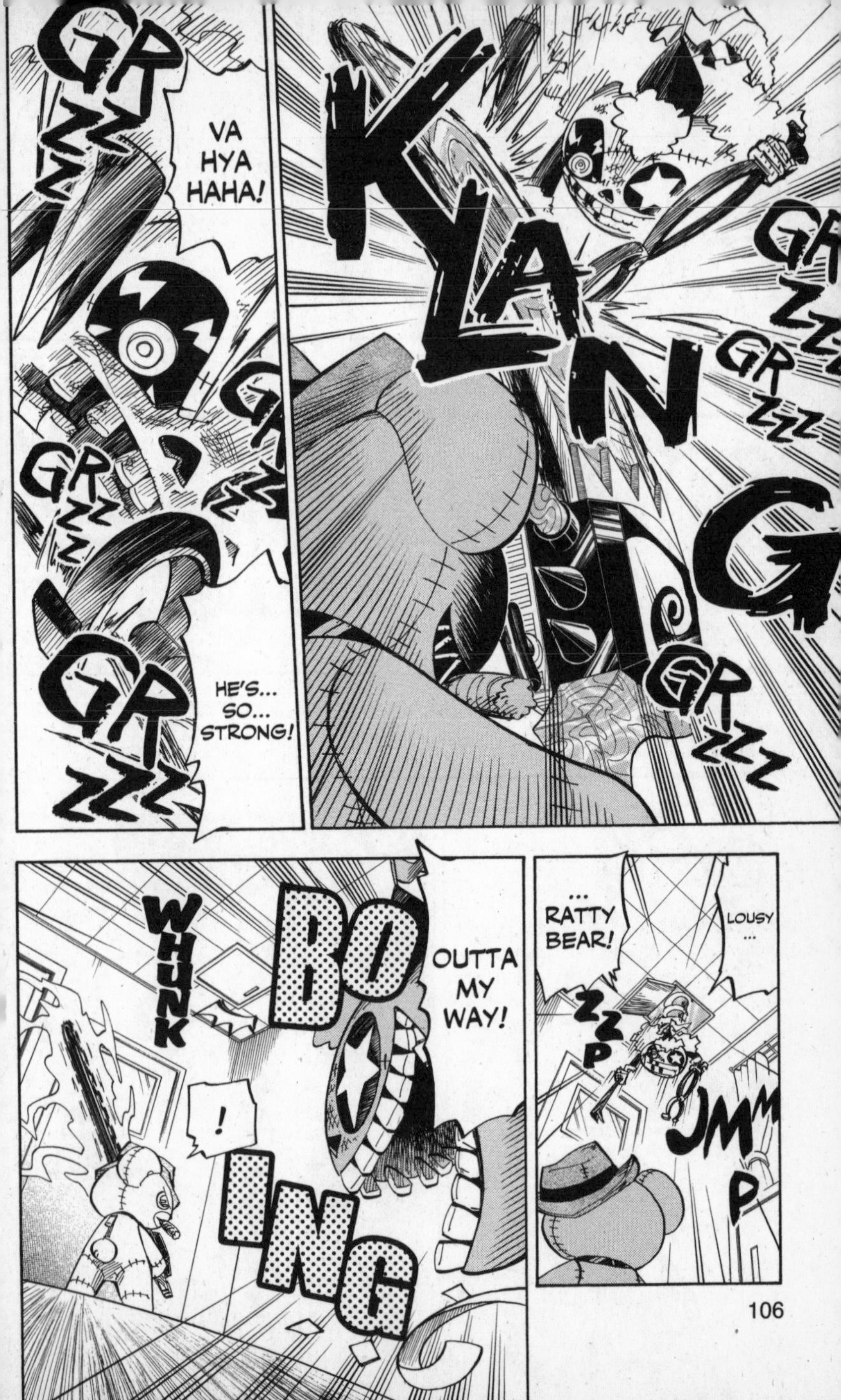
KYANG
GRZZZ
GRZZZ
G
GRZZZ
GRZZZ
VA HYA HAHA!
GRZZZ
GRZZZ
HE'S... SO... STRONG!
GRZZZ
LOUSY...
...RATTY BEAR!
ZZP
JMMP
OUTTA MY WAY!
BOING
WHUNK
!

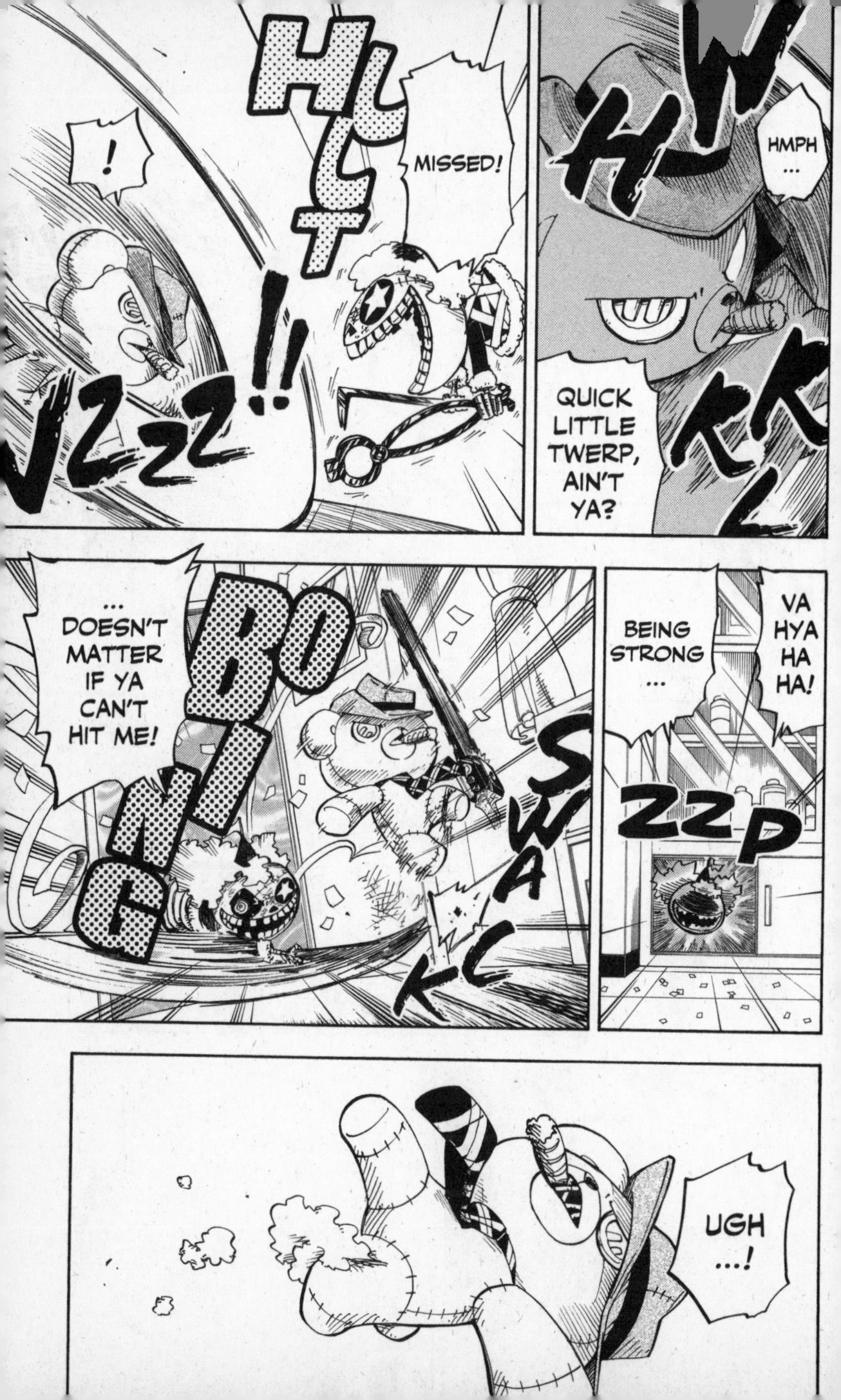
HMPH ...
QUICK LITTLE TWERP, AIN'T YA?
MISSED!
!
VA HYA HA HA!
BEING STRONG ...
ZZZP
... DOESN'T MATTER IF YA CAN'T HIT ME!
BOING!
UGH ...!

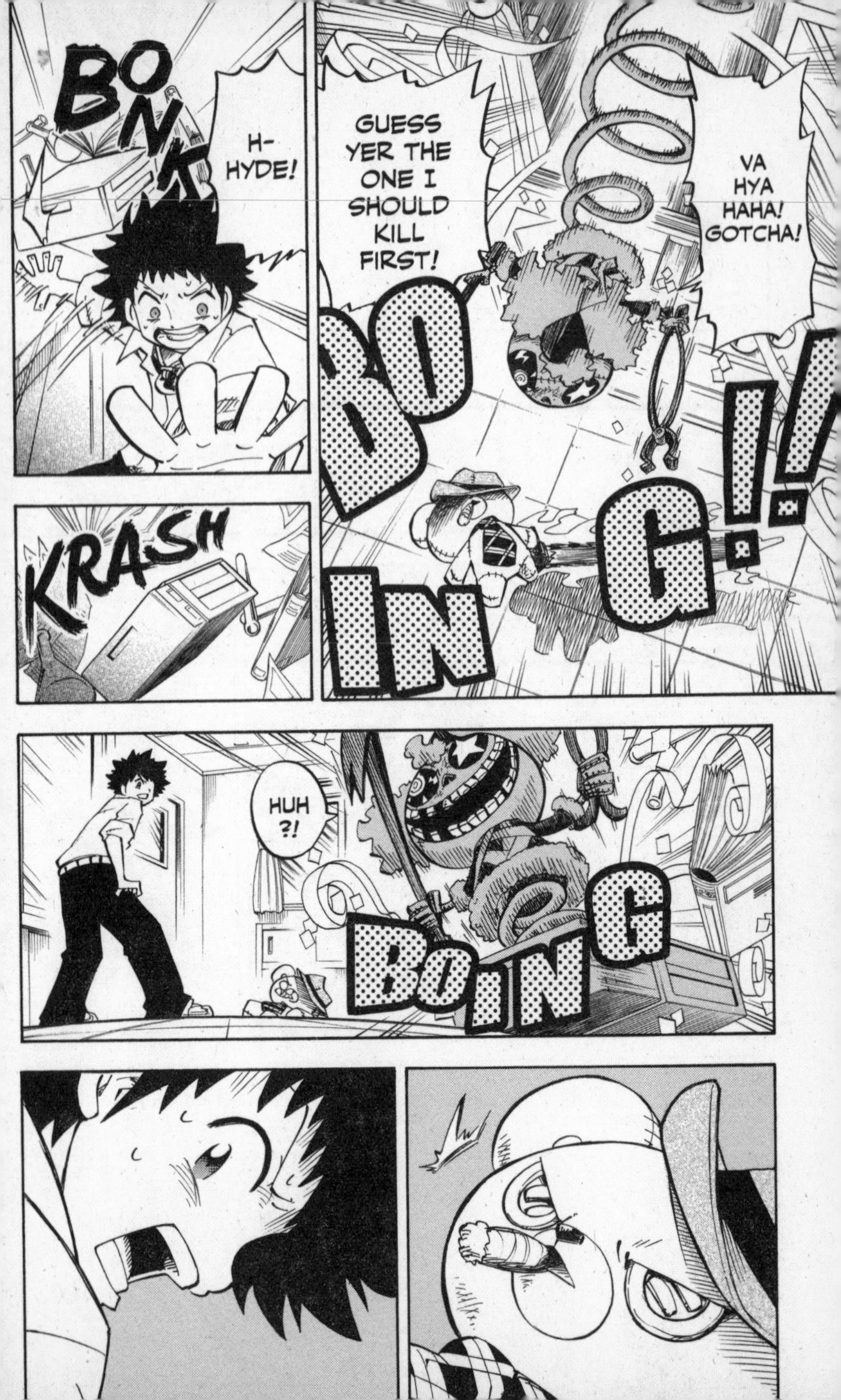
VA HYA HAHA! GOTCHA!
GUESS YER THE ONE I SHOULD KILL FIRST!
BOING!!
H- HYDE!
BONK
KRASH
HUH?!
BOING

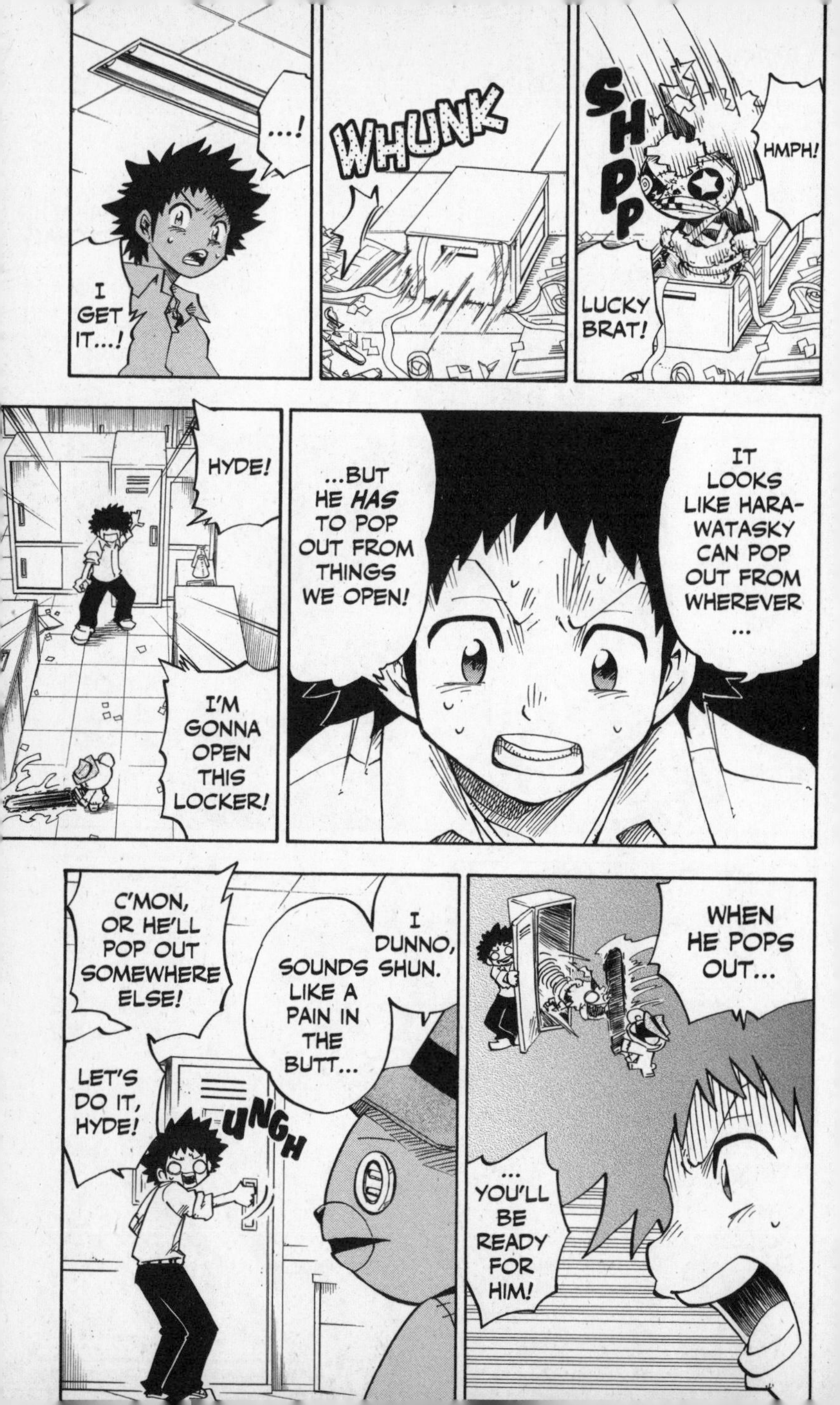
SHPP
HMPH!
LUCKY BRAT!
WHUNK
...!
I GET IT...!
IT LOOKS LIKE HARA-WATASKY CAN POP OUT FROM WHEREVER...
...BUT HE *HAS* TO POP OUT FROM THINGS WE OPEN!
HYDE!
I'M GONNA OPEN THIS LOCKER!
WHEN HE POPS OUT...
...YOU'LL BE READY FOR HIM!
I DUNNO, SHUN. SOUNDS LIKE A PAIN IN THE BUTT...
C'MON, OR HE'LL POP OUT SOMEWHERE ELSE!
LET'S DO IT, HYDE!
UNGH

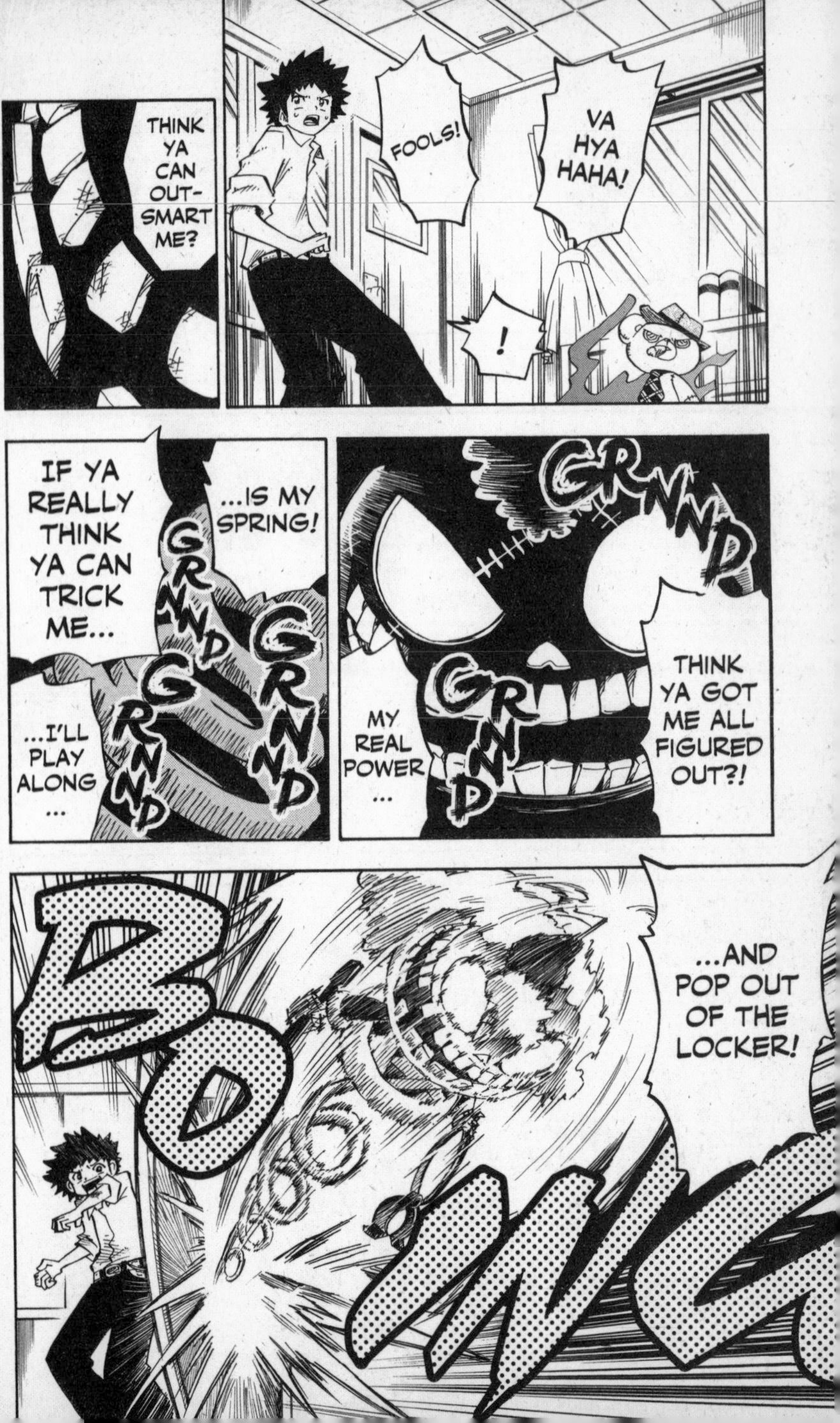

VA HYA HAHA!
FOOLS!
!
THINK YA CAN OUT-SMART ME?
GRNND
THINK YA GOT ME ALL FIGURED OUT?!
GRNND
MY REAL POWER ...
...IS MY SPRING!
IF YA REALLY THINK YA CAN TRICK ME...
GRNND
GRNND
GRNND
...I'LL PLAY ALONG ...
...AND POP OUT OF THE LOCKER!
BOING

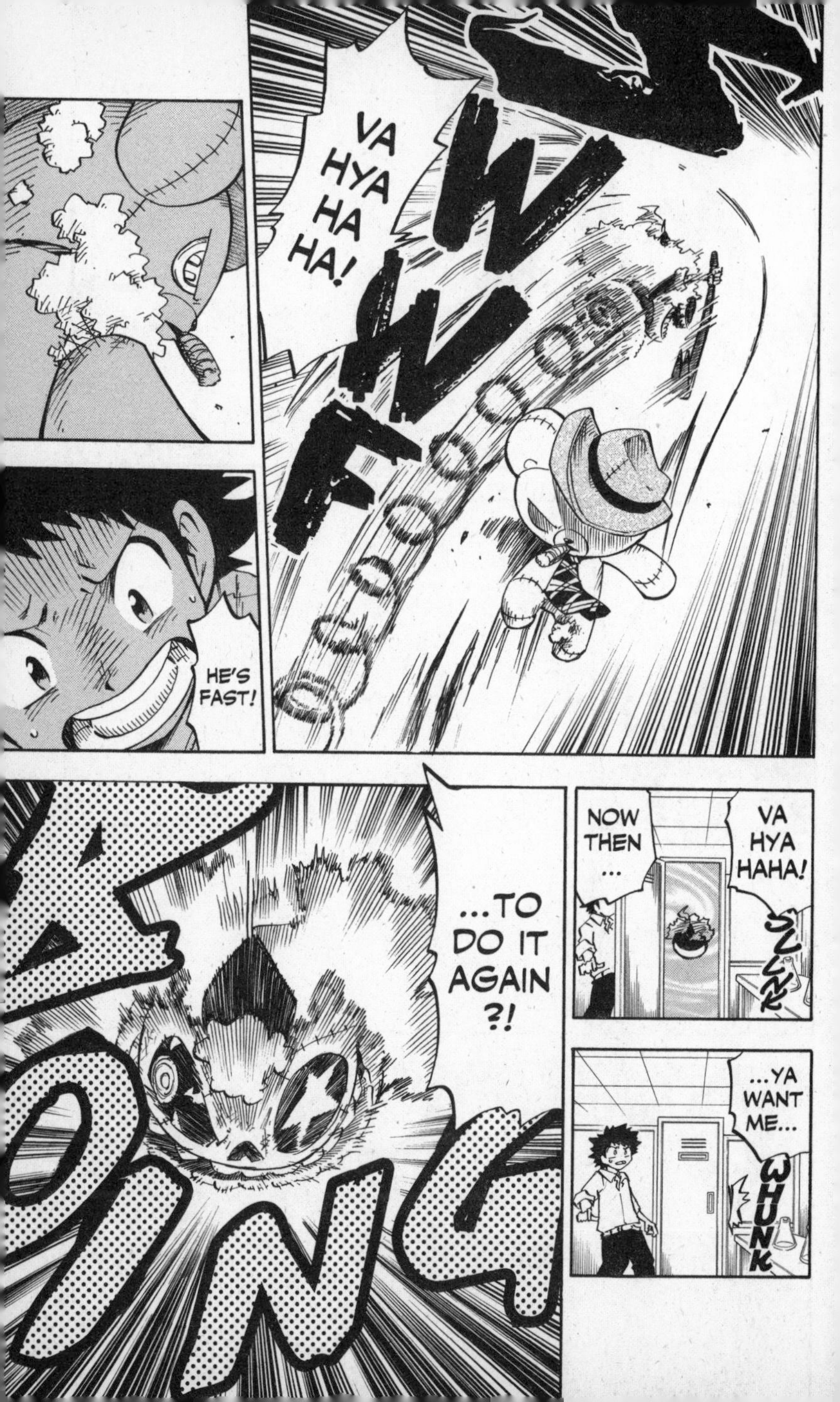
VA HYA HA HA HA!
FWWW
HE'S FAST!
VA HYA HAHA!
SLUNK
NOW THEN ...
...YA WANT ME...
WHUNK
...TO DO IT AGAIN?!

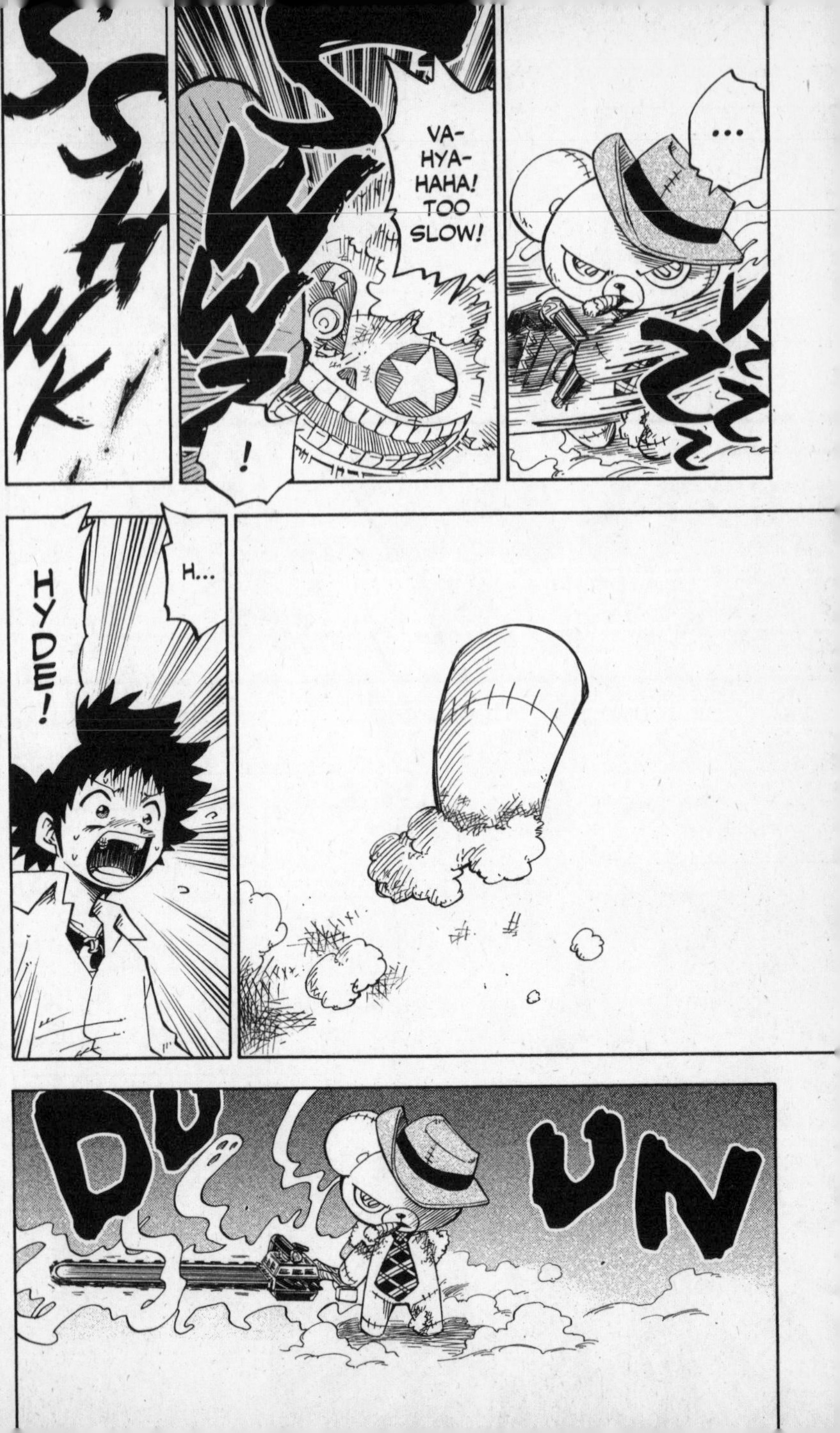
...
VA-HYA-HAHA! TOO SLOW!
!
H...
HYDE!
DUUN

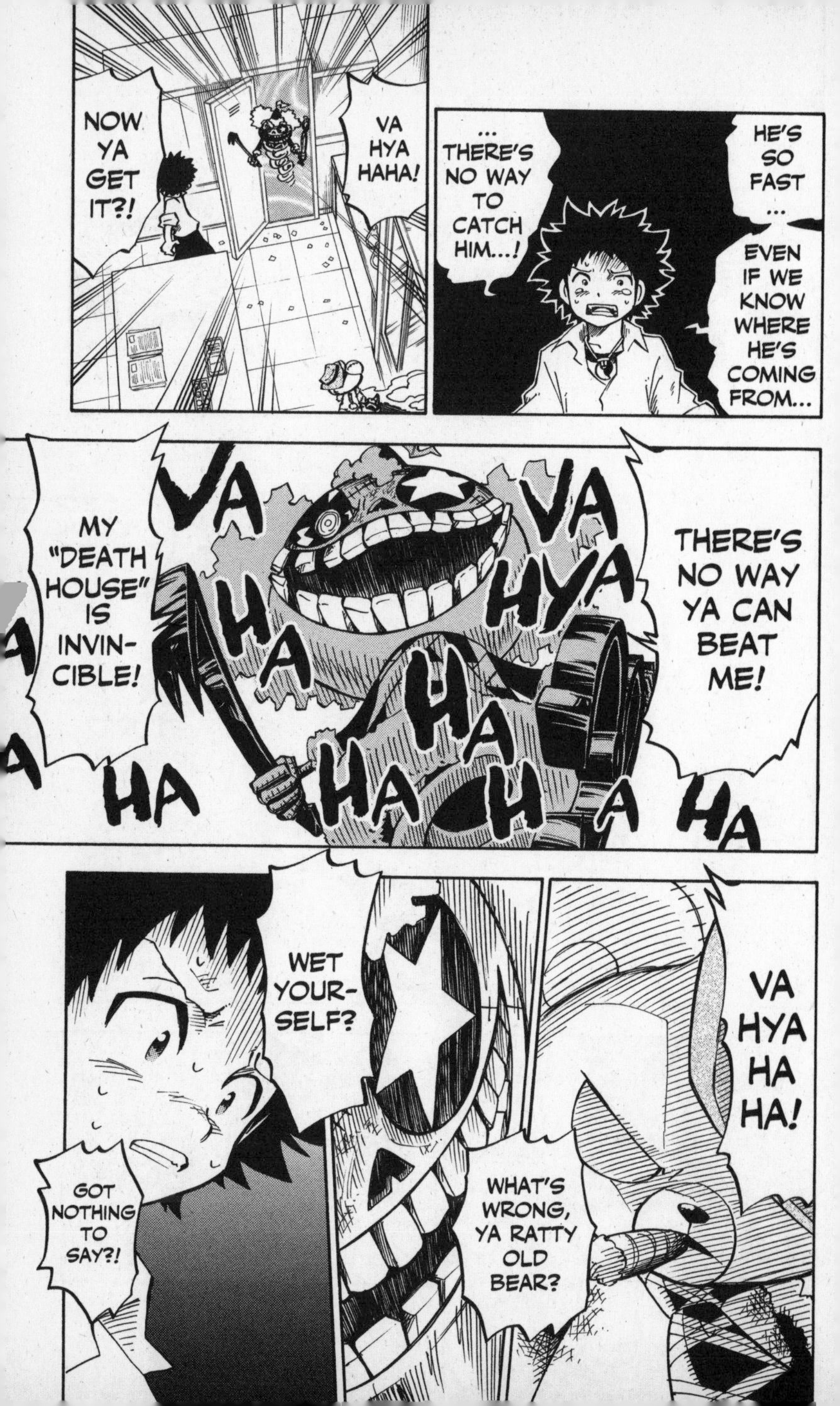
HE'S SO FAST... EVEN IF WE KNOW WHERE HE'S COMING FROM...
...THERE'S NO WAY TO CATCH HIM...!
VA HYA HAHA!
NOW YA GET IT?!
THERE'S NO WAY YA CAN BEAT ME!
VA HYA HA HA HA HA HA HA
MY "DEATH HOUSE" IS INVINCIBLE!
VA HYA HA HA!
WHAT'S WRONG, YA RATTY OLD BEAR?
WET YOURSELF?
GOT NOTHING TO SAY?!

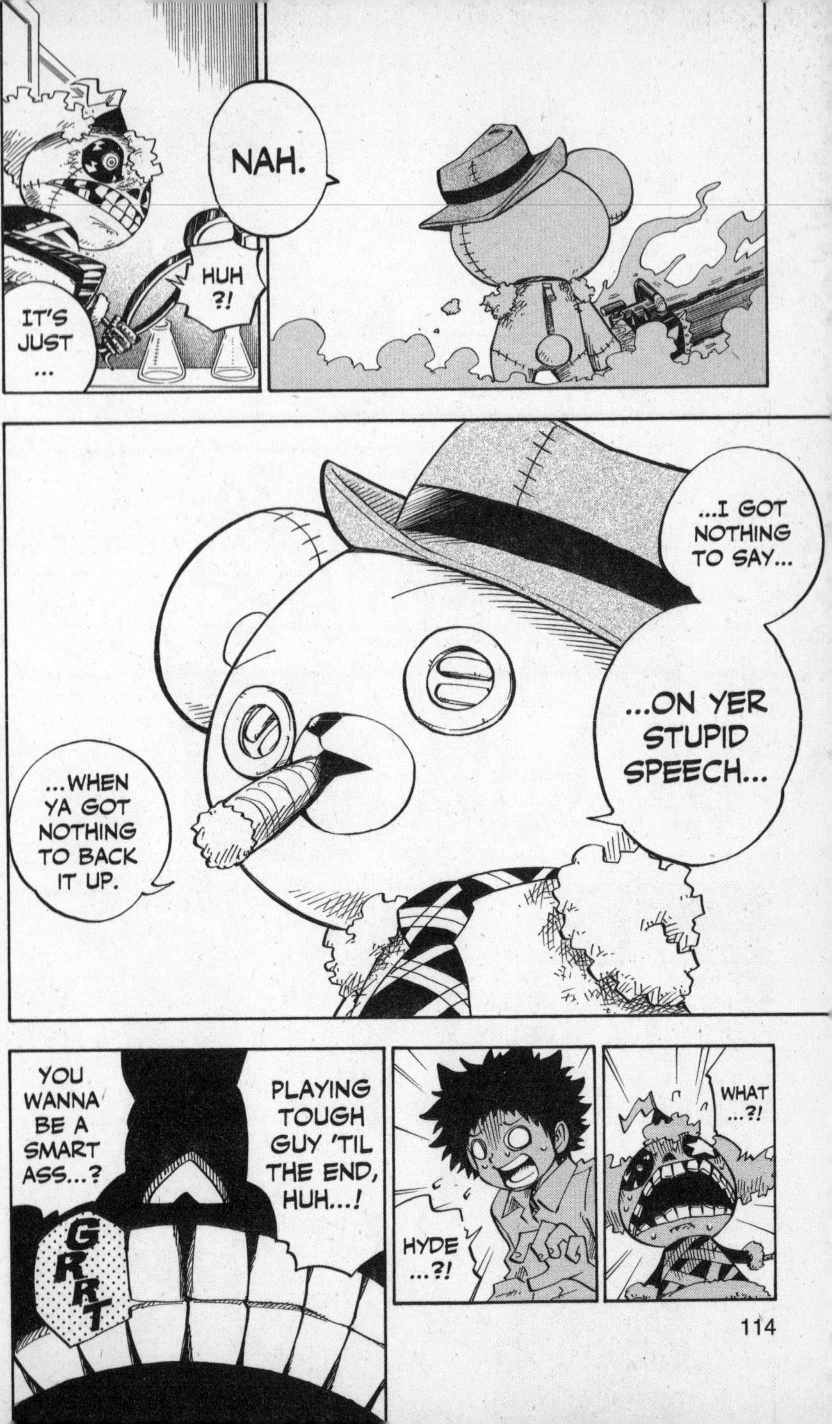
NAH.
HUH ?!
IT'S JUST ...
...I GOT NOTHING TO SAY...
...ON YER STUPID SPEECH...
...WHEN YA GOT NOTHING TO BACK IT UP.
WHAT ...?!
HYDE ...?!
PLAYING TOUGH GUY 'TIL THE END, HUH...!
YOU WANNA BE A SMART ASS...?
GRRT

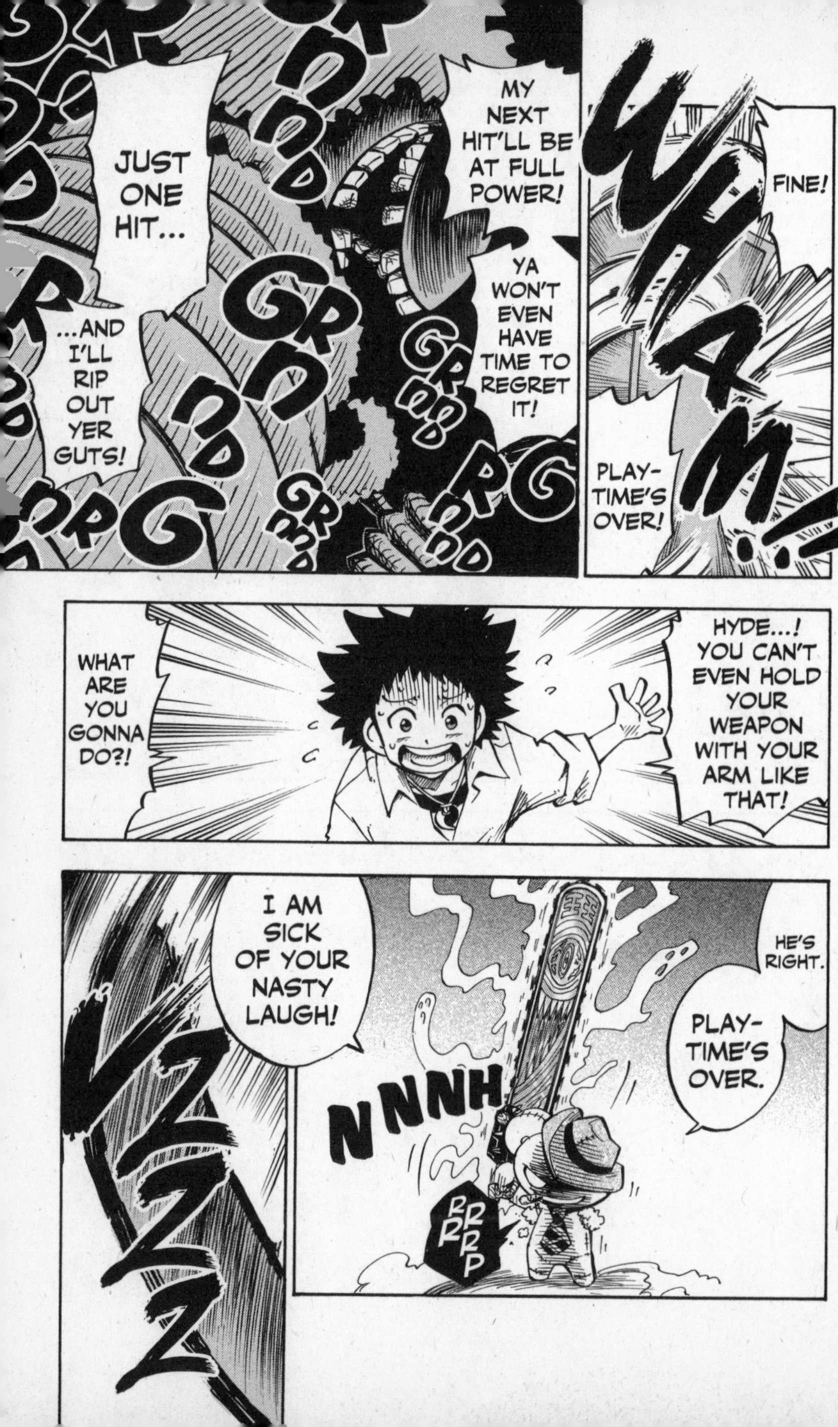
WHAM!!
FINE!
PLAY-TIME'S OVER!
MY NEXT HIT'LL BE AT FULL POWER!
YA WON'T EVEN HAVE TIME TO REGRET IT!
JUST ONE HIT...
...AND I'LL RIP OUT YER GUTS!
HYDE...! YOU CAN'T EVEN HOLD YOUR WEAPON WITH YOUR ARM LIKE THAT!
WHAT ARE YOU GONNA DO?!
HE'S RIGHT.
PLAY-TIME'S OVER.
I AM SICK OF YOUR NASTY LAUGH!
NNNH
RRRRP

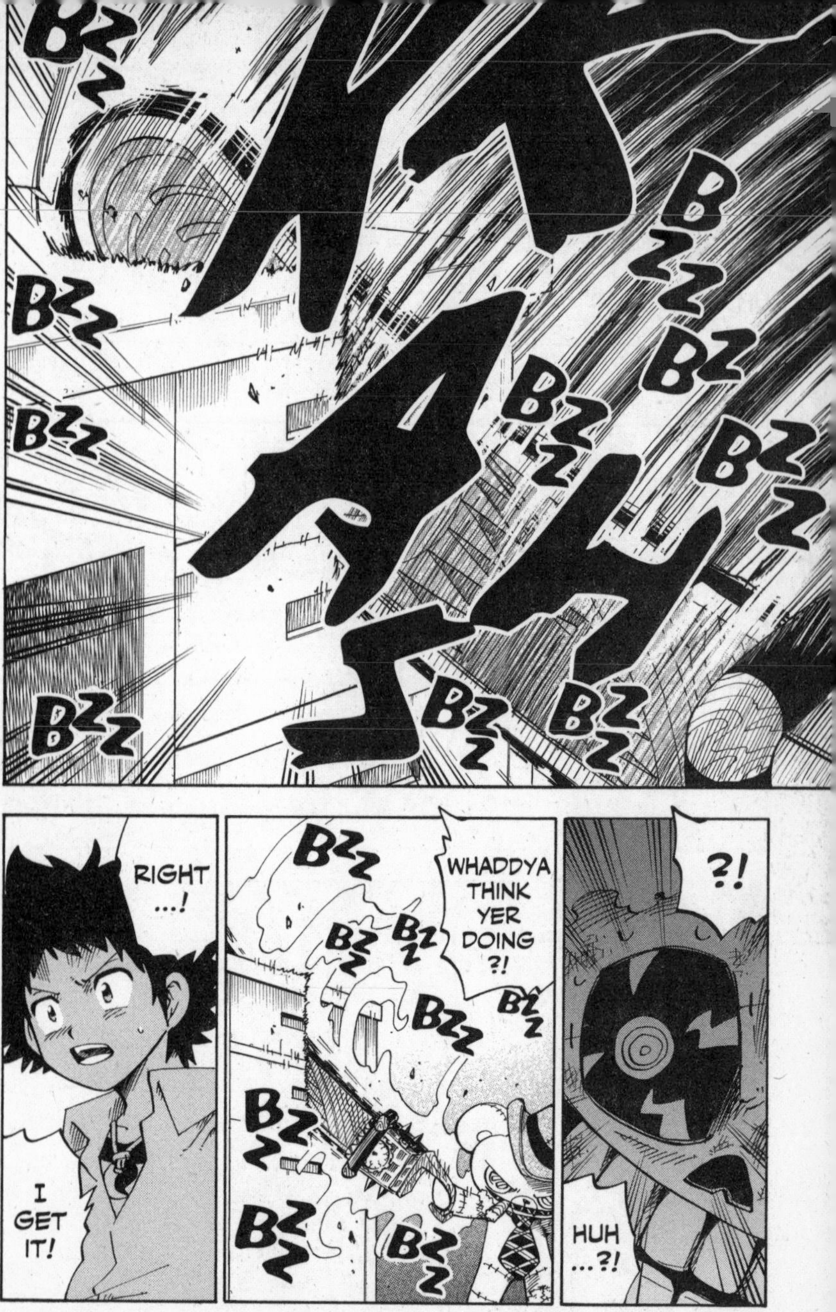
BZZ
BZZ
BZ
BZZ
BZZ
BZZ
BZZ
BZZ
BZZ
BZZ
?!
HUH ...?!
WHADDYA THINK YER DOING ?!
BZZ
BZZ
BZZ
BZZ
BZZ
BZZ
BZZ
BZZ
RIGHT ...!
I GET IT!

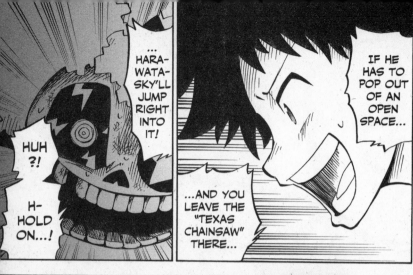

IF HE HAS TO POP OUT OF AN OPEN SPACE...
...AND YOU LEAVE THE "TEXAS CHAINSAW" THERE...
...HARA-WATA-SKY'LL JUMP RIGHT INTO IT!
HUH?!
H-HOLD ON...!
LISTEN TO YA, GOING ON AND ON ABOUT BEING INVINCIBLE...
...BUT REALLY, PAL...
...YER JUST ANOTHER DAMN CURSE.
Why didn't I think of that?
W-WAIT...!
DON'T...!
GUESS A GIANT COULDN'T HANDLE THIS JOB.
SWWF
SEE YA.

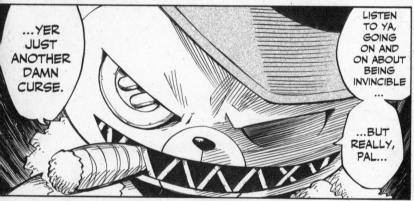

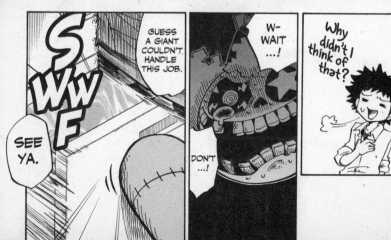

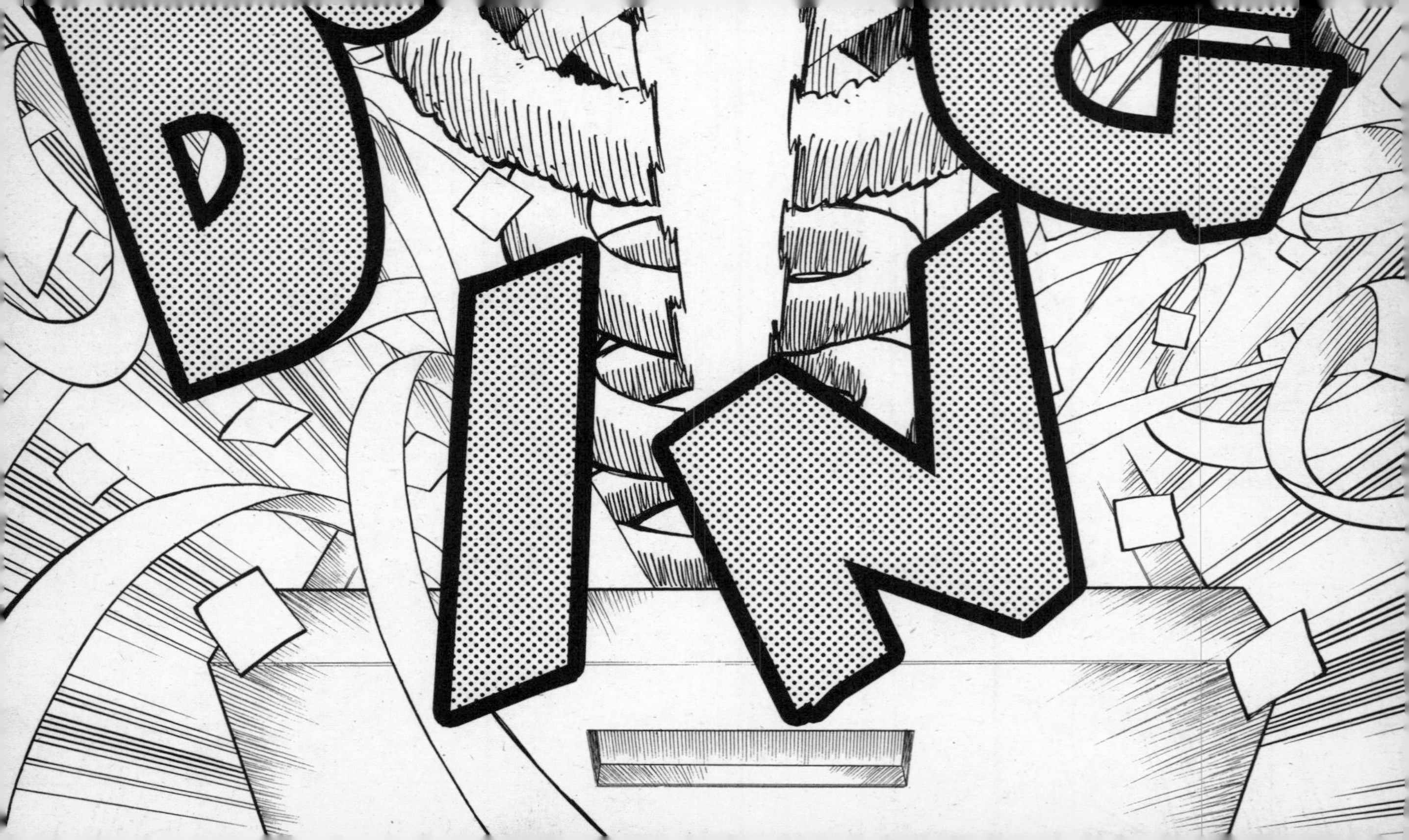
DING

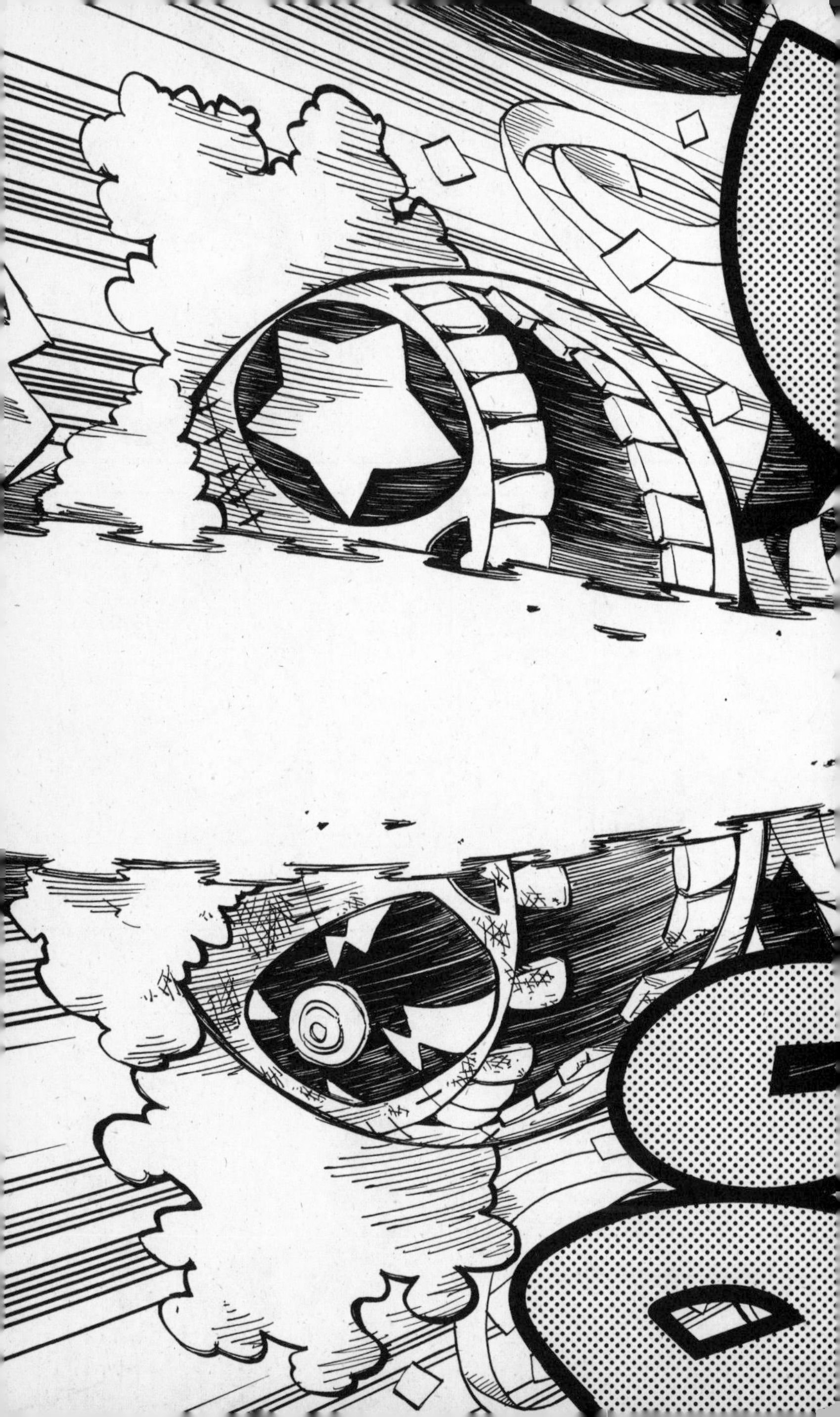

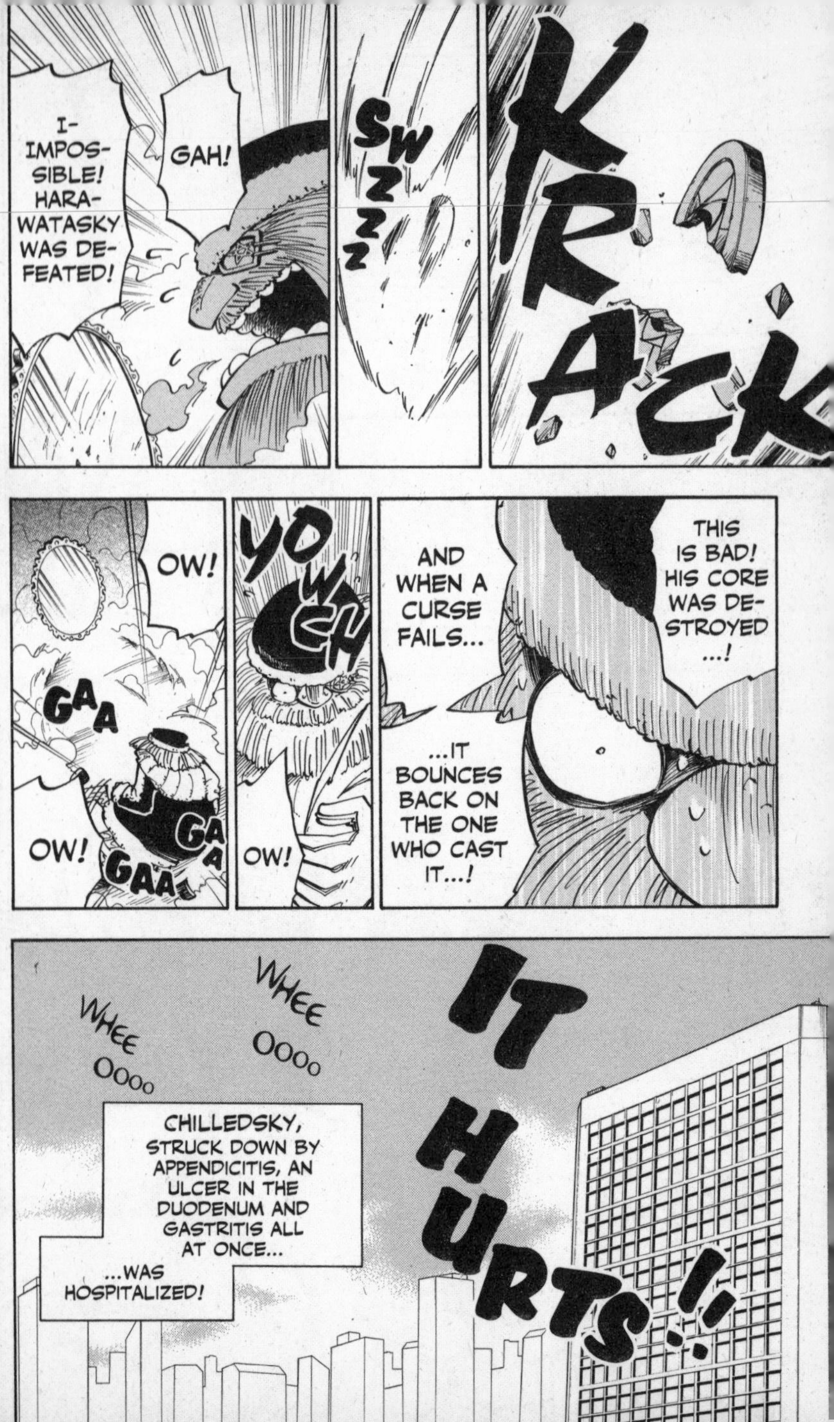
KRACK
SWZZZZ
GAH!
I- IMPOSSIBLE! HARAWATASKY WAS DEFEATED!
THIS IS BAD! HIS CORE WAS DESTROYED ...!
AND WHEN A CURSE FAILS...
...IT BOUNCES BACK ON THE ONE WHO CAST IT...!
YOWCH
OW!
OW!
GAA
OW!
GA A
GAA
IT HURTS!!
WHEE OOOo
WHEE OOOo
CHILLEDSKY, STRUCK DOWN BY APPENDICITIS, AN ULCER IN THE DUODENUM AND GASTRITIS ALL AT ONCE...
...WAS HOSPITALIZED!

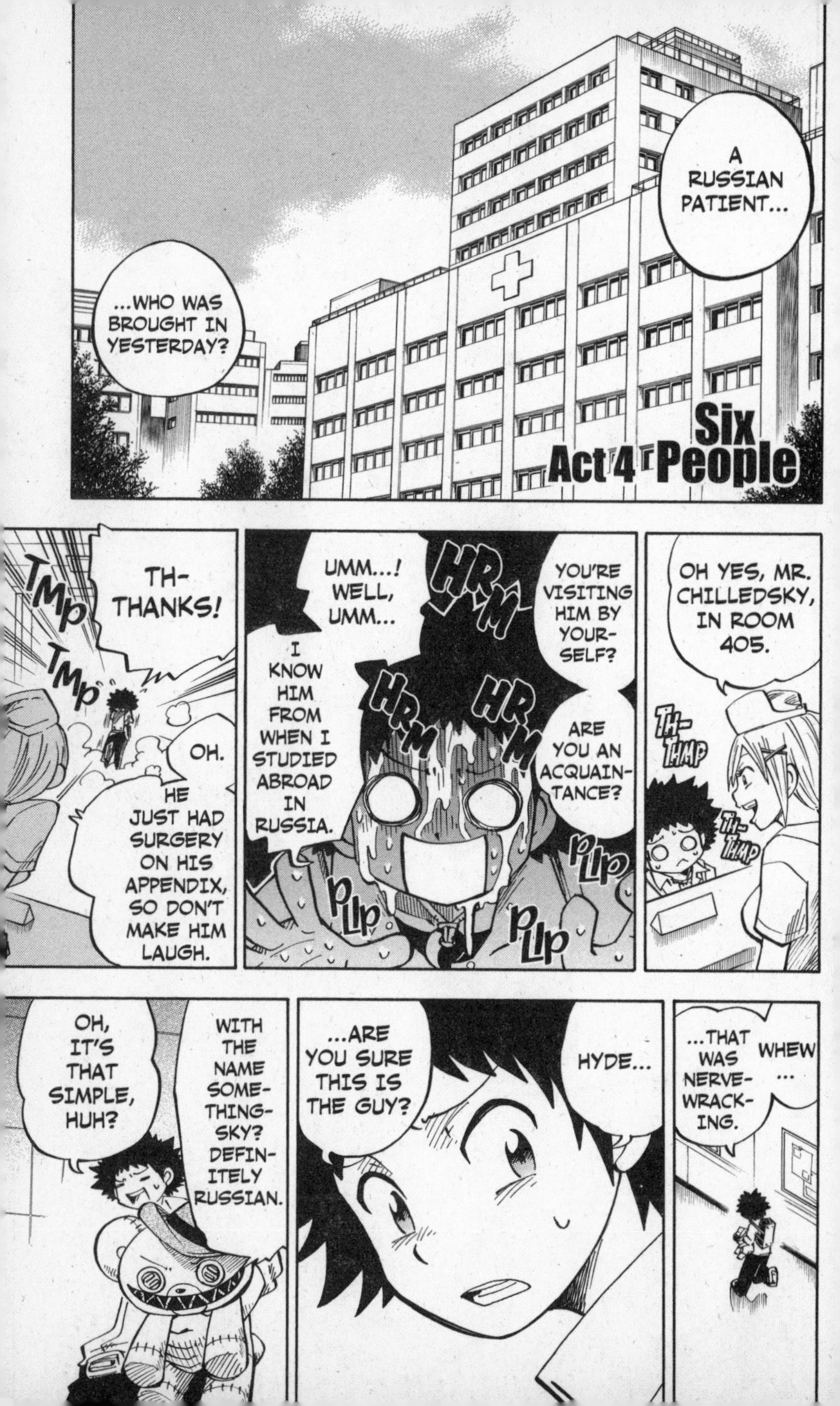
A RUSSIAN PATIENT...
...WHO WAS BROUGHT IN YESTERDAY?
Act 4 Six People
OH YES, MR. CHILLEDSKY, IN ROOM 405.
TH-THMP
TH-THMP
YOU'RE VISITING HIM BY YOURSELF?
ARE YOU AN ACQUAINTANCE?
HRM
HRM
HRM
UMM...! WELL, UMM...
I KNOW HIM FROM WHEN I STUDIED ABROAD IN RUSSIA.
PLIP
PLIP
PLIP
OH.
HE JUST HAD SURGERY ON HIS APPENDIX, SO DON'T MAKE HIM LAUGH.
TH-THANKS!
TMP
TMP
...THAT WAS NERVE-WRACKING.
WHEW ...
HYDE...
...ARE YOU SURE THIS IS THE GUY?
WITH THE NAME SOMETHING-SKY? DEFINITELY RUSSIAN.
OH, IT'S THAT SIMPLE, HUH?

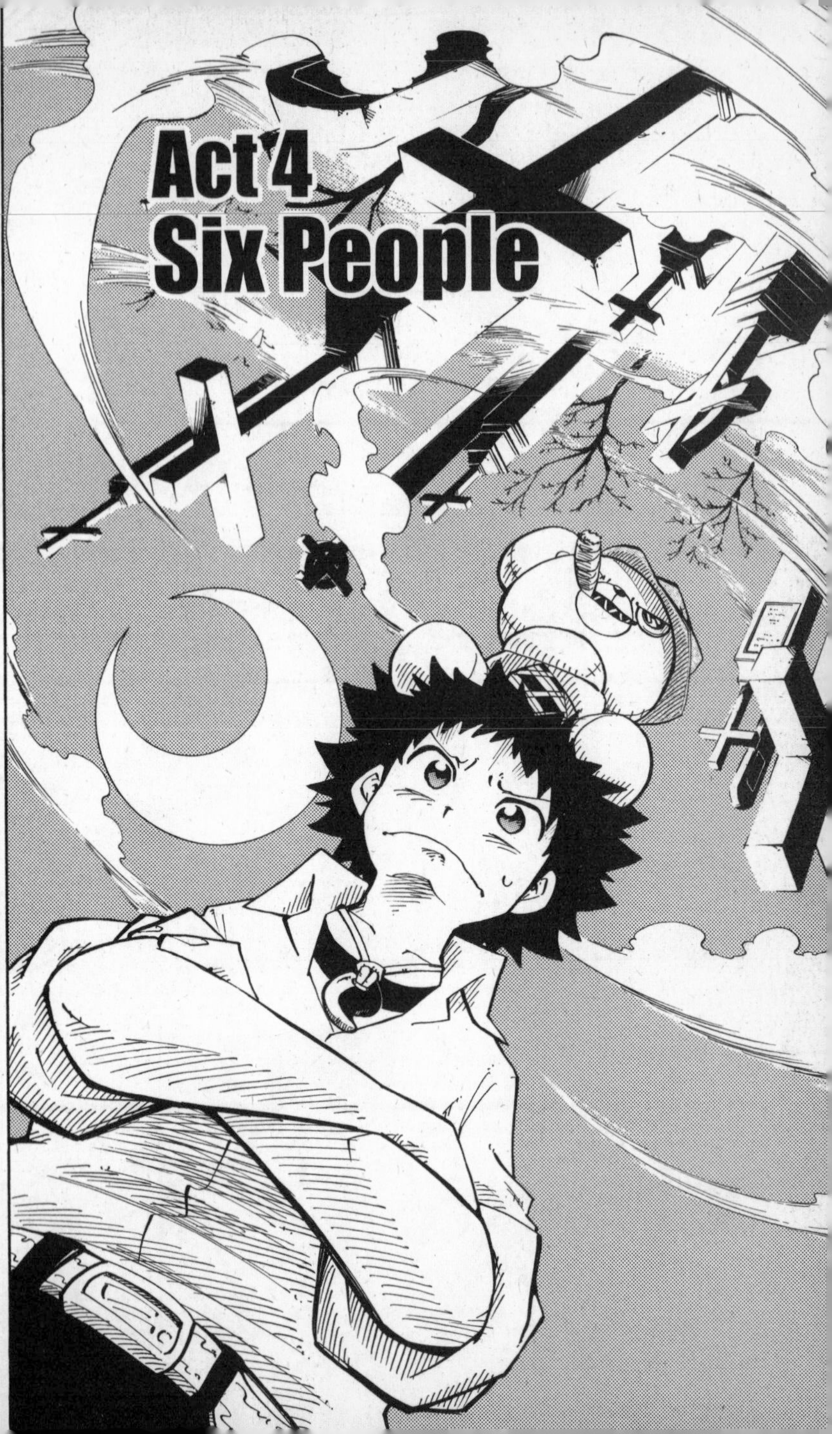
Act 4
Six People

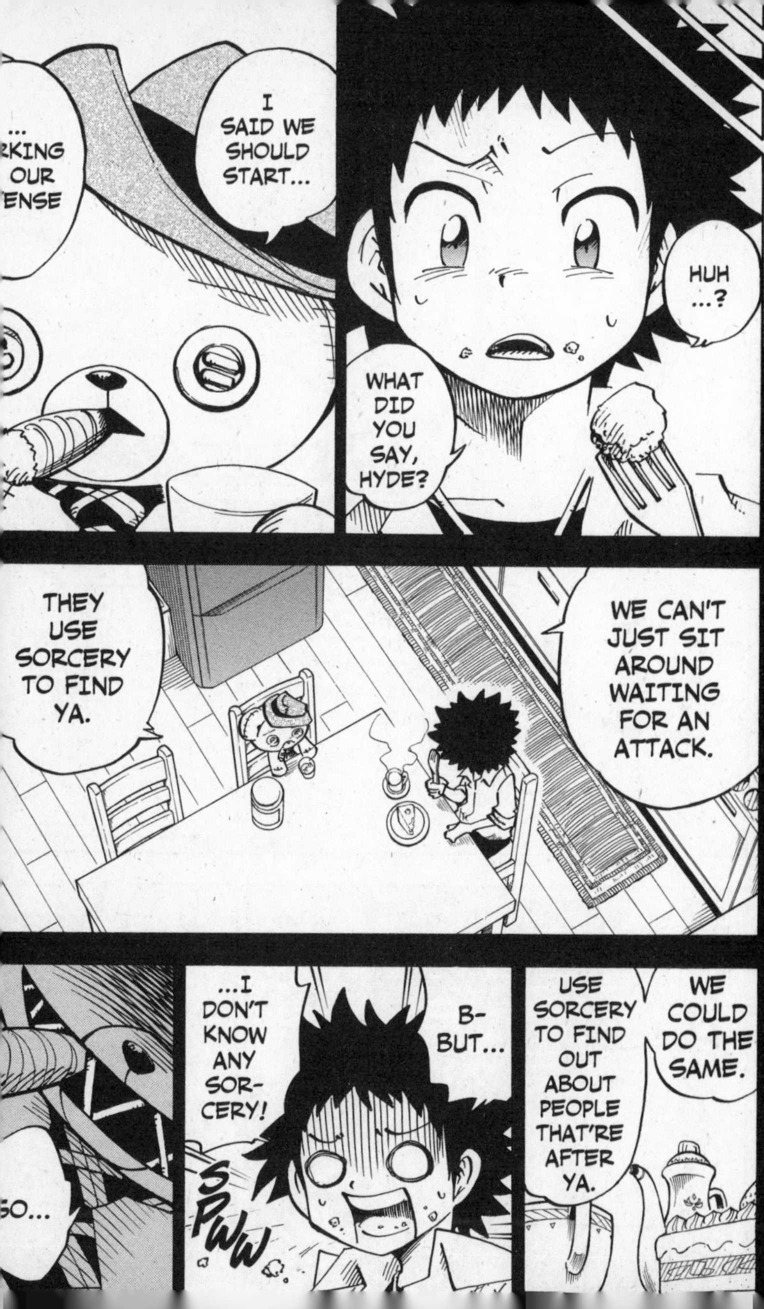
HUH ...?
WHAT DID YOU SAY, HYDE?
I SAID WE SHOULD START...
...RKING OUR ENSE
WE CAN'T JUST SIT AROUND WAITING FOR AN ATTACK.
THEY USE SORCERY TO FIND YA.
WE COULD DO THE SAME.
USE SORCERY TO FIND OUT ABOUT PEOPLE THAT'RE AFTER YA.
B-BUT...
...I DON'T KNOW ANY SOR-CERY!
SPWW
SO...

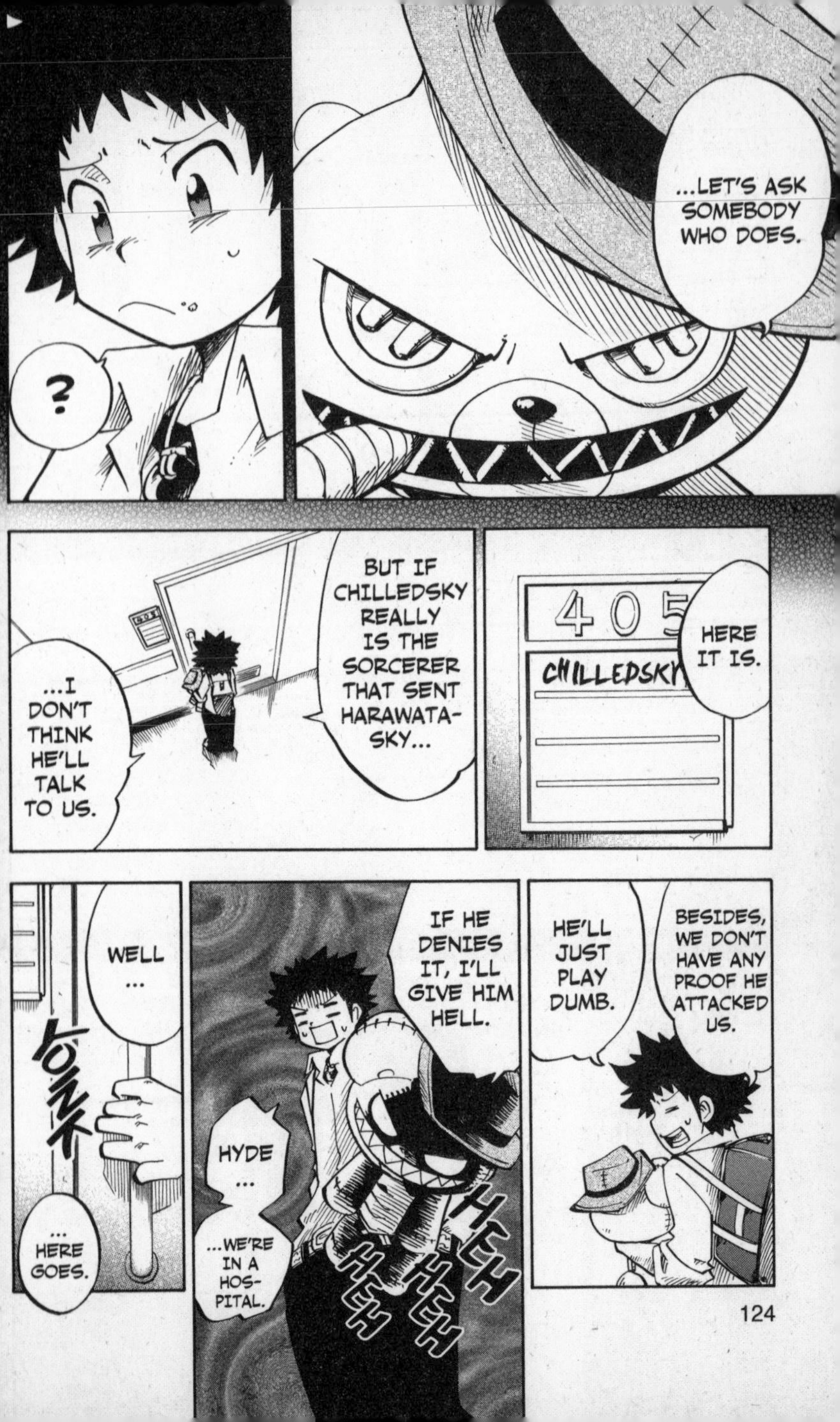
...LET'S ASK SOMEBODY WHO DOES.
?
405
CHILLEDSKY
HERE IT IS.
BUT IF CHILLEDSKY REALLY IS THE SORCERER THAT SENT HARAWATA-SKY...
...I DON'T THINK HE'LL TALK TO US.
BESIDES, WE DON'T HAVE ANY PROOF HE ATTACKED US.
HE'LL JUST PLAY DUMB.
IF HE DENIES IT, I'LL GIVE HIM HELL.
HEH HEH HEH
HYDE...
...WE'RE IN A HOS-PITAL.
WELL...
YOINK
...HERE GOES.

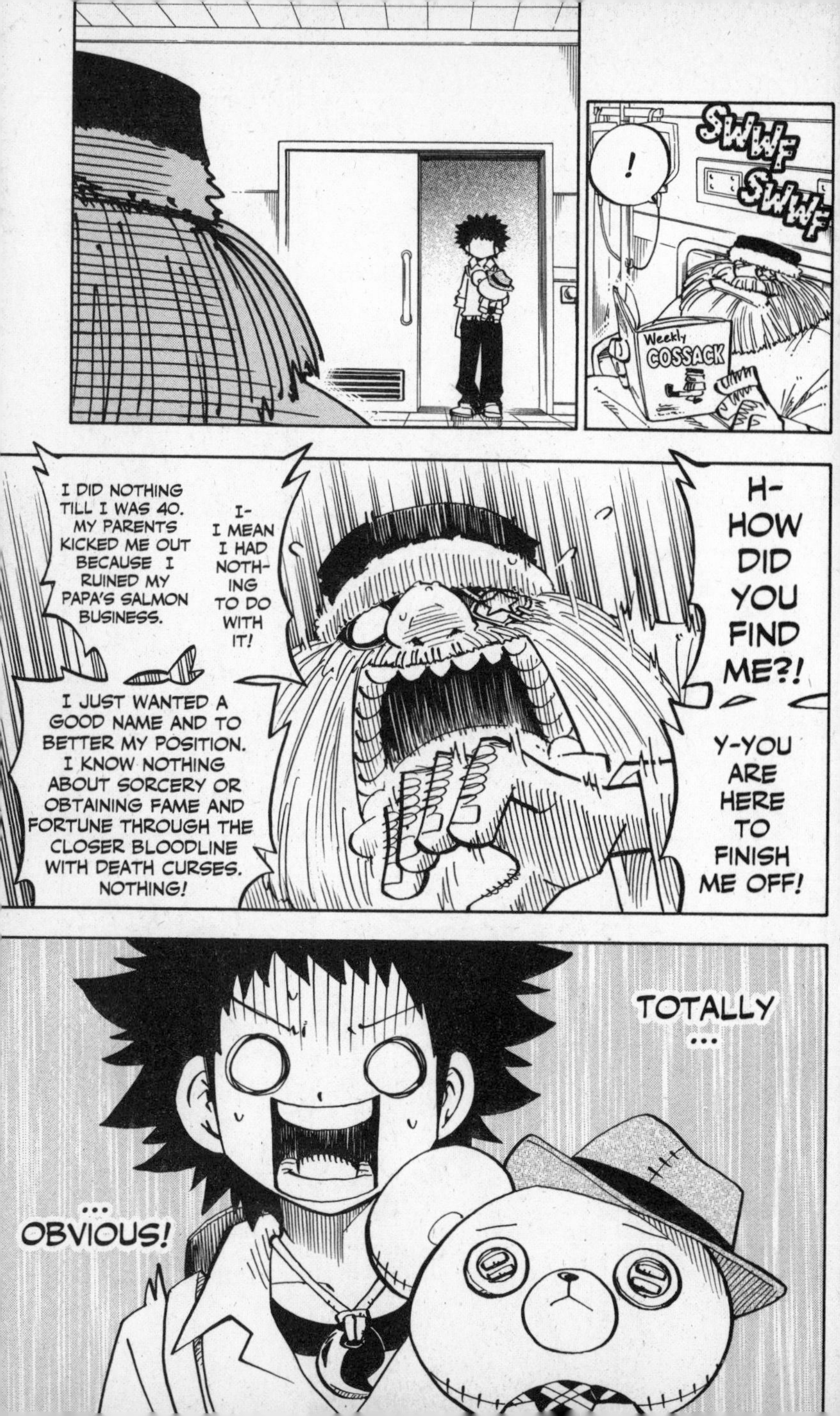

SWWF SWWF
!
Weekly COSSACK
H-HOW DID YOU FIND ME?!
Y-YOU ARE HERE TO FINISH ME OFF!
I- I MEAN I HAD NOTHING TO DO WITH IT!
I DID NOTHING TILL I WAS 40. MY PARENTS KICKED ME OUT BECAUSE I RUINED MY PAPA'S SALMON BUSINESS.
I JUST WANTED A GOOD NAME AND TO BETTER MY POSITION. I KNOW NOTHING ABOUT SORCERY OR OBTAINING FAME AND FORTUNE THROUGH THE CLOSER BLOODLINE WITH DEATH CURSES. NOTHING!
TOTALLY ...
... OBVIOUS!

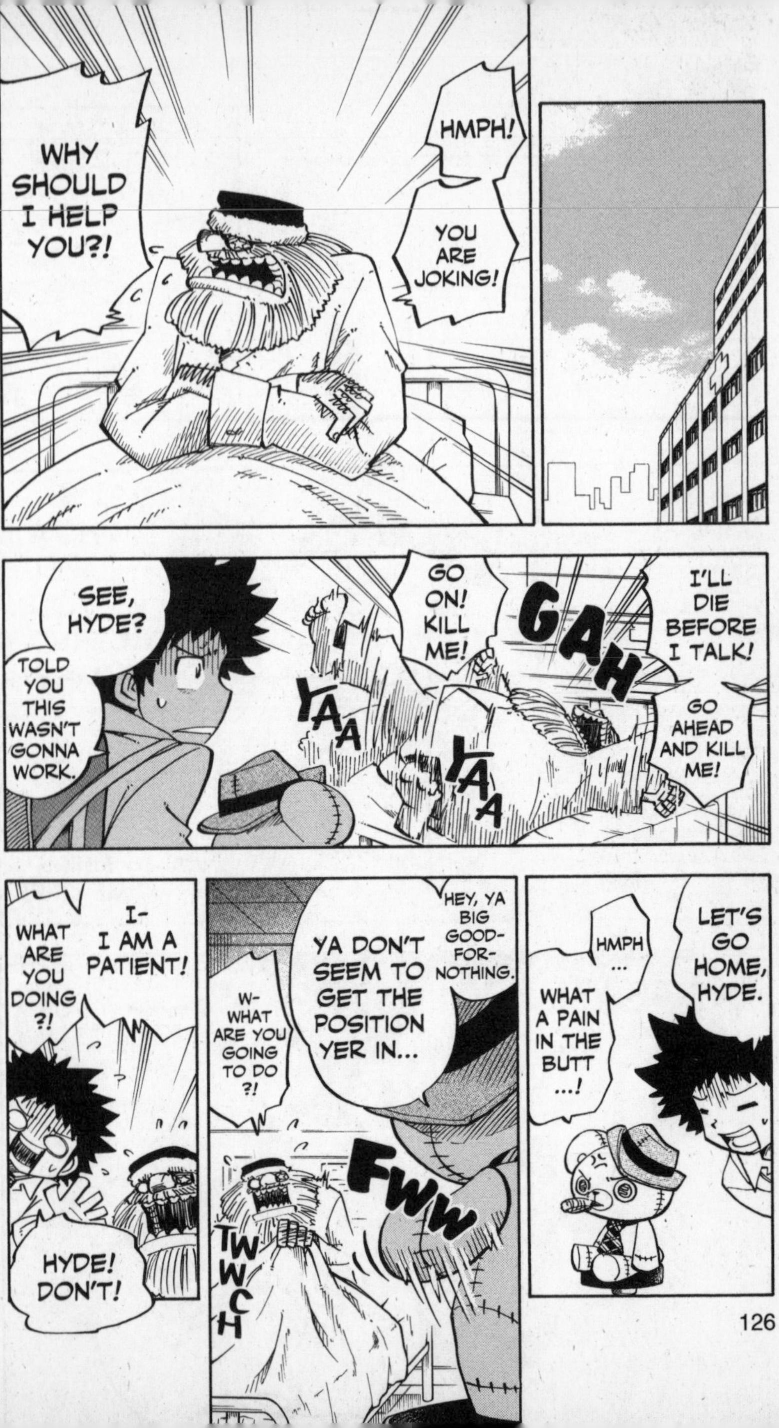
HMPH!
YOU ARE JOKING!
WHY SHOULD I HELP YOU?!
I'LL DIE BEFORE I TALK!
GAH
GO AHEAD AND KILL ME!
GO ON! KILL ME!
YAA
YAA
SEE, HYDE?
TOLD YOU THIS WASN'T GONNA WORK.
LET'S GO HOME, HYDE.
HMPH...
WHAT A PAIN IN THE BUTT...!
HEY, YA BIG GOOD-FOR-NOTHING.
YA DON'T SEEM TO GET THE POSITION YER IN...
W-WHAT ARE YOU GOING TO DO?!
FWW
TWWCH
I- I AM A PATIENT!
WHAT ARE YOU DOING?!
HYDE! DON'T!

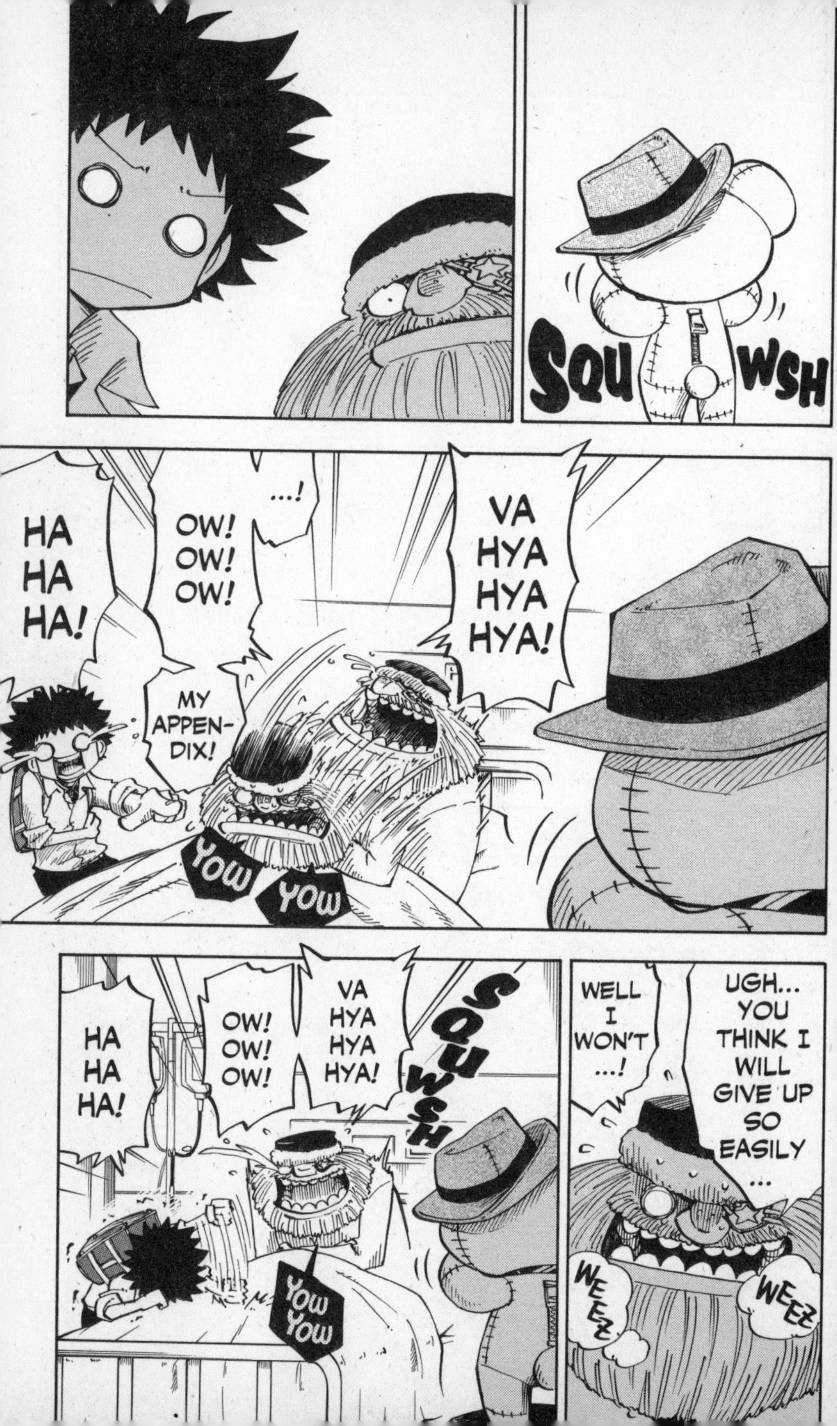
SQU WSH
VA HYA HYA HYA!
...!
OW! OW! OW!
HA HA HA!
MY APPEN-DIX!
YOW
YOW
UGH... YOU THINK I WILL GIVE UP SO EASILY ...
WELL I WON'T ...!
WEEZ
WEEZ
SQUWSH
VA HYA HYA HYA!
OW! OW! OW!
HA HA HA!
YOW YOW

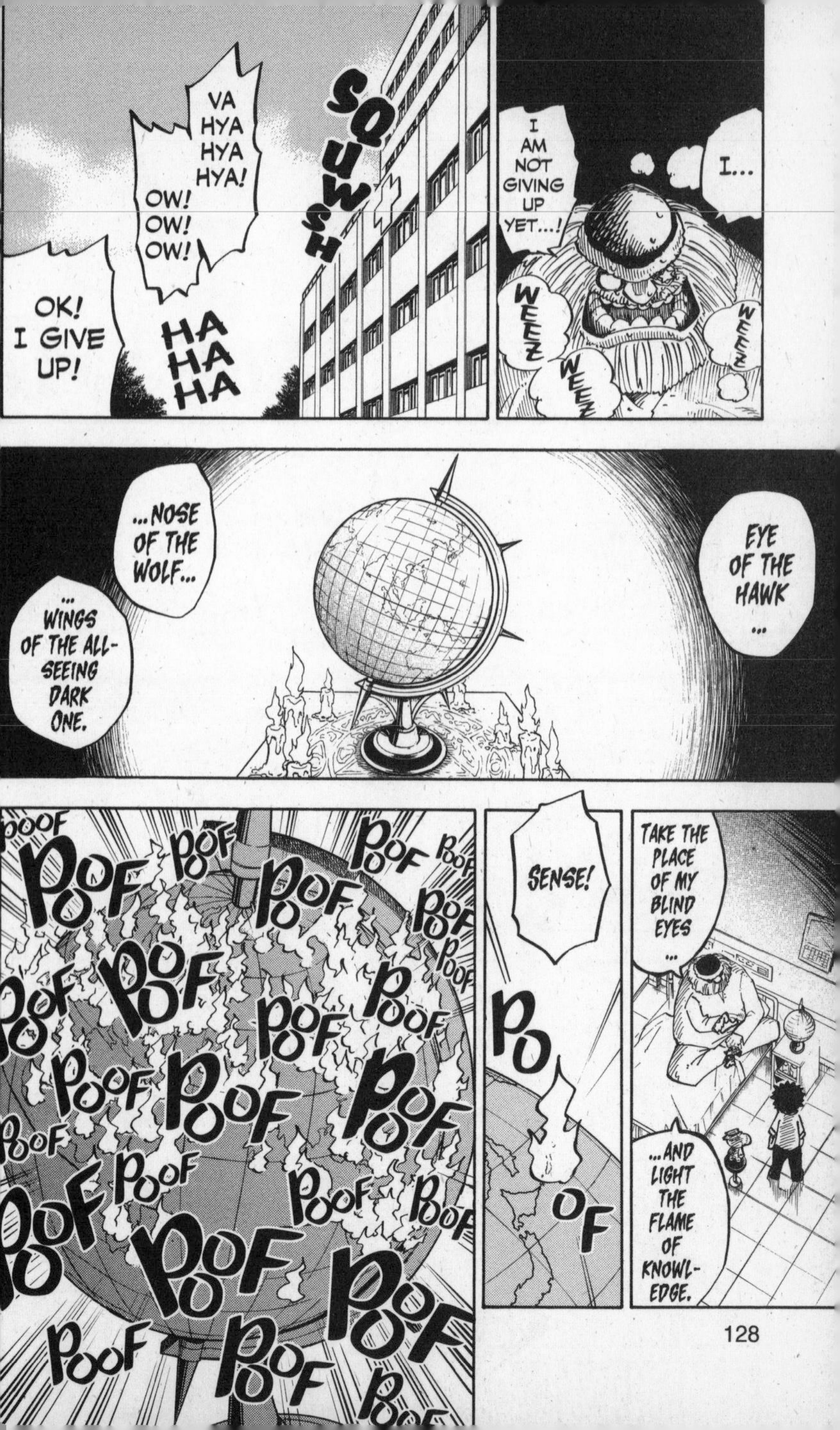
I...
I AM NOT GIVING UP YET...!
WEEZ
WEEZ
WEEZ
SQUWSH
VA HYA HYA HYA!
OW! OW! OW!
HA HA HA
OK! I GIVE UP!
EYE OF THE HAWK...
...NOSE OF THE WOLF...
...WINGS OF THE ALL-SEEING DARK ONE.
TAKE THE PLACE OF MY BLIND EYES...
...AND LIGHT THE FLAME OF KNOWLEDGE.
SENSE!
PO OF
POOF POOF POOF POOF POOF POOF POOF POOF POOF POOF POOF POOF POOF POOF POOF POOF POOF POOF POOF POOF

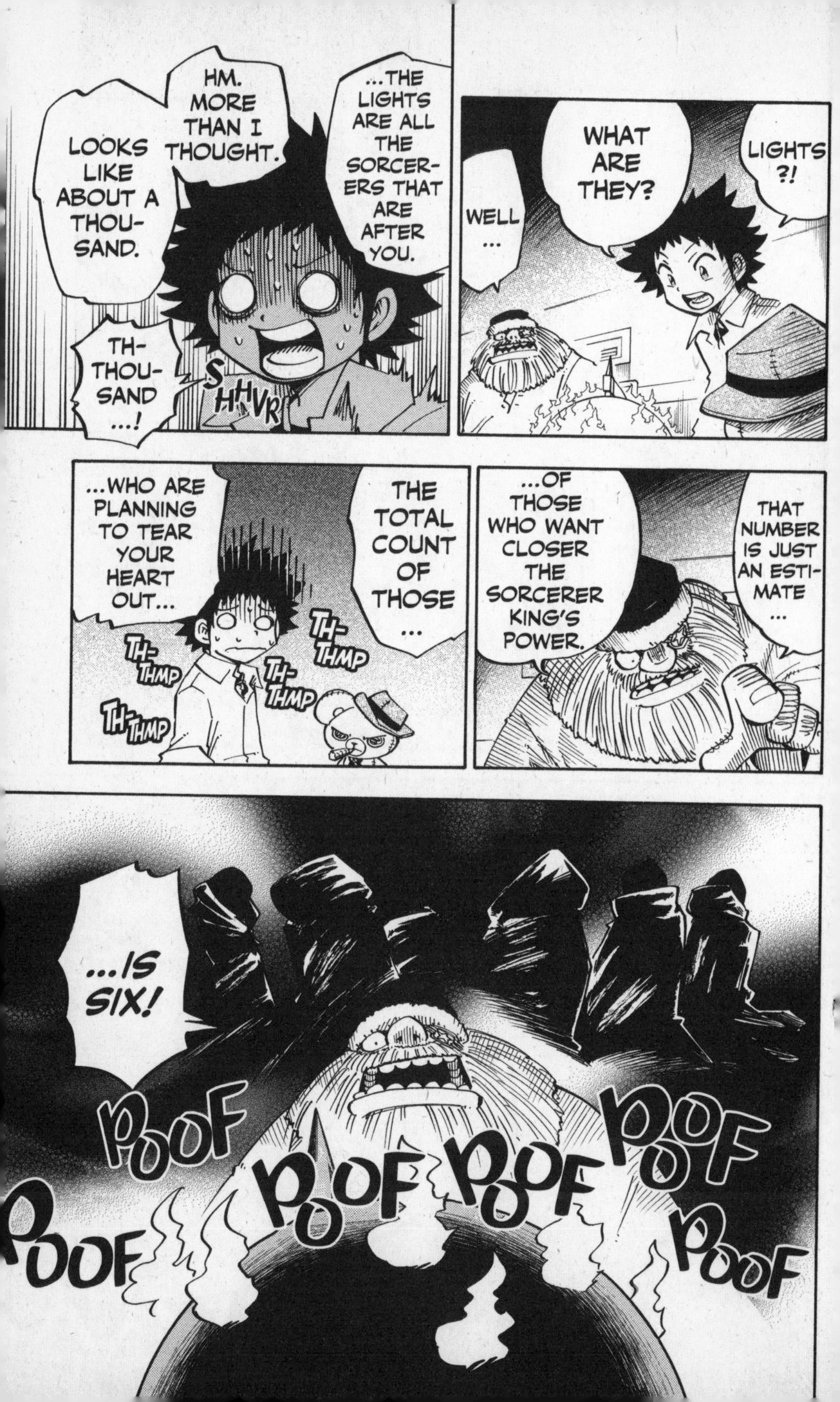
LIGHTS?!
WHAT ARE THEY?
WELL...
...THE LIGHTS ARE ALL THE SORCERERS THAT ARE AFTER YOU.
HM. MORE THAN I THOUGHT.
LOOKS LIKE ABOUT A THOUSAND.
TH-THOUSAND...!
SHHVR
THAT NUMBER IS JUST AN ESTIMATE...
...OF THOSE WHO WANT CLOSER THE SORCERER KING'S POWER.
THE TOTAL COUNT OF THOSE...
...WHO ARE PLANNING TO TEAR YOUR HEART OUT...
TH-THMP
TH-THMP
TH-THMP
TH-THMP
...IS SIX!
POOF
POOF
POOF
POOF
POOF
POOF

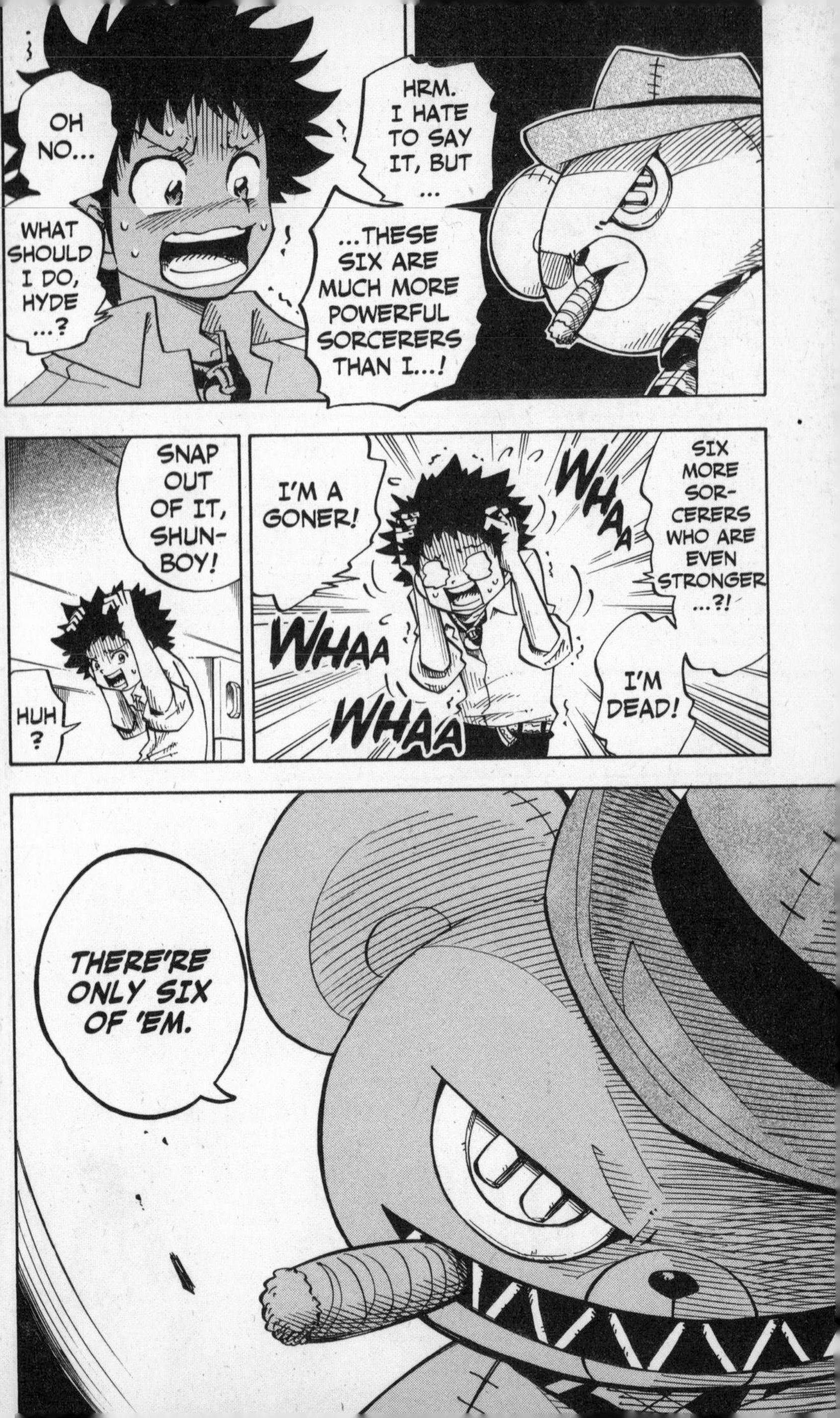
HRM. I HATE TO SAY IT, BUT ...
...THESE SIX ARE MUCH MORE POWERFUL SORCERERS THAN I...!
OH NO...
WHAT SHOULD I DO, HYDE ...?
SIX MORE SOR-CERERS WHO ARE EVEN STRONGER ...?!
WHAA
I'M A GONER!
WHAA
WHAA
I'M DEAD!
SNAP OUT OF IT, SHUN-BOY!
HUH ?
THERE'RE ONLY SIX OF 'EM.

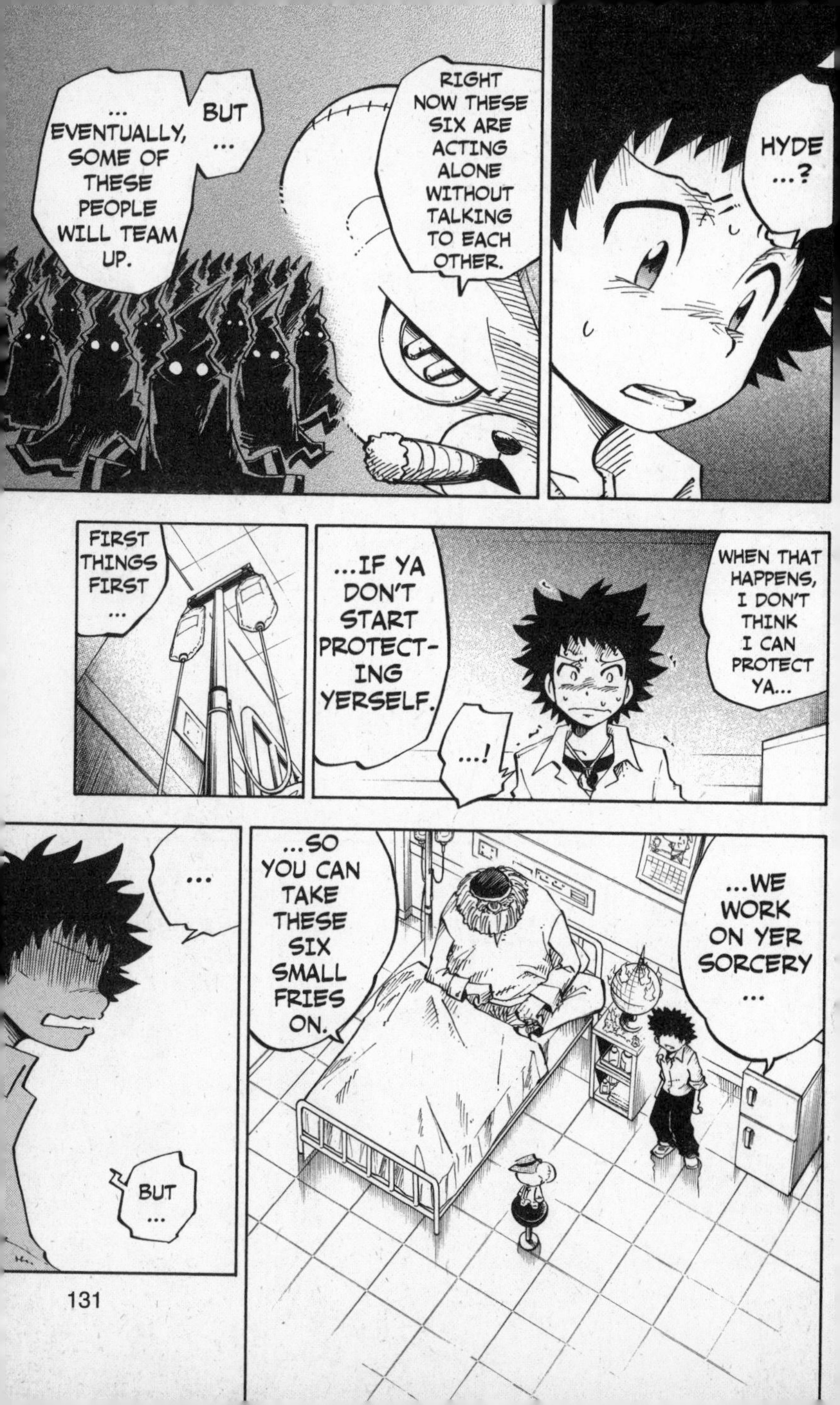
HYDE ...?
RIGHT NOW THESE SIX ARE ACTING ALONE WITHOUT TALKING TO EACH OTHER.
BUT ...
... EVENTUALLY, SOME OF THESE PEOPLE WILL TEAM UP.
WHEN THAT HAPPENS, I DON'T THINK I CAN PROTECT YA...
...IF YA DON'T START PROTECT-ING YERSELF.
...!
FIRST THINGS FIRST ...
...WE WORK ON YER SORCERY ...
...SO YOU CAN TAKE THESE SIX SMALL FRIES ON.
...
BUT ...

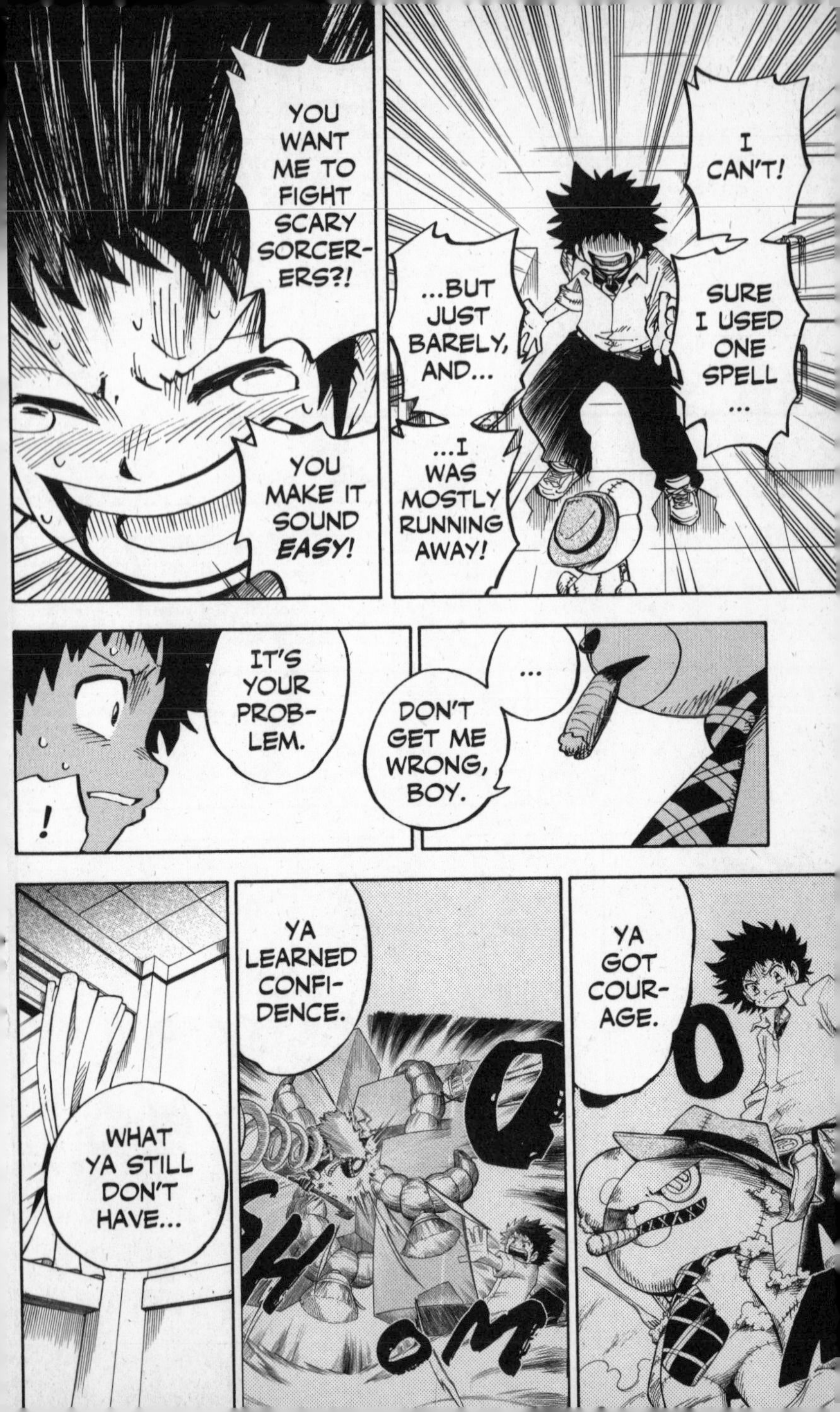
I CAN'T!
SURE I USED ONE SPELL ...
...BUT JUST BARELY, AND...
...I WAS MOSTLY RUNNING AWAY!
YOU WANT ME TO FIGHT SCARY SORCERERS?!
YOU MAKE IT SOUND *EASY*!
...
DON'T GET ME WRONG, BOY.
IT'S YOUR PROBLEM.
!
YA GOT COURAGE.
YA LEARNED CONFIDENCE.
WHAT YA STILL DON'T HAVE...

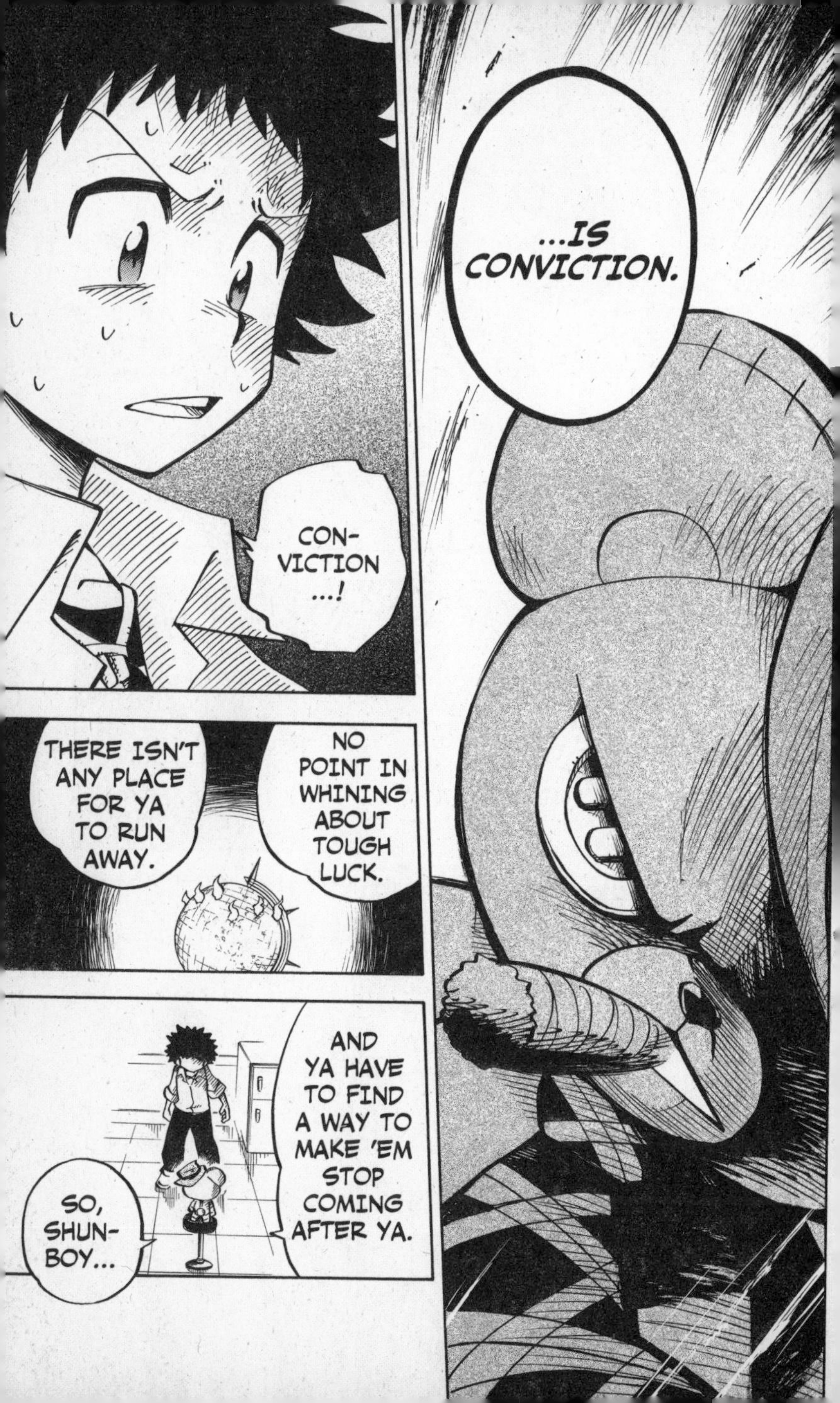
...IS CONVICTION.
CON-VICTION ...!
NO POINT IN WHINING ABOUT TOUGH LUCK.
THERE ISN'T ANY PLACE FOR YA TO RUN AWAY.
AND YA HAVE TO FIND A WAY TO MAKE 'EM STOP COMING AFTER YA.
SO, SHUN-BOY...

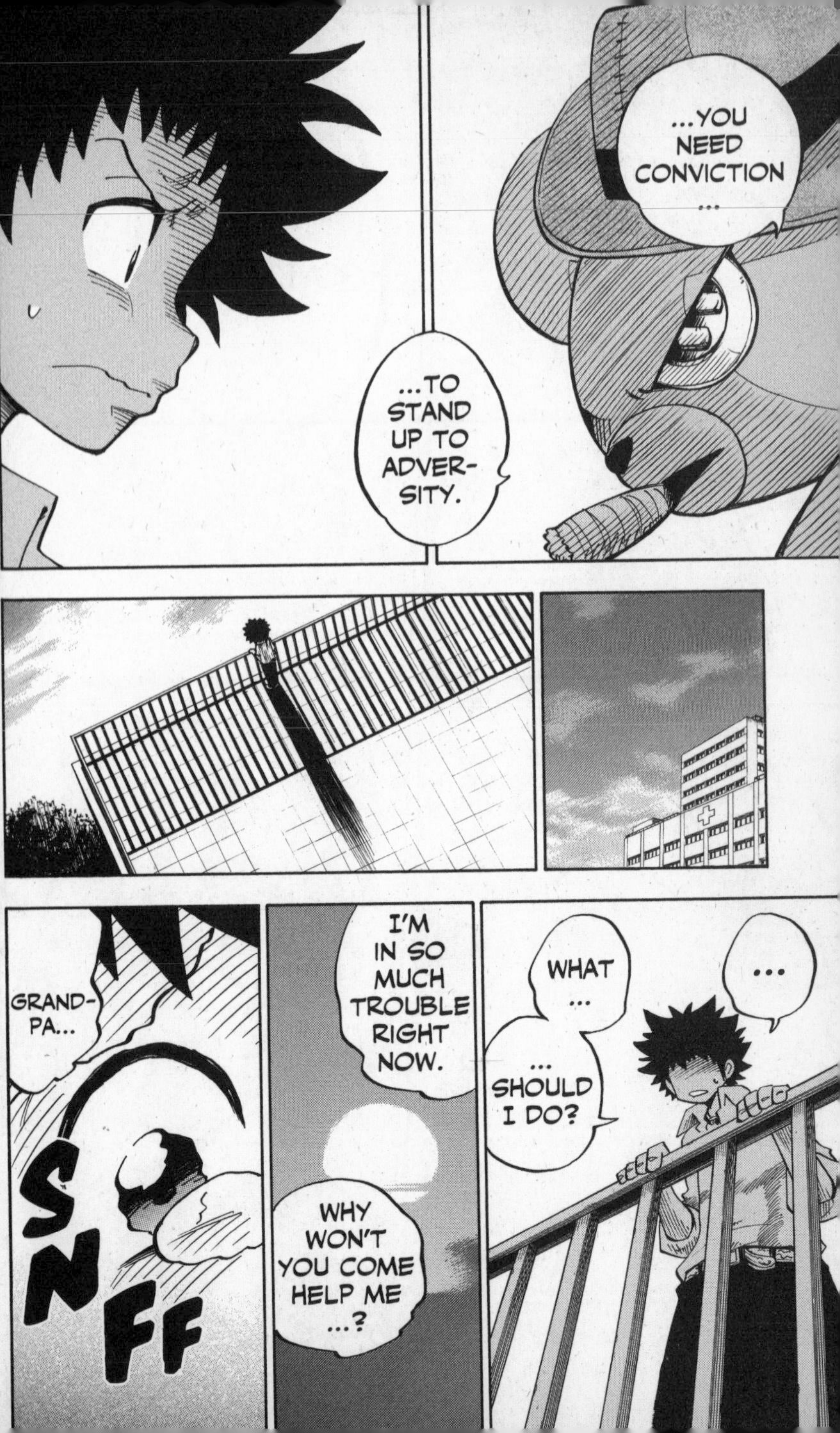
...YOU NEED CONVICTION ...
...TO STAND UP TO ADVER-SITY.
...
WHAT ...
... SHOULD I DO?
I'M IN SO MUCH TROUBLE RIGHT NOW.
WHY WON'T YOU COME HELP ME ...?
GRAND-PA...
SNFF

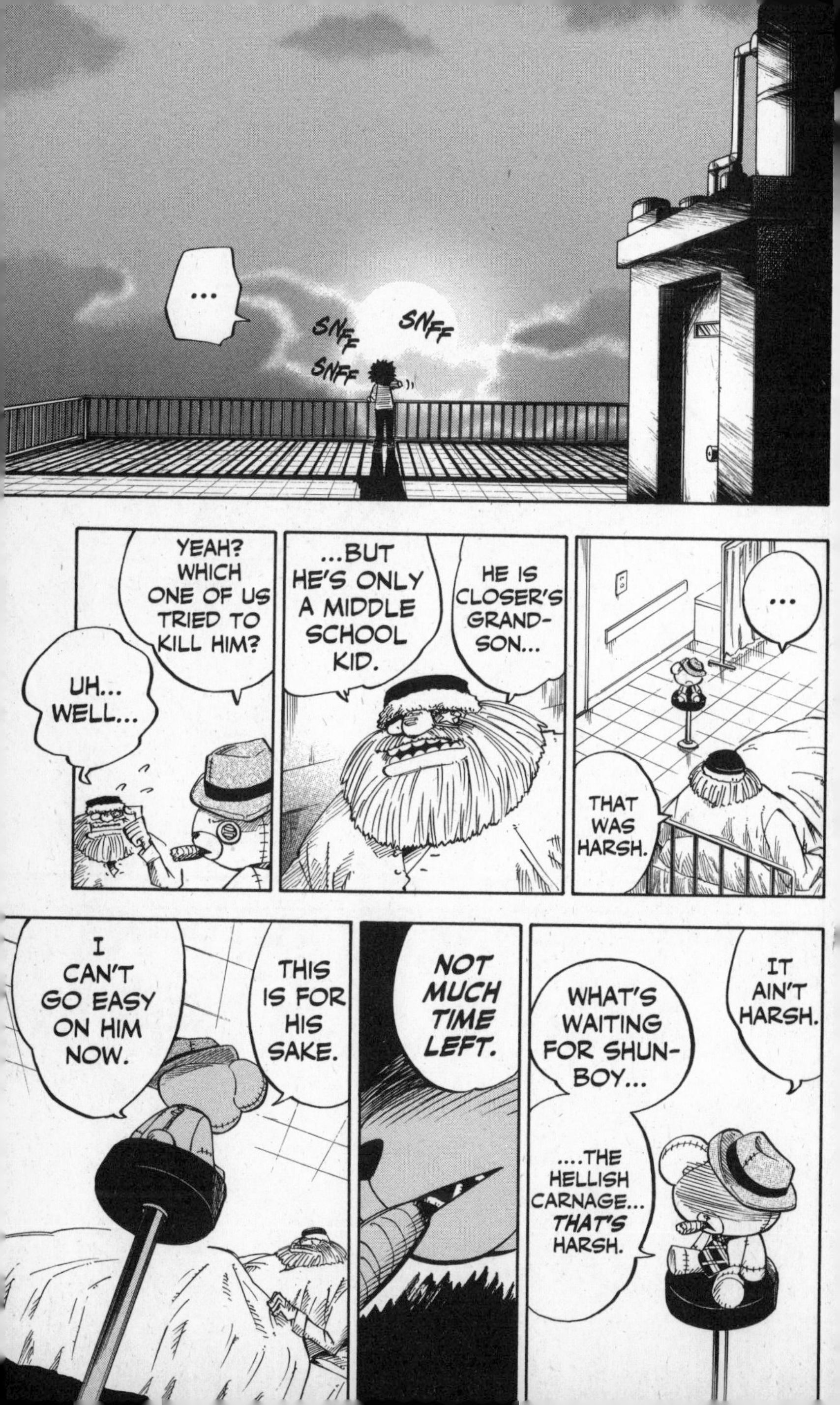
...
SNFF
SNFF
SNFF
...
THAT WAS HARSH.
HE IS CLOSER'S GRAND-SON...
...BUT HE'S ONLY A MIDDLE SCHOOL KID.
YEAH? WHICH ONE OF US TRIED TO KILL HIM?
UH... WELL...
IT AIN'T HARSH.
WHAT'S WAITING FOR SHUN-BOY...
....THE HELLISH CARNAGE... *THAT'S* HARSH.
NOT MUCH TIME LEFT.
THIS IS FOR HIS SAKE.
I CAN'T GO EASY ON HIM NOW.

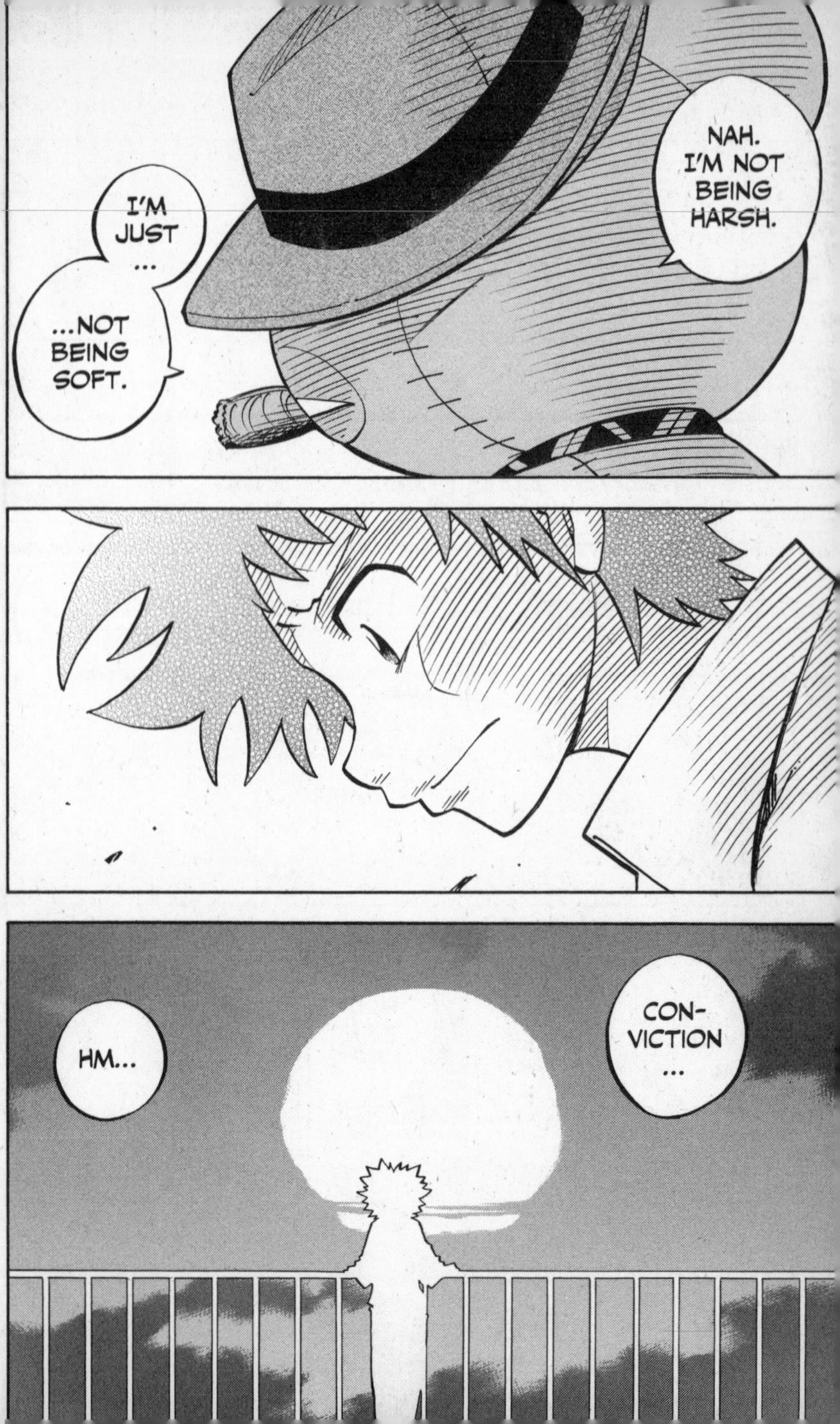
NAH. I'M NOT BEING HARSH.
I'M JUST ...
...NOT BEING SOFT.
CON-VICTION ...
HM...

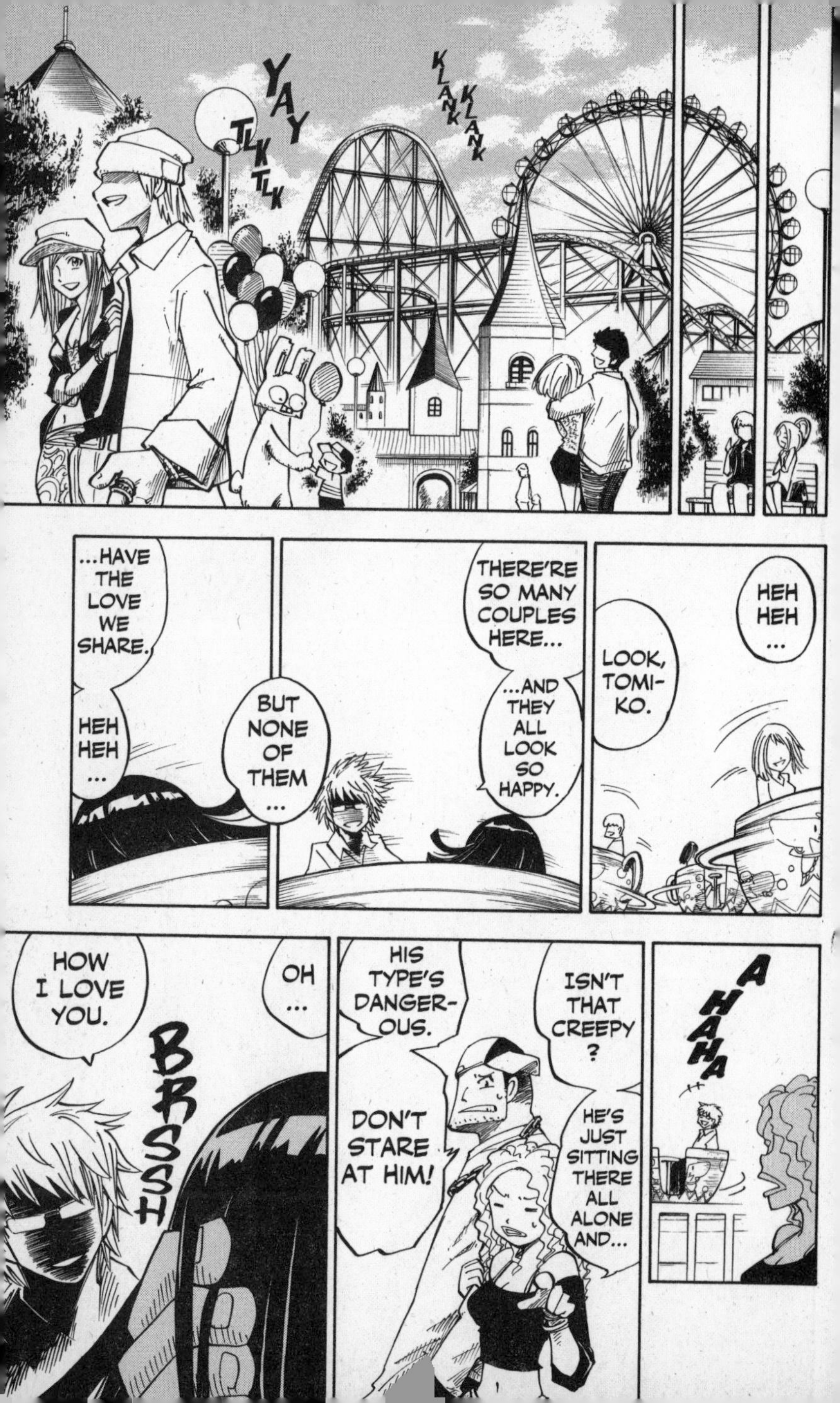
KLANK KLANK
YAY
TLKTLK
HEH HEH ...
LOOK, TOMI-KO.
THERE'RE SO MANY COUPLES HERE...
...AND THEY ALL LOOK SO HAPPY.
BUT NONE OF THEM ...
...HAVE THE LOVE WE SHARE.
HEH HEH ...
AHAHA
ISN'T THAT CREEPY?
HE'S JUST SITTING THERE ALL ALONE AND...
HIS TYPE'S DANGER-OUS.
DON'T STARE AT HIM!
OH ...
HOW I LOVE YOU.
BRSSH

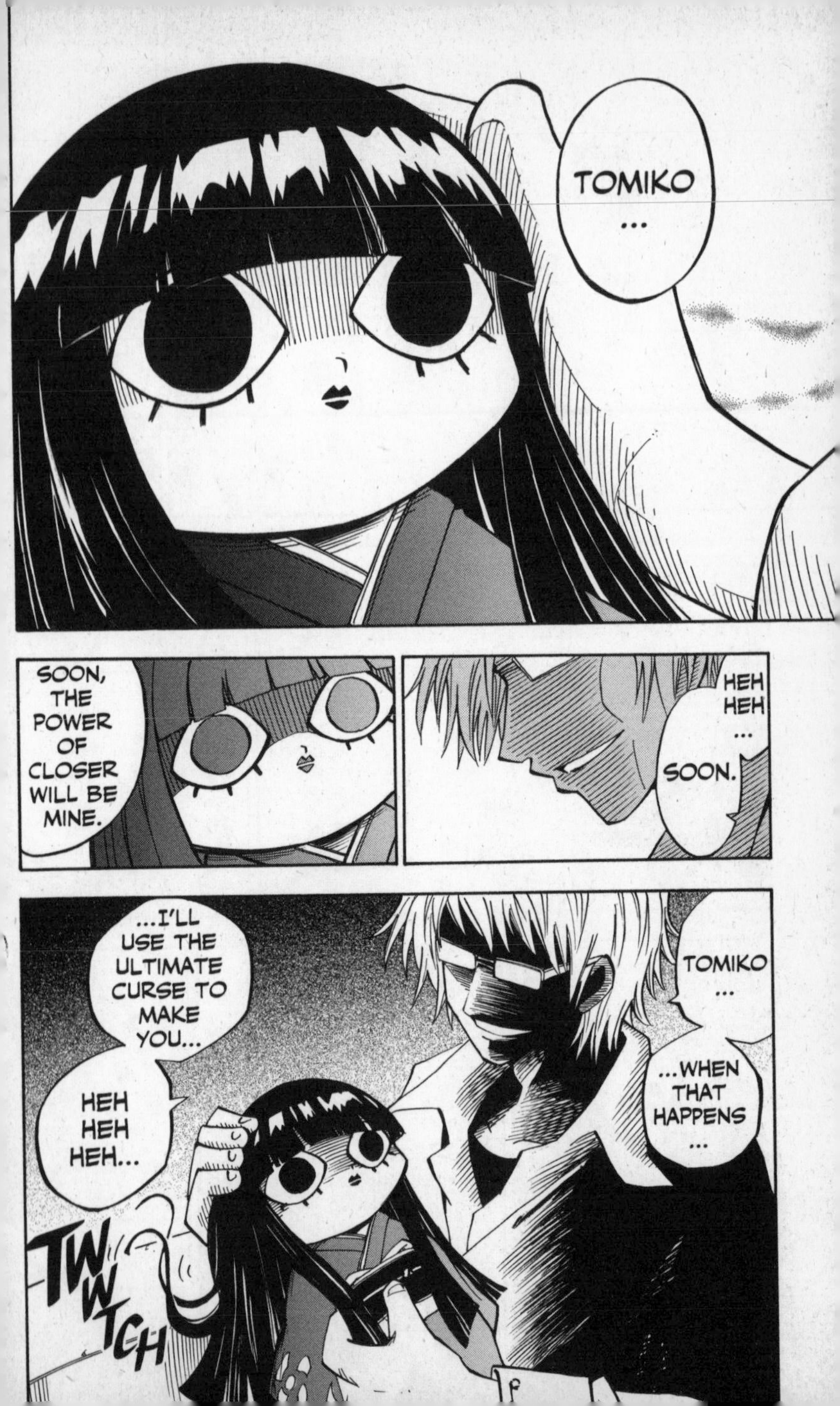
TOMIKO ...
HEH HEH ... SOON.
SOON, THE POWER OF CLOSER WILL BE MINE.
TOMIKO ...
...WHEN THAT HAPPENS ...
...I'LL USE THE ULTIMATE CURSE TO MAKE YOU...
HEH HEH HEH...
TWITCH

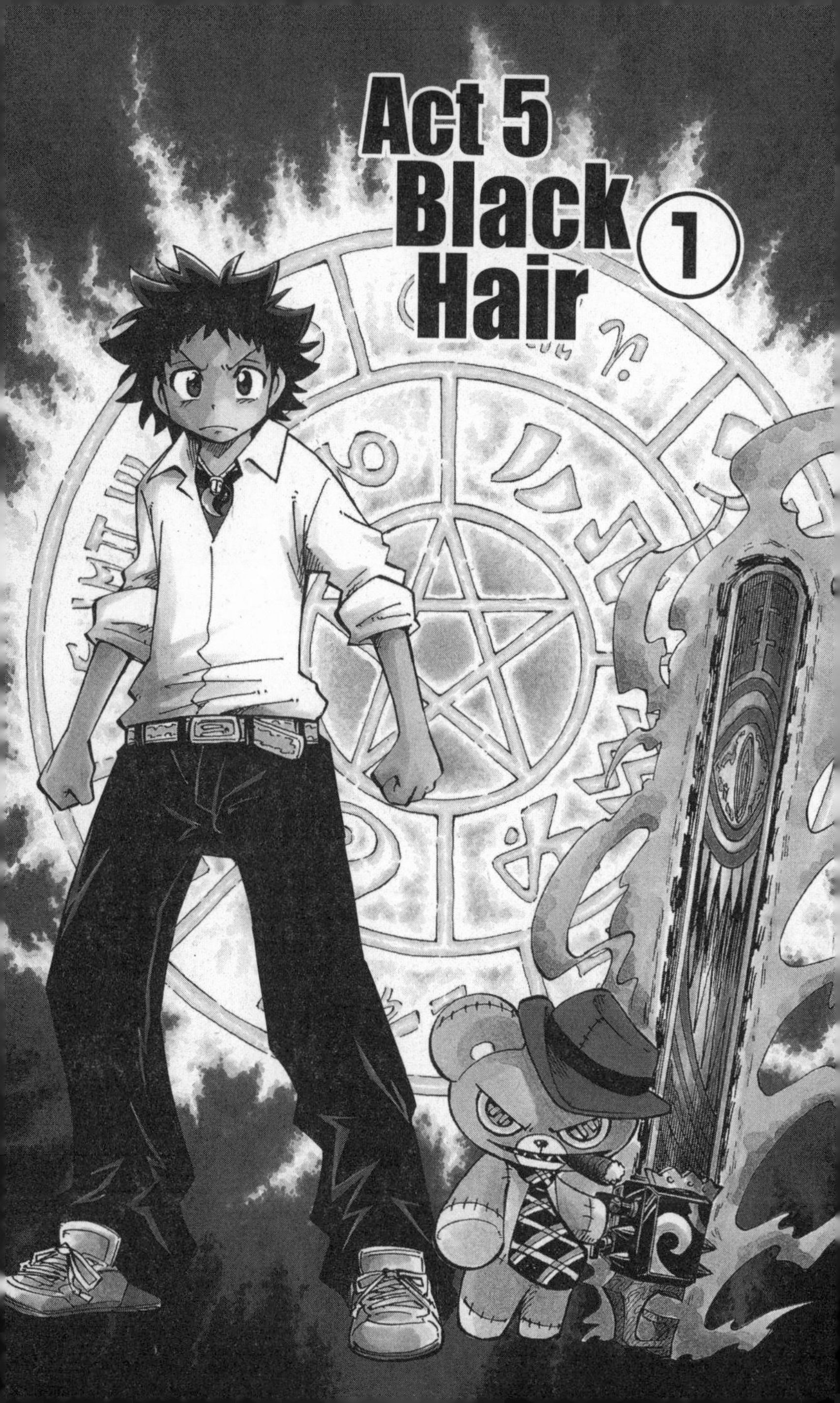
Act 5
Black
Hair
1

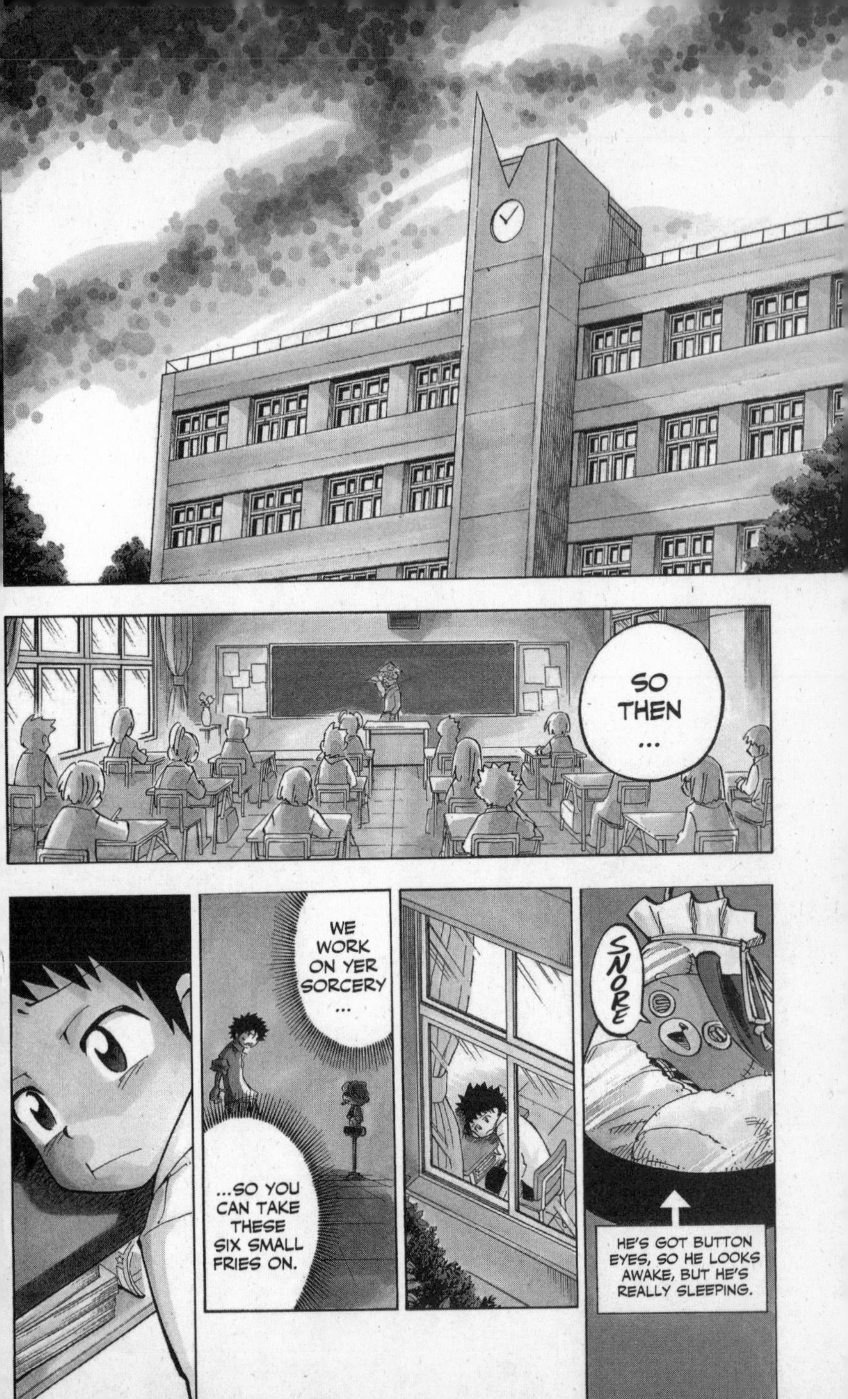
SO THEN ...
SNORE
HE'S GOT BUTTON EYES, SO HE LOOKS AWAKE, BUT HE'S REALLY SLEEPING.
WE WORK ON YER SORCERY ...
...SO YOU CAN TAKE THESE SIX SMALL FRIES ON.

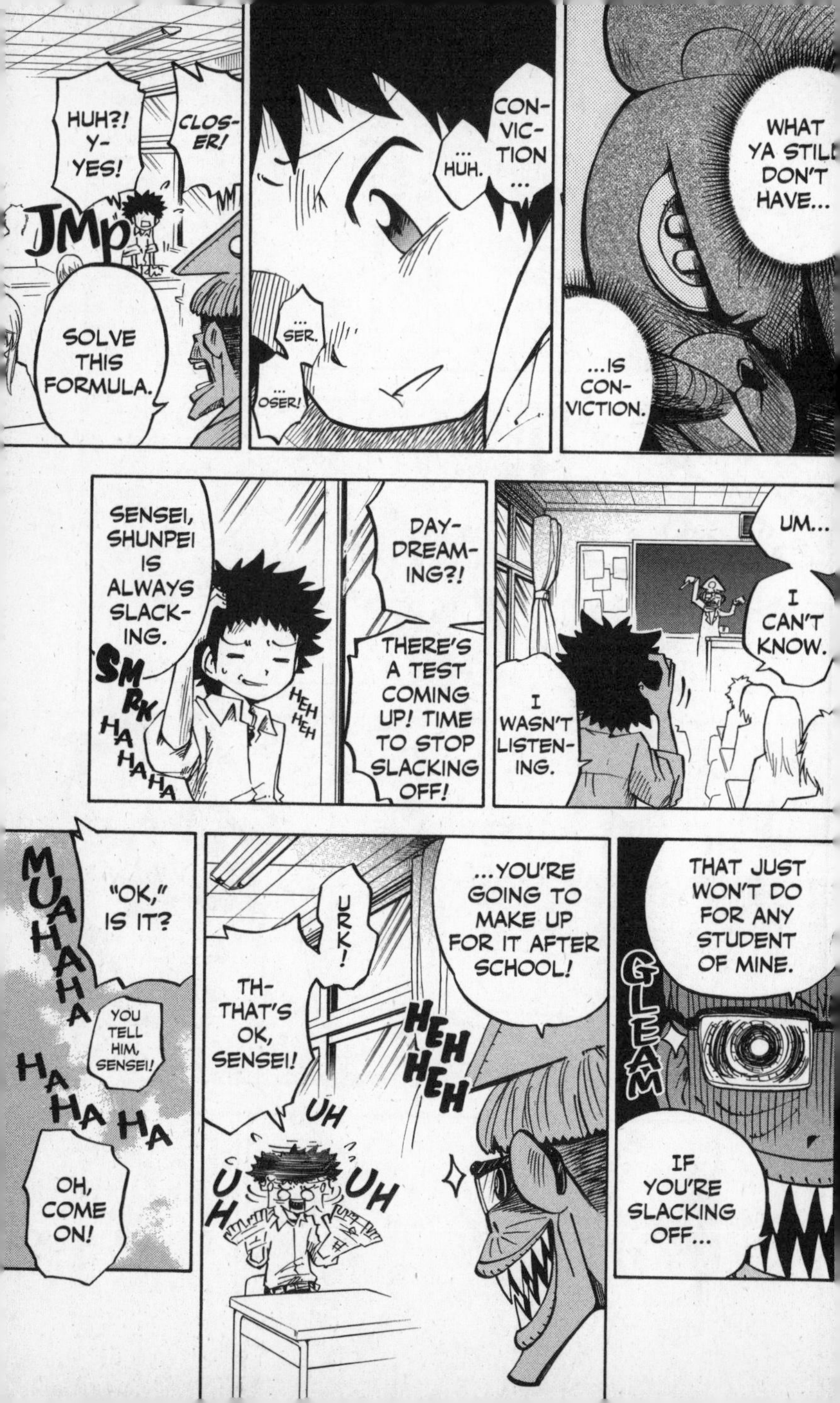

WHAT YA STILL DON'T HAVE...
...IS CONVICTION.
CONVICTION...
...HUH.
...SER.
...OSER!
CLOSER!
HUH?! Y-YES!
JMP
SOLVE THIS FORMULA.
UM...
I CAN'T KNOW.
I WASN'T LISTENING.
DAYDREAMING?!
THERE'S A TEST COMING UP! TIME TO STOP SLACKING OFF!
SENSEI, SHUNPEI IS ALWAYS SLACKING.
SMRK
HEH HEH
HA HA HA HA
THAT JUST WON'T DO FOR ANY STUDENT OF MINE.
GLEAM
IF YOU'RE SLACKING OFF...
...YOU'RE GOING TO MAKE UP FOR IT AFTER SCHOOL!
HEH HEH HEH
URK!
TH-THAT'S OK, SENSEI!
UH UH UH UH
"OK," IS IT?
MUAHAHAHA
YOU TELL HIM, SENSEI!
HA HA HA HA
OH, COME ON!

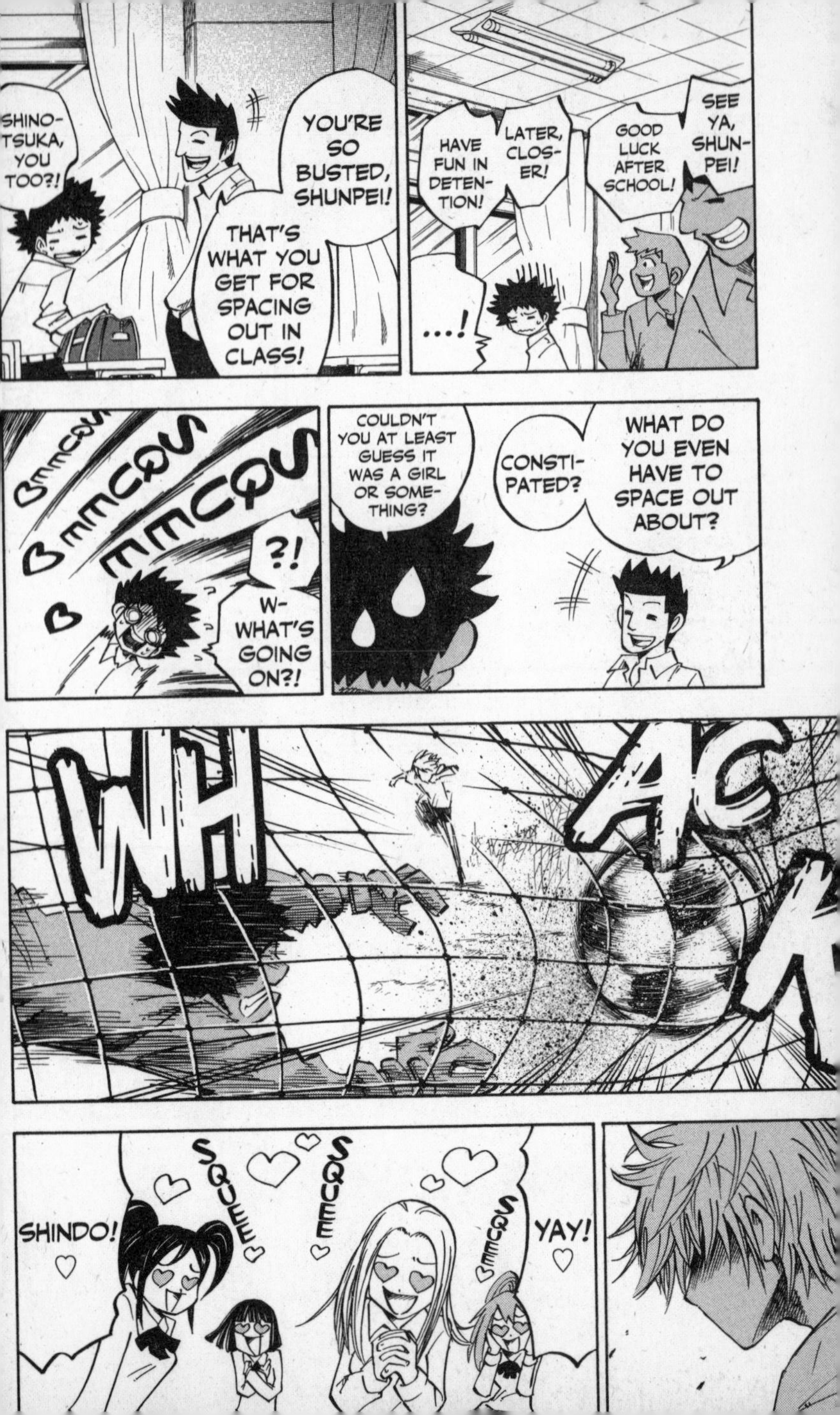
SEE YA, SHUN-PEI!
GOOD LUCK AFTER SCHOOL!
LATER, CLOS-ER!
HAVE FUN IN DETEN-TION!
...!
YOU'RE SO BUSTED, SHUNPEI!
THAT'S WHAT YOU GET FOR SPACING OUT IN CLASS!
SHINO-TSUKA, YOU TOO?!
WHAT DO YOU EVEN HAVE TO SPACE OUT ABOUT?
CONSTI-PATED?
COULDN'T YOU AT LEAST GUESS IT WAS A GIRL OR SOME-THING?
?!
W-WHAT'S GOING ON?!
WHACK
YAY!
SQUEE
SQUEE
SQUEE
SHINDO!

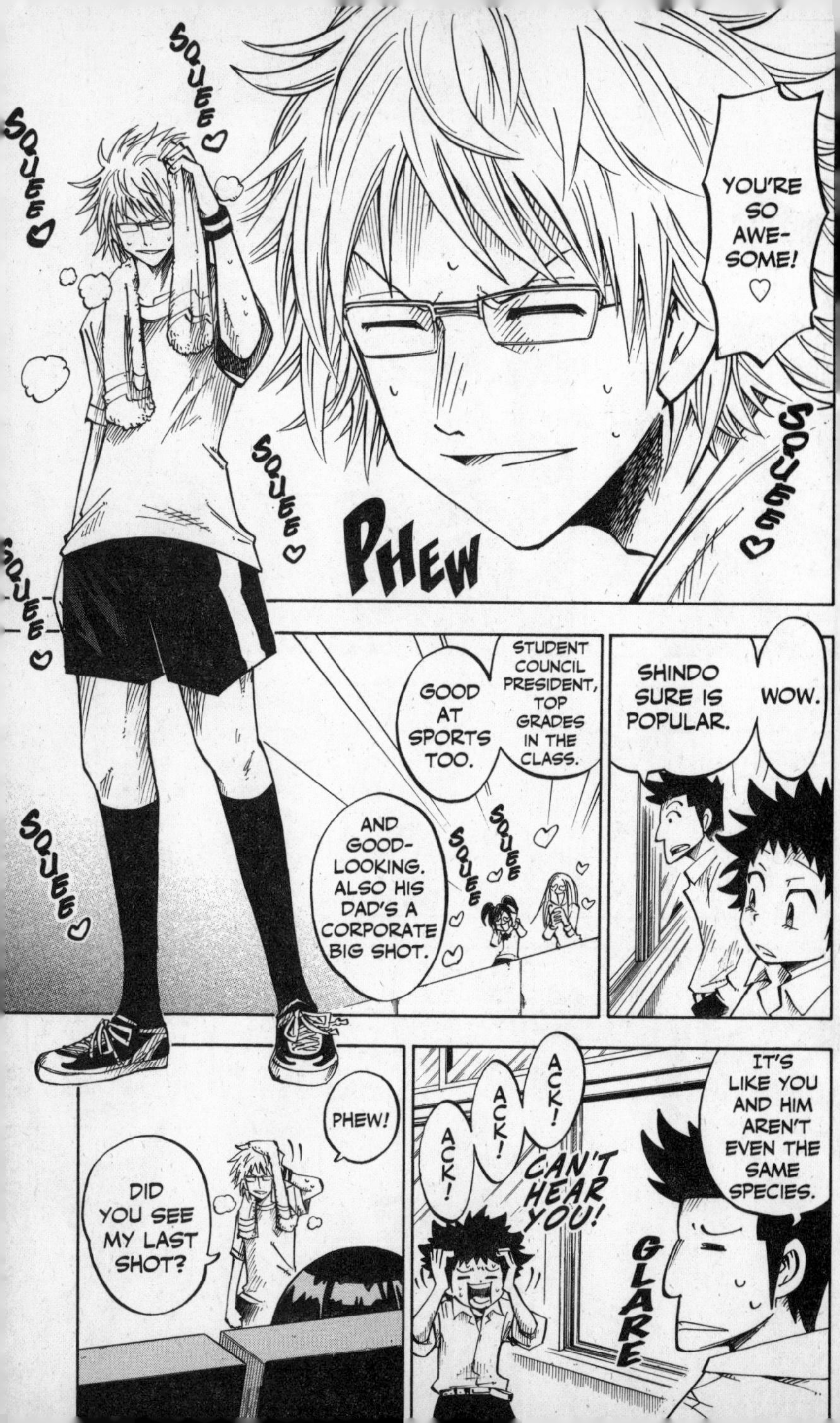
YOU'RE SO AWESOME! ♡
SQUEE ♡
PHEW
WOW.
SHINDO SURE IS POPULAR.
STUDENT COUNCIL PRESIDENT, TOP GRADES IN THE CLASS.
GOOD AT SPORTS TOO.
SQUEE
SQUEE
AND GOOD-LOOKING. ALSO HIS DAD'S A CORPORATE BIG SHOT.
SQUEE ♡
SQUEE ♡
SQUEE ♡
SQUEE ♡
SQUEE ♡
IT'S LIKE YOU AND HIM AREN'T EVEN THE SAME SPECIES.
GLARE
ACK!
ACK!
ACK!
CAN'T HEAR YOU!
PHEW!
DID YOU SEE MY LAST SHOT?

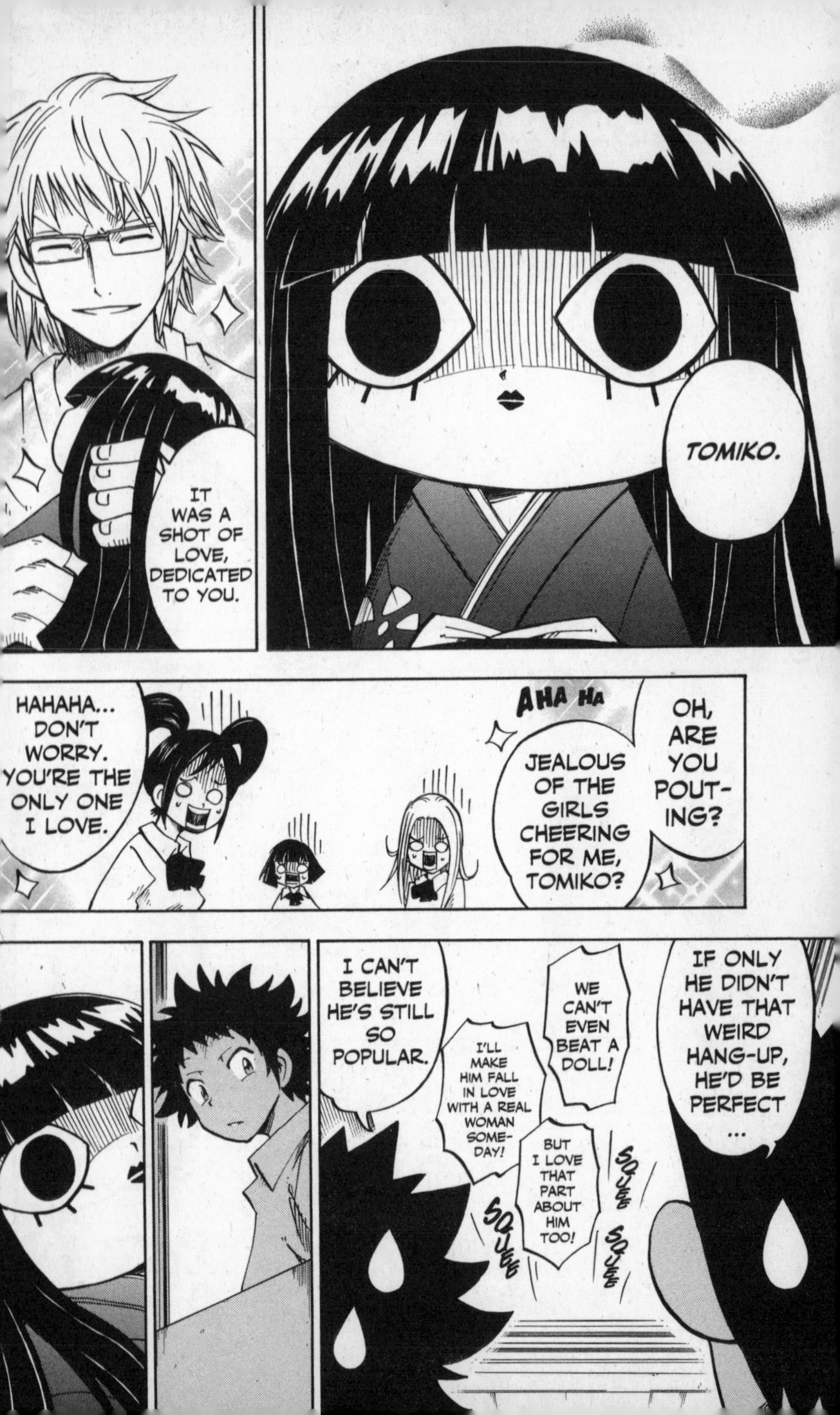
TOMIKO.
IT WAS A SHOT OF LOVE, DEDICATED TO YOU.
OH, ARE YOU POUT-ING?
AHA HA
JEALOUS OF THE GIRLS CHEERING FOR ME, TOMIKO?
HAHAHA... DON'T WORRY. YOU'RE THE ONLY ONE I LOVE.
IF ONLY HE DIDN'T HAVE THAT WEIRD HANG-UP, HE'D BE PERFECT...
WE CAN'T EVEN BEAT A DOLL!
BUT I LOVE THAT PART ABOUT HIM TOO!
SQUEE
SQUEE
SQUEE
I'LL MAKE HIM FALL IN LOVE WITH A REAL WOMAN SOME-DAY!
I CAN'T BELIEVE HE'S STILL SO POPULAR.

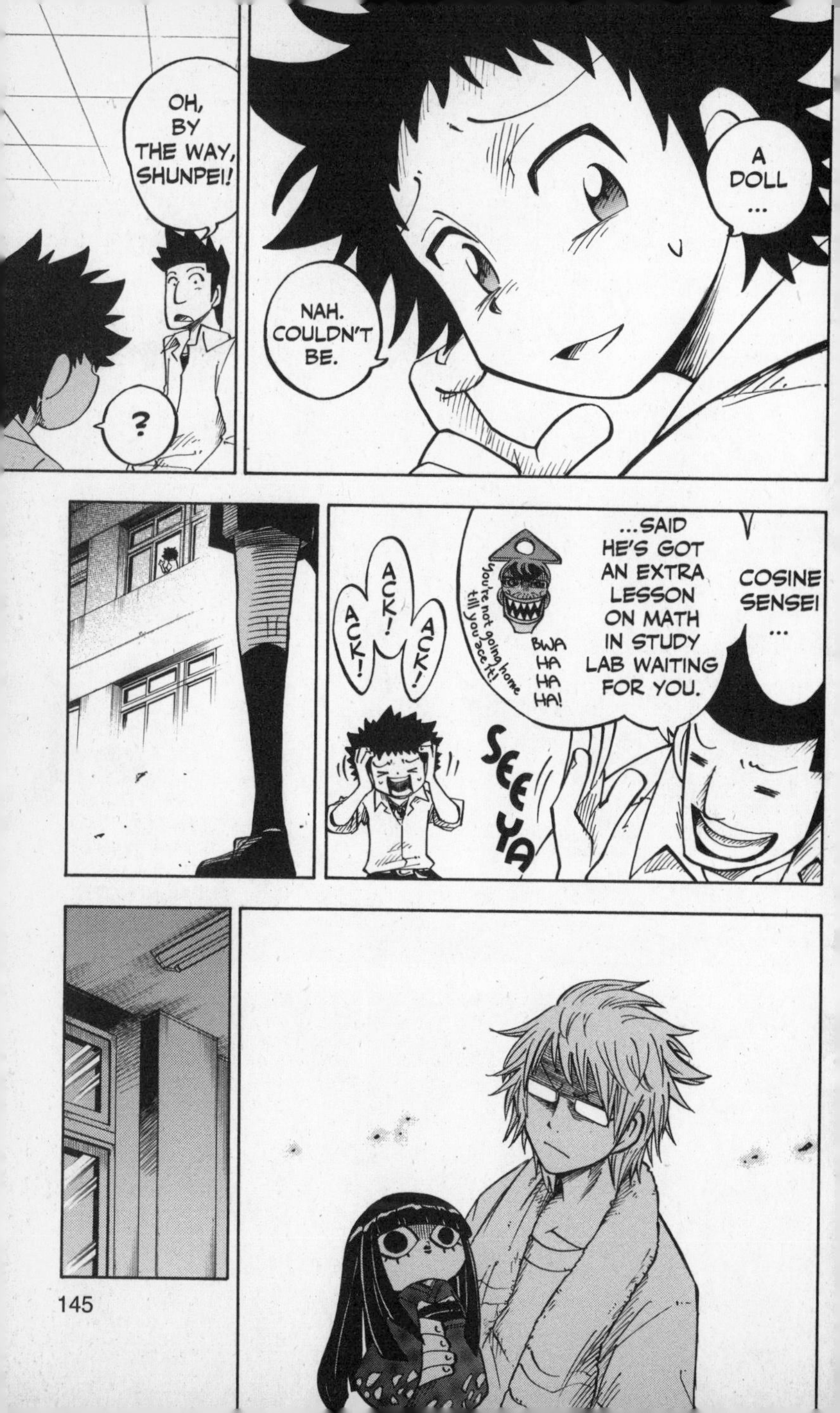
A DOLL ...
NAH. COULDN'T BE.
OH, BY THE WAY, SHUNPEI!
?
COSINE SENSEI ...
...SAID HE'S GOT AN EXTRA LESSON ON MATH IN STUDY LAB WAITING FOR YOU.
BWA HA HA HA!
You're not going home till you ace it!
ACK! ACK! ACK! ACK!
SEE YA

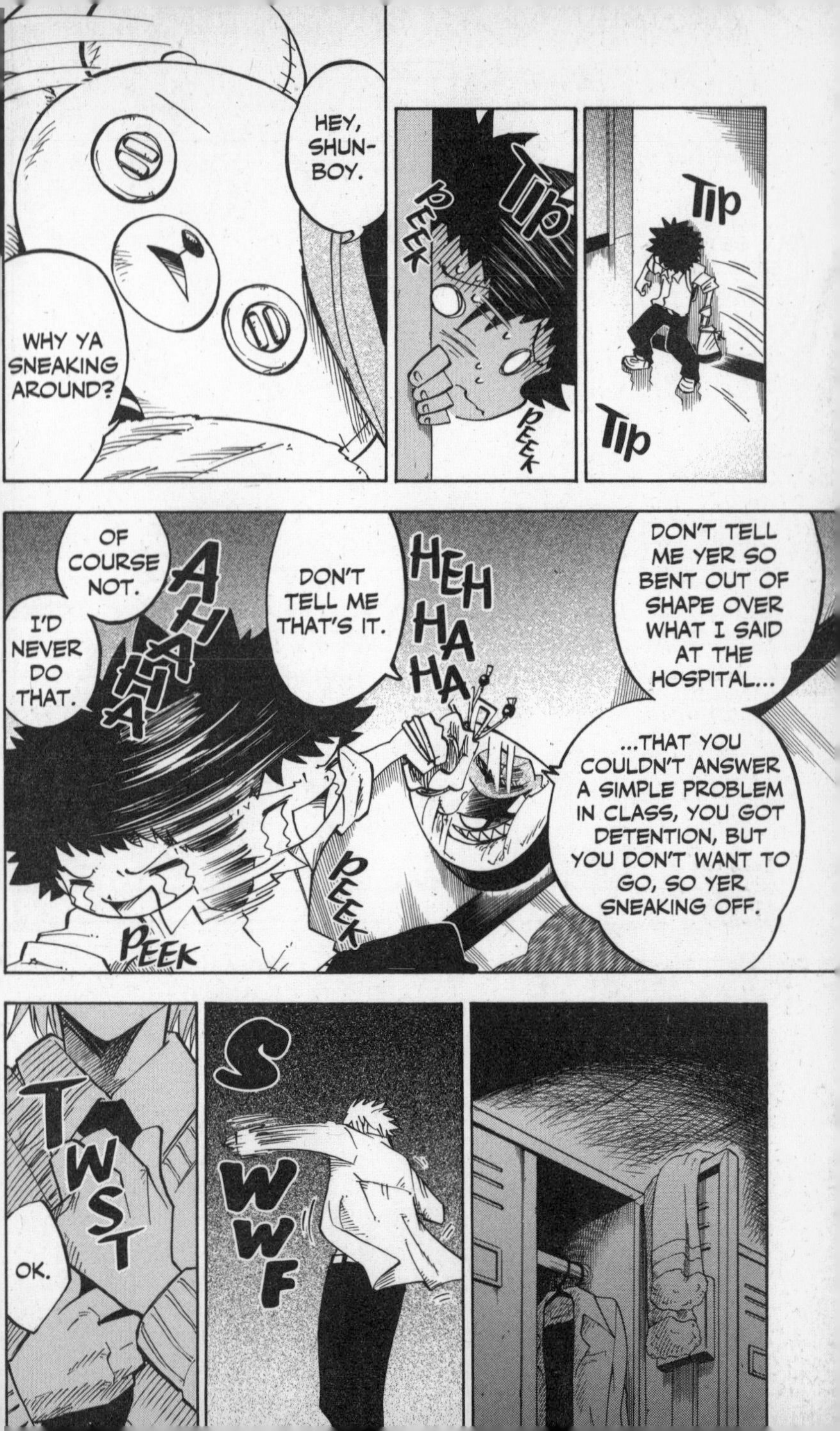
Tip
Tip
Tip
PEEK
PEEK
HEY, SHUN-BOY.
WHY YA SNEAKING AROUND?
DON'T TELL ME YER SO BENT OUT OF SHAPE OVER WHAT I SAID AT THE HOSPITAL...
...THAT YOU COULDN'T ANSWER A SIMPLE PROBLEM IN CLASS, YOU GOT DETENTION, BUT YOU DON'T WANT TO GO, SO YER SNEAKING OFF.
HEH HA HA HA
DON'T TELL ME THAT'S IT.
PEEK
OF COURSE NOT.
AHAHAHA
I'D NEVER DO THAT.
PEEK
SWWF
TWST
OK.

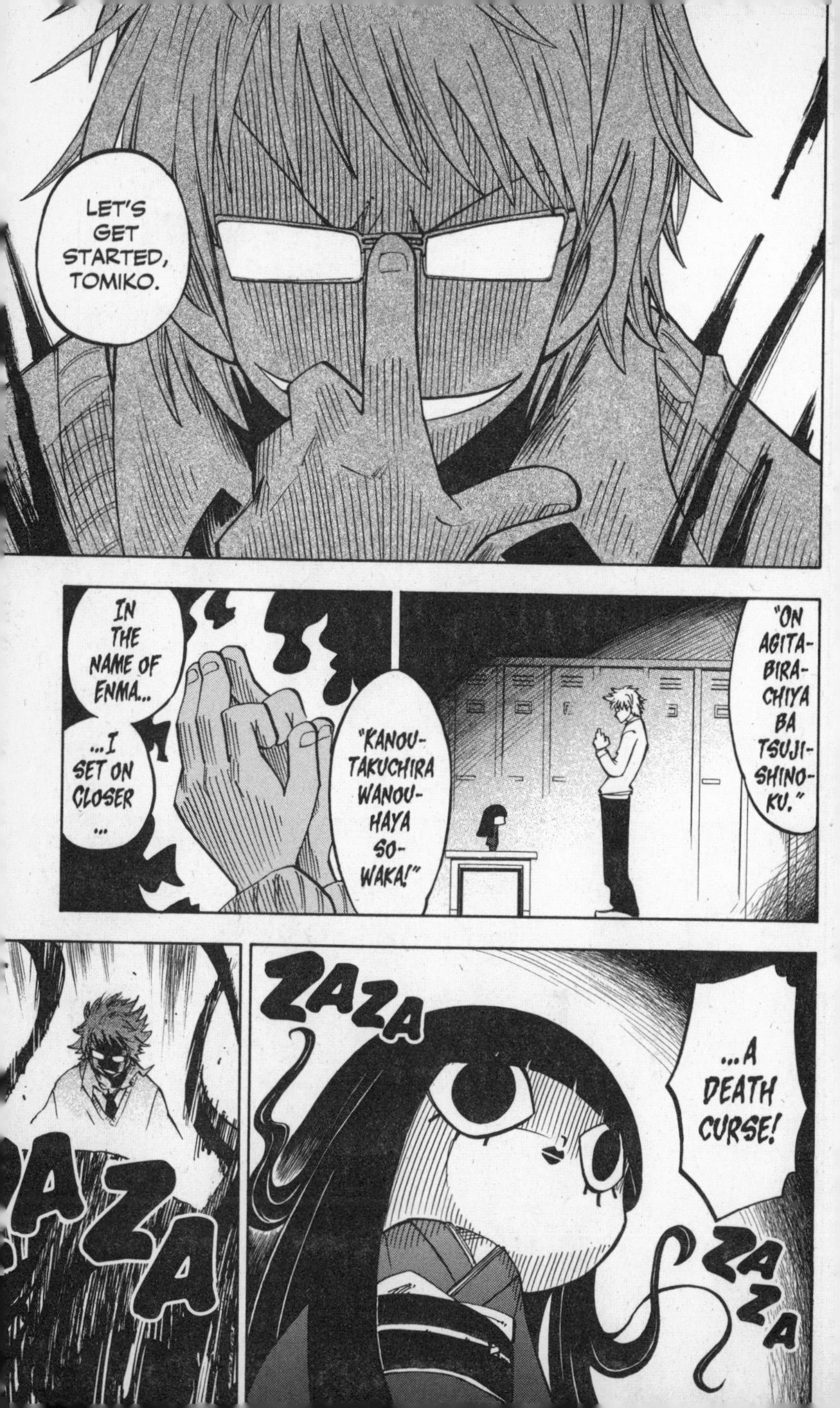
LET'S GET STARTED, TOMIKO.
"ON AGITA-BIRA-CHIYA BA TSUJI-SHINO-KU."
"KANOU-TAKUCHIRA WANOU-HAYA SO-WAKA!"
IN THE NAME OF ENMA...
...I SET ON CLOSER...
ZAZA
...A DEATH CURSE!
ZAZA
ZAZA

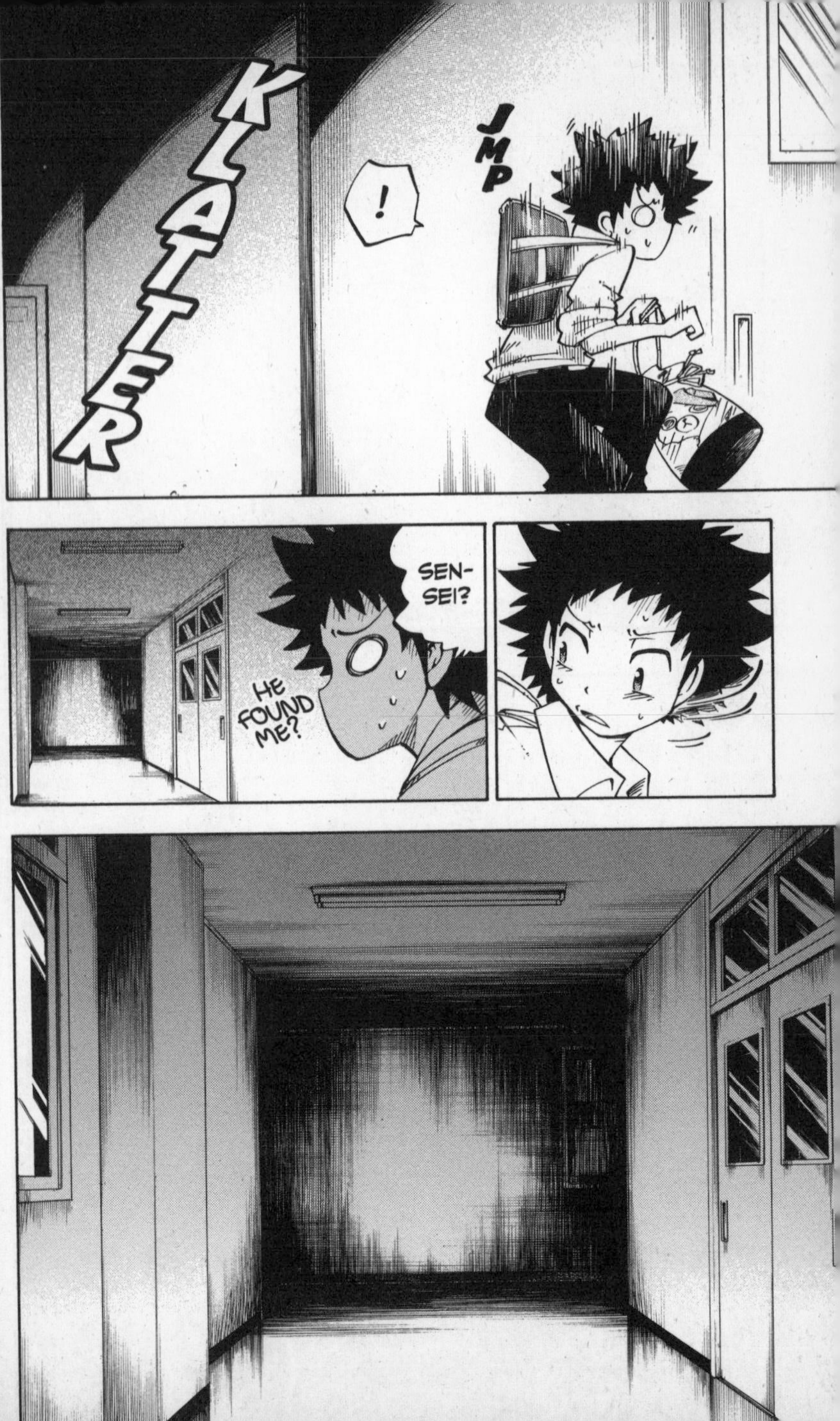
JMP
!
KLATTER
SEN-SEI?
HE FOUND ME?

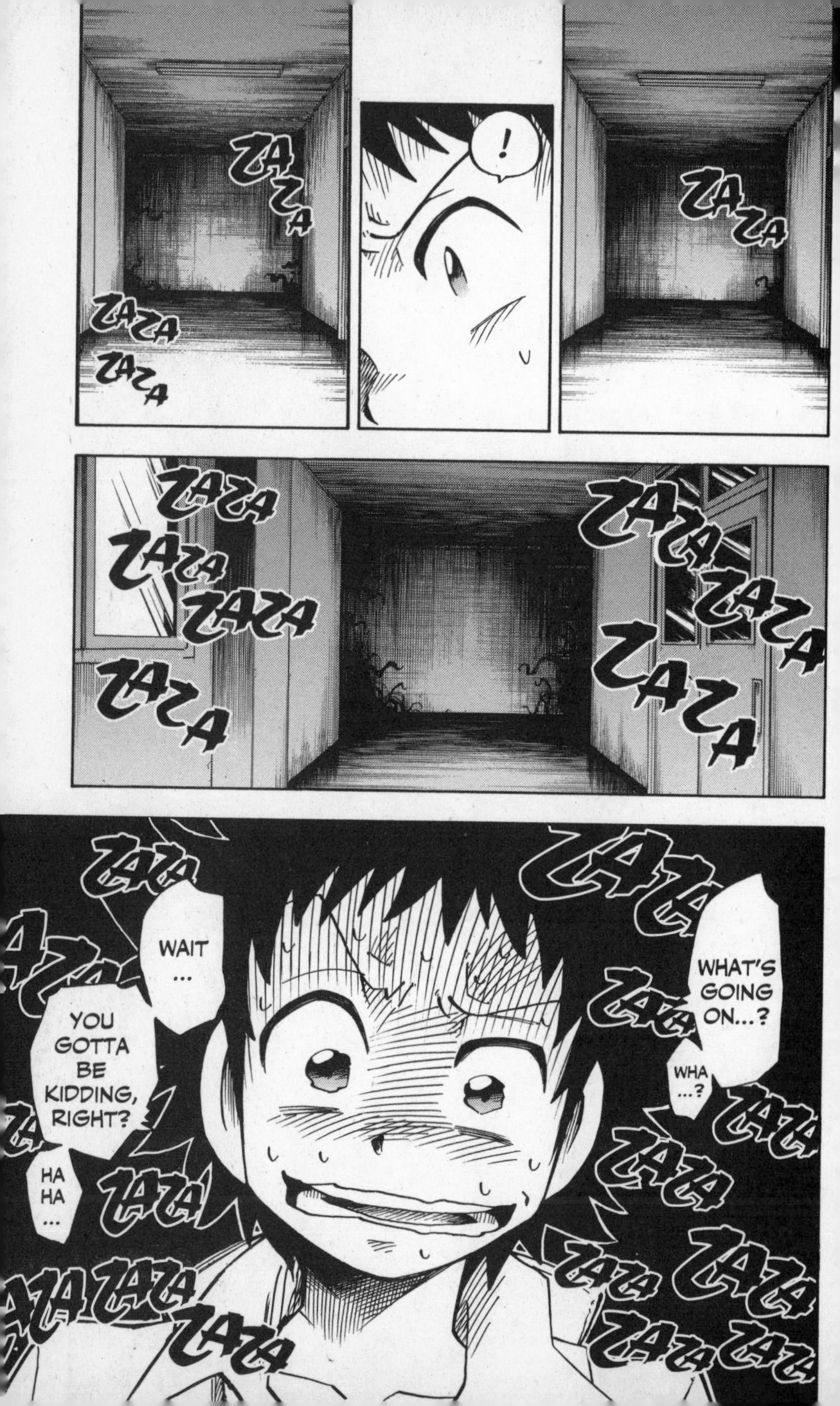

ZAZA
!
ZAZA
ZAZA
ZAZA
ZAZA
ZAZA
ZAZA
ZAZA
ZAZA
ZAZA
ZAZA
ZAZA
WHAT'S GOING ON...?
WHA...?
WAIT...
YOU GOTTA BE KIDDING, RIGHT?
HA HA...
ZAZA
ZAZA
ZAZA
ZAZA
ZAZA
ZAZA
ZAZA
ZAZA

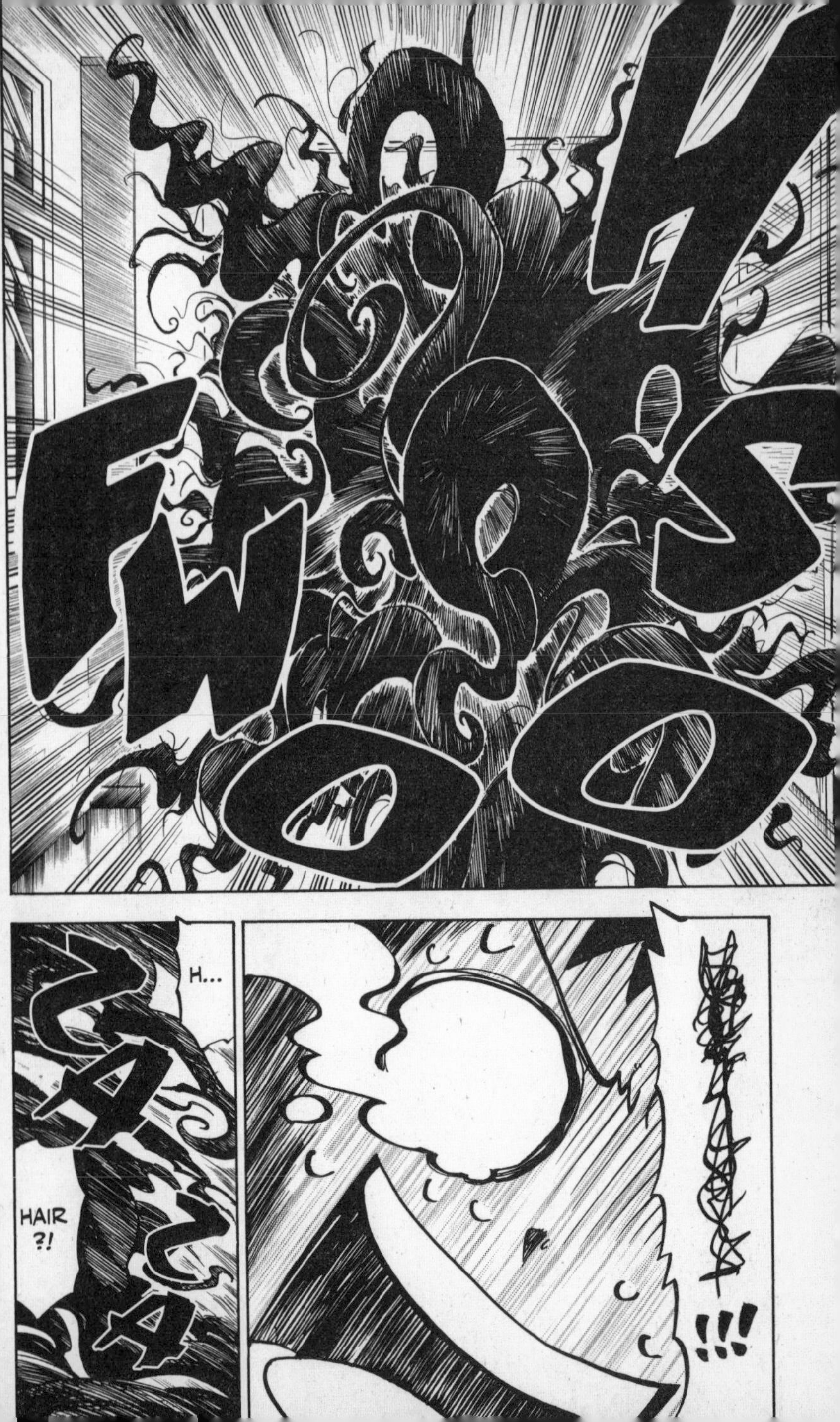
!!!
H...
HAIR ?!

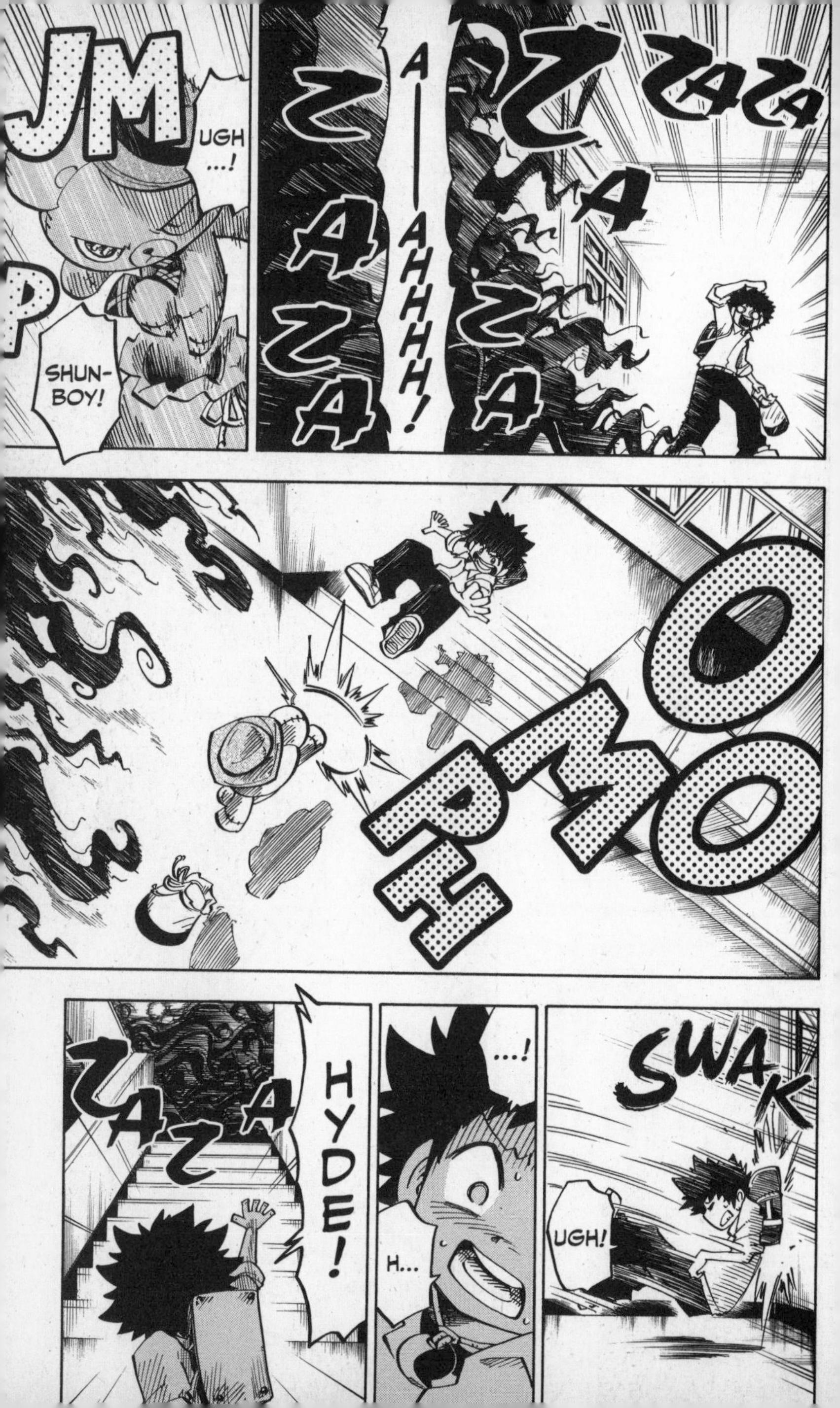

ZAZA
A—AHHHH!
UGH ...!
SHUN-BOY!
SWAK
UGH!
...!
H...
HYDE!

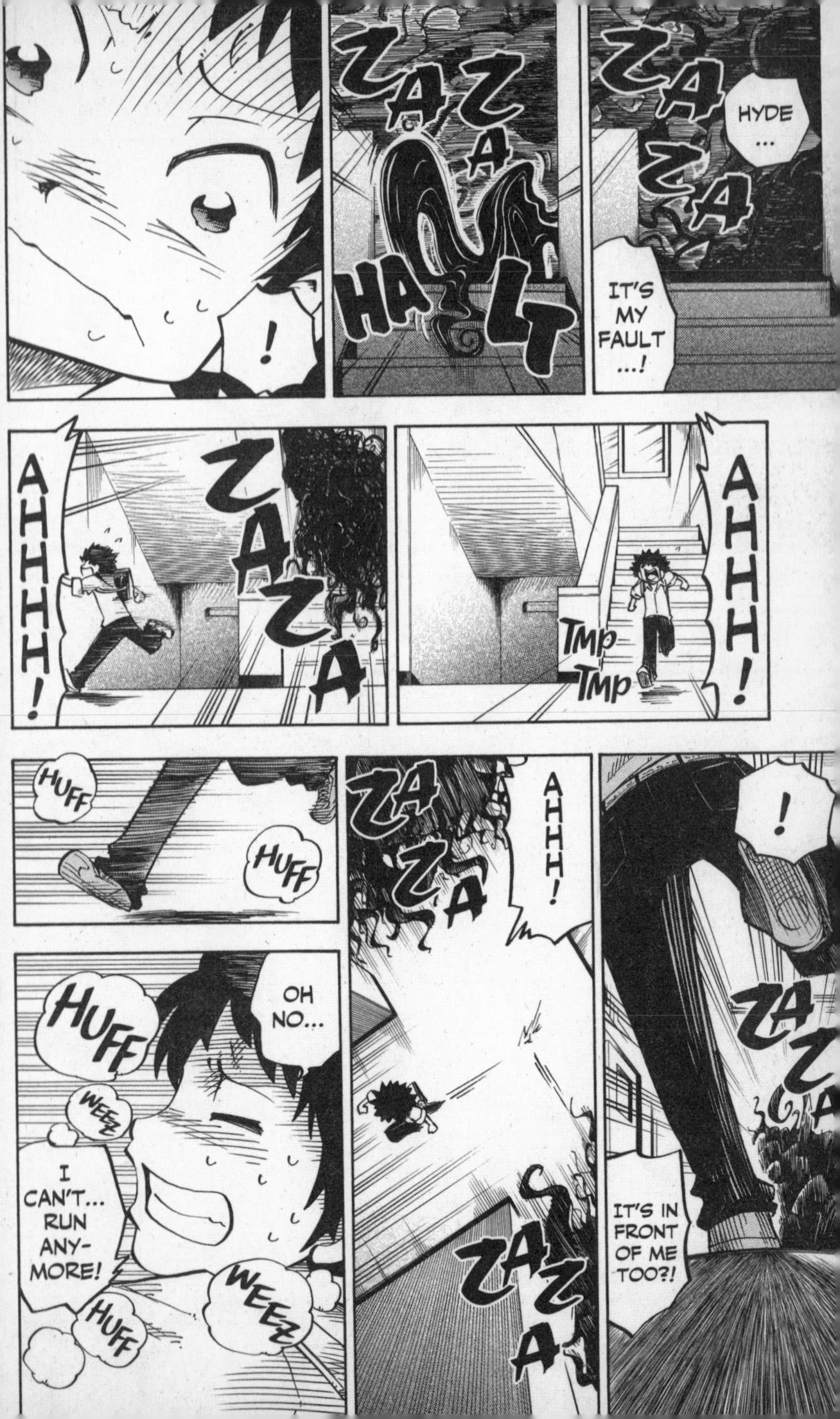
ZA ZA ZA ZA
HYDE...
IT'S MY FAULT...!
ZA ZA ZA
HALT
!
AHHHH!
TMP TMP
AHHHHH!
ZA ZA ZA
!
ZA ZA ZA
IT'S IN FRONT OF ME TOO?!
ZA ZA ZA
AHHH!
ZA ZA
HUFF
HUFF
OH NO...
HUFF
WEEZ
I CAN'T... RUN ANYMORE!
WEEZ
HUFF

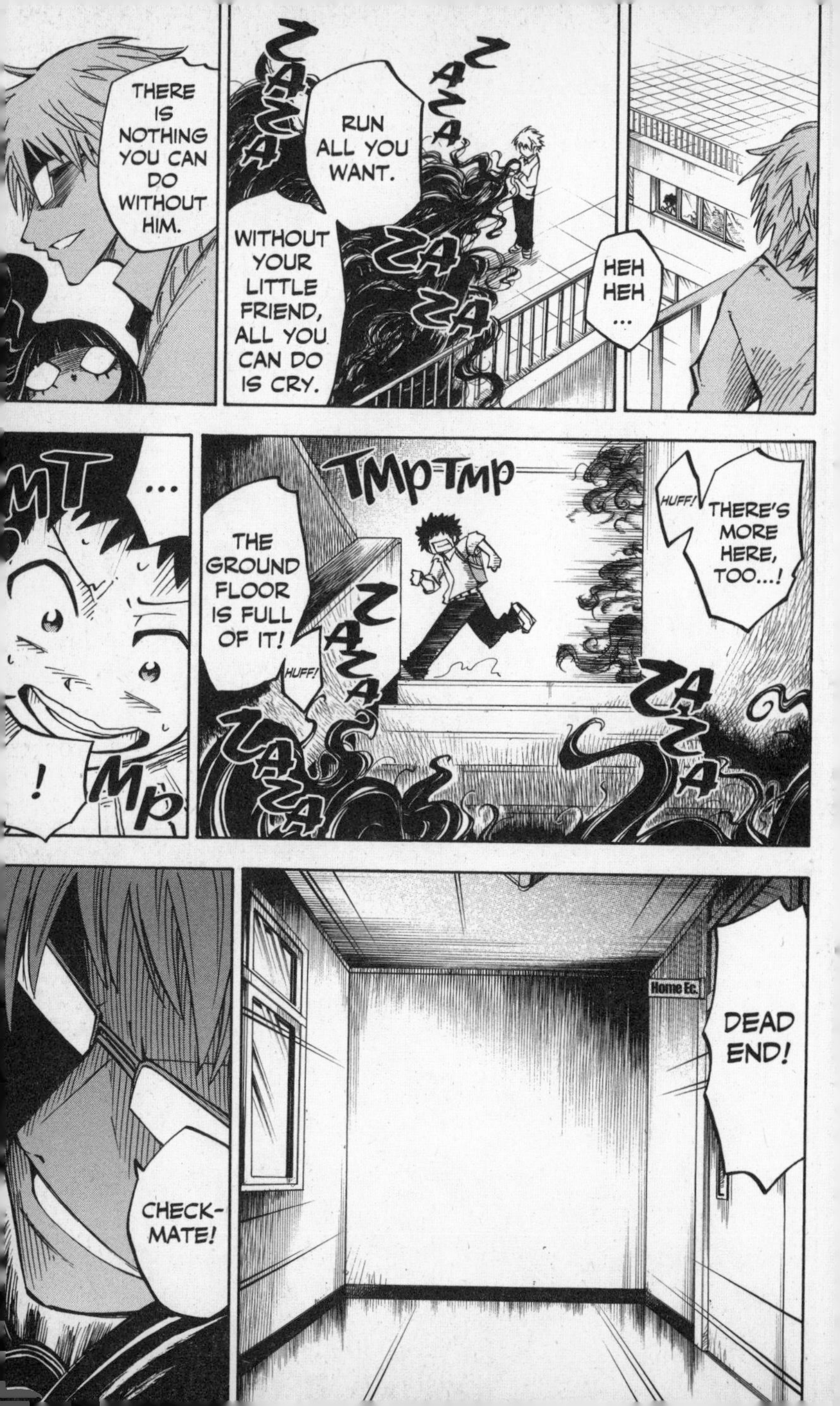
HEH HEH ...
ZA ZA ZA
RUN ALL YOU WANT.
WITHOUT YOUR LITTLE FRIEND, ALL YOU CAN DO IS CRY.
ZA ZA ZA
ZA ZA
THERE IS NOTHING YOU CAN DO WITHOUT HIM.
HUFF!
THERE'S MORE HERE, TOO...!
TMP TMP
ZA ZA ZA
THE GROUND FLOOR IS FULL OF IT!
HUFF!
ZA ZA ZA
ZA ZA ZA
MT
...
!
MP
Home Ec.
DEAD END!
CHECK-MATE!

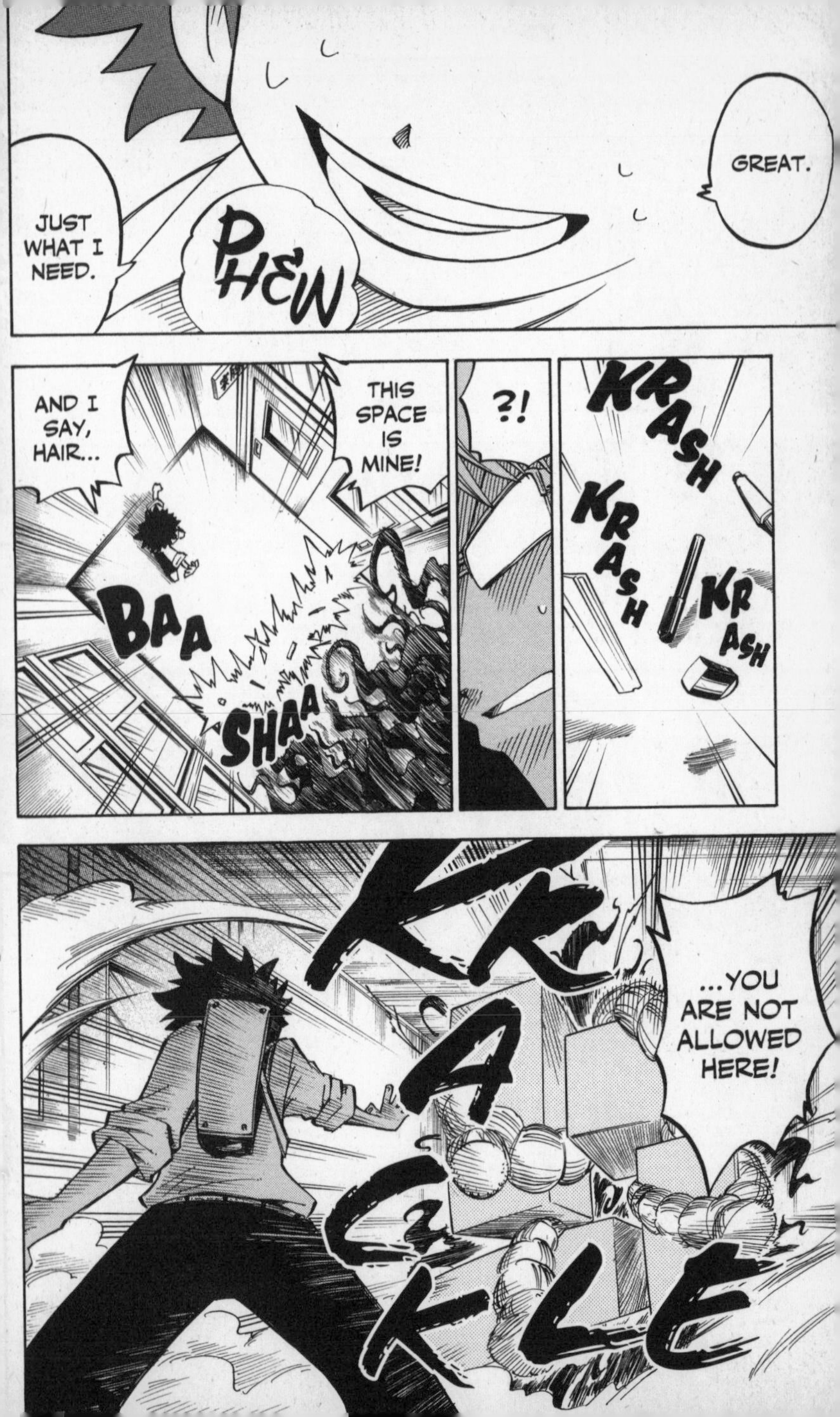
GREAT.
PHEW
JUST WHAT I NEED.
KRASH
KRASH
KRASH
?!
THIS SPACE IS MINE!
AND I SAY, HAIR...
BAA
SHAA
...YOU ARE NOT ALLOWED HERE!
KRACKLE

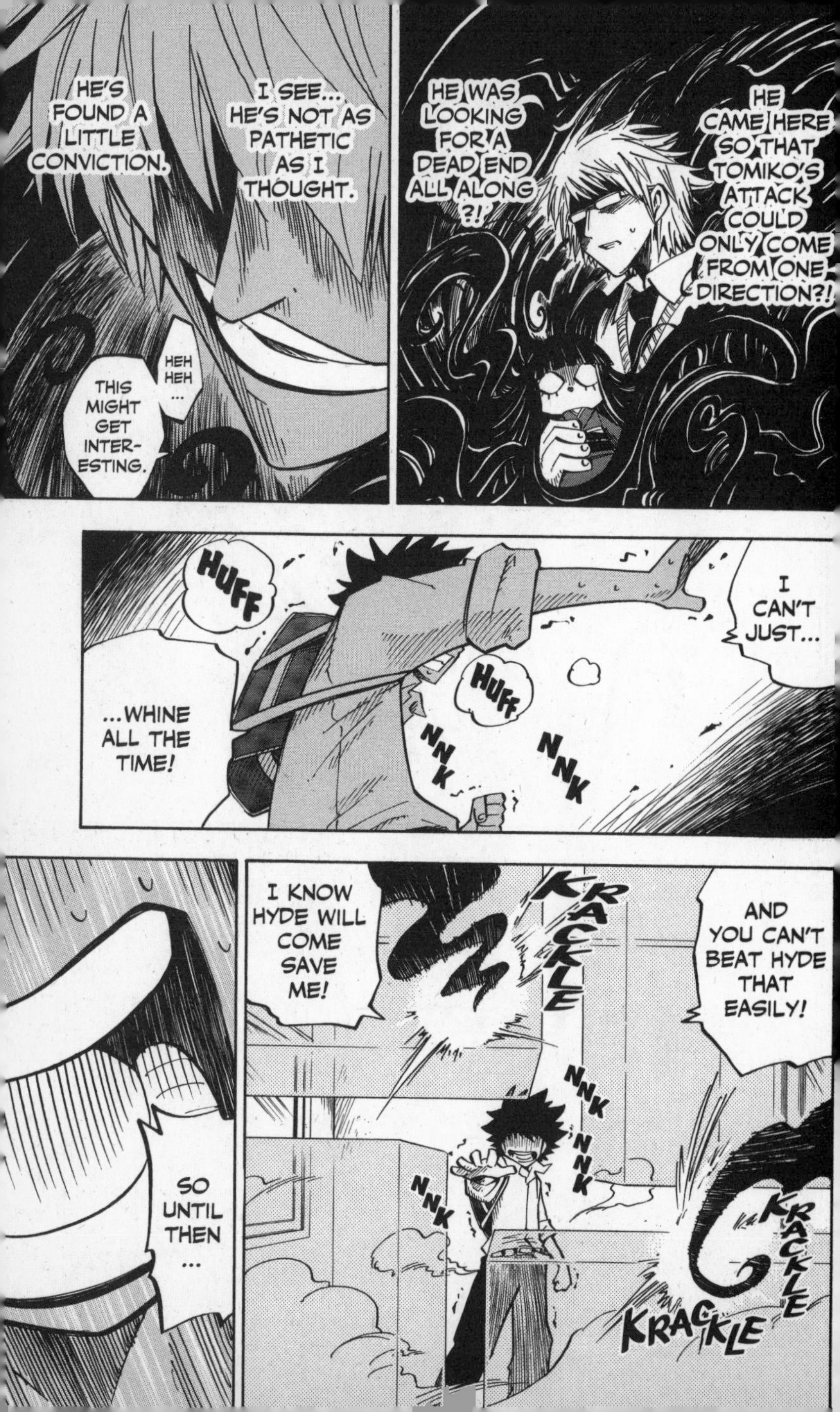
HE CAME HERE SO THAT TOMIKO'S ATTACK COULD ONLY COME FROM ONE DIRECTION?!
HE WAS LOOKING FOR A DEAD END ALL ALONG?!
I SEE... HE'S NOT AS PATHETIC AS I THOUGHT.
HE'S FOUND A LITTLE CONVICTION.
HEH HEH...
THIS MIGHT GET INTER-ESTING.
I CAN'T JUST...
HUFF
HUFF
NNK
NNK
...WHINE ALL THE TIME!
AND YOU CAN'T BEAT HYDE THAT EASILY!
KRACKLE
I KNOW HYDE WILL COME SAVE ME!
KRACKLE
KRACKLE
NNK
NNK
NNK
NNK
SO UNTIL THEN...

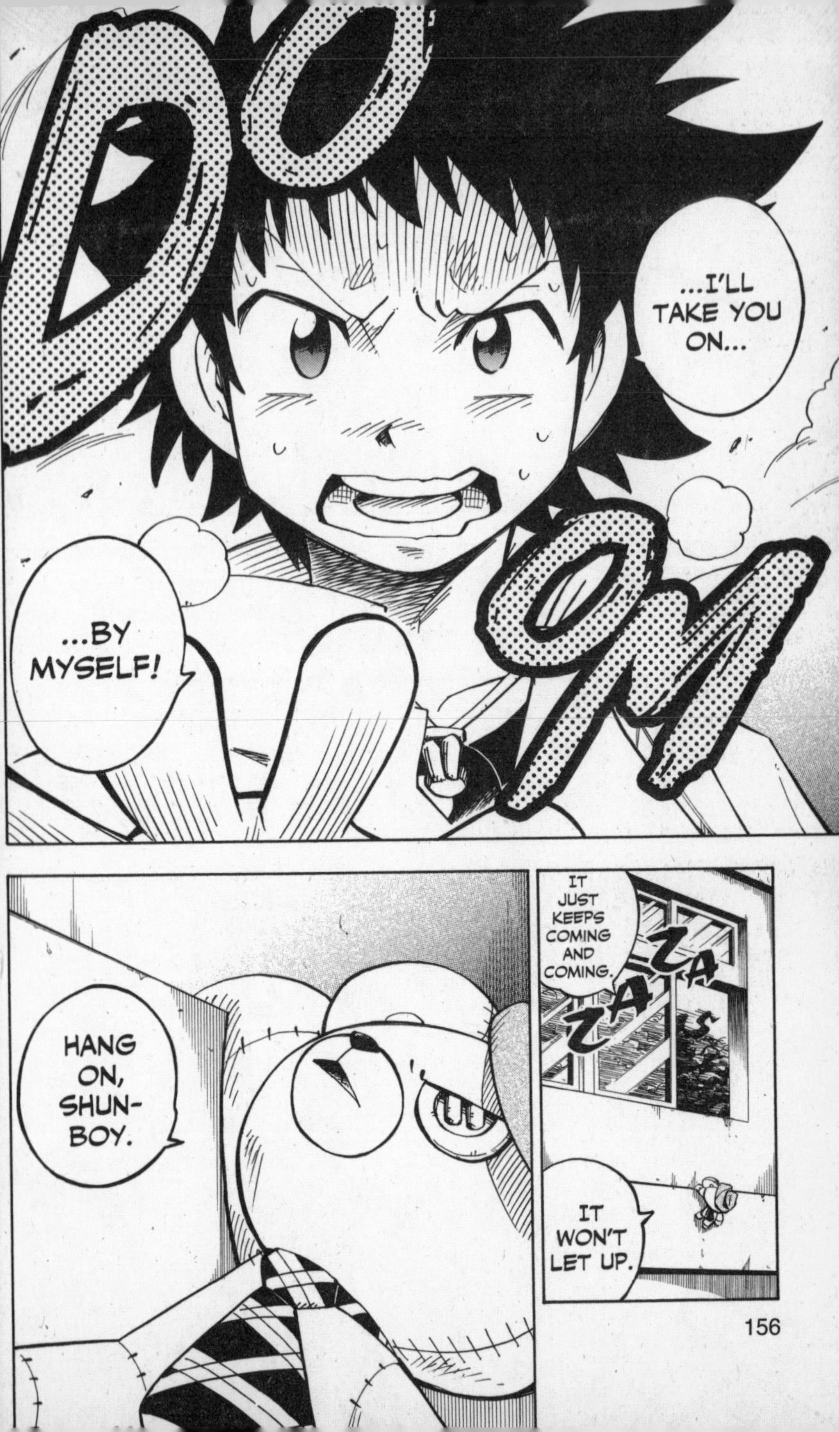
DOOM
...I'LL TAKE YOU ON...
...BY MYSELF!
IT JUST KEEPS COMING AND COMING.
ZA ZA ZA
IT WON'T LET UP.
HANG ON, SHUN-BOY.

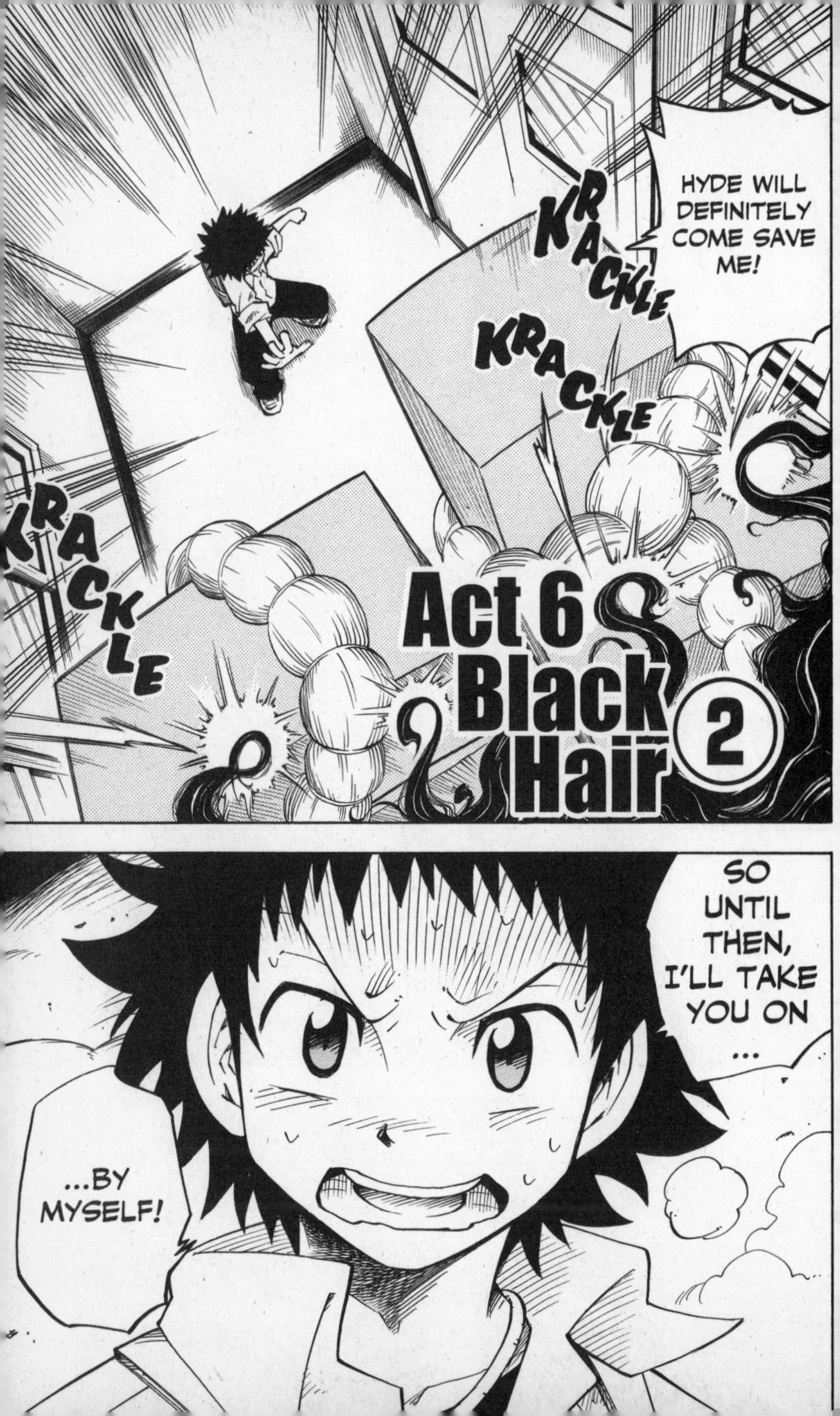
HYDE WILL DEFINITELY COME SAVE ME!
KRACKLE
KRACKLE
KRACKLE
Act 6 Black Hair 2
SO UNTIL THEN, I'LL TAKE YOU ON ...
...BY MYSELF!

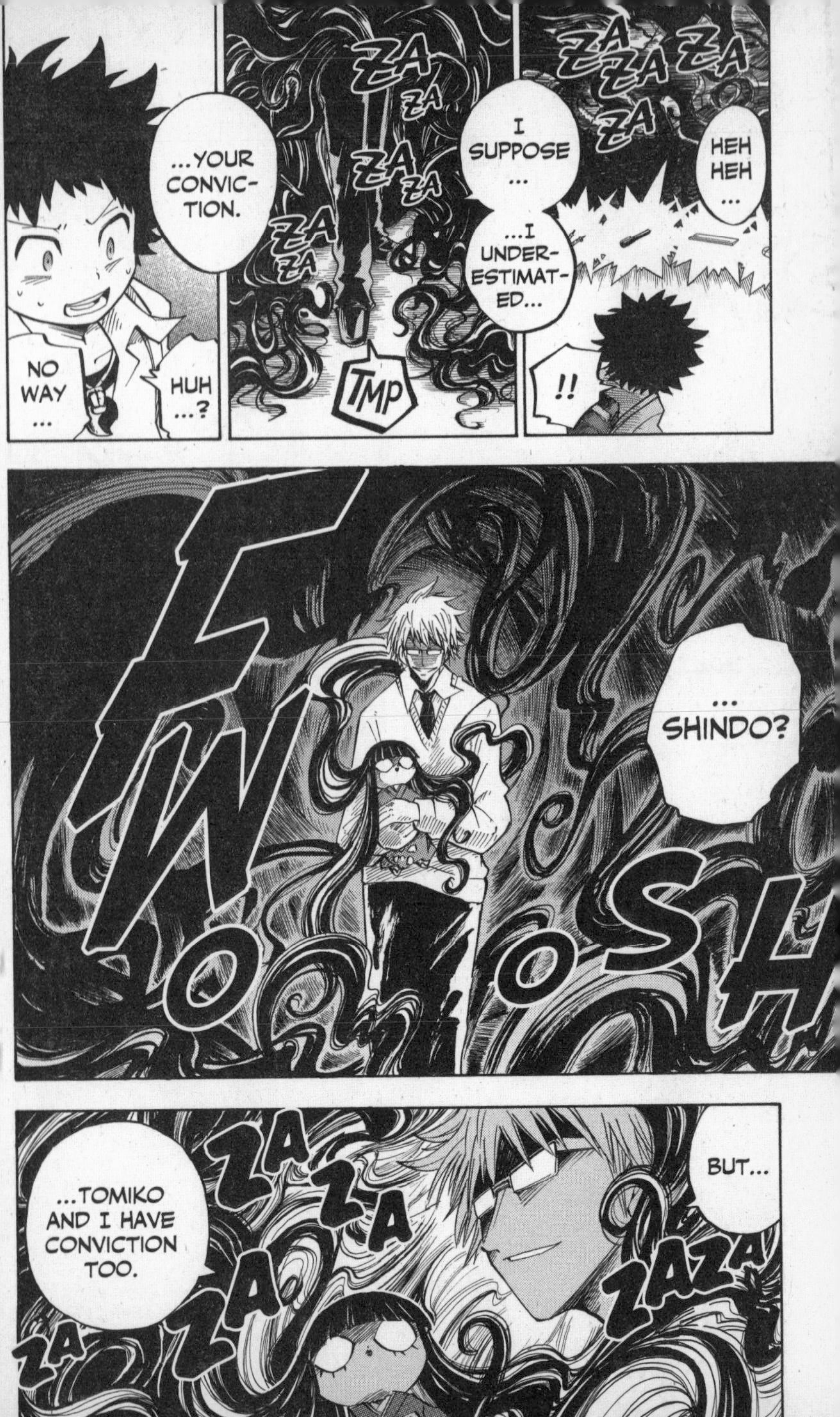
ZA ZA ZA ZA ZA
HEH HEH ...
!!
ZA ZA ZA ZA ZA ZA ZA ZA
I SUPPOSE ...
...I UNDER-ESTIMAT-ED...
TMP
...YOUR CONVIC-TION.
HUH ...?
NO WAY ...
WHOOOSH
... SHINDO?
BUT...
...TOMIKO AND I HAVE CONVICTION TOO.
ZAZA ZA ZA ZA ZA

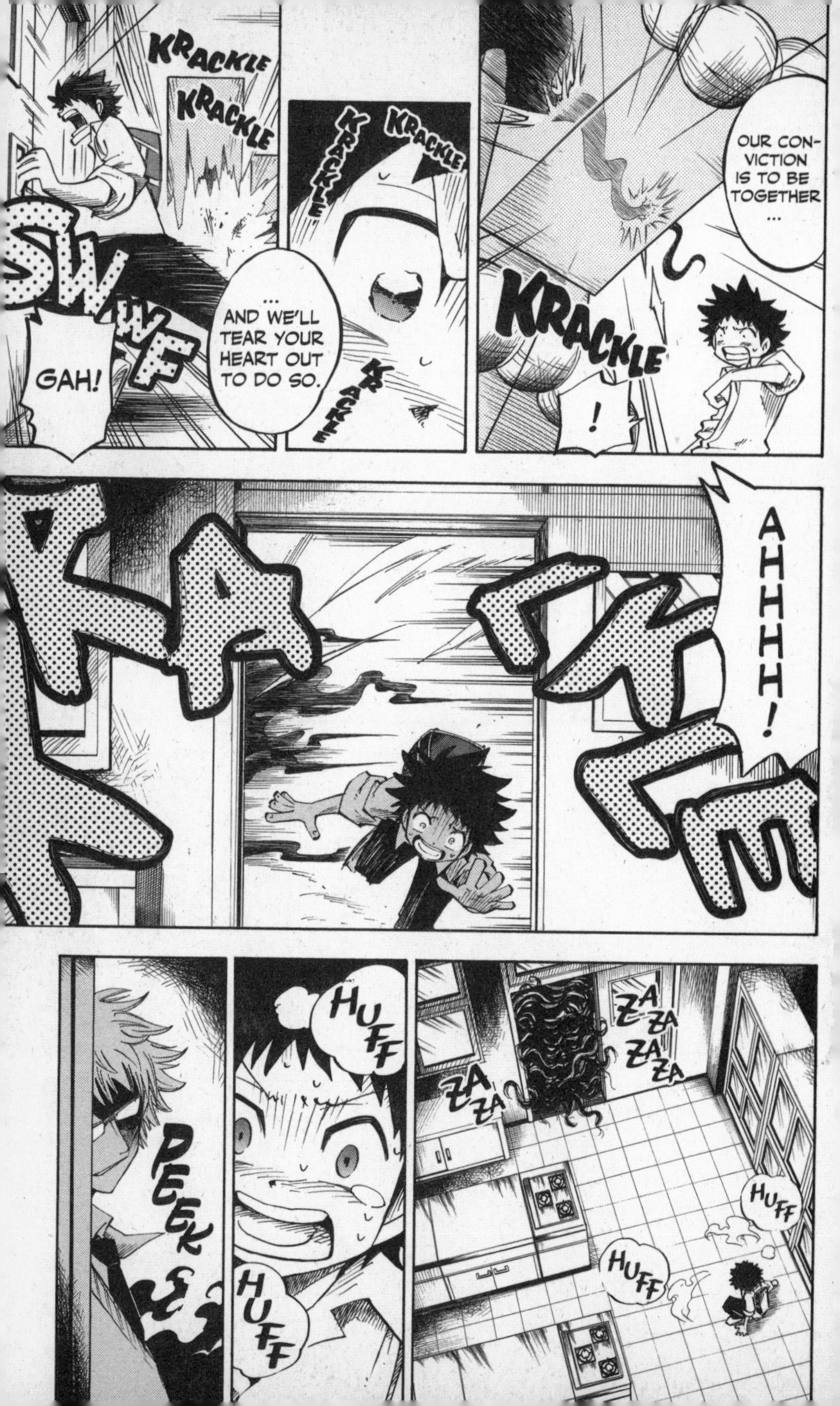
OUR CONVICTION IS TO BE TOGETHER...
KRACKLE
!
KRACKLE
KRACKLE
... AND WE'LL TEAR YOUR HEART OUT TO DO SO.
KRACKLE
KRACKLE
KRACKLE
GAH!
AHHHH!
ZA ZA ZA ZA ZA
ZA ZA
HUFF
HUFF
HUFF
HUFF
PEEEK

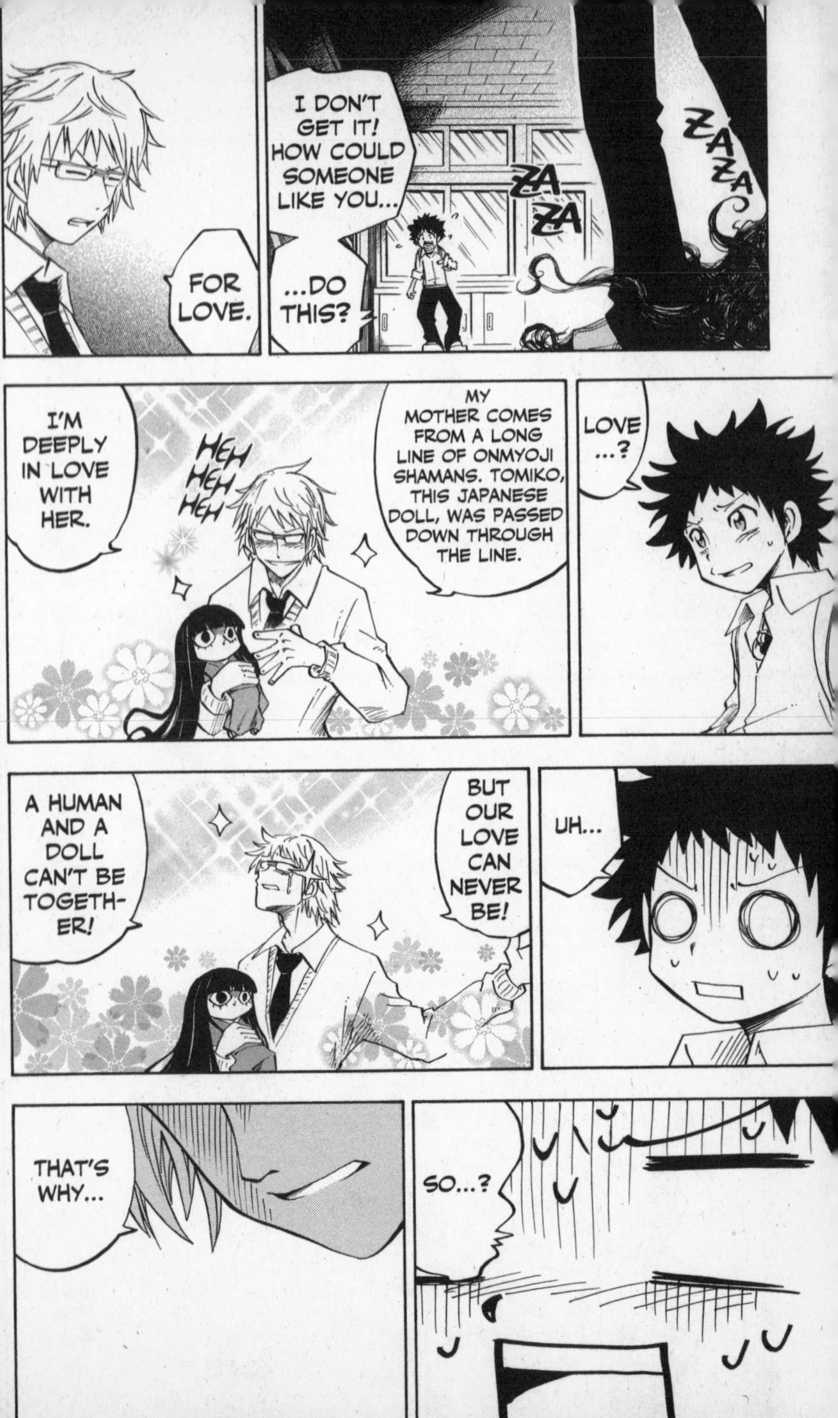
ZAZA
I DON'T GET IT! HOW COULD SOMEONE LIKE YOU...
ZA ZA
...DO THIS?
FOR LOVE.
LOVE ...?
MY MOTHER COMES FROM A LONG LINE OF ONMYOJI SHAMANS. TOMIKO, THIS JAPANESE DOLL, WAS PASSED DOWN THROUGH THE LINE.
HEH HEH HEH
I'M DEEPLY IN LOVE WITH HER.
UH...
BUT OUR LOVE CAN NEVER BE!
A HUMAN AND A DOLL CAN'T BE TOGETH-ER!
SO...?
THAT'S WHY...

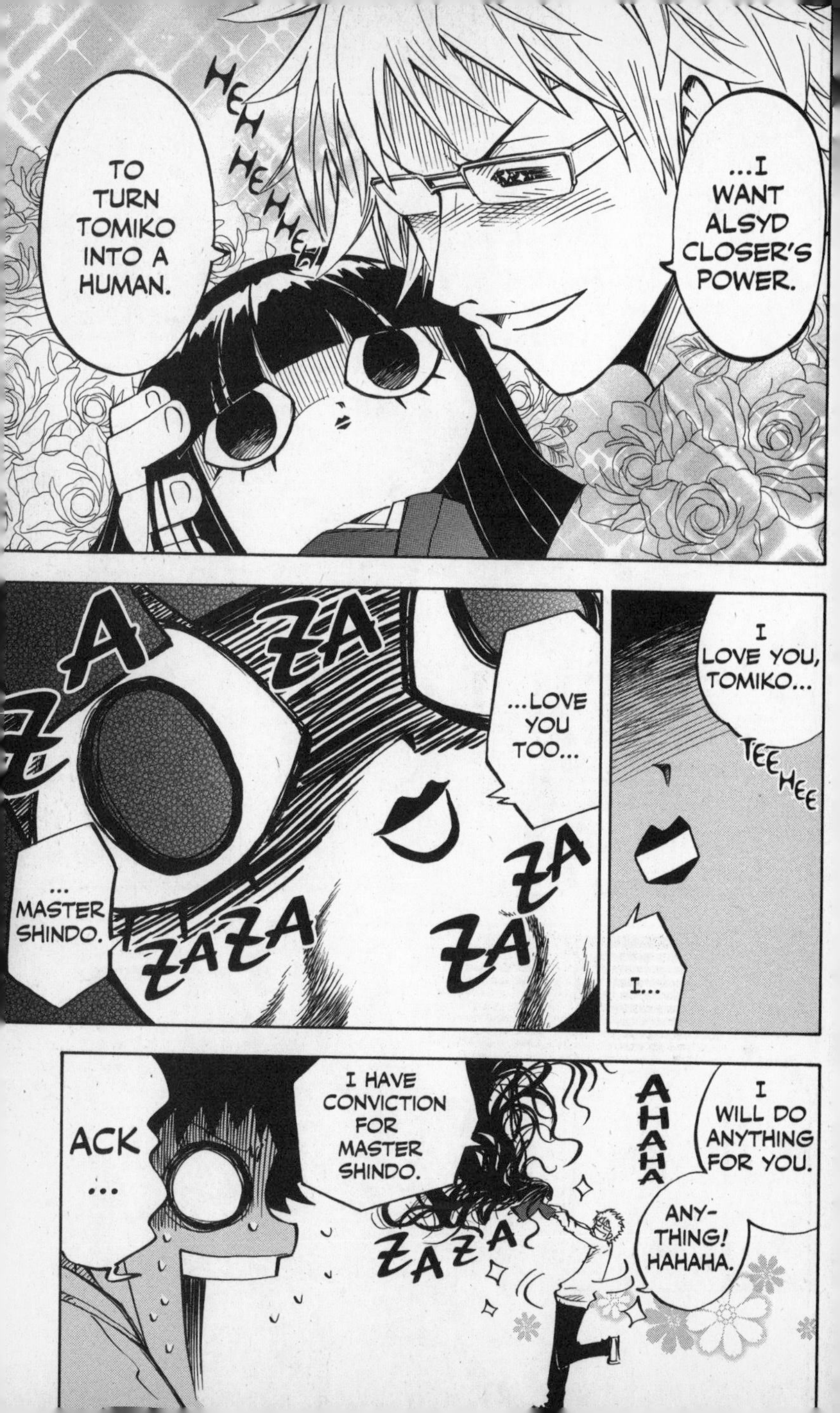
...I WANT ALSYD CLOSER'S POWER.
HEH HEH HEH HEH
TO TURN TOMIKO INTO A HUMAN.
I LOVE YOU, TOMIKO...
TEE HEE
I...
...LOVE YOU TOO...
ZAZA
ZAZA
ZAZA
... MASTER SHINDO.
ZAZA
I WILL DO ANYTHING FOR YOU.
AHAHA
ANY-THING! HAHAHA.
ZAZA
I HAVE CONVICTION FOR MASTER SHINDO.
ACK ...

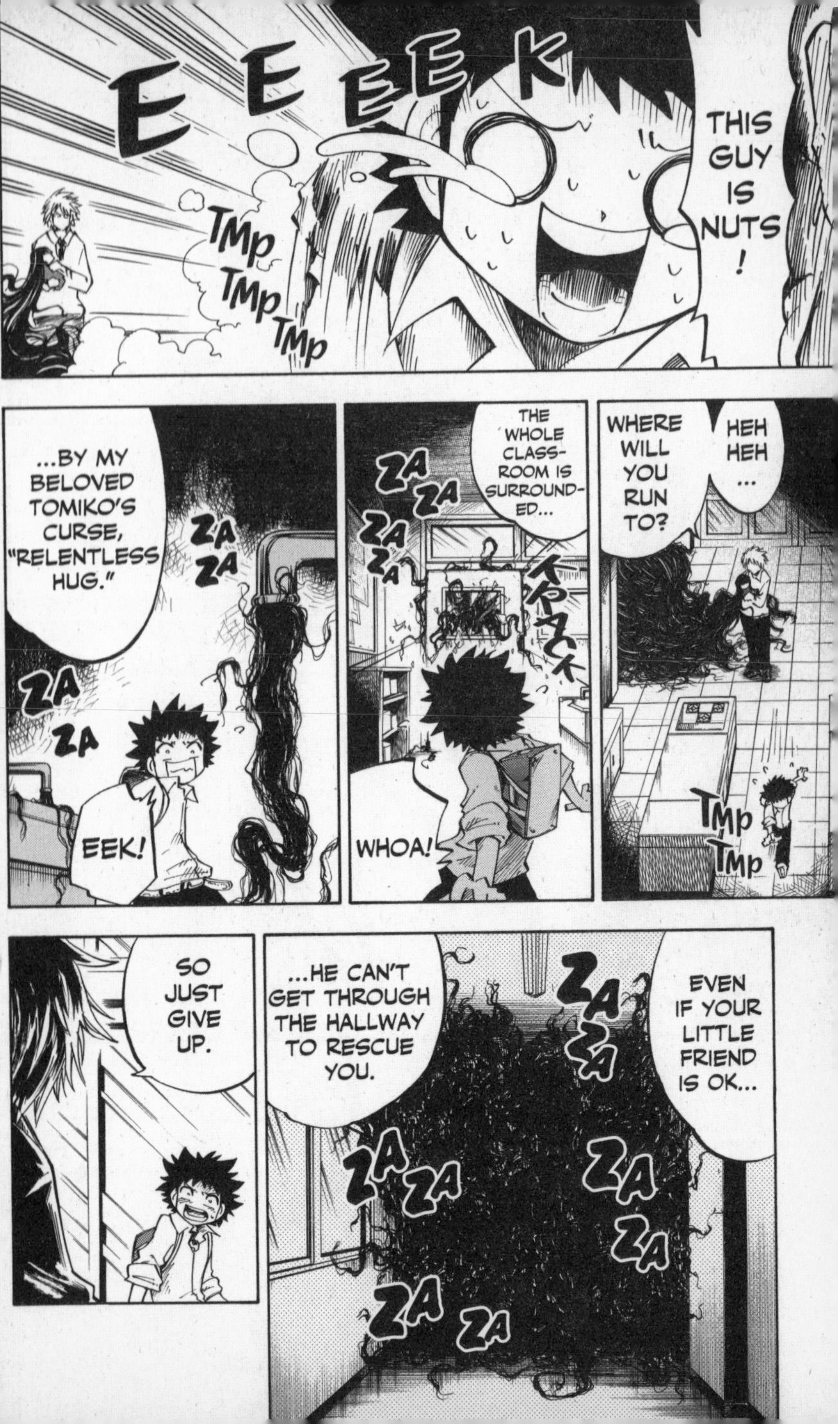
THIS GUY IS NUTS!
EEEEK
TMp TMp TMp
HEH HEH ...
WHERE WILL YOU RUN TO?
TMp TMp
THE WHOLE CLASS-ROOM IS SURROUND-ED...
ZA ZA ZA ZA
KRACK
WHOA!
...BY MY BELOVED TOMIKO'S CURSE, "RELENTLESS HUG."
ZA ZA
ZA ZA
EEK!
EVEN IF YOUR LITTLE FRIEND IS OK...
...HE CAN'T GET THROUGH THE HALLWAY TO RESCUE YOU.
ZA ZA
ZA ZA
ZA ZA
ZA ZA
SO JUST GIVE UP.

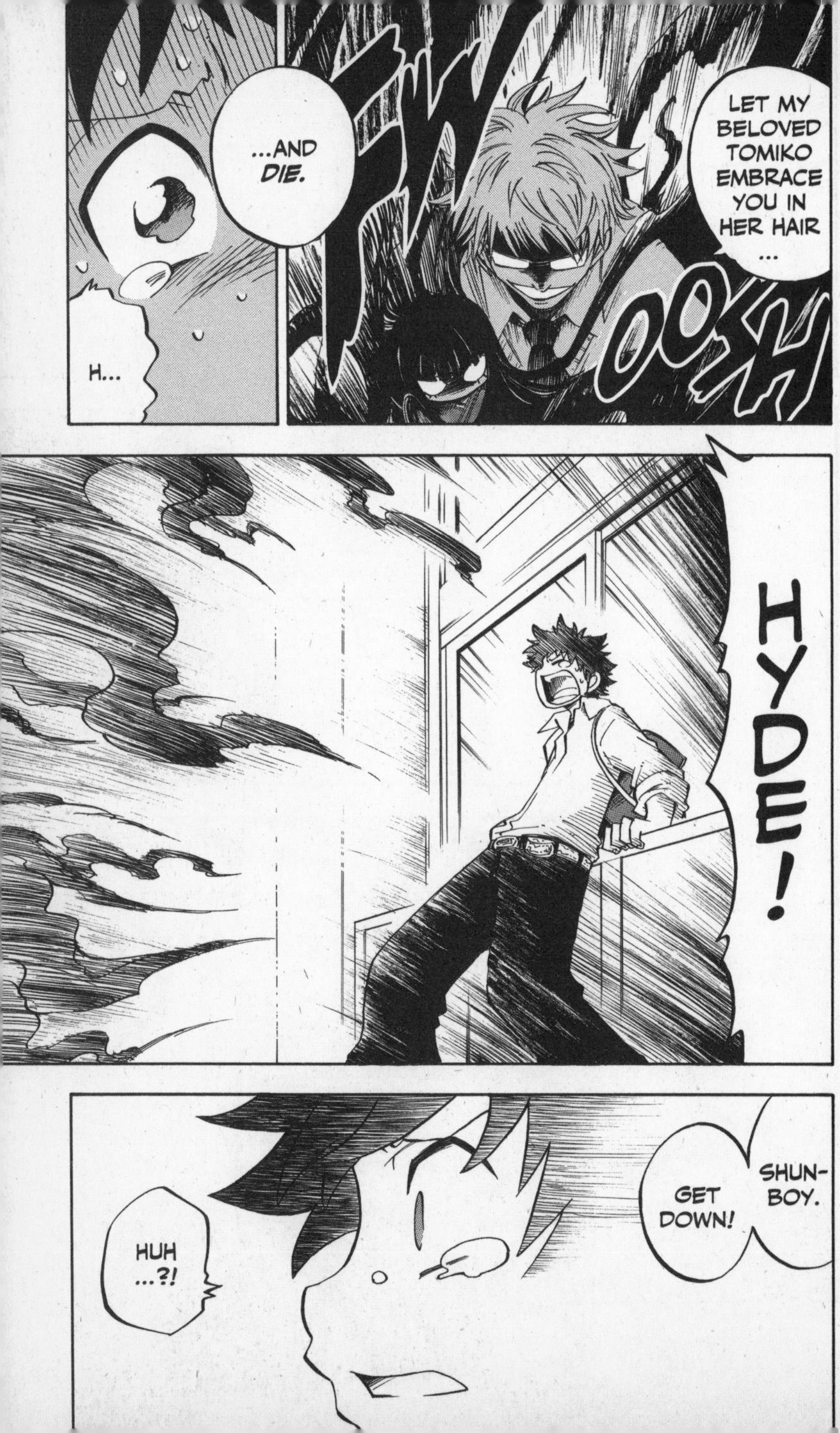

LET MY BELOVED TOMIKO EMBRACE YOU IN HER HAIR ...
...AND DIE.
H...
HYDE!
SHUN-BOY.
GET DOWN!
HUH ...?!

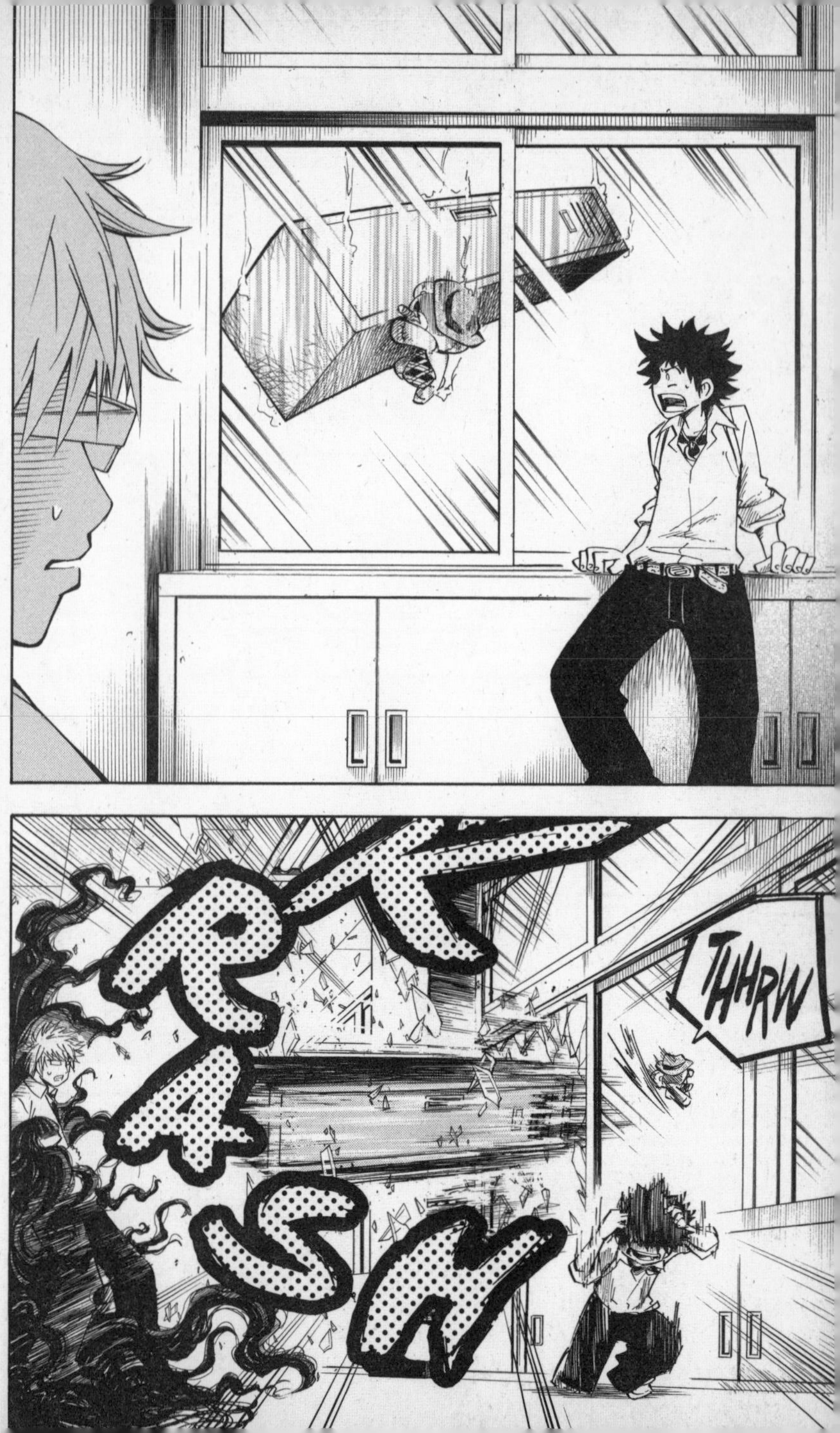
THHRW
KRASH

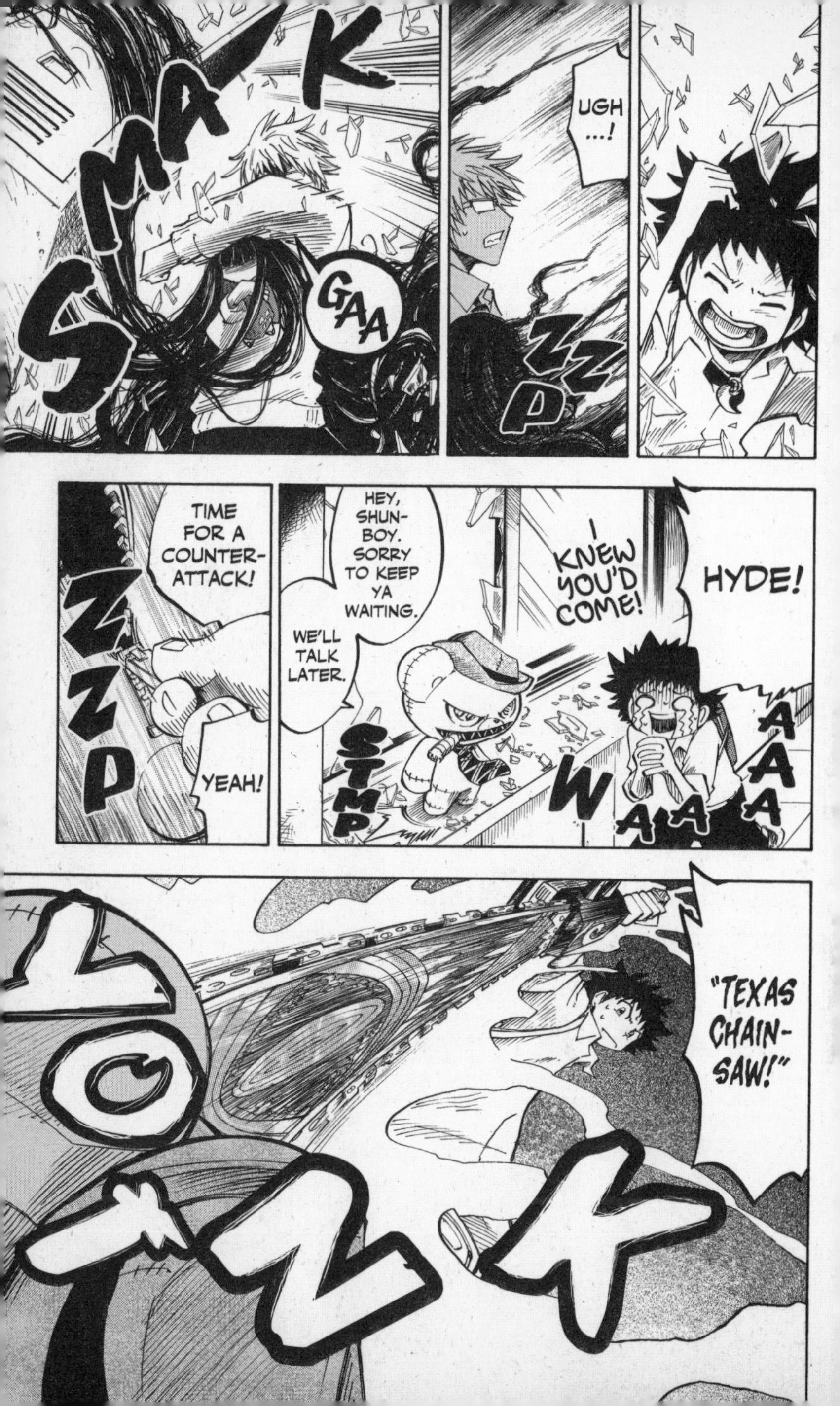
UGH ...!
ZZZP
SMAK
GAA
HYDE!
I KNEW YOU'D COME!
WAAAAAA
HEY, SHUN-BOY. SORRY TO KEEP YA WAITING.
WE'LL TALK LATER.
STMP
TIME FOR A COUNTER-ATTACK!
ZZZP
YEAH!
"TEXAS CHAIN-SAW!"

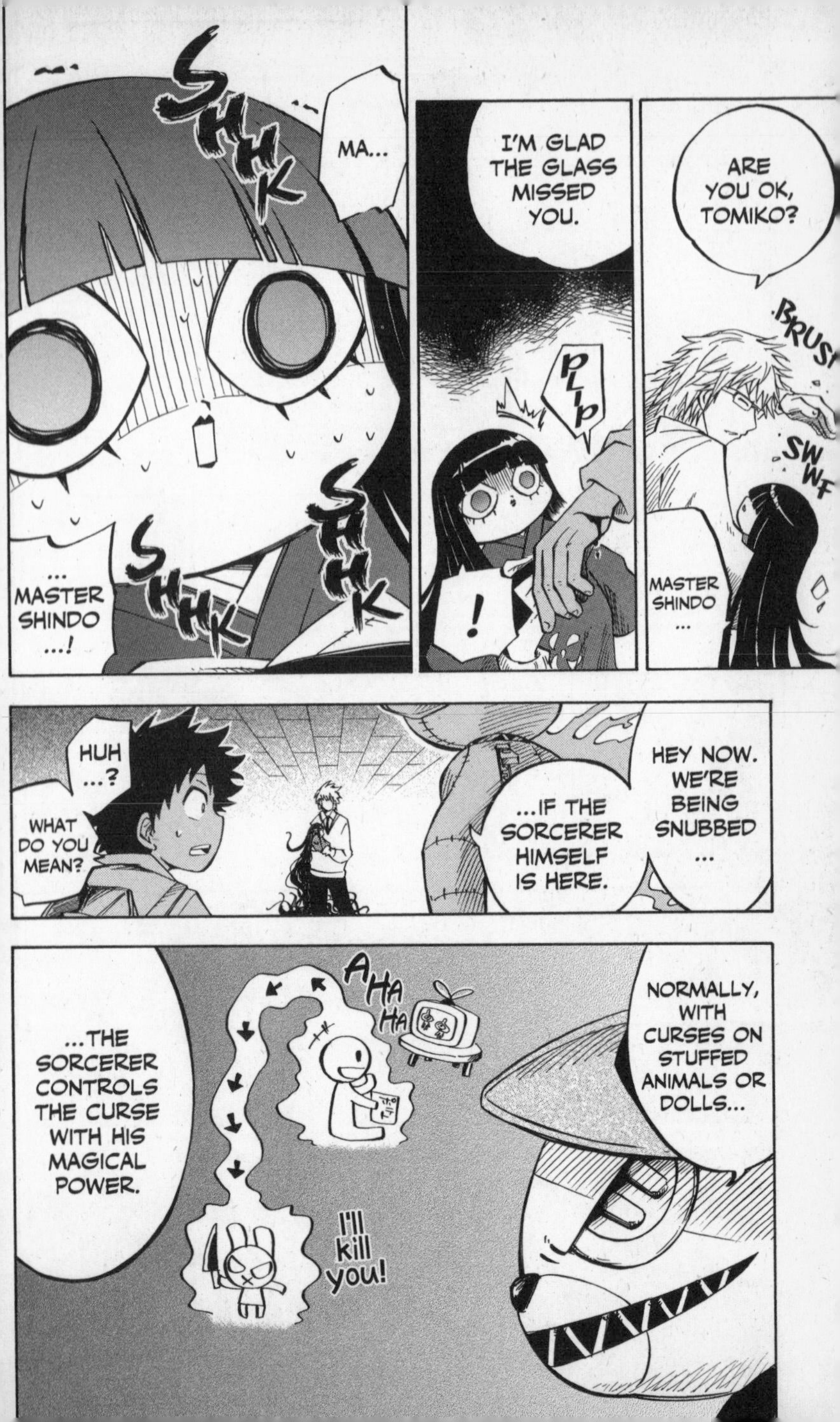

ARE YOU OK, TOMIKO?
BRUS
SWWF
MASTER SHINDO ...
I'M GLAD THE GLASS MISSED YOU.
PLIP
!
MA...
SHHK
SHHK
SHHK
... MASTER SHINDO ...!
HEY NOW. WE'RE BEING SNUBBED ...
...IF THE SORCERER HIMSELF IS HERE.
HUH ...?
WHAT DO YOU MEAN?
NORMALLY, WITH CURSES ON STUFFED ANIMALS OR DOLLS...
AHAHA
...THE SORCERER CONTROLS THE CURSE WITH HIS MAGICAL POWER.
I'll kill you!

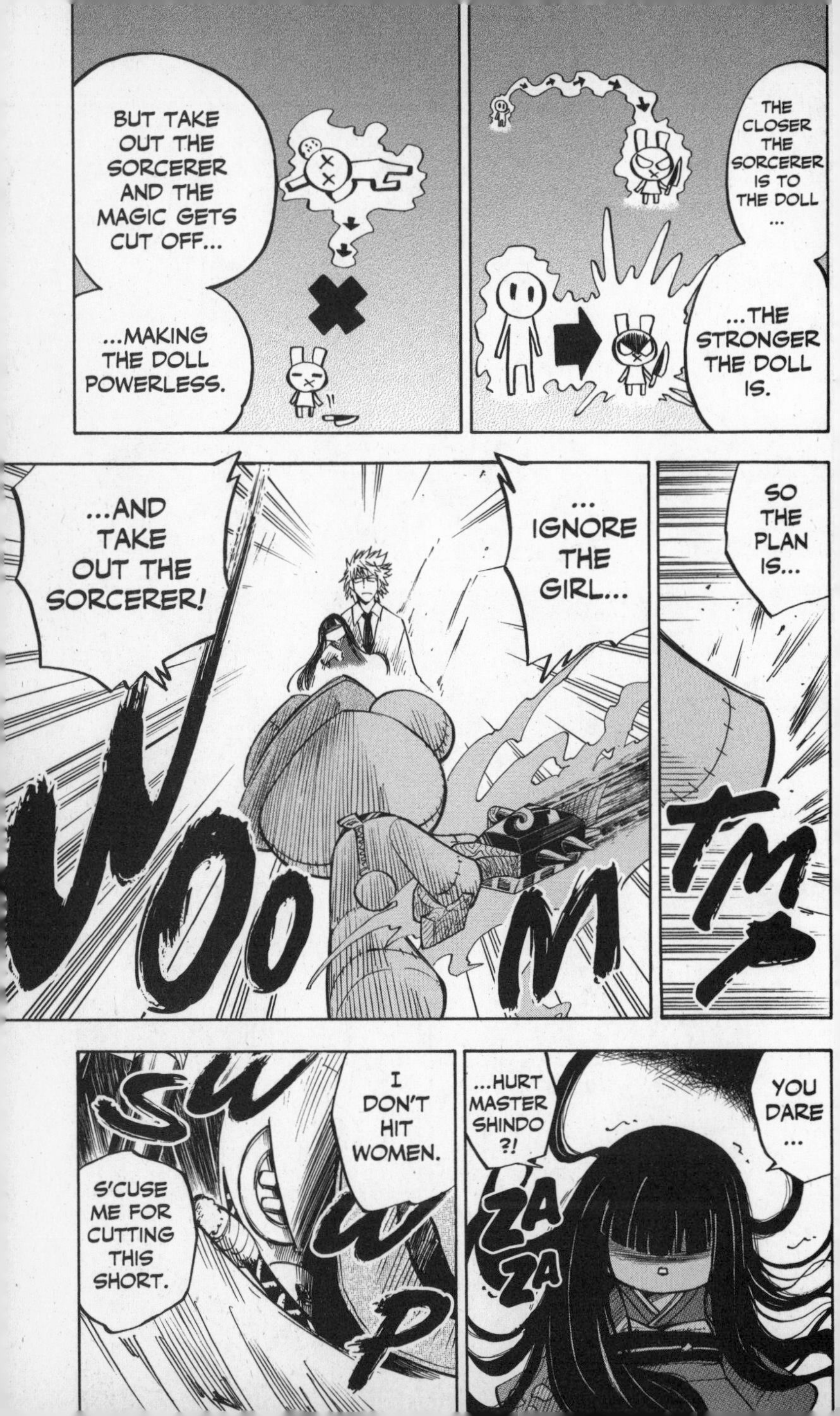
THE CLOSER THE SORCERER IS TO THE DOLL ...
...THE STRONGER THE DOLL IS.
BUT TAKE OUT THE SORCERER AND THE MAGIC GETS CUT OFF...
...MAKING THE DOLL POWERLESS.
SO THE PLAN IS...
TMP
... IGNORE THE GIRL...
...AND TAKE OUT THE SORCERER!
VOOM
YOU DARE ...
...HURT MASTER SHINDO ?!
ZA ZA
I DON'T HIT WOMEN.
S'CUSE ME FOR CUTTING THIS SHORT.

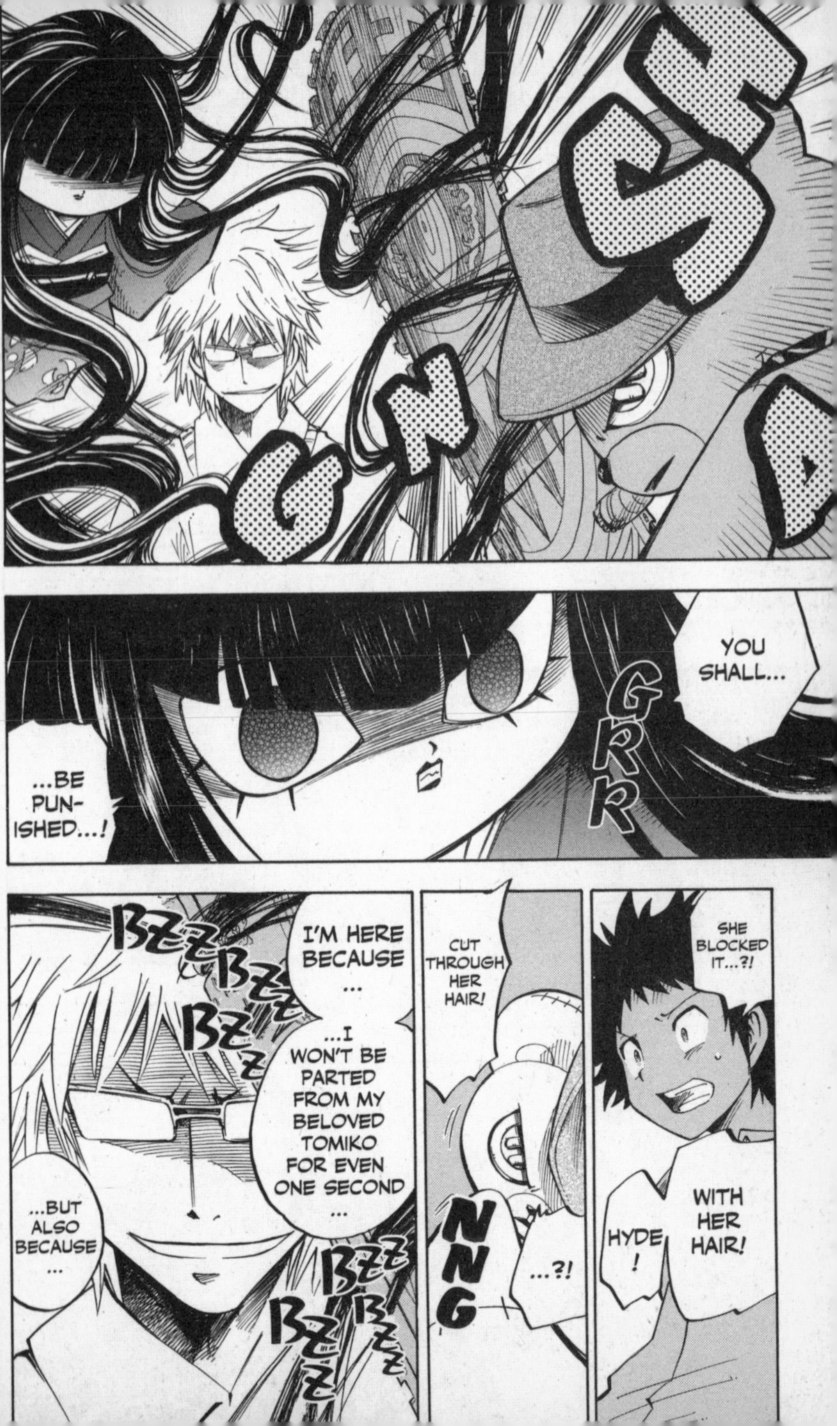
YOU SHALL...
GRRR
...BE PUN-ISHED...!
SHE BLOCKED IT...?!
WITH HER HAIR!
HYDE!
CUT THROUGH HER HAIR!
NNG
...?!
BZZ BZZ BZZ
I'M HERE BECAUSE ...
...I WON'T BE PARTED FROM MY BELOVED TOMIKO FOR EVEN ONE SECOND ...
...BUT ALSO BECAUSE ...
BZZ BZZ BZZ

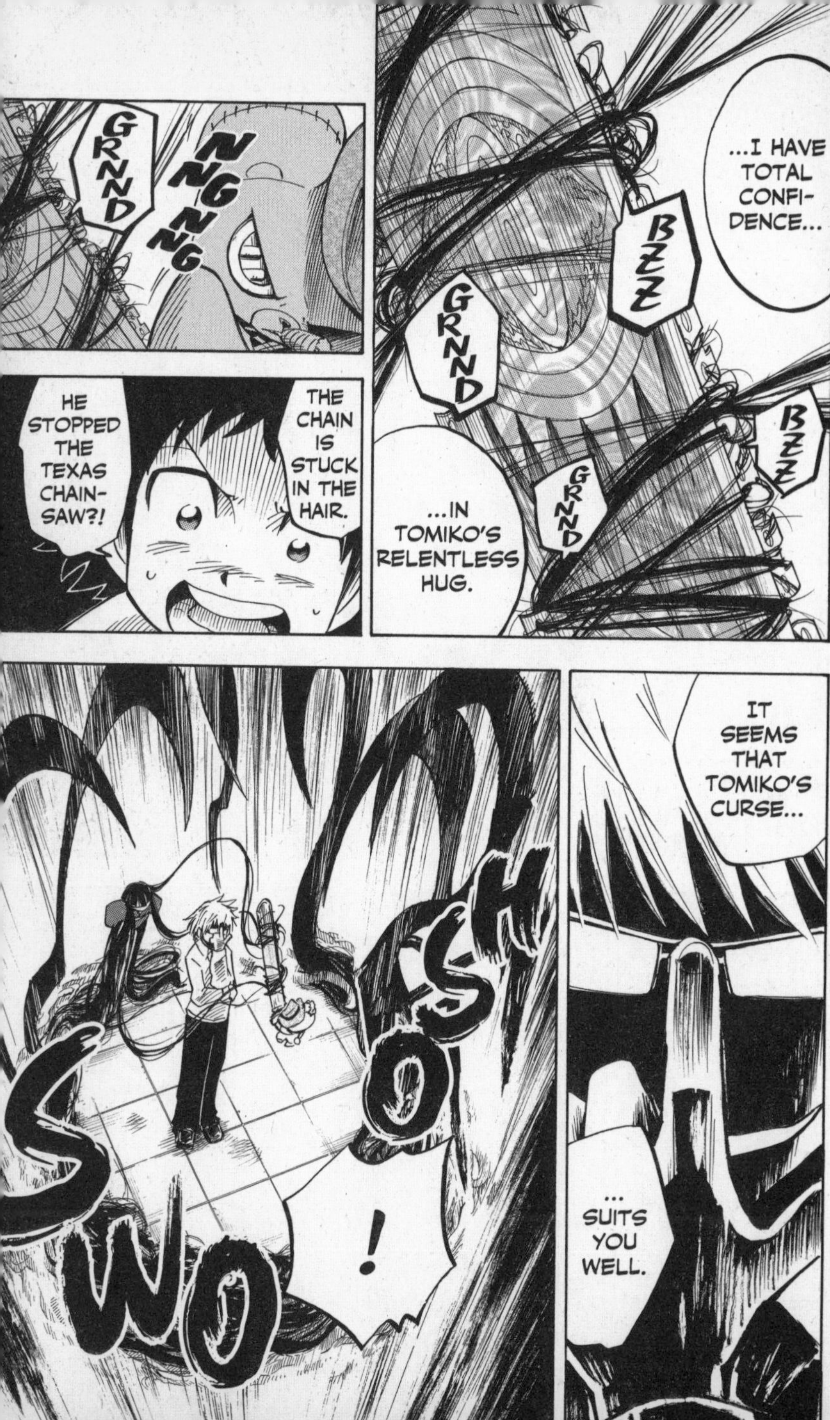
...I HAVE TOTAL CONFIDENCE...
BZZZ
GRNND
BZZZ
...IN TOMIKO'S RELENTLESS HUG.
GRNND
NNGNGNG
GRNND
THE CHAIN IS STUCK IN THE HAIR.
HE STOPPED THE TEXAS CHAIN-SAW?!
IT SEEMS THAT TOMIKO'S CURSE...
... SUITS YOU WELL.
SWOOSH
!

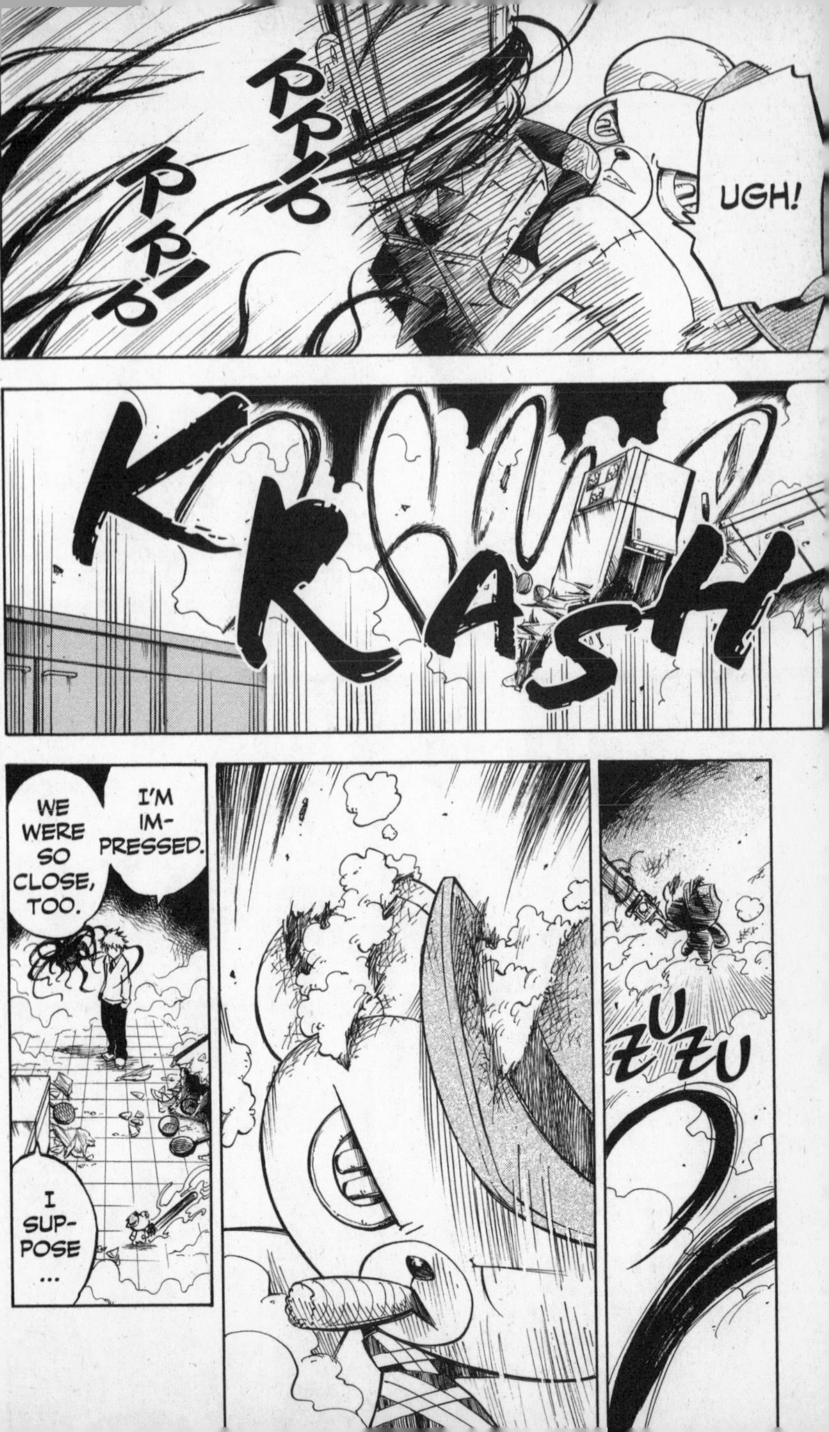
UGH!
KRASH
ZUZU
I'M IM-PRESSED.
WE WERE SO CLOSE, TOO.
I SUP-POSE ...

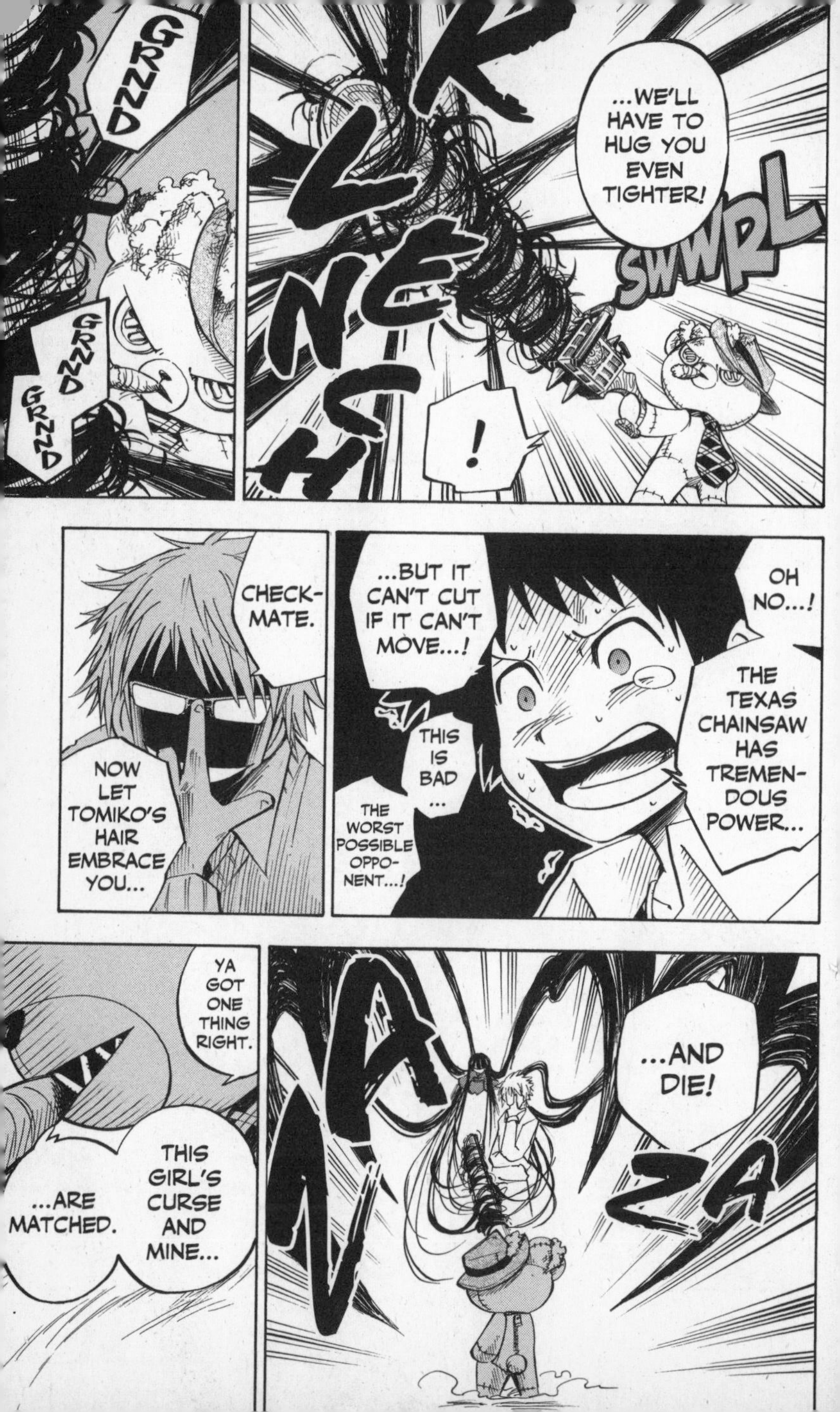
...WE'LL HAVE TO HUG YOU EVEN TIGHTER!
SWWRL
!
GRNND
GRNND
GRNND
OH NO...!
THE TEXAS CHAINSAW HAS TREMEN-DOUS POWER...
...BUT IT CAN'T CUT IF IT CAN'T MOVE...!
THIS IS BAD...
THE WORST POSSIBLE OPPO-NENT...!
CHECK-MATE.
NOW LET TOMIKO'S HAIR EMBRACE YOU...
...AND DIE!
YA GOT ONE THING RIGHT.
THIS GIRL'S CURSE AND MINE...
...ARE MATCHED.

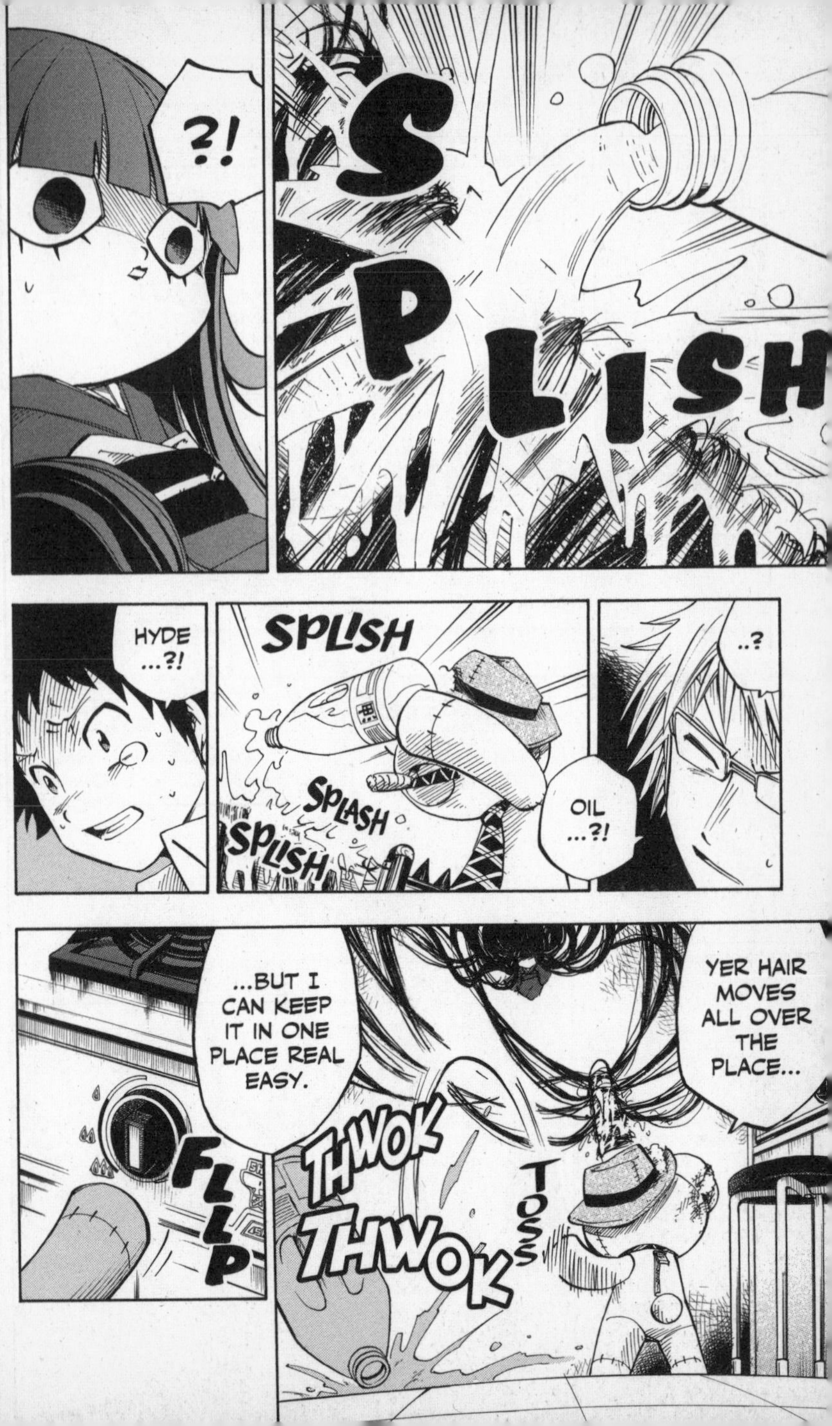
SPLISH
?!
..?
SPLISH
OIL ...?!
SPLASH
SPLISH
HYDE ...?!
YER HAIR MOVES ALL OVER THE PLACE...
...BUT I CAN KEEP IT IN ONE PLACE REAL EASY.
TOSS
THWOK
THWOK
FLIP

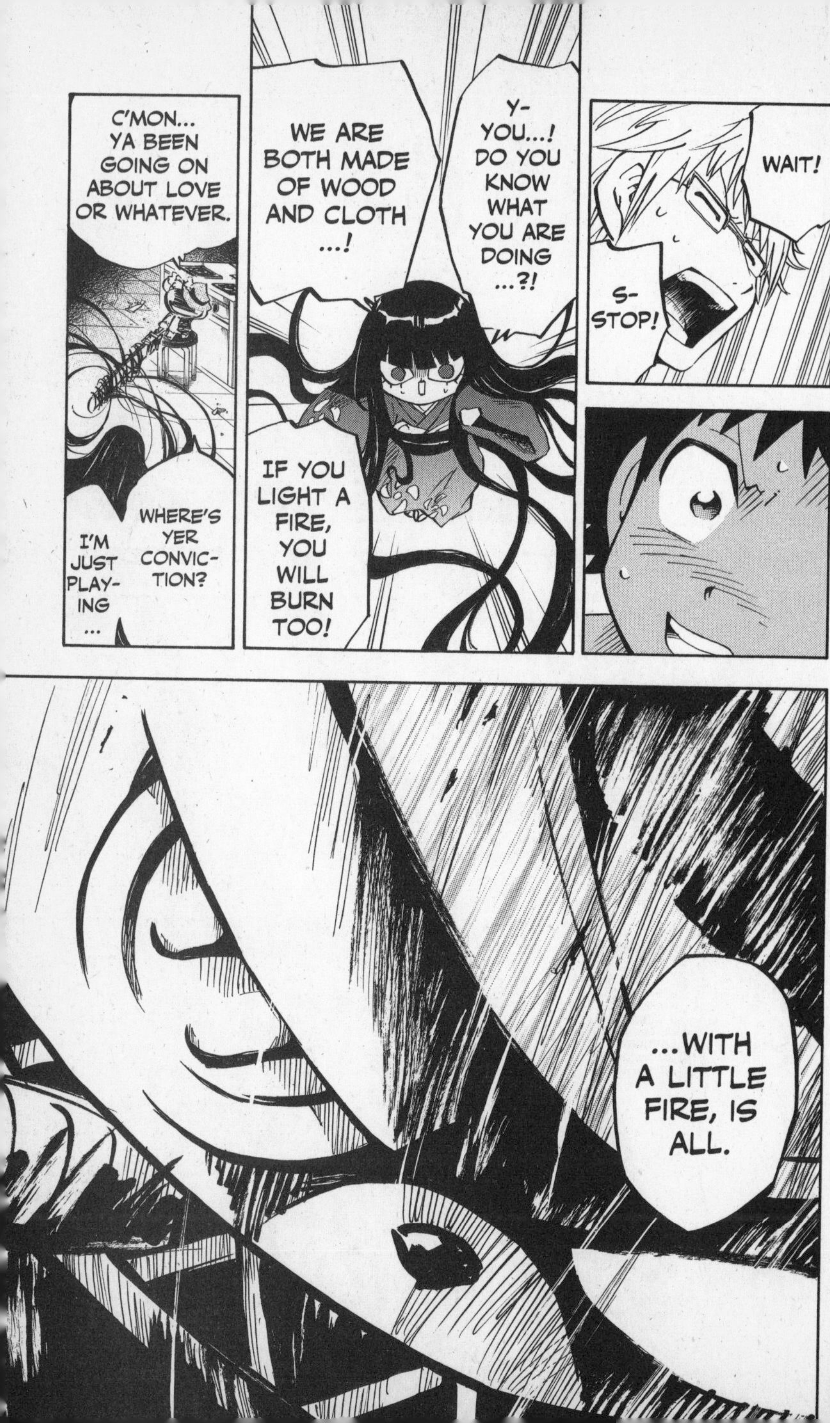
WAIT!
S-STOP!
Y-YOU...! DO YOU KNOW WHAT YOU ARE DOING...?!
WE ARE BOTH MADE OF WOOD AND CLOTH...!
IF YOU LIGHT A FIRE, YOU WILL BURN TOO!
C'MON... YA BEEN GOING ON ABOUT LOVE OR WHATEVER.
WHERE'S YER CONVICTION?
I'M JUST PLAYING...
...WITH A LITTLE FIRE, IS ALL.

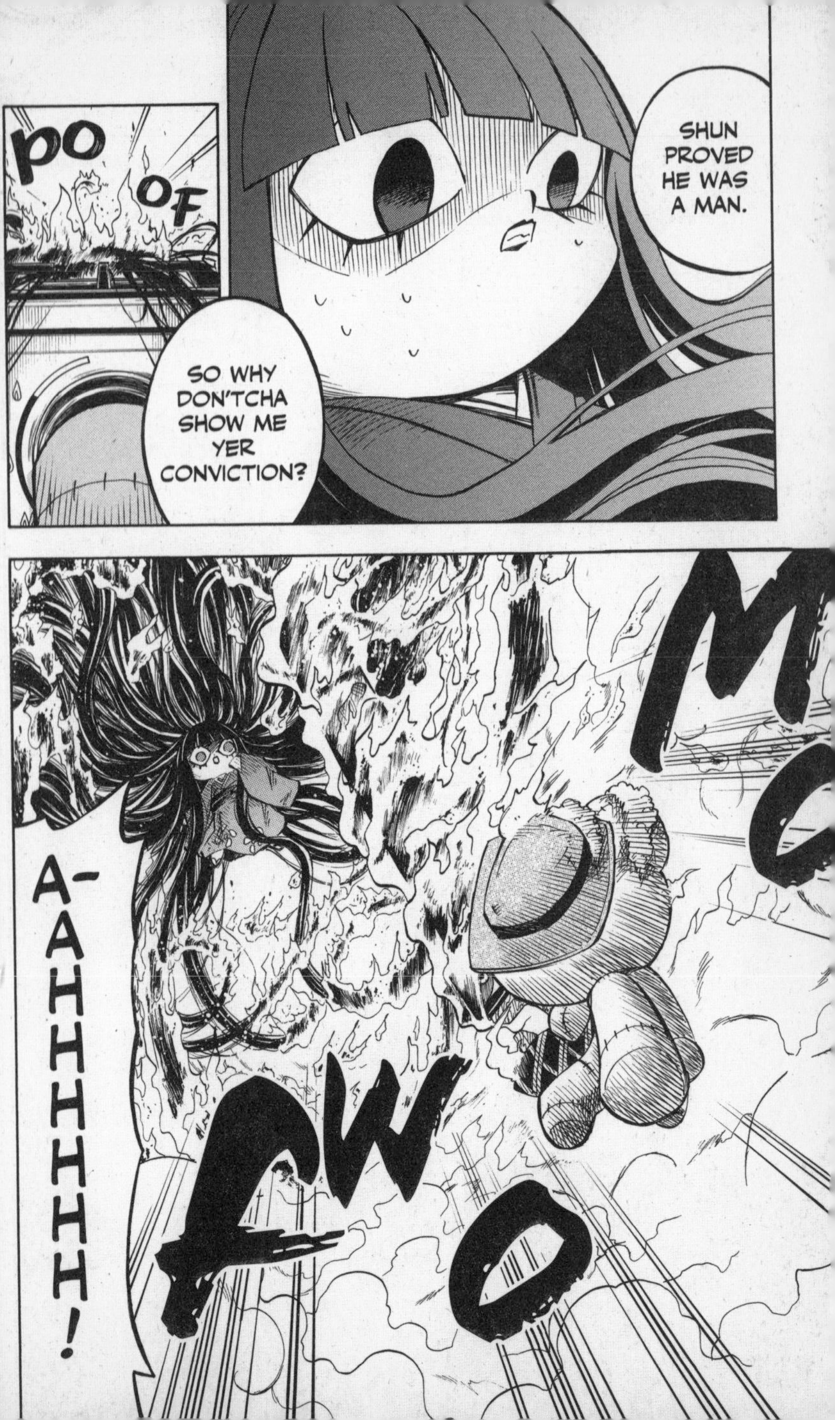
SHUN PROVED HE WAS A MAN.
SO WHY DON'TCHA SHOW ME YER CONVICTION?
POOF
A-AHHHHHH!

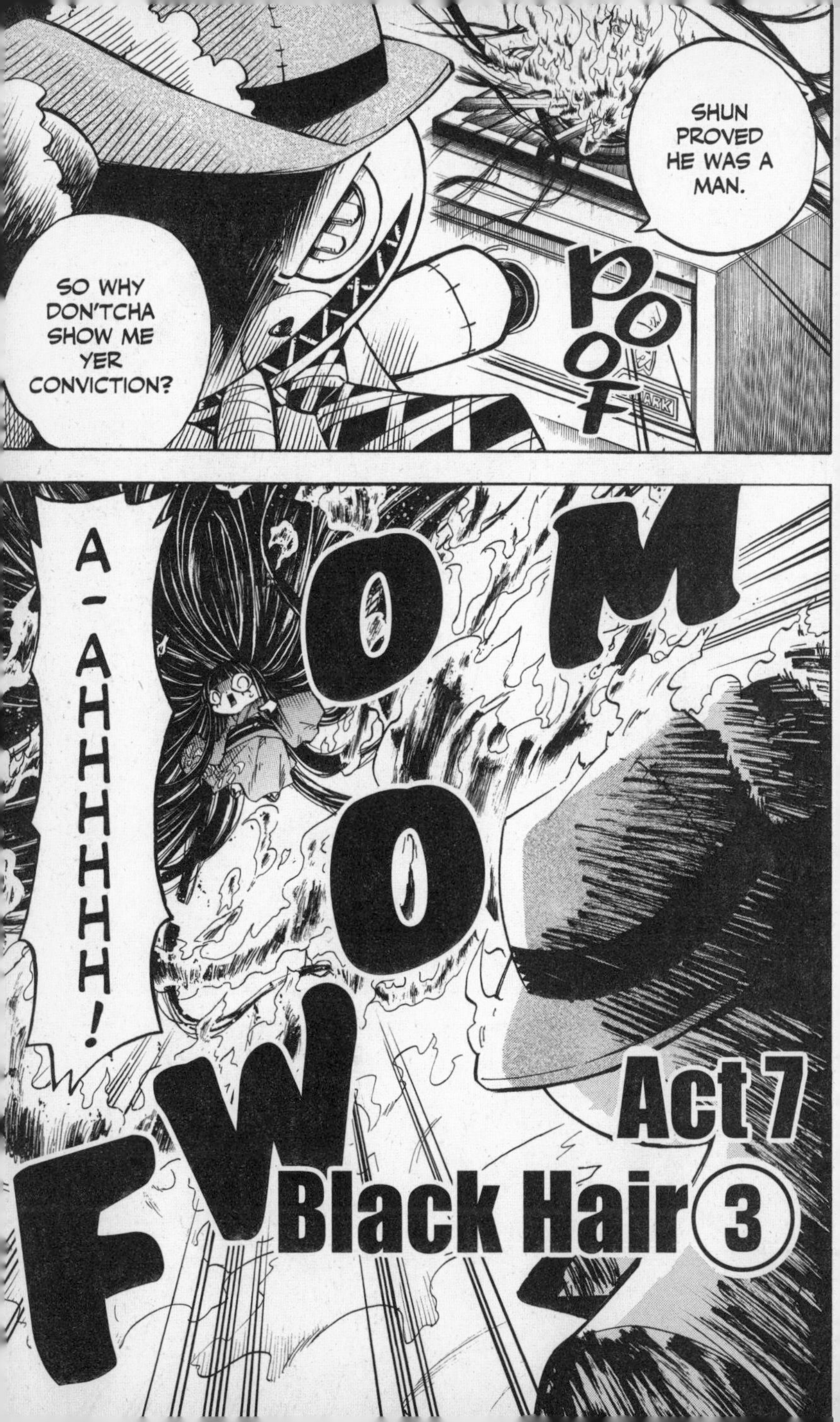
SHUN PROVED HE WAS A MAN.
POOF
SO WHY DON'TCHA SHOW ME YER CONVICTION?
A-AHHHHH!
FWOOM
Act 7
Black Hair ③

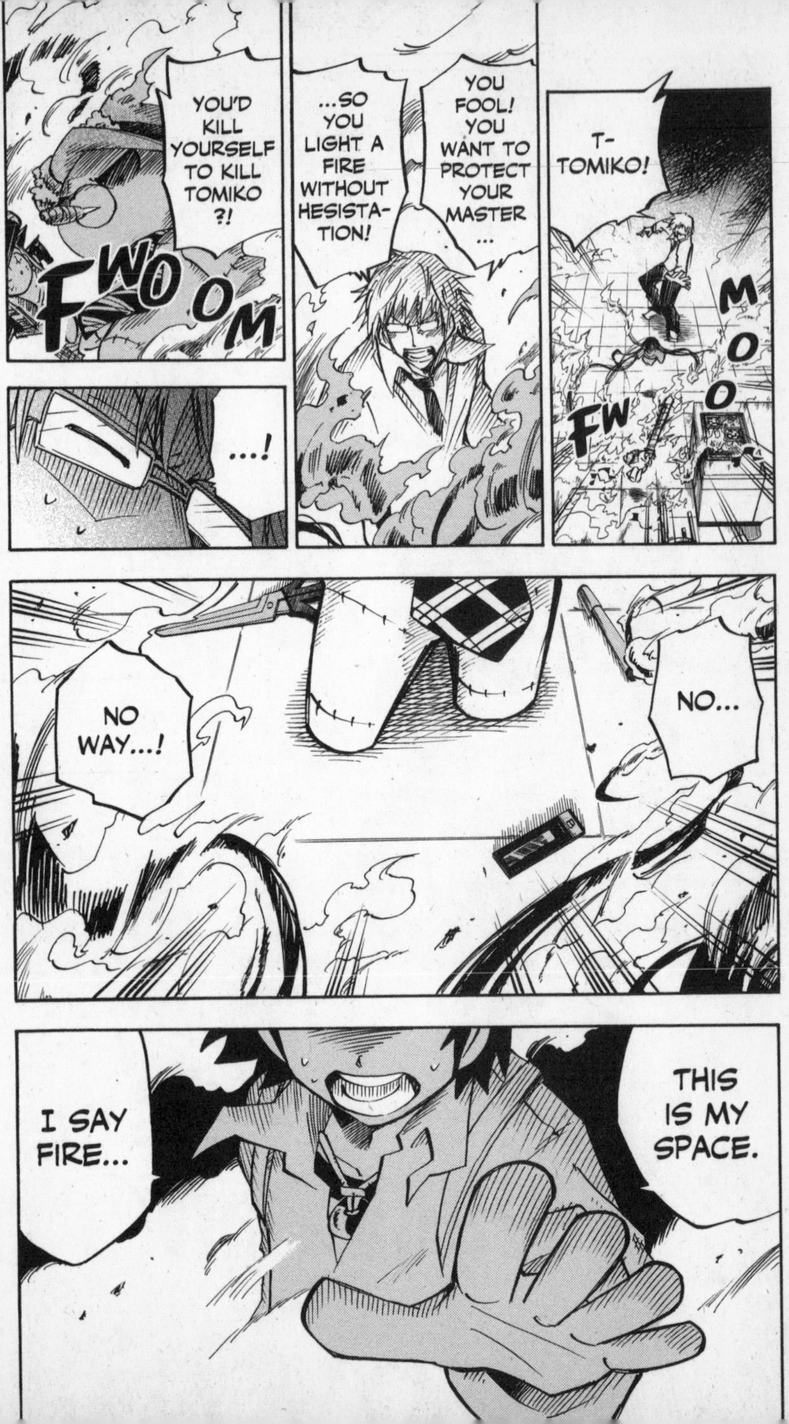
T-TOMIKO!
FWOOM
YOU FOOL! YOU WANT TO PROTECT YOUR MASTER...
...SO YOU LIGHT A FIRE WITHOUT HESISTA-TION!
YOU'D KILL YOURSELF TO KILL TOMIKO?!
FWOOM
...!
NO...
NO WAY...!
THIS IS MY SPACE.
I SAY FIRE...

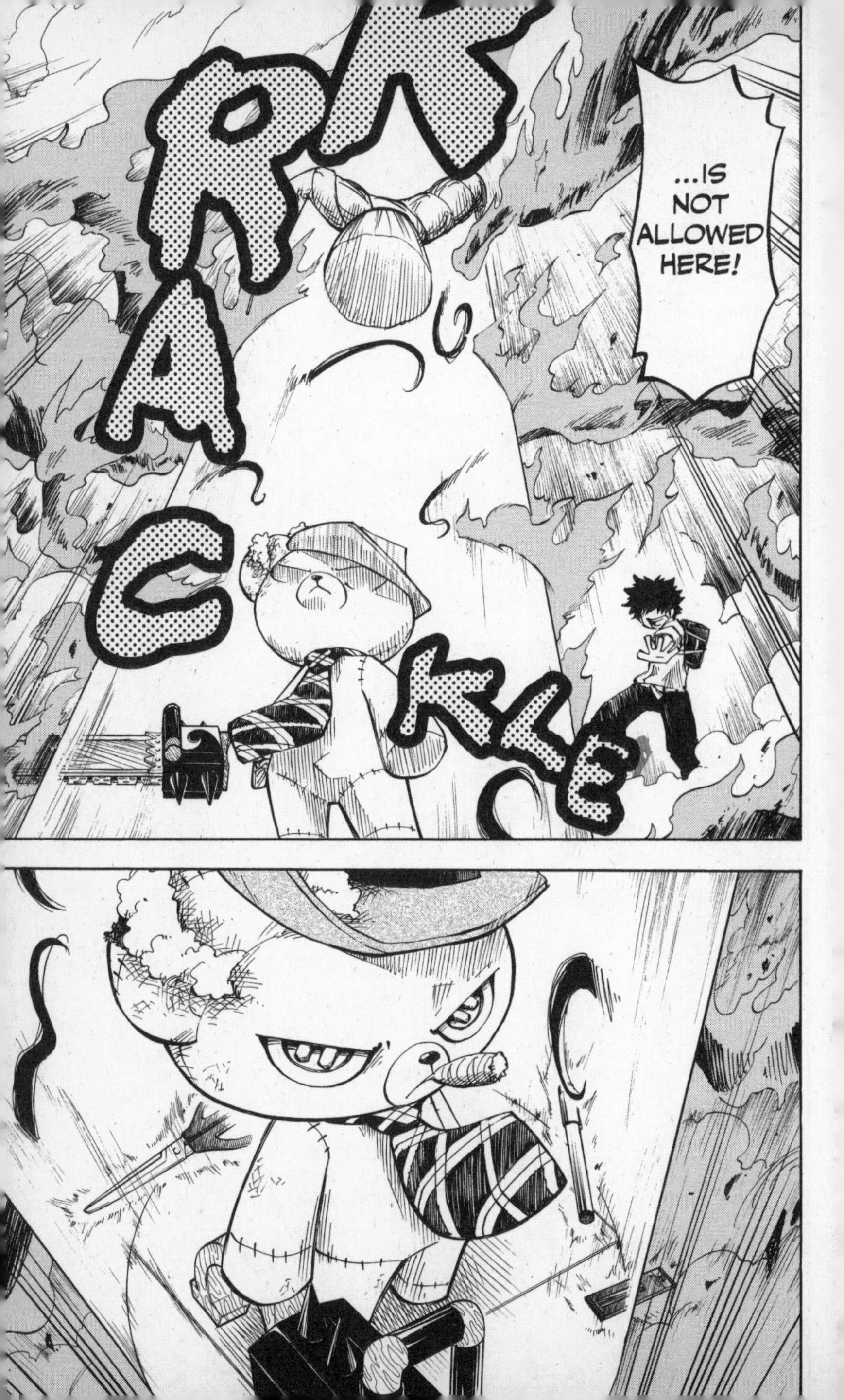
...IS NOT ALLOWED HERE!
RACKLE

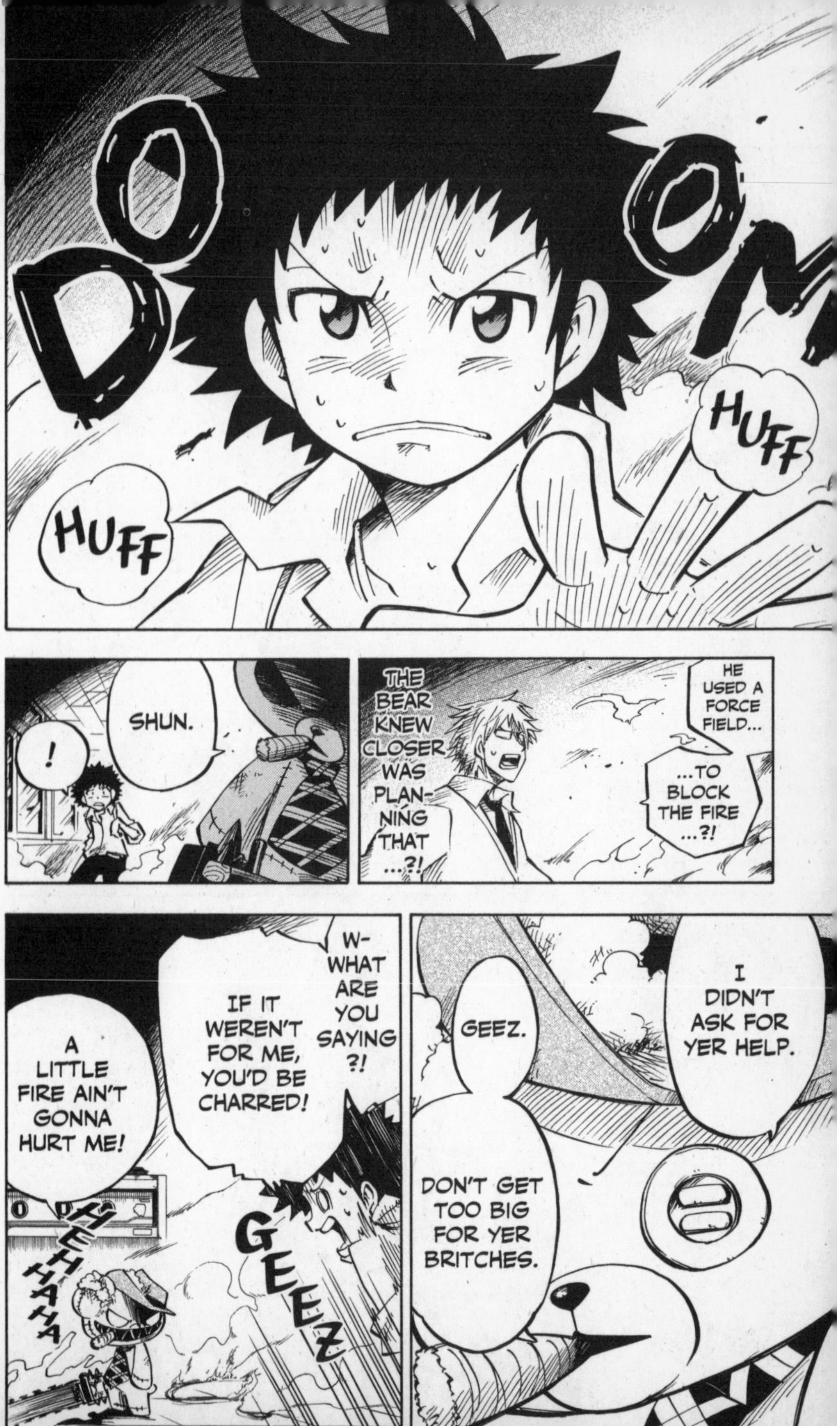
DOOOM
HUFF
HUFF
HE USED A FORCE FIELD...
...TO BLOCK THE FIRE ...?!
THE BEAR KNEW CLOSER WAS PLAN-NING THAT ...?!
SHUN.
!
I DIDN'T ASK FOR YER HELP.
GEEZ.
DON'T GET TOO BIG FOR YER BRITCHES.
W-WHAT ARE YOU SAYING ?!
IF IT WEREN'T FOR ME, YOU'D BE CHARRED!
GEEZ
A LITTLE FIRE AIN'T GONNA HURT ME!
HEHEHAHAHA

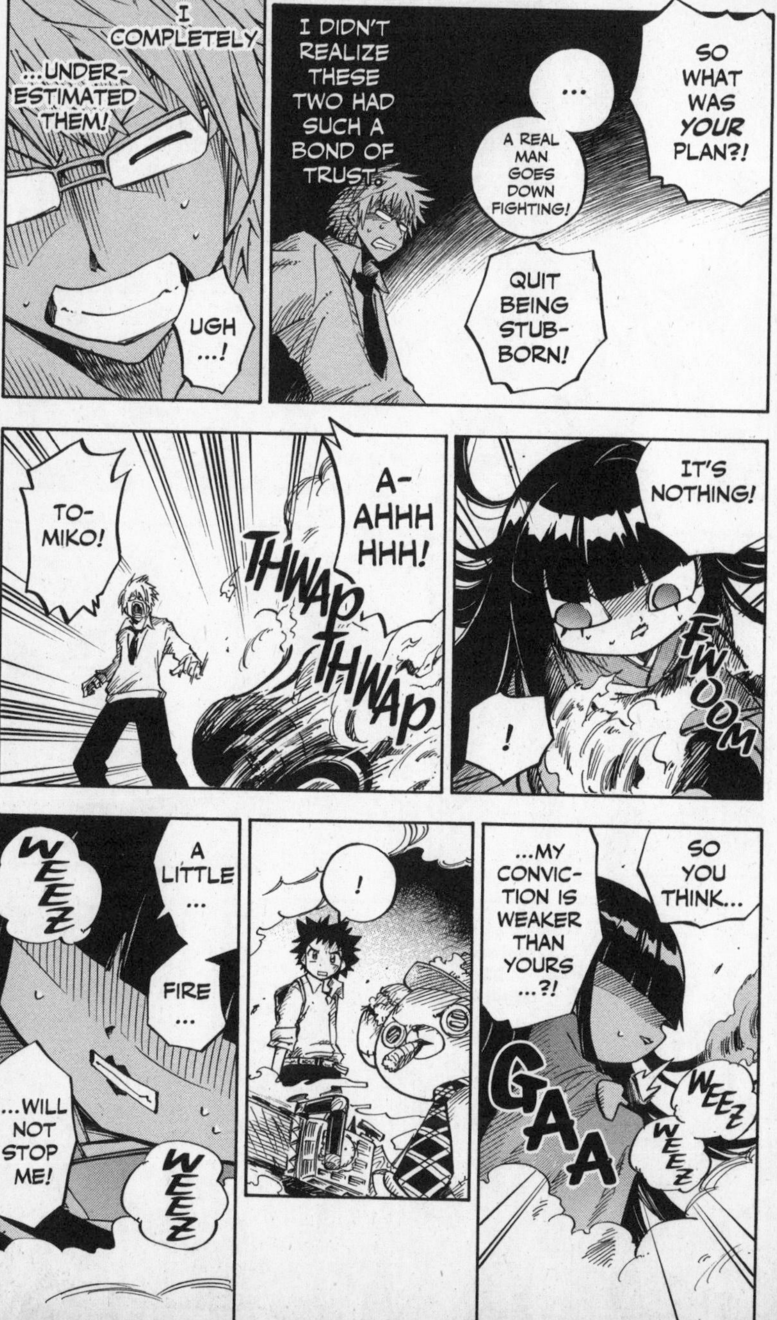
SO WHAT WAS YOUR PLAN?!
...
A REAL MAN GOES DOWN FIGHTING!
QUIT BEING STUBBORN!
I DIDN'T REALIZE THESE TWO HAD SUCH A BOND OF TRUST.
I COMPLETELY ...UNDER-ESTIMATED THEM!
UGH ...!
IT'S NOTHING!
FWOOM
!
A-AHHHHHH!
THWAP THWAP
TO-MIKO!
SO YOU THINK...
...MY CONVICTION IS WEAKER THAN YOURS ...?!
GAA
WEEZ WEEZ
!
A LITTLE ...
FIRE ...
WEEZ
...WILL NOT STOP ME!
WEEZ

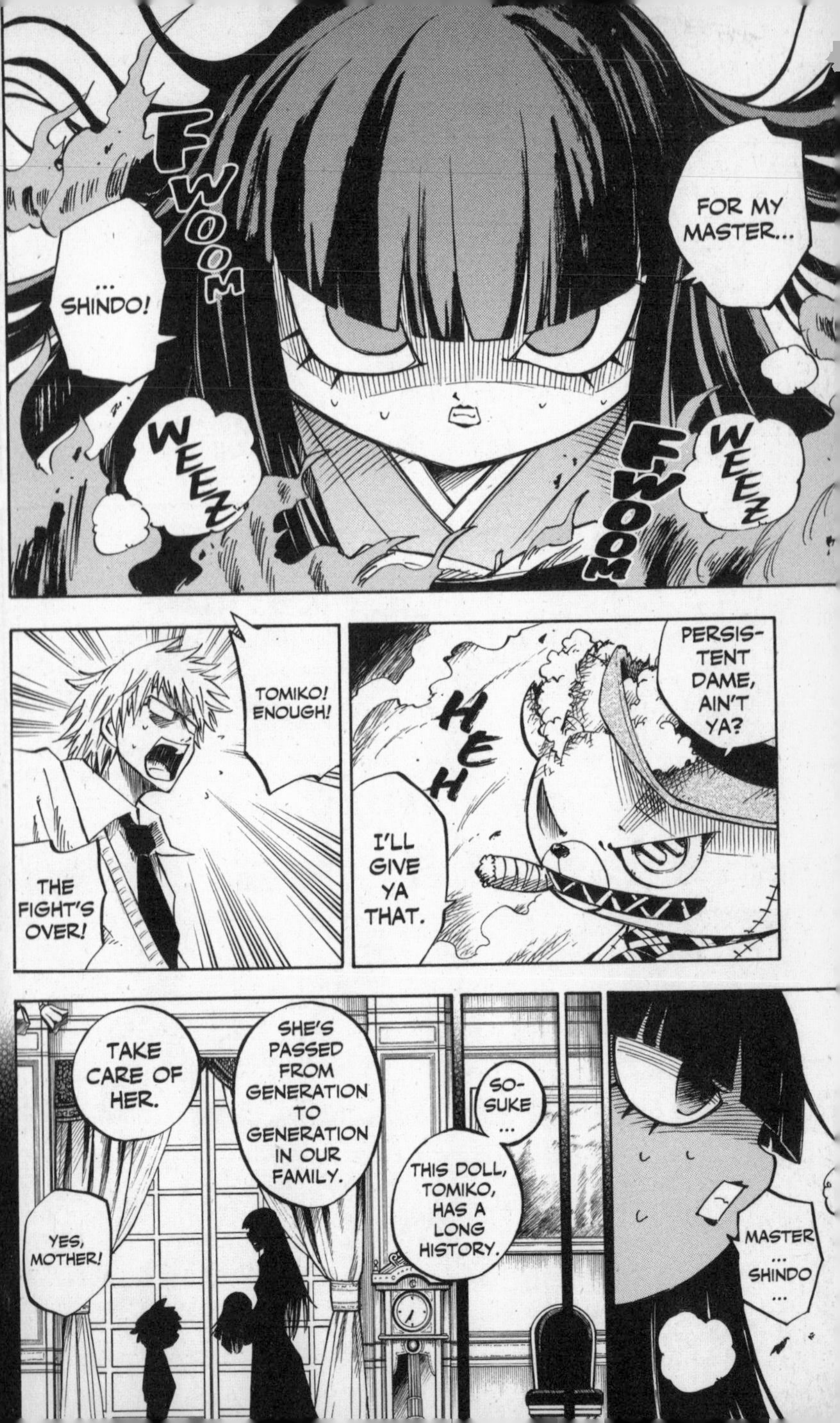
FOR MY MASTER...
FWOOM
WEEZ
... SHINDO!
FWOOM
WEEZ
PERSIS-TENT DAME, AIN'T YA?
HEH
I'LL GIVE YA THAT.
TOMIKO! ENOUGH!
THE FIGHT'S OVER!
MASTER ... SHINDO ...
SO-SUKE ...
THIS DOLL, TOMIKO, HAS A LONG HISTORY.
SHE'S PASSED FROM GENERATION TO GENERATION IN OUR FAMILY.
TAKE CARE OF HER.
YES, MOTHER!

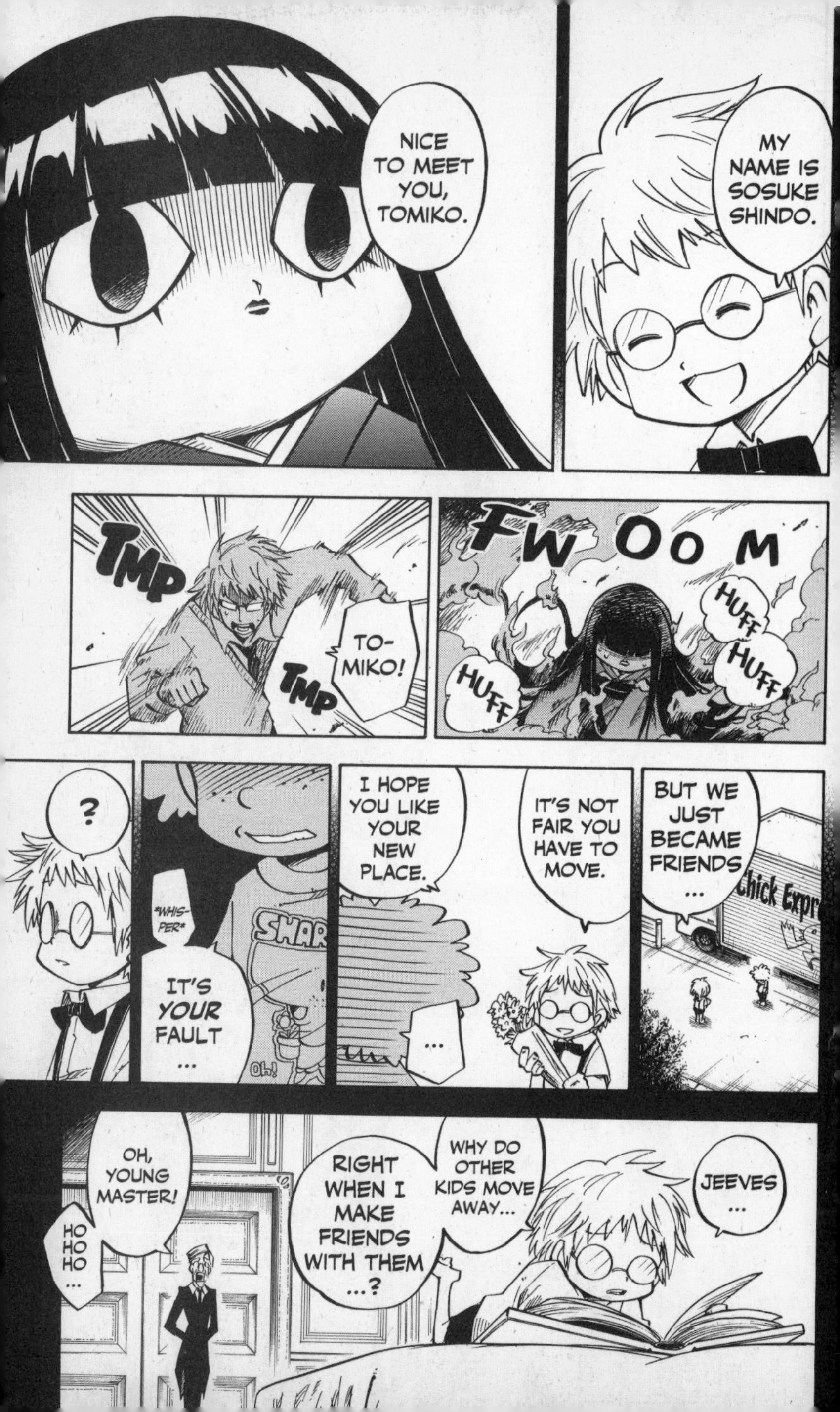
MY NAME IS SOSUKE SHINDO.
NICE TO MEET YOU, TOMIKO.
FWOOM
HUFF
HUFF
HUFF
TMP
TO-MIKO!
TMP
BUT WE JUST BECAME FRIENDS ...
Chick Expr
IT'S NOT FAIR YOU HAVE TO MOVE.
I HOPE YOU LIKE YOUR NEW PLACE.
...
Oh!
WHIS-PER
IT'S *YOUR* FAULT ...
?
JEEVES ...
WHY DO OTHER KIDS MOVE AWAY...
RIGHT WHEN I MAKE FRIENDS WITH THEM ...?
OH, YOUNG MASTER!
HO HO HO ...

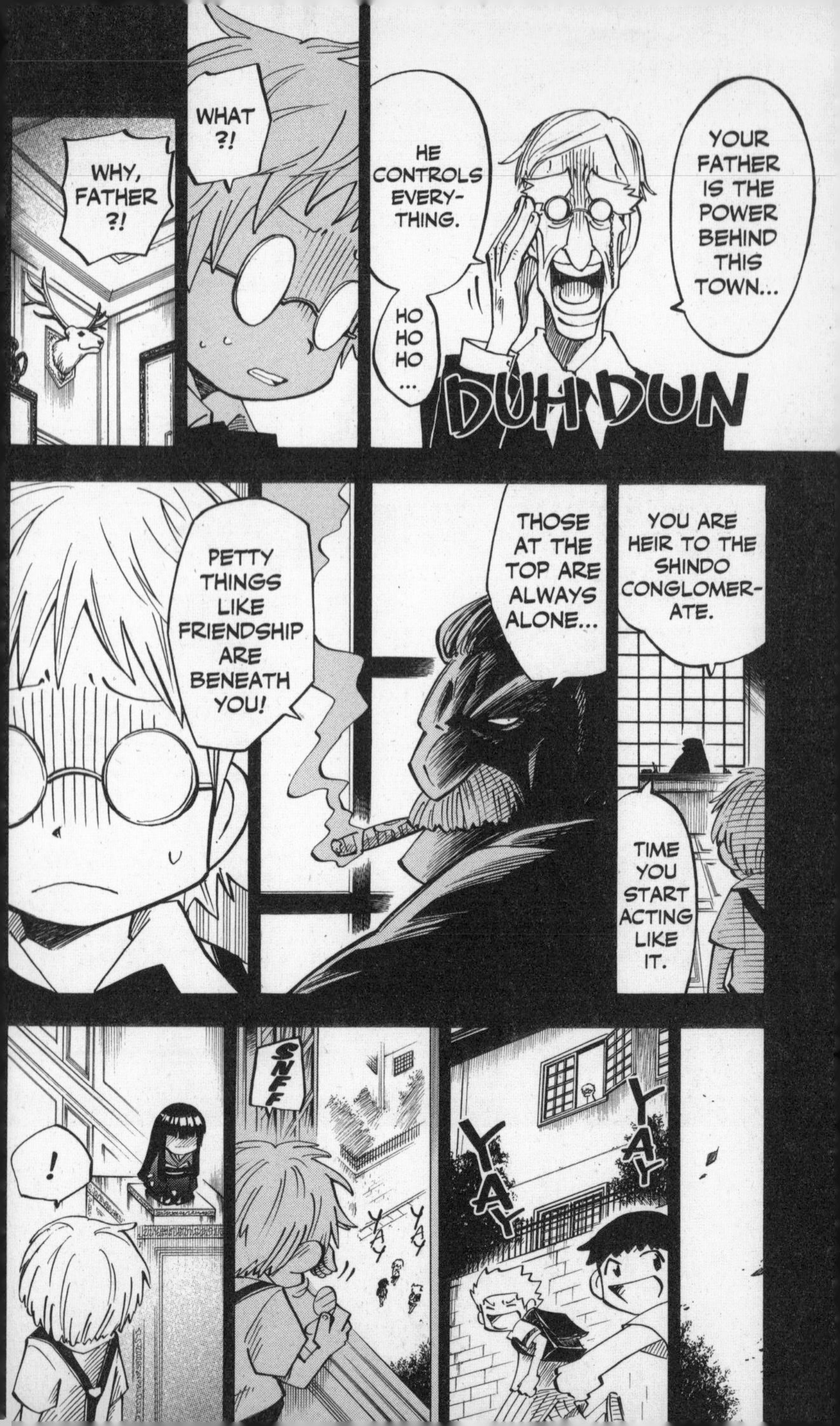
YOUR FATHER IS THE POWER BEHIND THIS TOWN...
HE CONTROLS EVERY-THING.
HO HO HO ...
DUH DUN
WHAT ?!
WHY, FATHER ?!
YOU ARE HEIR TO THE SHINDO CONGLOMER-ATE.
TIME YOU START ACTING LIKE IT.
THOSE AT THE TOP ARE ALWAYS ALONE...
PETTY THINGS LIKE FRIENDSHIP ARE BENEATH YOU!
YAY
YAY
SNFF
YAY
YAY
!

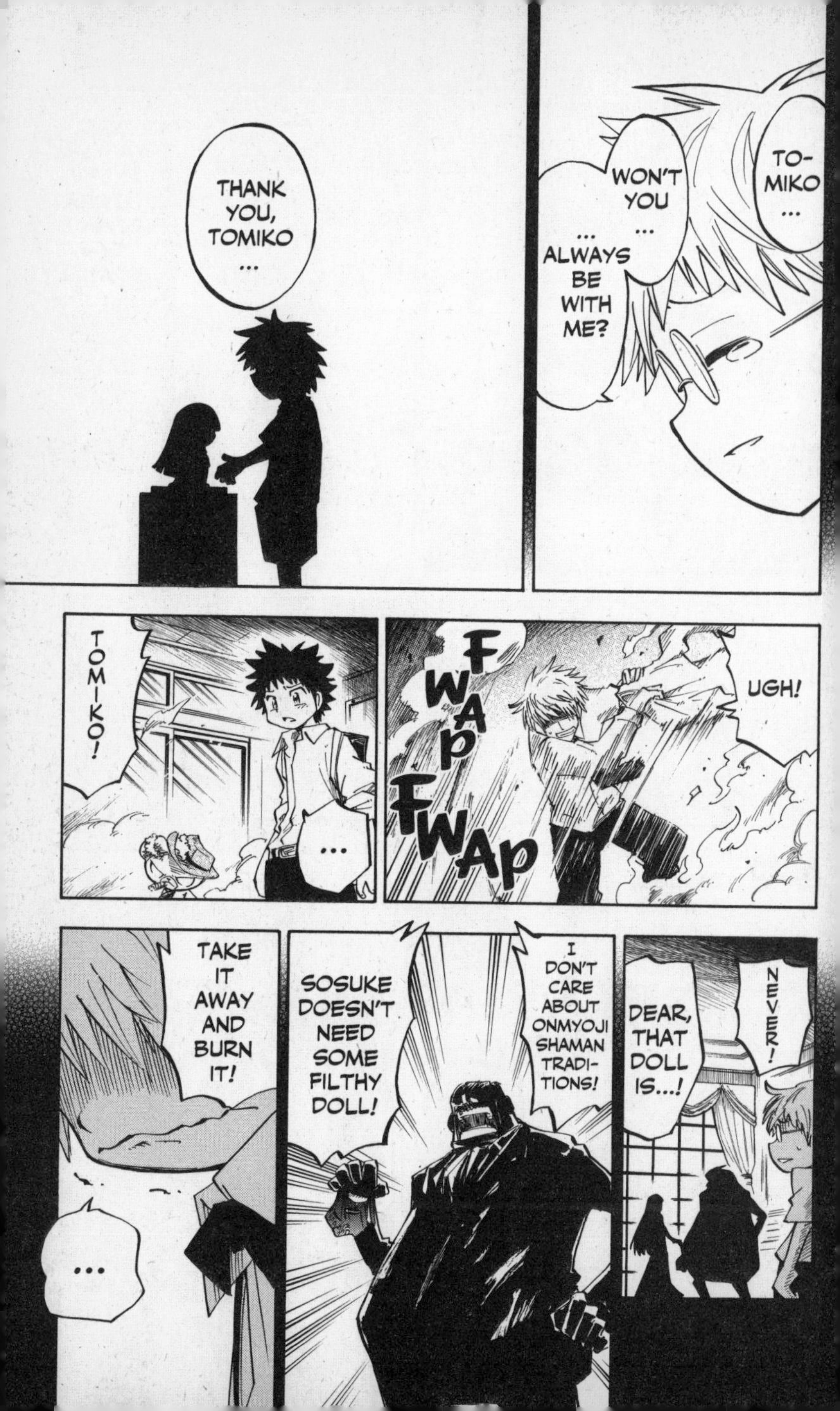
TO-MIKO ...
WON'T YOU ... ... ALWAYS BE WITH ME?
THANK YOU, TOMIKO ...
UGH!
FWAP FWAP
TOMIKO!
...
NEVER!
DEAR, THAT DOLL IS...!
I DON'T CARE ABOUT ONMYOJI SHAMAN TRADI-TIONS!
SOSUKE DOESN'T NEED SOME FILTHY DOLL!
TAKE IT AWAY AND BURN IT!
...

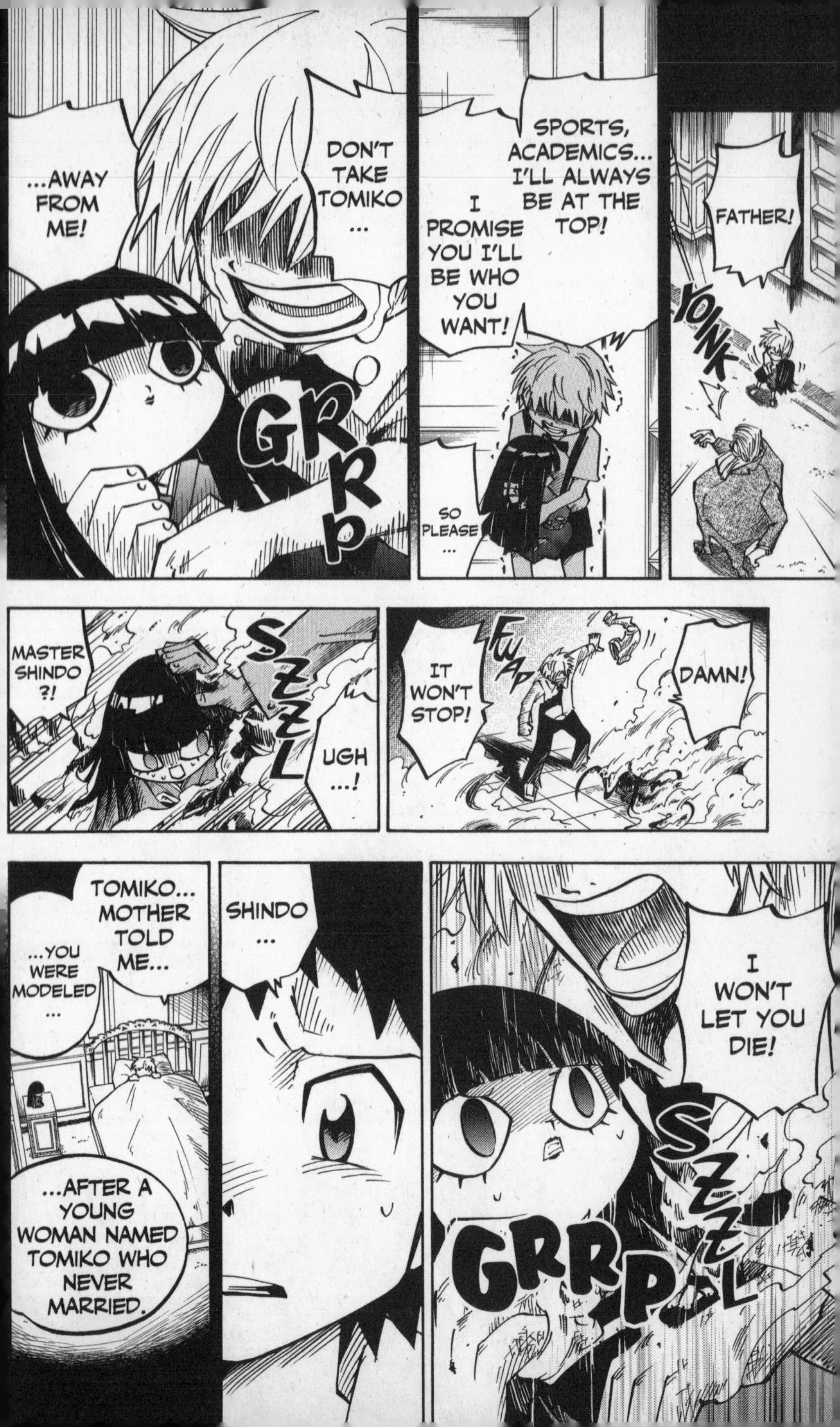
FATHER!
YOINK
SPORTS, ACADEMICS... I'LL ALWAYS BE AT THE TOP!
I PROMISE YOU I'LL BE WHO YOU WANT!
SO PLEASE ...
DON'T TAKE TOMIKO ...
...AWAY FROM ME!
GRRP
DAMN!
FWAP
IT WON'T STOP!
UGH ...!
SZZZL
MASTER SHINDO ?!
I WON'T LET YOU DIE!
SZZZL
GRRP
SHINDO ...
TOMIKO... MOTHER TOLD ME...
...YOU WERE MODELED ...
...AFTER A YOUNG WOMAN NAMED TOMIKO WHO NEVER MARRIED.

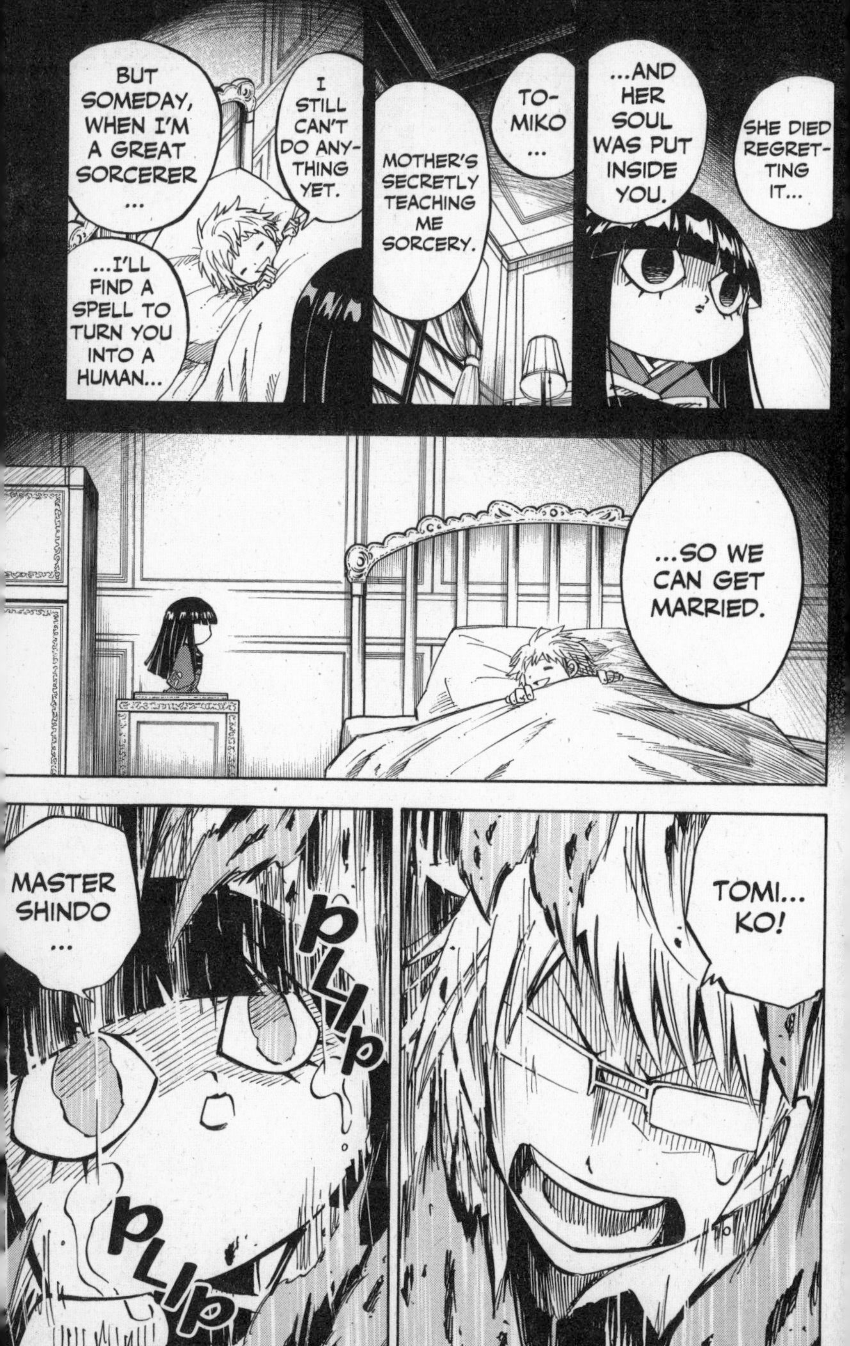
SHE DIED REGRETTING IT...
...AND HER SOUL WAS PUT INSIDE YOU.
TO-MIKO ...
MOTHER'S SECRETLY TEACHING ME SORCERY.
I STILL CAN'T DO ANYTHING YET.
BUT SOMEDAY, WHEN I'M A GREAT SORCERER ...
...I'LL FIND A SPELL TO TURN YOU INTO A HUMAN...
...SO WE CAN GET MARRIED.
TOMI... KO!
MASTER SHINDO ...
PLIP
PLIP

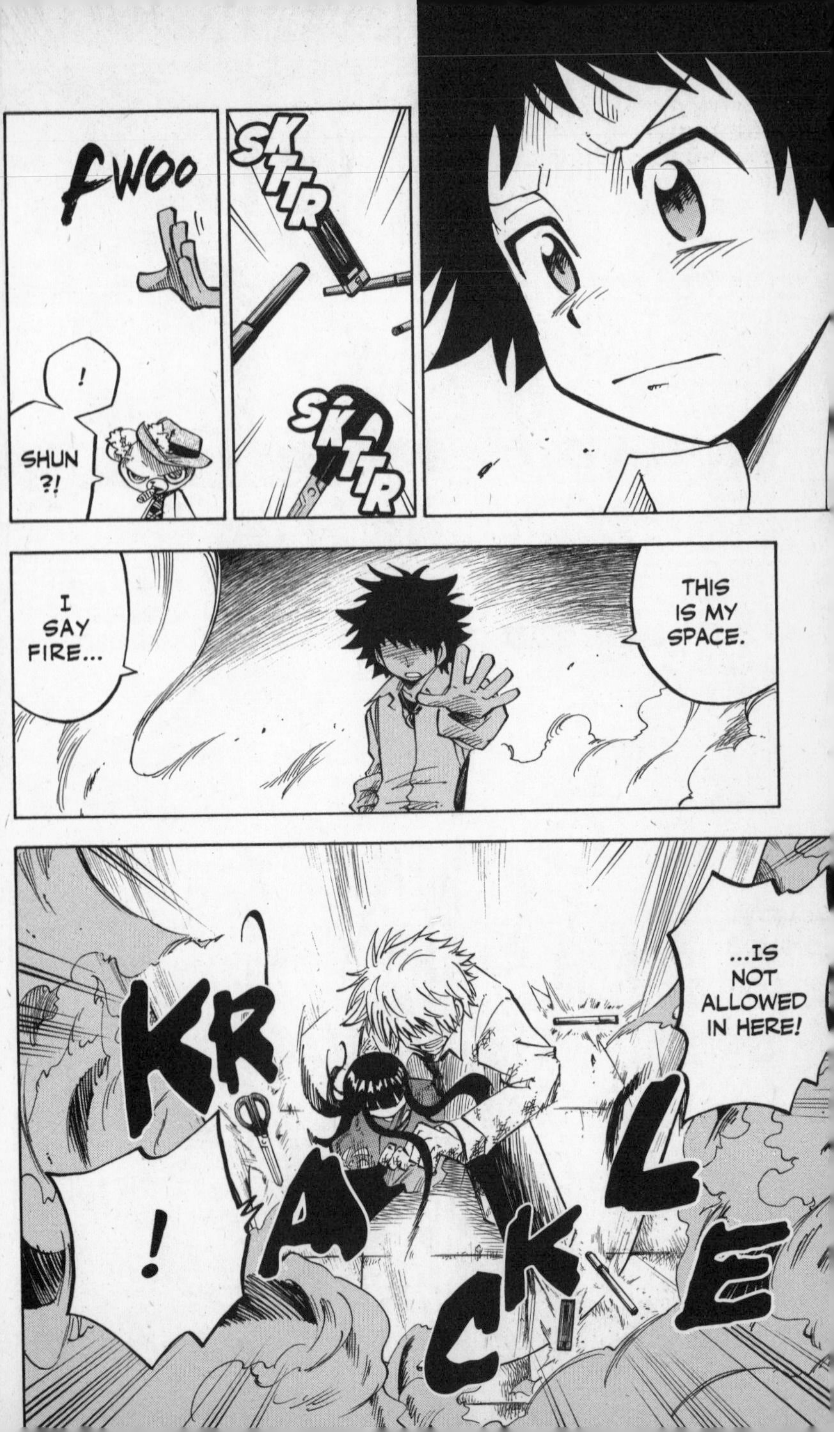
SKTTR
SKTTR
FWOO
!
SHUN ?!
THIS IS MY SPACE.
I SAY FIRE...
...IS NOT ALLOWED IN HERE!
KRACKLE
!

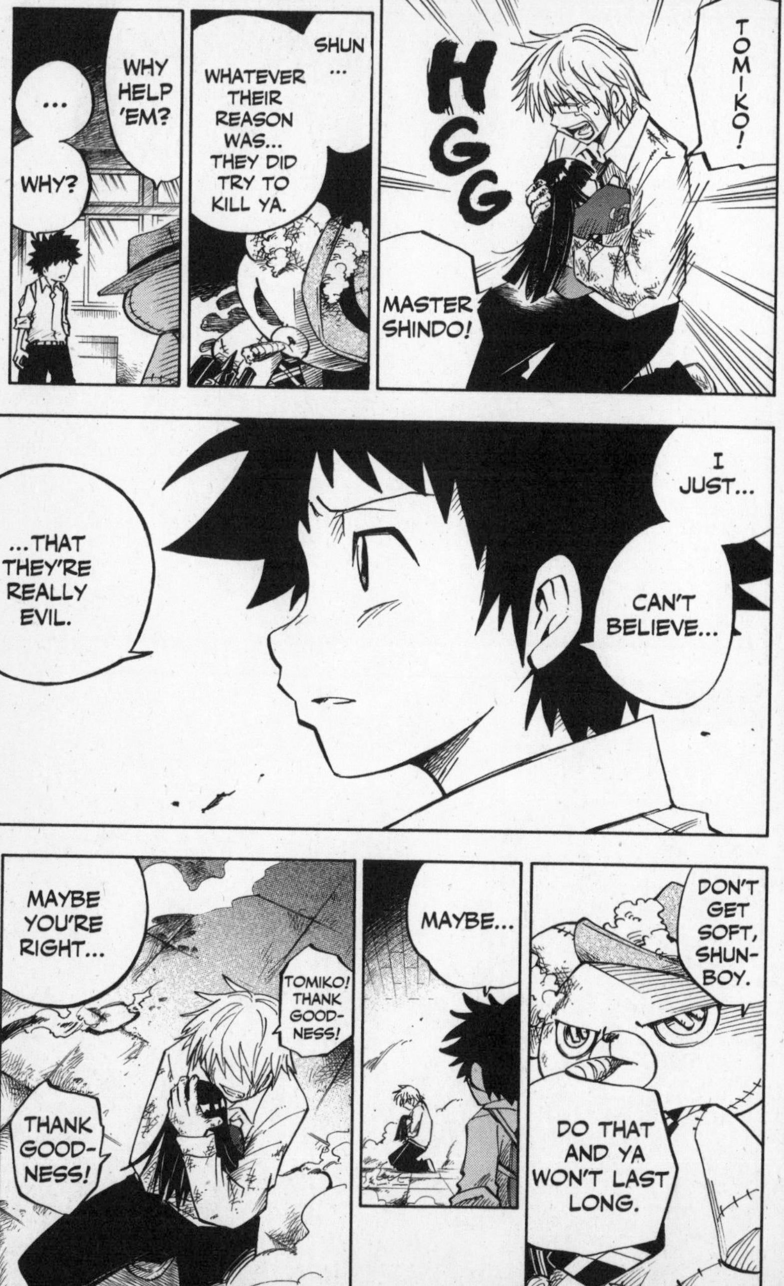

TOMIKO!
HGG
MASTER SHINDO!
SHUN...
WHATEVER THEIR REASON WAS... THEY DID TRY TO KILL YA.
WHY HELP 'EM?
...
WHY?
I JUST...
CAN'T BELIEVE...
...THAT THEY'RE REALLY EVIL.
DON'T GET SOFT, SHUN-BOY.
DO THAT AND YA WON'T LAST LONG.
MAYBE...
MAYBE YOU'RE RIGHT...
TOMIKO! THANK GOODNESS!
THANK GOOD-NESS!

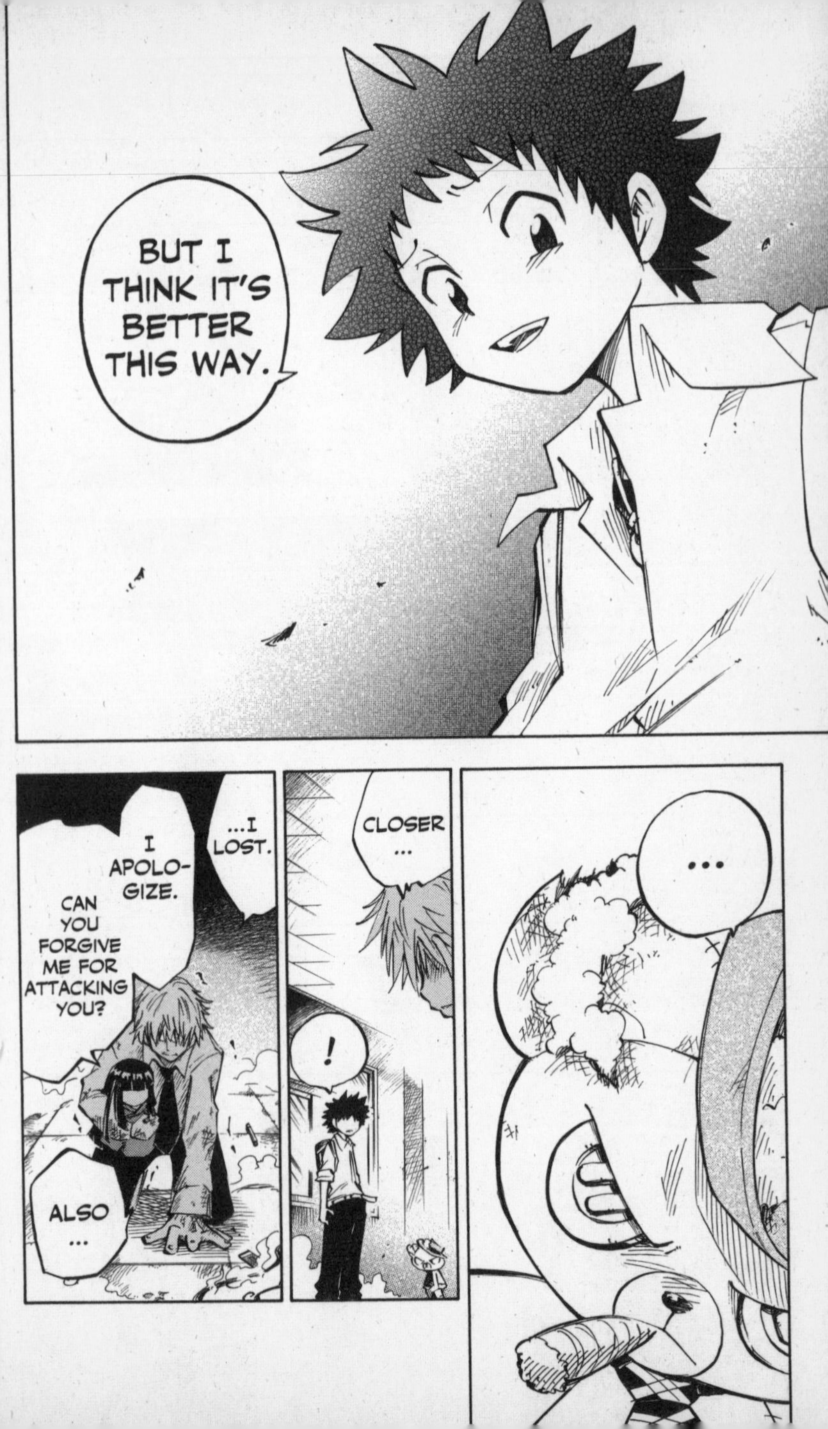
BUT I THINK IT'S BETTER THIS WAY.
...
CLOSER ...
!
...I LOST.
I APOLO-GIZE.
CAN YOU FORGIVE ME FOR ATTACKING YOU?
ALSO ...

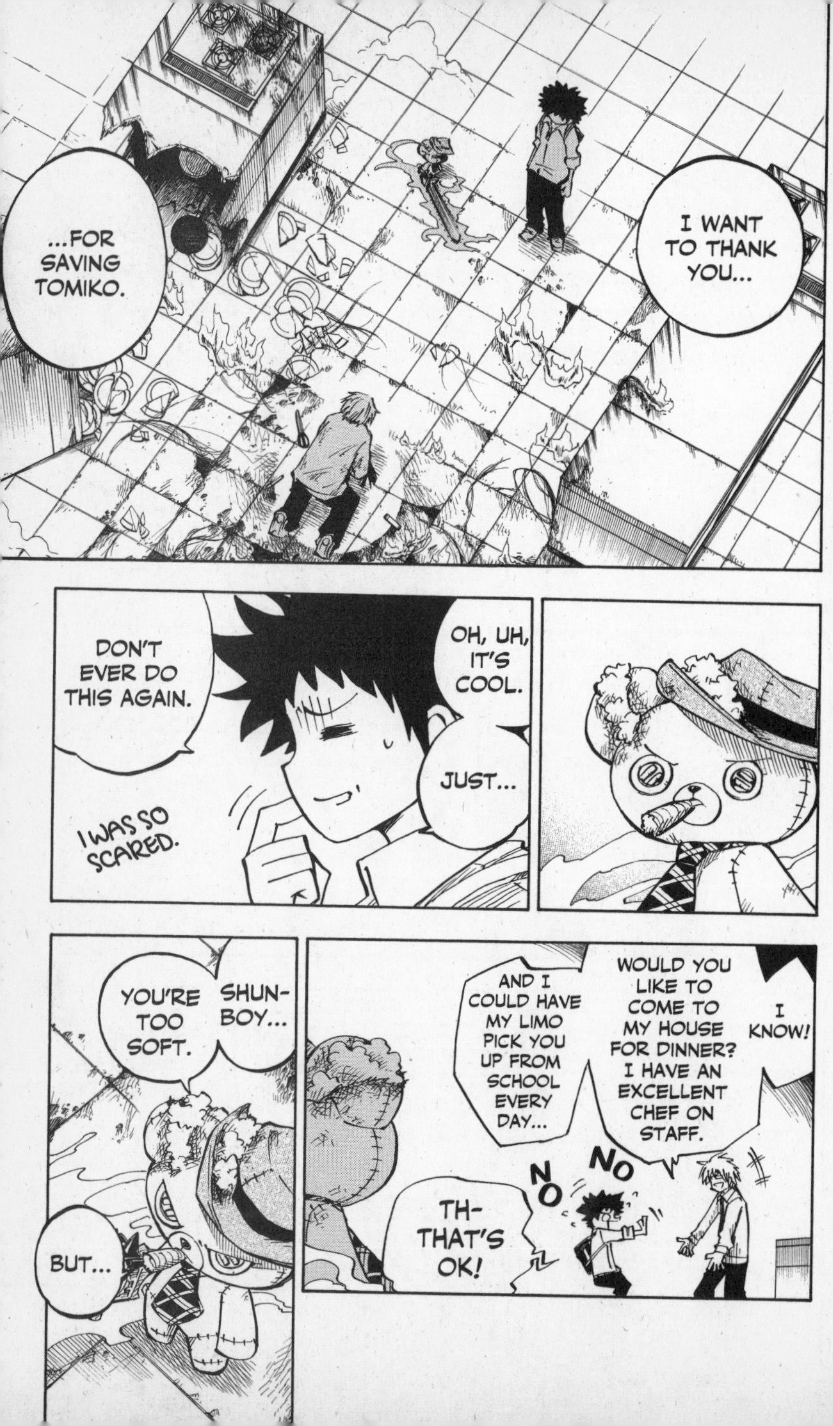
I WANT TO THANK YOU...
...FOR SAVING TOMIKO.
OH, UH, IT'S COOL.
JUST...
DON'T EVER DO THIS AGAIN.
I WAS SO SCARED.
I KNOW!
WOULD YOU LIKE TO COME TO MY HOUSE FOR DINNER? I HAVE AN EXCELLENT CHEF ON STAFF.
AND I COULD HAVE MY LIMO PICK YOU UP FROM SCHOOL EVERY DAY...
NO
NO
TH-THAT'S OK!
SHUN-BOY...
YOU'RE TOO SOFT.
BUT...

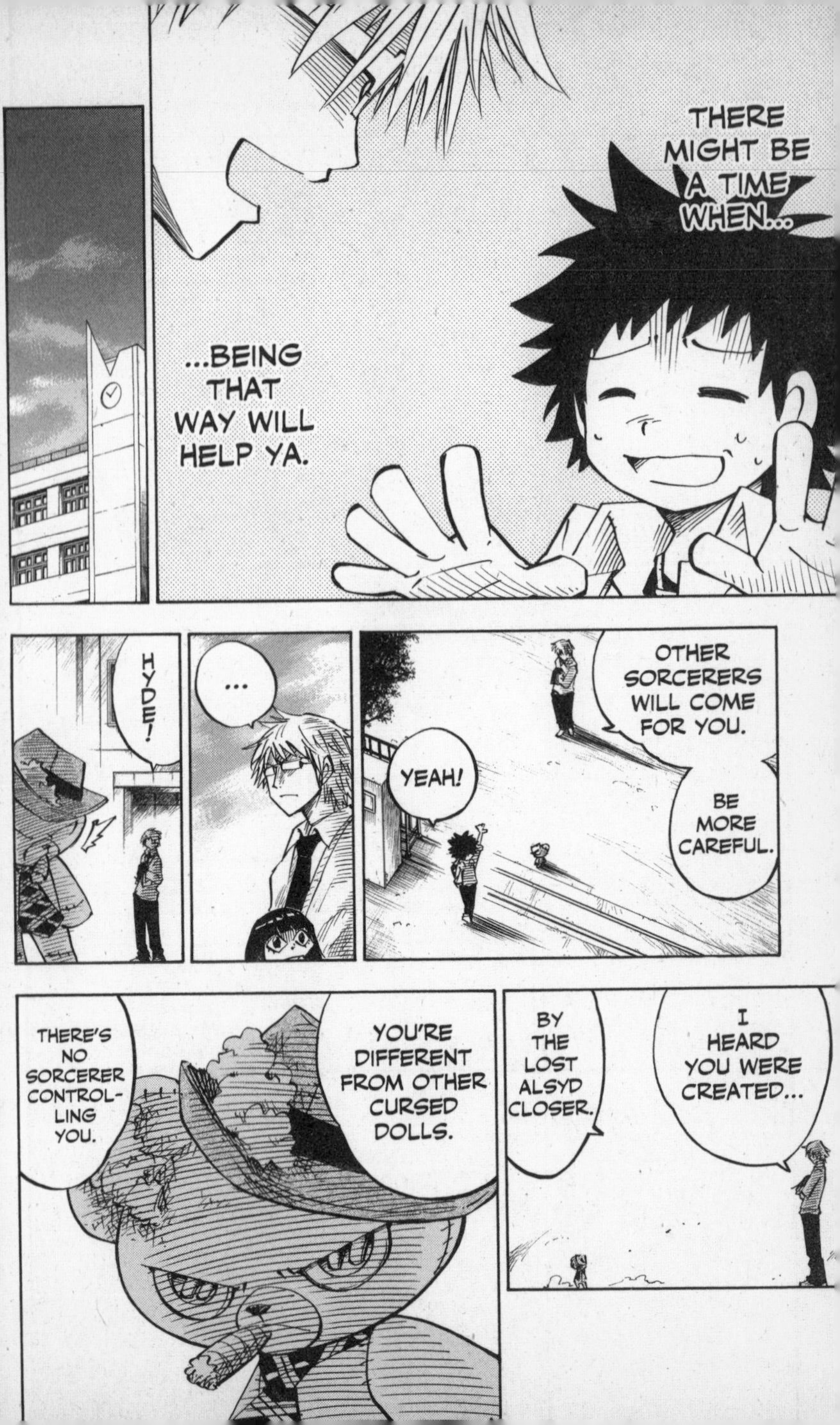
THERE MIGHT BE A TIME WHEN...
...BEING THAT WAY WILL HELP YA.
OTHER SORCERERS WILL COME FOR YOU.
BE MORE CAREFUL.
YEAH!
...
HYDE!
I HEARD YOU WERE CREATED...
BY THE LOST ALSYD CLOSER.
YOU'RE DIFFERENT FROM OTHER CURSED DOLLS.
THERE'S NO SORCERER CONTROL-LING YOU.

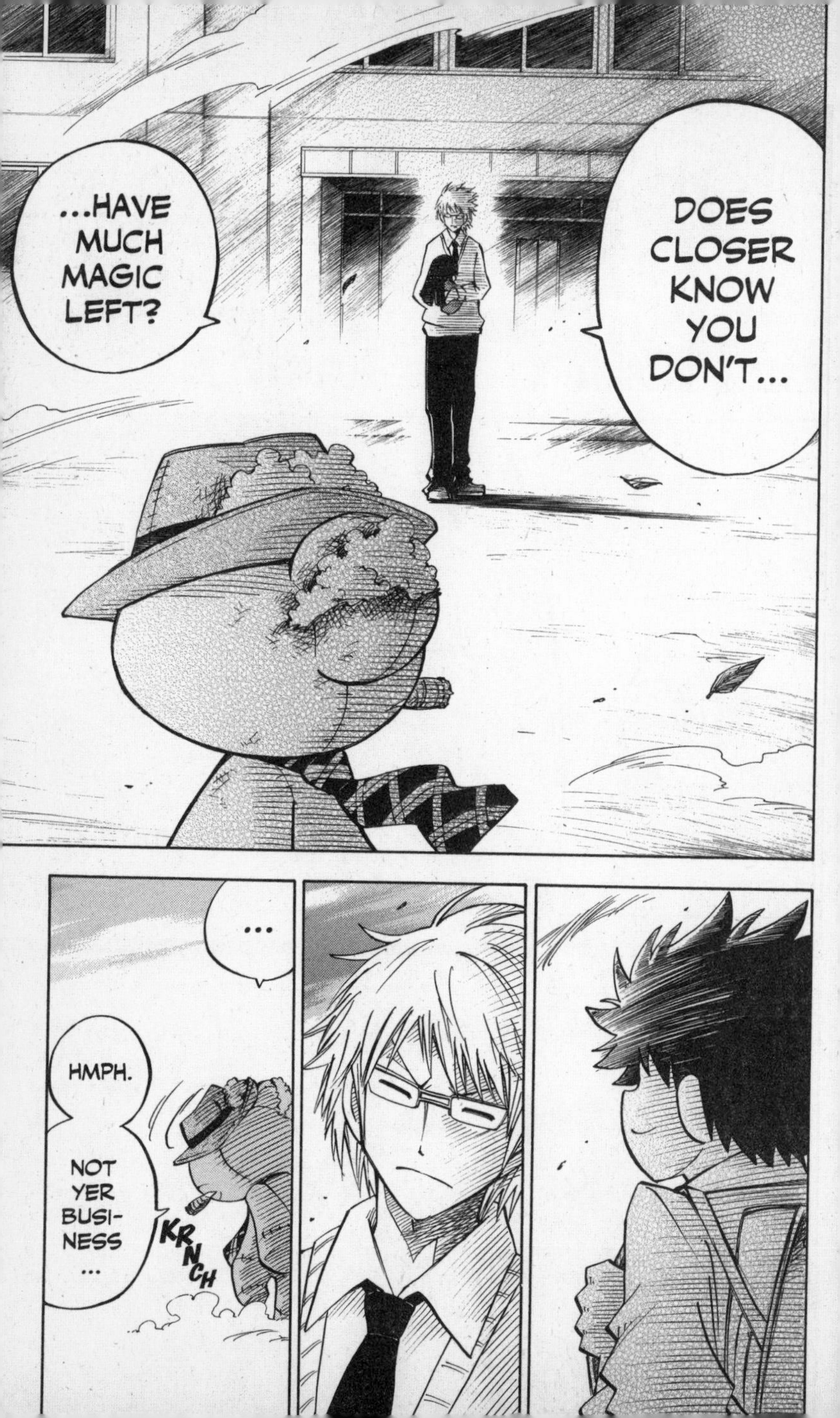
DOES CLOSER KNOW YOU DON'T...
...HAVE MUCH MAGIC LEFT?
...
HMPH.
NOT YER BUSI-NESS...
KRNCH

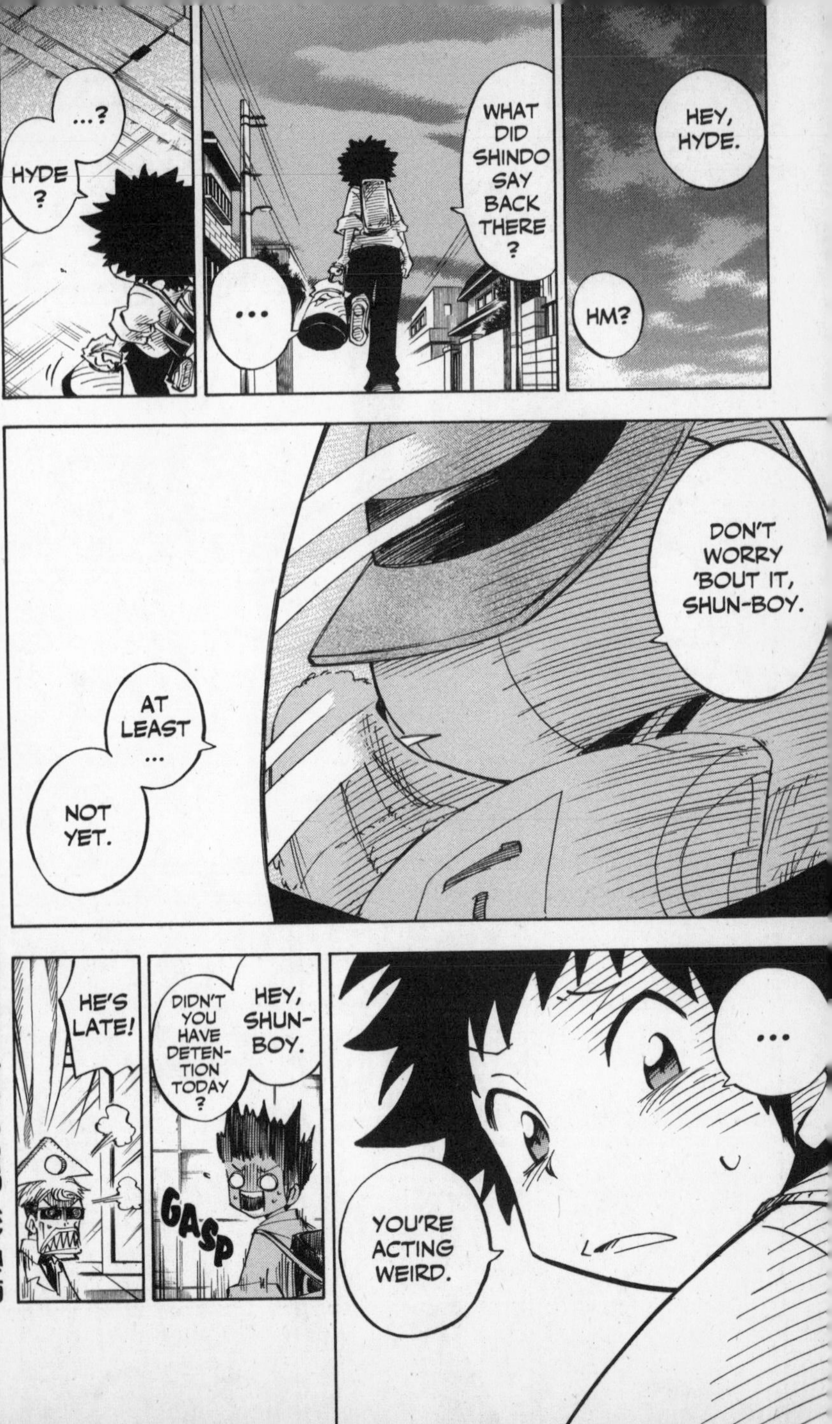
HEY, HYDE.
HM?
WHAT DID SHINDO SAY BACK THERE?
...
...?
HYDE?
DON'T WORRY 'BOUT IT, SHUN-BOY.
AT LEAST...
NOT YET.
...
YOU'RE ACTING WEIRD.
HEY, SHUN-BOY.
DIDN'T YOU HAVE DETENTION TODAY?
GASP
HE'S LATE!

HYDE & CLOSER (1) END

HY-CLO EXTRA THEATER

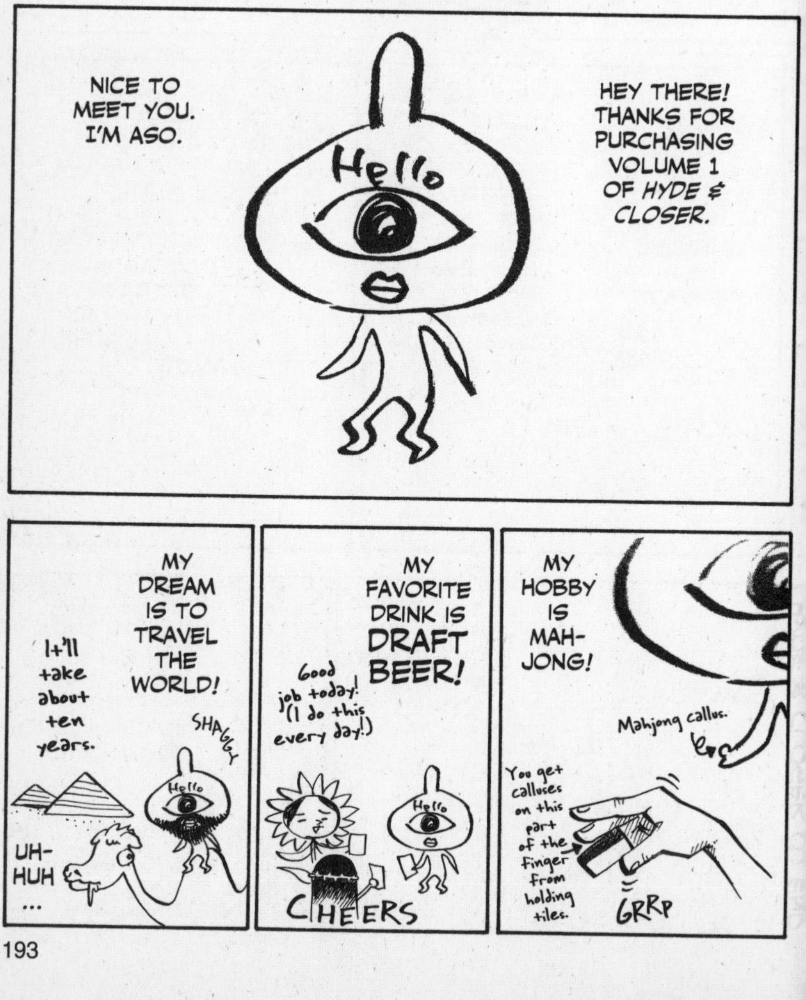
HEY THERE! THANKS FOR PURCHASING VOLUME 1 OF *HYDE & CLOSER.*
NICE TO MEET YOU. I'M ASO.
Hello
MY HOBBY IS MAH-JONG!
Mahjong callus.
You get calluses on this part of the finger from holding tiles.
GRRP
MY FAVORITE DRINK IS DRAFT BEER!
Good job today! (I do this every day!)
Hello
CHEERS
MY DREAM IS TO TRAVEL THE WORLD!
SHAGGY
It'll take about ten years.
Hello
UH-HUH ...

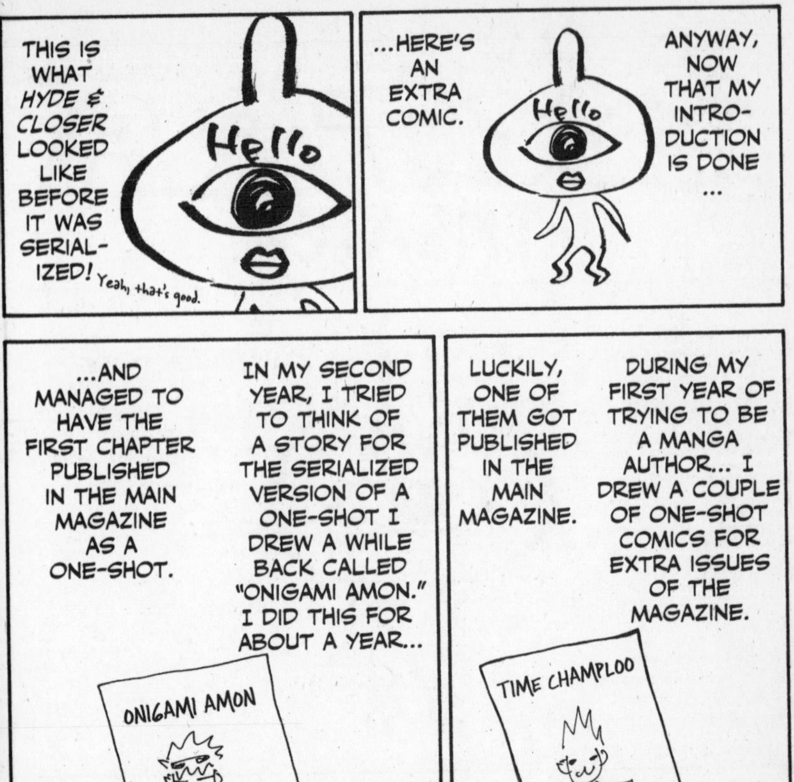
ANYWAY, NOW THAT MY INTRO- DUCTION IS DONE ...
...HERE'S AN EXTRA COMIC.
Hello
THIS IS WHAT HYDE & CLOSER LOOKED LIKE BEFORE IT WAS SERIAL- IZED!
Yeah, that's good.
Hello
DURING MY FIRST YEAR OF TRYING TO BE A MANGA AUTHOR... I DREW A COUPLE OF ONE-SHOT COMICS FOR EXTRA ISSUES OF THE MAGAZINE.
LUCKILY, ONE OF THEM GOT PUBLISHED IN THE MAIN MAGAZINE.
TIME CHAMPLOO
IN MY SECOND YEAR, I TRIED TO THINK OF A STORY FOR THE SERIALIZED VERSION OF A ONE-SHOT I DREW A WHILE BACK CALLED "ONIGAMI AMON." I DID THIS FOR ABOUT A YEAR...
...AND MANAGED TO HAVE THE FIRST CHAPTER PUBLISHED IN THE MAIN MAGAZINE AS A ONE-SHOT.
ONIGAMI AMON
TECHNICALLY, "ONIGAMI AMON" DID WELL IN THE FAN SURVEYS... BUT, STILL... YOU KNOW...
Do something different.
BUMMER
Hello
EDITOR
I TOOK A GAMBLE AND TRIED DOING A FANTASY COMIC...
So... what? Boy's magazines prefer fantasy?!
Hello

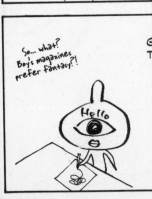

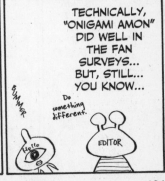

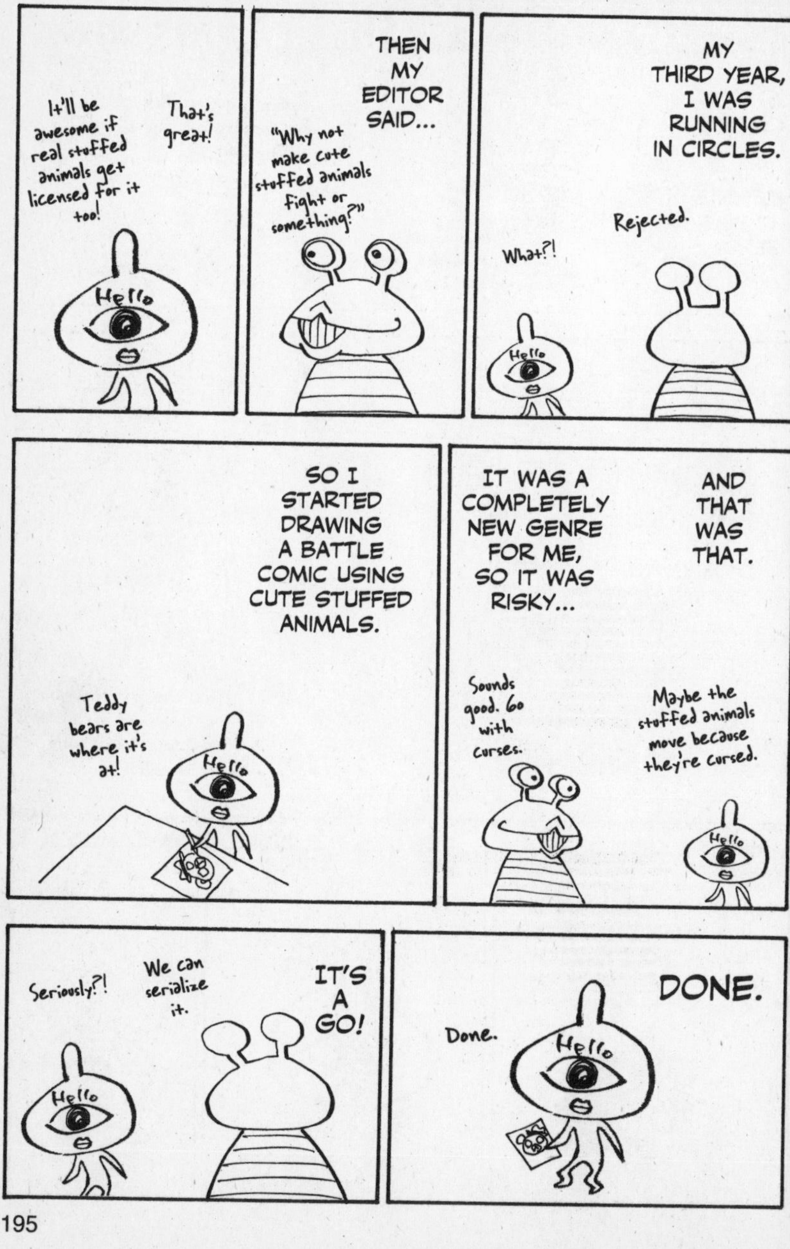
MY THIRD YEAR, I WAS RUNNING IN CIRCLES.
Rejected.
What?!
Hello
THEN MY EDITOR SAID...
"Why not make cute stuffed animals fight or something?"
That's great!
It'll be awesome if real stuffed animals get licensed for it too!
Hello
AND THAT WAS THAT.
IT WAS A COMPLETELY NEW GENRE FOR ME, SO IT WAS RISKY...
Maybe the stuffed animals move because they're cursed.
Sounds good. Go with curses.
Hello
SO I STARTED DRAWING A BATTLE COMIC USING CUTE STUFFED ANIMALS.
Teddy bears are where it's at!
Hello
DONE.
Done.
Hello
IT'S A GO!
We can serialize it.
Seriously?!
Hello

First HYDE ROUGH DRAFT Revealed!

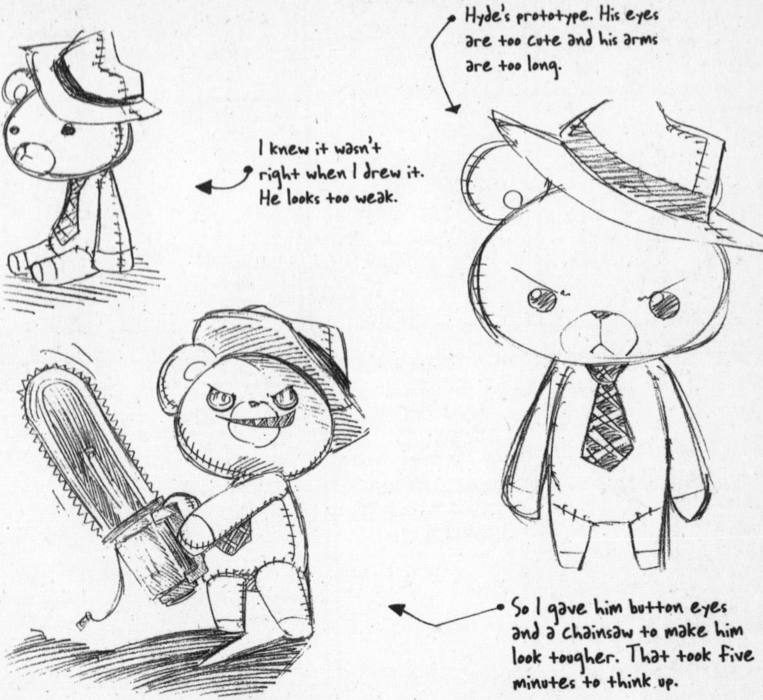
Hyde's prototype. His eyes are too cute and his arms are too long.
I knew it wasn't right when I drew it. He looks too weak.
So I gave him button eyes and a chainsaw to make him look tougher. That took five minutes to think up.

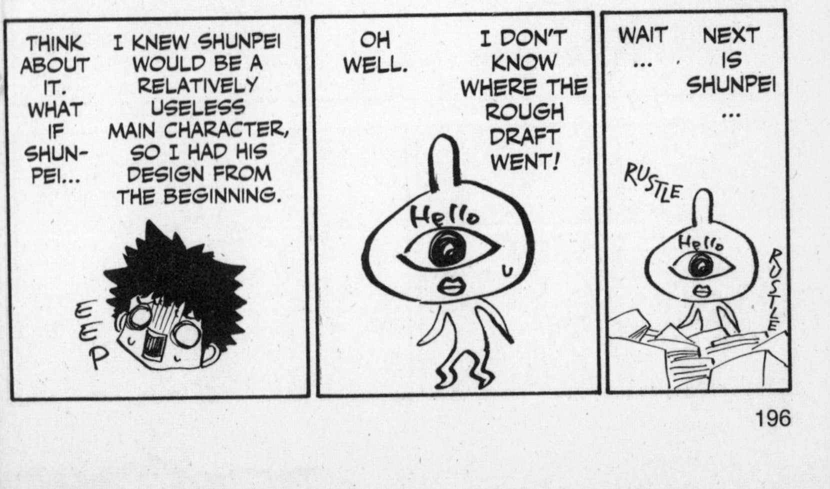
NEXT IS SHUNPEI ...
WAIT ...
RUSTLE
Hello
RUSTLE
I DON'T KNOW WHERE THE ROUGH DRAFT WENT!
OH WELL.
Hello
I KNEW SHUNPEI WOULD BE A RELATIVELY USELESS MAIN CHARACTER, SO I HAD HIS DESIGN FROM THE BEGINNING.
THINK ABOUT IT. WHAT IF SHUN-PEI...
EEP

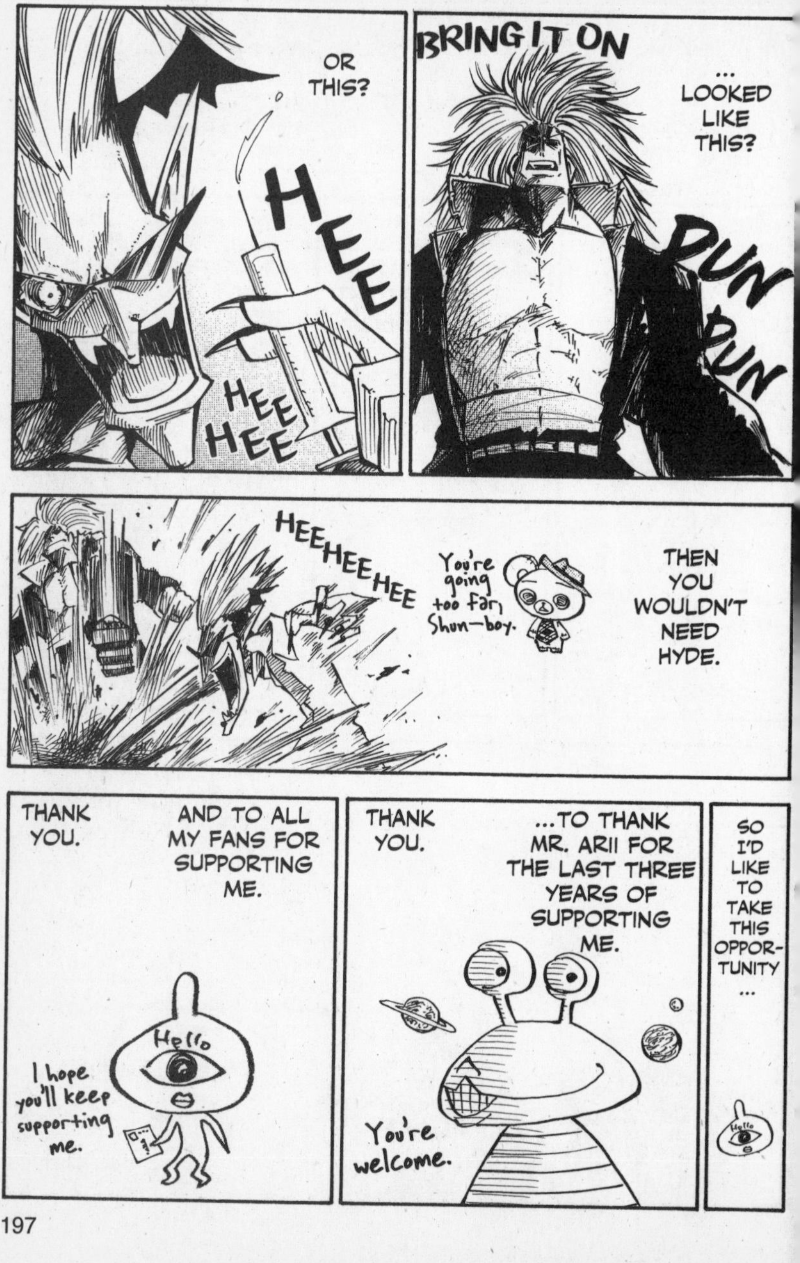
BRING IT ON
...LOOKED LIKE THIS?
DUN DUN
OR THIS?
HEE
HEE HEE HEE
THEN YOU WOULDN'T NEED HYDE.
You're going too far, Shun-boy.
HEEHEEHEE
SO I'D LIKE TO TAKE THIS OPPORTUNITY...
...TO THANK MR. ARII FOR THE LAST THREE YEARS OF SUPPORTING ME.
THANK YOU.
Hello
You're welcome.
AND TO ALL MY FANS FOR SUPPORTING ME.
THANK YOU.
Hello
I hope you'll keep supporting me.

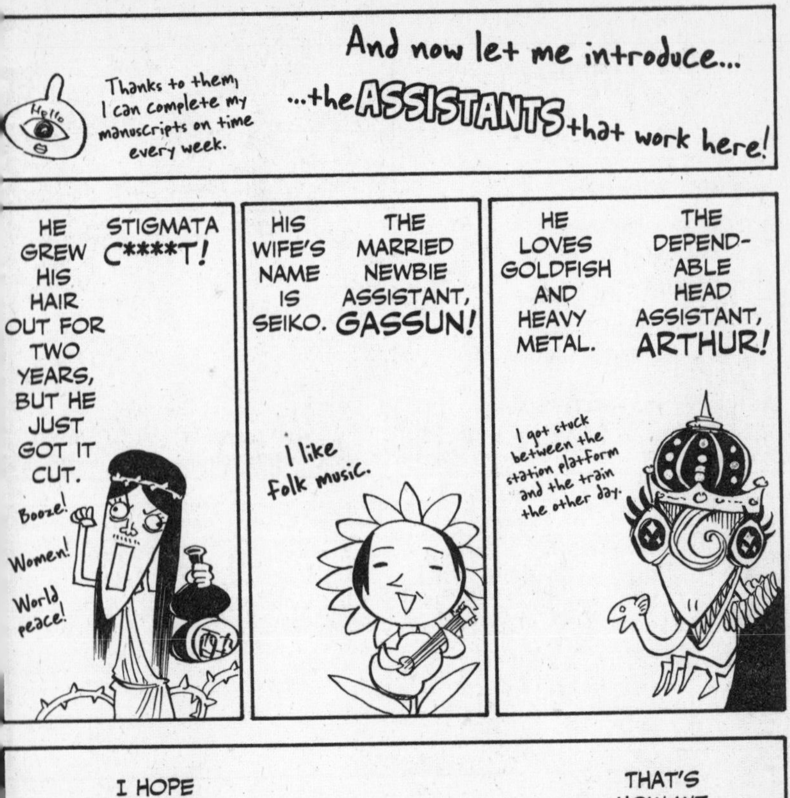
And now let me introduce...
...the ASSISTANTS that work here!
Thanks to them, I can complete my manuscripts on time every week.
Hello
THE DEPENDABLE HEAD ASSISTANT, ARTHUR!
HE LOVES GOLDFISH AND HEAVY METAL.
I got stuck between the station platform and the train the other day.
THE MARRIED NEWBIE ASSISTANT, GASSUN!
HIS WIFE'S NAME IS SEIKO.
I like folk music.
STIGMATA C****T!
HE GREW HIS HAIR OUT FOR TWO YEARS, BUT HE JUST GOT IT CUT.
Booze!
Women!
World peace!
THAT'S HOW WE WORK.
I HOPE WE MEET AGAIN IN VOLUME 2... BYE!
So warm...
...I want to go outside to play.
Back to work.
Hello
TOASTY
TOASTY
Booze!
Women!
World peace!

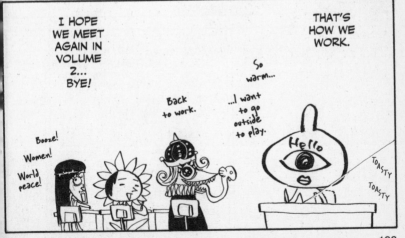

Sorcerer Bio

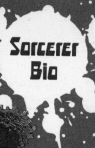

Sorcerer: Anthonio

His name never appears in the comic, so he gets an introduction here.

Born in Kenya. Thirty-eight years old, single.

Favorite food: junk food

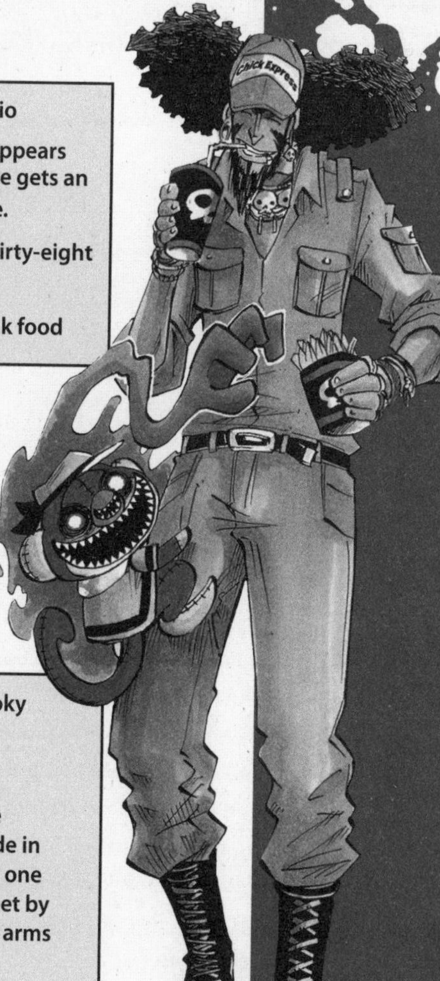
Chick Express

Curse Doll: Chamoky

Curse Name:
Bad Monkey Play

Chamoky can take control of any blade in a space of roughly one hundred square feet by sprouting shadow arms from his body.

Haro Aso

Born in 1980 in Osaka Prefecture, Haro Aso played around too much at Kansai University and was held back twice in the Engineering Department. Eventually he dropped out of college and started drawing comics full-time. He received Shogakukan's Manga College award for "YUNGE!" in 2004. He then moved to Tokyo, where he trained for three years and now draws *Hyde & Closer*.